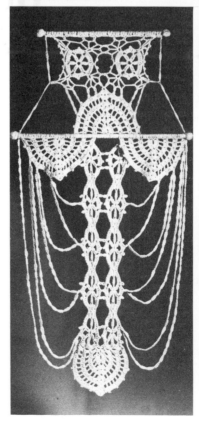

The Woman's Day Book of Designer Crochet

by Jacqueline Henderson

Photographs by Robert Epstein

The Bobbs-Merrill Company, Inc.
New York/Indianapolis

All photographs in the book are taken by Robert Epstein with the
exception of the following, for which the author gratefully acknowledges
permission to reprint:

    Lacy Vest (p.52 and in color section), photographed by Carmen
      Schiavone

    Dresses (p.58), photographed by Les Caron

    Pinwheel Pillow Bag (p.123), photographed by Arnold Maucher

    Trellis Wall Hanging (p.202), photographed by Woman's Day
      Studios

    Rugs (pp.190 and 193), photographed by Jacqueline Henderson

Published by The Bobbs-Merrill Company, Inc.
Indianapolis   New York
Manufactured in the United States of America
First printing

Designed by Marcia Ben-Eli

Library of Congress Cataloging in Publication Data
Henderson, Jacqueline.
   The Woman's day book of designer crochet.
   1. Crocheting. I. Woman's day. II. Title.
TT820.H5   746.43'4   80-693
ISBN 0-672-52580-1

Contents

Home Decoration — 161

Appendix — 208

To John-Roger

Acknowledgments

Without the assistance and support of others, this book could not have come into being.

I would like to thank Theresa Capuana, creative crafts editor, and her assistant, Lina Morielli, for their encouragement and support of my work over the years. Thanks to Helen Donnally and Ruth Jacksier of the How-To Department, and their assistants, for their part in editing the instructions that have appeared in *Woman's Day* magazine.

Thanks to Dina von Zweck for originating the concept of this book and to Lisa Lefever for her work on production.

Thanks to Barbara Reiss of Bobbs-Merrill whose editorial expertise and encouragement have been invaluable.

My gratitude and special thanks to the following friends who have given assistance on many levels: To Joan Witkowski, especially for her encouragement and good criticism; Sylvia Bhourne who spent hours at the typewriter; Diane Goodstein who helped in the preparation of the manuscript; Helen Witkowski for crocheting projects that had to be remade; and to my aunt, Margaret Walton, who has, over the years, generously assisted me in executing some of these pieces.

Thanks also to Robert Epstein for photography and Marcia Ben-Eli for art direction.

Finally, thanks to the many readers who have sent encouraging mail.

J. M. H.
New York, June 1980

Introduction

Experience the delight of "drawing in crochet." This collection of unique designs offers you the opportunity to create with "modular crochet," a technique in which dynamic effects are achieved by working in units. This method opens up a whole range of possibilities in crochet patterns and transforms easily obtained knitting worsted and cotton yarns into rare and beautiful objects.

This book contains many of my designs which have been published in *Woman's Day* and also presents over twenty new projects. Among the patterns are designs for wearing and for decorating the home. They run the gamut from a simple necklace to a tour de force coat of many colors. For your home you might choose a relatively easy wall hanging or go all out with an afghan reminiscent of Persian carpets. In each piece I have sought a perfect blend of art and function.

Traditionally, these patterns would be labeled "fancy" or "difficult." However, I see the major difference between this work and "plain" crochet as primarily one of length. Simple crochet requires fewer lines of instruction, whereas the more complex design demands a rather lengthy explanation with numerous illustrations. It is important to remember that all stitch patterns are composed of one or more of the basic stitches. Therefore, if you know your basic stitches, you will, with sustained effort, be able to do any pattern. As you proceed, you will find this an excellent way to build up your stitch vocabulary and to increase your knowledge of construction.

Whether you pursue the craft as a leisure time activity or as a serious art, the possibilities presented in these designs are meant ultimately to inspire you to develop a greater facility and a deeper understanding of the structural and aesthetic aspects of the medium, while experiencing the joy of creating.

Tools and Supplies

YARNS

In each project we have given the generic name for the yarn used and where possible the specific yarn used for the project. Substitutions for the generic yarn can be made, and in some projects the substitutions are listed in the instructions. Whenever substitutions are made, be sure your material yields the stitch gauge given in the directions. It is advisable to work up a test swatch before you begin working the pattern.

Most of these yarns are available at yarn shops, art needlework section in department stores, or craft supply stores. If you cannot find a particular yarn in your local yarn shop, write to the manufacturer or distributor and request a list of retailers in your area or ask for information about ordering directly. A list of manufacturers' and distributors' addresses is given in the appendix.

It is important to remember that colors of yarn may vary from one dye lot to another. Therefore, it is best to purchase all the yarn needed for a given project at the same time.

The following list describes generic yarns and mentions brand name examples in some cases. It is difficult to guarantee the availability of a brand name yarn, since a manufacturer may discontinue the yarn from its line at any time.

STANDARD WEIGHT WOOLS AND SYNTHETICS

The following yarns are available in many brands:

Knitting Worsted: A medium-weight 4-ply yarn which is generally sold in 3½- or 4-oz. skeins. It is a soft and smooth yarn.

Sport Yarn: This yarn is about half the thickness of knitting worsted. It is also a soft, smooth yarn. It may come in 3-ply or 4-ply and is usually sold in 2-oz. skeins.

Fingering or Baby Yarn: Another soft, smooth yarn, finer than sport yarn, it is sold in 1-oz. skeins and may come in 3-ply or 4-ply.

Bulky Yarn: This is a fluffy, heavyweight yarn which is much thicker than knitting worsted. The heavy handspuns are sometimes categorized as bulky yarns. These yarns vary in plys and number of ounces per skein.

Rug Yarn: A heavyweight yarn, denser and coarser than bulky yarn, it usually comes in 3-ply and varies in the number of ounces per skein. The following are examples of economical brands of rug yarns which are available at five-and-ten stores: American Thread's Aunt Lydia Rug Yarn, Coats and Clark's Craft and Rug Yarn, and January and Wood's Kentucky Rug Yarn.

Tapestry Wool: Approximately the same size as knitting worsted, it is a soft, luxurious yarn which comes in a great variety of color tones. It is usually packaged in small skeins and the number of ounces per skein varies.

Mohair: A soft, fuzzy yarn which comes in wool or a blend of wool and synthetics. It is usually packaged in 40-gram balls.

COTTONS

Cotton Thread: A thin-weight, plyed and twisted cotton thread, it comes in a variety of sizes from 100 (the finest) to 10 (the heaviest). The heavier sizes are the sizes most commonly used today and are usually labeled mercurized knit and crochet cotton or "bedspread cotton." Examples of this thread are Coats and Clark's Knit-Cro-Sheen and Lily's Glo-Tone.

Quick-Crochet Cotton: This yarn is a hard cable-twist string. It is packaged in yards and in a variety of colors. Examples of this yarn are Lily's Double Quick and Coats and Clark's Speed-Cro-Sheen.

Pearl Cotton: A thin-weight, lustrous cotton, it ranges from sizes 8 to 1. It comes on small cardboard cones in varying yardage. Examples of pearl cottons of similar weights are DMC Pearl Cotton No. 5 and Coats and Clark's Pearl Cotton.

Cotton String: A soft, loosely twisted, package-wrapping string, it is sometimes called butcher's twine. The ply and thickness vary. Hardware or stationery stores are sources for this yarn.

Lightweight Cotton Yarn: This yarn is slightly heavier than cotton thread. It is usually imported. Examples of this yarn are Joseph Galler's Parisian Cotton and Armen's Chatbotté Loto.

Medium-Weight Cotton Yarn: "Bedspread cotton," pearl cotton, or lightweight cotton worked in multiple strands will give a weight equivalent to worsted weight. Another medium-weight cotton yarn is Lily's Sugar-'n-Cream. Slightly heavier than medium-weight is Tahki's Creole.

RAYON

Medium-Weight Rayon: Kentucky All-Purpose Yarn is a cross between yarn and string. It is a worsted-weight yarn ideal for summer crochet. Coyote's Xochitl is a medium-weight yarn with silky, slippery, and shiny qualities, and will work well for elegant crochet.

LINEN

Lightweight Linen: This yarn is fine, soft, and strong and has no stretch. An example is Frederick Fawcett's Linen Yarn. Worked double, it approximates medium-weight cotton.

Medium-Weight Linen: A coarse, thick, and heavy yarn which varies in twist, it is suitable for wall hangings, bags, and similar projects.

NOVELTY YARNS

Bouclé: A bumpy, soft yarn, it comes in wools, cottons, linens, and synthetics. The weight varies. Sometimes loop yarns are put in this category. Examples of bouclés that are between lightweight and medium-weight are Joseph Galler's Margaret, Stanley Berroco's Que Linda and 100% cotton or 100% rayon bouclés from Scott's Woolen Mill.

Chainette: Chained rayon, it is a slippery, shiny yarn which is slightly heavier than lightweight yarn. It is available in specialty yarn shops or through distributors of yarns for trimmings' manufacturers.

Chenille: This is a velvet-like yarn which comes in cotton, silk, or synthetics. Generally medium-weight, it can vary in weight.

Cordé: This is a stiff, shiny cord, which is rayon wrapped around cotton. It is suitable for such projects as bags, belts, and wall hangings.

Jute: A rope-like yarn of slightly heavier than medium-weight, it comes in a variety of colors. It is coarse and stiff and works best for rugs, wall hangings, and planters. An example is Lily's Jute-Tone.

Metallic Yarn: Metallics come in a variety of weights. The heavier weights are made with plastic over a thick cotton center. These yarns come in silver, gold, or other metallic colors.

Macrame Braided Cord: Rayon around cotton, this yarn comes flat and soft or round and stiff. It is a heavy-weight cord which can be found in specialty shops or through distributors of yarns to trimmings' manufacturers. An example is Lily's Macrame Cord Fine.

Raffia or Synthetic Straw: Raffia comes in two forms, rounded into a string or flattened in a ribbon-like yarn. It can have a sheen or mat finish and is appropriate for summer hats and bags or placemats.

Rattail: This satiny cord is made from rayon wrapped around cotton. It comes in two weights, lightweight and heavyweight. Examples are Lawrence Schiff's Satin Cord and Lily's Rattail Macrame Cord. The latter comes in heavyweight only.

Soutache: A flat yarn with a sheen, it is made from rayon wrapped around two strands of cotton with a seam down the center. It is pliable and feels like elastic, although it actually has no stretch.

3-Line: This is a flat, rayon braid which has a ribbon-like quality. It is about ¾ inch wide.

CROCHET HOOKS

Crochet hooks come in a variety of sizes, materials, and lengths. The patterns presented in this book call for only steel crochet hooks and aluminum hooks. Steel crochet hooks are mainly used for cotton thread and come in sizes 00, the largest, through 14, the smallest. Aluminum hooks which are used for heavier cotton, wool, or other yarns, are sometimes sized differently by manufacturers, so it is wise to select from well-known brand names. Some man-ufacturers size their hooks by number, others size by letter, and some by both letter and number. The numbers, however, are not standardized. Aluminum hooks come in sizes B through K, K being the largest. They usually come numbered 1 through 10½, the latter being the largest. Larger sizes are made by a few manufacturers. Because the sizing of hooks is not the same in the United States, England, or Canada, a listing of comparative sizes of crochet hooks and numbering systems is given on the next page.

The English/Canadian sizing has two systems which have been set up side by side for easy reference.

CROCHET HOOKS

Aluminum Hooks

American		English/Canadian		Continental-mm	International-mm
—	—	—	14	2	—
—	—	—	13	2¼	—
B	1	14	12	2½	2:00
C	2	13	11	3–2¾	2:50
D	3	12	10	3¼	3:00
E	4	11	9	3½	3:50
F	5	10	8	4	4:00
G	6–7	9	7	4½	4:50
H	7–8	8	6	5	—
H	8	—	5	5½	5:00
I	8–9	7	4	6	5:50
J	9–10	6	3	6½	6:00–6:50
K	10¼–10½	4	2	7–7½	7:00
					8:00
					9:00
					10:00

Steel Hooks

American	English/Canadian		Continental-mm
00	—	—	—
0	—	—	—
1	0	3/0	3
2	1	2/0	2.5
3	1½	1/0	—
4	2	1	2
5	2½	1½	—
6	3	2	1.75
7	3½	2½	1.5
8	4	3	1.25
9	4½	4	1
10	5	5	0.75
11	5½	5½	—
12	6	6	0.6
13	6½	6½	—
14	7	7	—

General Instructions

ABBREVIATIONS AND TERMS

The following are the abbreviations commonly used in crochet directions.

beg	beginning
bl	block
dec	decrease
incl	inclusive
inc	increase
lp	loop
rep	repeat
rnd	round
sk	skip
sp	space
tog	together
y o	yarn over hook
st(s)	stitch(es)
sl st	slip stitch
ch	chain
sc	single crochet
dc	double crochet
hdc	half double crochet
tr	treble crochet
dtr	double treble crochet
tr tr	triple treble crochet
cl	cluster
p	picot
pc	popcorn

* **Asterisk** means that you are to repeat the instructions following the asterisk as many times as is specified in addition to the first time.

** or *** **Double or Triple Asterisks** are sometimes given in a pattern when there are repeats within repeats. You are to repeat the instructions following the ** or *** as indicated.

† **Dagger** is used in the same manner as the asterisk.

( ) **Parentheses** mean that you are to repeat the instructions in the parentheses as many times as specified.

[ ] **Brackets** indicate changes in size when directions are given for more than one size.

Even When directions say "work even" continue without increasing or decreasing.

Multiple of stitches refers to the number of stitches a pattern stitch requires for each repeat. When directions call for "multiple of," it means the number of stitches to be made must be divisible by this number. For example, "multiple of 5" would be 10, 15, 20, etc.; "multiple of 5 plus 2" would be 12, 17, 22, etc.

BEGINNING TO CROCHET

The following seven diagrams with accompanying step-by-step directions show you how to make a slip knot, which anchors yarn on the hook, exact positions for holding the yarn and the hook, and how to do the chain stitch, which is a foundation for other stitches. To practice, use knitting worsted and a size G aluminum or plastic hook.

While you learn, hold your hands in the positions shown in the Diagrams. As you become more proficient, you will adjust to the positions most comfortable for you.

Left-handed crochet work comes out in reverse. If you are left-handed, try to crochet with your right hand—directions are written for right-handed crocheters and you'll find it easier to follow more complex patterns and shaping later on. However, if using your right hand is impossible, hold Diagrams in front of a mirror to reverse hands. With the basic stitches and designs featured here, working with your left hand shouldn't be difficult.

Hold the hook in your right hand as you would a pencil; bring middle finger forward to rest on hook near tip (Diagram 1).

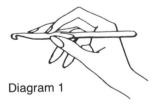

Diagram 1

SLIP KNOT

A. To make a slip knot, hold yarn end with left thumb and forefinger. Bring yarn up and around to make a ring—with yarn dropping behind ring. Put hook through ring; catch yarn and draw through ring toward you (Diagram 2).

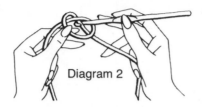

Diagram 2

B. With yarn loop on hook, pull short yarn end and long working yarn in opposite directions to tighten. You have now made the starting slip knot. Insert long working yarn between ring and little fingers of left hand. Wrap yarn around little finger toward back of hand and bring out between ring and middle fingers (Diagram 3).

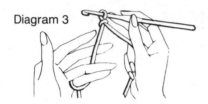

Diagram 3

C. Weave yarn around middle finger toward back of hand; bring it forward between forefinger and thumb. This weaving of the working yarn enables you to control the tension as you feed the yarn onto the hook (Diagram 4).

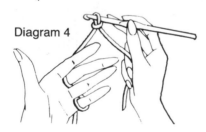

Diagram 4

D. To begin crocheting, grasp short yarn end between left thumb and middle finger under knot (Diagram 5).

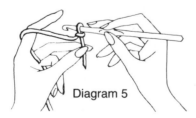

Diagram 5

CHAIN STITCH (ch)
A. Pass hook under yarn and catch yarn with hook. This is called yarn over (y o) (Diagram 6).

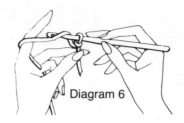

Diagram 6

B. Draw yarn through loop on hook. This makes one chain (ch) (Diagram 7).

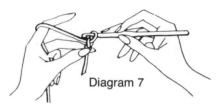

Diagram 7

Repeat Steps A and B until you have as many chain stitches as you need. One loop always remains on the hook. Practice making chains until they are uniform.

THE BASIC STITCHES

SINGLE CROCHET (sc)
Make a foundation chain of 10 or more stitches for practice.
A. Working from front, insert hook under 2 top threads of second chain from hook; yarn over hook (Diagram 8).

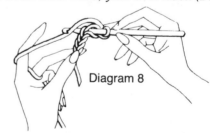

Diagram 8

B. Draw yarn through chain. There are now 2 loops on hook (Diagram 9).

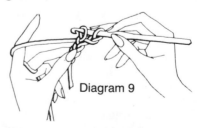

Diagram 9

C. Yarn over hook (Diagram 10).

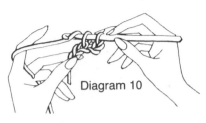

Diagram 10

D. Draw yarn through 2 loops on hook. One loop now remains on hook. One single crochet (sc) is completed (Diagram 11).

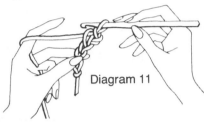

Diagram 11

E. To work next single crochet, insert hook under 2 top threads of next chain (Diagram 12).

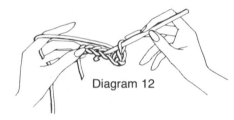

Diagram 12

F. Yarn over hook. Repeat Steps B through F until you have made a single crochet in each chain.

G. At end of row of single crochet, chain one to turn (Diagram 13).

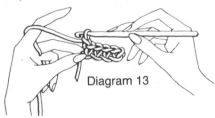

Diagram 13

H. Turn work so reverse side is facing you (Diagram 14).

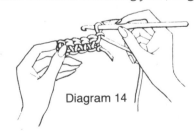

Diagram 14

I. Insert hook under 2 top threads of first single crochet. Repeat Steps B through F, inserting hook into single crochet instead of chain, to complete second row of single crochet, ending with a chain one. Turn. Continue in this manner until work is uniform and the stitch is familiar.

J. On last row do not make a turning chain. Cut yarn about 3 inches from work; bring cut end through remaining loop on hook. Pull tight (Diagram 15).

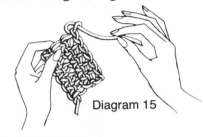

Diagram 15

DOUBLE CROCHET (dc)

Make a foundation chain of 15 stitches for practice piece.

A. Yarn over hook (Diagram 16).

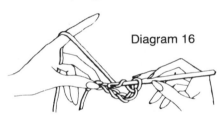

Diagram 16

B. Insert hook under 2 top threads of fourth chain from hook. Yarn over hook (Diagram 17).

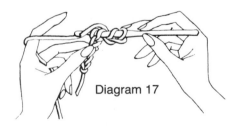

Diagram 17

C. Draw yarn through chain. There are 3 loops on hook. Yarn over hook (Diagram 18).

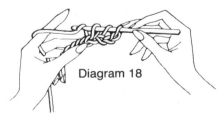

Diagram 18

D. Draw yarn through first 2 loops on hook. Two loops remain on hook. Yarn over hook (Diagram 19).

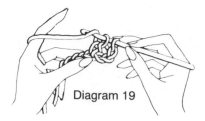

Diagram 19

E. Draw yarn through remaining 2 loops. One loop remains on hook. One double crochet (dc) is now completed (Diagram 20).

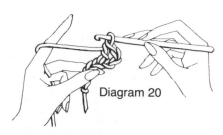

Diagram 20

F. To work next double crochet, yarn over hook, insert hook under 2 top threads of next chain. Yarn over hook and repeat steps C through E. Repeat until you have made a double crochet in each chain.

G. At end of row of double crochet, chain 3 (Diagram 21).

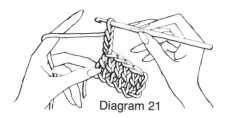

Diagram 21

H. Turn work. On next row, yarn over hook. Skip first double crochet, insert hook under 2 top threads of second double crochet (Diagram 22).

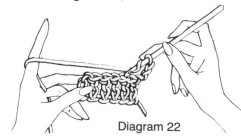

Diagram 22

I. Yarn over hook. Repeat steps C through E, inserting hook into double crochet instead of chain; complete double crochet. Work a double crochet in top of each remaining double crochet across (Diagram 23).

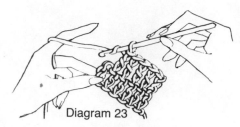

Diagram 23

J. Work a double crochet in top chain stitch of turning chain. Continue in this manner until work is uniform and you feel familiar with the stitch. On last row do not make a turning chain. Cut yarn about 3 inches from work; bring cut end through remaining loop on hook. Pull tight.

HALF DOUBLE CROCHET (hdc)

Make a foundation chain of 10 or more stitches for practice piece.

A. Yarn over hook; insert hook under 2 top threads of third chain from hook. Yarn over hook, draw yarn through chain. There are 3 loops on hook. Yarn over hook; draw through all 3 loops at once. A half double crochet (hdc) is now completed (Diagram 24).

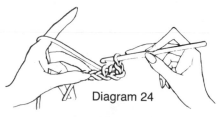

Diagram 24

B. Work a half double crochet in each remaining chain. At the end of row, chain 2 to turn.

C. Skip first half double crochet; work half double crochet in each half double crochet across; half double crochet in top stitch of turning chain. Chain 2 to turn. Continue in this manner until you are familiar with the stitch. End off as before.

TREBLE CROCHET (tr)

Make a foundation chain of 15 or more stitches for practice.

A. Yarn over hook twice (Diagram 25).

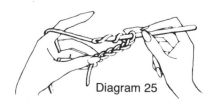

Diagram 25

B. Insert hook under 2 top threads of fifth chain from hook. Yarn over hook (Diagram 26).

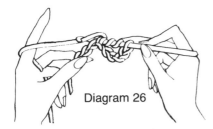

Diagram 26

C. Draw loop through chain. There are 4 loops on hook. Yarn over hook (Diagram 27).

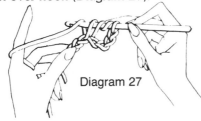

Diagram 27

D. Draw yarn through first 2 loops on hook. Three loops remain. Yarn over hook (Diagram 28).

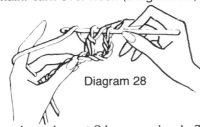

Diagram 28

E. Draw through next 2 loops on hook. Two loops remain. Yarn over hook (Diagram 29).

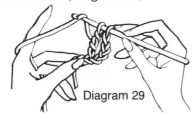

Diagram 29

F. Draw through remaining 2 loops on hook. One loop remains. One treble crochet (tr) is now completed.

G. Work a treble crochet in each remaining chain. At end of row, chain 4 to turn.

H. Skip first treble crochet, work treble crochet in each treble crochet across; treble crochet in top stitch of turning chain. Chain 4 to turn. Continue in this manner until you are familiar with the stitch. End off as before.

DOUBLE TREBLE CROCHET (dtr)

Make a foundation chain of 15 or more stitches for practice. Yarn over hook 3 times; insert hook under 2 top threads of sixth chain from hook. Yarn over hook and draw loop through chain. There are 5 loops on hook. Yarn over hook and draw through 2 loops at a time, 4 times.

One loop remains on hook. One double treble (dtr) is now completed (Diagram 30). Work double treble crochet in each remaining chain. At the end of the row, chain 5 to turn.

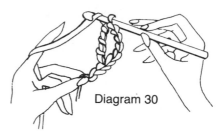

Diagram 30

TRIPLE TREBLE CROCHET (tr tr)

Make a foundation chain of 15 or more stitches for practice. Yarn over hook 4 times; insert hook under 2 top threads of seventh chain stitch from hook. Yarn over hook and draw loop through chain. There are 6 loops on hook. Yarn over hook and draw through 2 loops at a time, 5 times. One loop remains on hook. One triple treble (tr tr) is now completed (Diagram 31). Work triple treble crochet in each remaining chain. At the end of the row, chain 6 to turn.

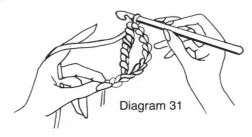

Diagram 31

THE BASIC TECHNIQUES

DECREASING (dec) SINGLE CROCHET

A. Draw up a loop in next single crochet; 2 loops on hook. Draw up loop in following single crochet. There are 3 loops on hook. Yarn over hook (Diagram 32).

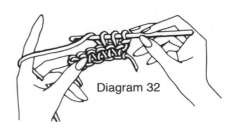

Diagram 32

B. Draw yarn through all 3 loops at once. One single crochet decrease is completed (Diagram 33).

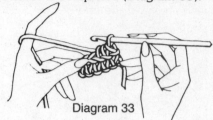

Diagram 33

DECREASING (dec) DOUBLE CROCHET

A. Work one double crochet to point where 2 loops remain on hook. Begin another double crochet in next stitch, work until 4 loops are on hook. Yarn over hook (Diagram 34).

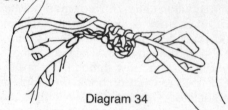

Diagram 34

B. Draw yarn through 2 loops. Yarn over hook (Diagram 35).

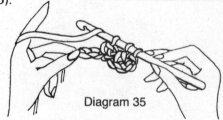

Diagram 35

C. Draw through all 3 loops at once. One double crochet decrease is completed (Diagram 36).

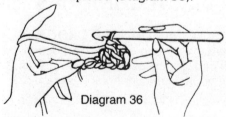

Diagram 36

INCREASING (inc)

Where directions indicate an increase, work 2 stitches in the same stitch. This forms one extra stitch.

SLIP STITCH (sl st)

Make a foundation chain of 10 or more stitches for practice.

A. Insert hook under top thread of second chain from hook. Yarn over hook. With one motion draw yarn through both chain and loop on hook. One slip stitch (sl st) is completed.

B. Insert hook under top thread of next chain (Diagram 37).

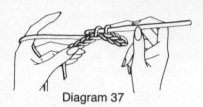

Diagram 37

C. Yarn over. Draw through chain and loop on hook. Work a slip stitch in each remaining chain.

Slip Stitch for Joining Rings: Use when directions say join in a ring. Make a chain of 10 stitches for practice.

A. Insert hook through 2 top threads of last chain from hook. Yarn over (Diagram 38).

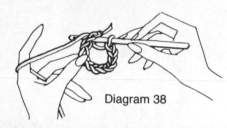

Diagram 38

B. With one motion draw yarn through chain and loop on hook (Diagram 39).

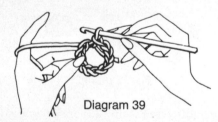

Diagram 39

Slip Stitch for Joining Rounds: Use when working around as for a hat, rather than across in rows. Following any set of crochet directions, work to end of round; then to join, insert hook under 2 top threads of first stitch on this same round and work slip stitch. First and last stitches of round are now joined.

Slip Stitch for Other Uses: The slip stitch has other purposes besides joining. Since the slip stitch adds no height to a row, it can be used to decrease several stitches at the beginning of a row, eliminating the need to cut the yarn and rejoin it. For a firm edge, a slip stitch can be worked as a final edging. The slip stitch is also used as a decorative stitch (Diagram 40).

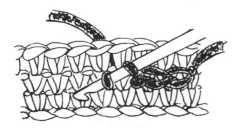

Diagram 40

FOUNDATION CHAIN LOOPS

This is sometimes referred to as purl foundation. Chain 4, work double crochet in fourth chain stitch from hook, make another chain 4 and work double crochet into fourth chain stitch from hook. Repeat to end of length desired (Diagram 41).

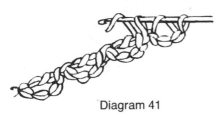

Diagram 41

TURNING WORK

Each stitch uses a different number of chain stitches to turn at the end of a row so as to bring the work into position for the next row. The length of the turning chain depends upon the height of the stitch that will be used to begin the row. Except for single crochet, the turning chain always counts as the first stitch of the new row, unless specified otherwise in directions. Follow the stitch table below for the number of chain stitches required to make a turn for each stitch:

single crochet (sc)	chain 1 to turn
half double crochet (hdc)	chain 2 to turn
double crochet (dc)	chain 3 to turn
treble crochet (tr)	chain 4 to turn
double treble (d tr)	chain 5 to turn
triple treble (tr tr)	chain 6 to turn

WORKING BOTH LOOPS

Unless directions specify otherwise, always insert hook under the 2 top loops (strands) of a stitch. Always insert hook from front to back. When directions call for working back loops, insert hook in loop farthest from you. To work front loops insert hook in loop closest to you. If back of stitch is facing you, the front loop will be termed top loop.

WORKING IN ROWS

This is the term used for working to and fro. The work is turned at the end of each row, unless otherwise specified.

If crochet is to be worked in one direction only, each row is begun in the first stitch of the preceding row.

WORKING IN ROUNDS (rnd)

This term describes working in a circular motion. Each round is completed by means of a slip stitch into the first stitch of the round, or as stated in the instructions. Directions will also indicate whether the work is to be turned or not.

STARTING A ROW

If first stitch is a single crochet, make a slip knot on hook, insert hook in stitch designated, draw yarn through, and complete as for single crochet. **If first stitch is a double crochet,** make a slip knot on hook, yarn over, insert hook in stitch designated, draw yarn through, and complete as for double crochet. **To start row with a chain,** make slip knot on hook, insert hook in stitch designated, draw yarn through stitch and through loop on hook as for a slip stitch, then make your chain.

CHANGING COLORS

When at the end of a row or round, cut the old color leaving a 3-inch end, then change to a new color in manner specified for starting a row. Crochet over ends of yarn as you work to avoid the nuisance of having to weave them in later. If stitch pattern does not allow for crocheting over the end, then weave it in later. When a change of color occurs in a row or round in progress, work the stitch immediately preceding color change to the point where 2 loops of that stitch remain, then work last yarn over with new color.

HOLDING BACK LAST LOOP

The phrase "holding back last loop on hook" means to work stitch to the point where only 2 loops remain on hook. This technique can be applied only to double crochet and the other tall crochet stitches.

WORKING AROUND POST OR BAR OF STITCH

When directions call for working around "post" or "bar" of a stitch on a previous row, insert hook around stitch instead of inserting it into the top of stitch. Hook A has been inserted with right side of stitch facing; Hook B has been inserted with wrong side of stitch facing (Diagram 42).

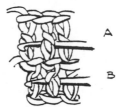

Diagram 42

EDGING WITH SINGLE CROCHET

When working edging over the vertical edge of a piece, work single crochet over the end-of-row stitches, distributing stitches evenly so that the edging will not cup or ruffle. When working along a foundation chain or an end row edge, work single crochet in each stitch. To turn corners, always work an increase such as three single crochet, or work one single crochet, chain two, and one single crochet.

WORKING TO GAUGE

At the beginning of all directions a gauge is given. Gauge refers to the number of stitches there are to 1 inch and the number of rows there are to 1 inch. It is very important that you crochet to the gauge specified if the finished article is to be the correct size. Because tension can vary with each crocheter, it is necessary to make a practice swatch to check your gauge against the gauge given in the directions. Make a swatch of at least 2 inches square, using the hook and material specified. Measure the number of stitches you have to 1 inch. If there is a discrepancy, try a hook of a different size. If you have more stitches to the inch than specified, you should use a larger hook. If you have fewer stitches to the inch, use a smaller hook. Keep changing hooks until you have the correct gauge.

When projects are made in sections, it is important that each section is the correct size. Measurements are usually given at the end of sections. Be sure duplicate pieces are the same size. If there is minor discrepancy in size, it can be corrected by blocking. As you finish each section, be sure it fits correctly to the adjacent section or that it can be blocked to fit. If you find your work begins to cup or ruffle, try to work a bit looser or tighter so that the pieces lie flat.

FASTENING ENDS

After you have completed an article, thread each loose yarn end in a needle and weave about 1 inch through solid part of reverse side of the crochet to fasten. Cut off remaining yarn end close to work. If yarn ends are too short for needle, use crochet hook to weave them into work.

JOINING MOTIFS OR SECTIONS

The most common method for attaching motifs or sections is sewing. Use a tapestry needle and the yarn specified. With right sides together, pin edges to be sewn, matching any pattern in rows or stitches. Begin sewing by anchoring yarn to the work with several small stitches. Sew straight edges with a whip stitch at edge of work. Sew shaped or uneven edges with a backstitch, sewing just inside edges of work. On woolen articles, work stitches loosely enough to match elasticity of pieces. On large sections, when sewing is completed, press seams lightly on the wrong side.

When edges are tops of stitches, pieces can also be attached by crocheting with slip stitch or single crochet. The use of either of these methods depends upon the desired effect. Sew or crochet two back loops along edges together, as shown (Diagram 43).

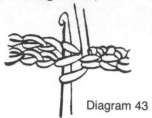

Diagram 43

Another method for attaching pieces is joining with picots (Diagram 44). This is commonly used to join motifs. When working last row on a second motif, work up to picot you wish to join. Place two motifs together as shown. Work to center chain stitch of picot, remove hook, and place it in corresponding picot of first motif. Place hook back in dropped loop, pull loop through, chain one, and finish picot. Continue working in pattern to second joining point; then join as for first joining.

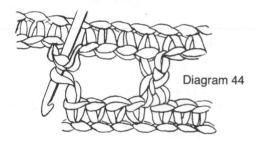

Diagram 44

LAUNDERING

If your work has become soiled, wash it by hand before blocking. Wash woolens in cold-water soap or mild soap and lukewarm water. Squeeze out water, but do not wring. Rinse in lukewarm water several times until all soap is removed. Roll in a towel to absorb some of the moisture.

BLOCKING

Since blocking is not always recommended for all yarns, especially synthetics, read the information on yarn wrapper. If blocking is suggested and an article is made up of several pieces, block each piece before sewing.

If you have laundered your work, block it while still damp. Place article wrong side up, on a flat, padded surface. Gently pat into shape; pin with rustproof pins. Let dry thoroughly before unpinning.

If you have not had to launder your work, pin the dry article, wrong side up, on a padded surface. Press through a damp cloth with a hot iron; do not let weight of iron rest on article. Let work dry.

THE PATTERN STITCHES

Pattern stitches are formed from various combinations of the basic stitches. A few of the more popular pattern stitches are presented here. When a pattern stitch is used in a particular project, the instructions may call for some variations in the making of the stitch.

BASIC SHELL STITCH

A shell is a group of 3 or more stitches worked in the same stitch or space (Diagram 45).

Diagram 45

Make a foundation chain which is a multiple of 6 plus 1.

1st row: Work 2 dc in 4th ch st from hook (**half shell made**), sk next 2 ch sts, sc in next ch st, * sk 2 ch sts, 5 dc in next ch st (**shell made**), sk next 2 ch sts, sc in next ch st. Rep from * across; ch 3, turn.

2nd row: 2 dc in same sp as turning ch, * sc in center dc of next shell, work a shell in next sc. Rep from * across, end sc in top of ch-3; ch 3, turn.

Rep 2nd row for pattern.

OPEN SHELL STITCH

Open shell stitches are made up of any even number of stitches with a chain space in the center (Diagram 46).

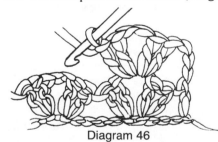

Diagram 46

Make a foundation chain which is a multiple of 6 plus 5.

1st row: In 7th ch st from hook work 2 dc, ch 3 and 2 dc (**open shell made**), * sk next 5 ch sts, work open shell in next st. Rep from * across to within last 4 ch sts, sk next 3 ch sts, dc in last ch st; ch 3, turn.

2nd row: Make an open shell in ch-sp of each open shell, sk 2 dc of last shell, dc in next ch st; ch 3, turn.

Rep 2nd row for pattern.

SLANT SHELL STITCH

This is one of a variety of slanting shell stitches (Diagram 47).

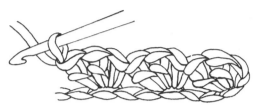

Diagram 47

Make a foundation chain which is a multiple of 3.

1st row: In 3rd ch st from hook work 2 dc, * sk next 2 ch sts, in next ch st work sc and 2 dc (**slant shell made**). Rep from * across to within last 3 ch sts, sk next 2 ch sts, sc in last ch st; ch 2, turn.

2nd row: In same sp as turning ch work 2 dc * sk next 2 dc, in sc work a slant shell. Rep from * across to within last 3 sts, sk 2 dc, sc in top of ch-2; ch 2, turn.

Rep 2nd row for pattern.

V-STITCH

This stitch can be worked with one or more chain stitches between two double crochet or two trebles or any two other tall stitches. It is worked here with one chain stitch between double crochet (Diagram 48).

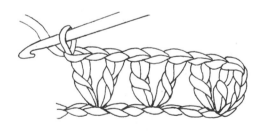

Diagram 48

Make a foundation chain which is a multiple of 3 plus 1.

1st row: In 5th ch st from hook work dc, ch 1 and dc (**V-st made**), * sk 2 ch sts, V-st in next ch st. Rep from * across to within last 2 ch sts, end dc in last ch st; ch 3, turn.

2nd row: * Work V-st in ch-1 sp of next V-st. Rep from * across, end dc in top of turning ch; ch 3, turn.

Rep 2nd row for pattern.

CLUSTER STITCH (cl)

A cluster is two or more stitches gathered into a group to form one stitch at the top, and can be worked in one space (Diagram 49).

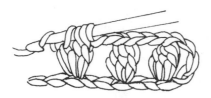

Diagram 49

Make a foundation chain which is a multiple of 3 plus 2.

1st row: Beg in 4th ch st from hook, work a dc until there are only 2 lps on hook, hold these 2 lps on hook, in same st work 2 more dc *holding back last lp of each dc on hook,* y o draw through all 4 lps on hook (**3-dc cl made**), * ch 2, sk 2 ch sts, 3-dc cl next st. Rep from * across, dc last ch st; ch 3, turn.

2nd row: Cl in top of first cl, * ch 2, cl in next cl. Rep from * across, dc in top of ch-3; ch 3, turn.

Rep 2nd row for pattern.

CLUSTER VARIATION

Another cluster stitch, sometimes called a 3-Joined Double Crochet, is worked over several stitches (Diagram 50).

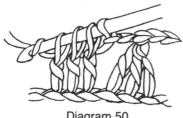

Diagram 50

Make a foundation chain which is a multiple of 3 plus 1.

1st row: Begin in 4th ch st from hook, * *holding back last lp of each st on hook* work 3 dc in each of the next 3 sts, y o draw through all 3 lps on hook (**cl made**), ch 2, * work cl, ch 2. Rep from * across, end dc in last ch st; ch 3, turn.

2nd row: * Work cl, ch 2. Rep from * across; end dc in top of turning ch; ch 3, turn.

Rep 2nd row for pattern.

PUFF STITCH

This stitch, another variation on the cluster, is sometimes called the Pineapple Stitch (Diagram 51).

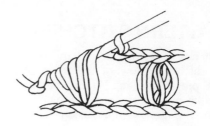

Diagram 51

Make a foundation chain which is a multiple of 3 plus 2.

1st row: Y o, insert hook in 4th ch st from hook, pull up a lp ½ inch high, (y o, insert hook in same st and pull up a lp to same height) twice, y o draw through all 7 lps on hook (**puff st made**), * ch 2, sk next 2 ch sts, work puff st in next ch st. Rep from * across, dc in last ch st; ch 3, turn.

2nd row: Puff st in top of first puff st, * ch 2, puff st in next puff st. Rep from * across, dc in top of ch-3; ch 3, turn.

Rep 2nd row for pattern.

POPCORN STITCH (pc)

This stitch begins as a shell and is then gathered into a fat cluster (Diagram 52).

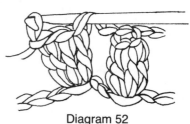

Diagram 52

Make a foundation chain which is a multiple of 3 plus 2.

1st row: In 4th ch st from hook work 4 dc, drop lp from hook, insert hook from **front to back** in first dc of 4-dc group and draw the dropped lp through, ch 1 to fasten (**pc made**), ch 1; * sk next 2 ch sts, work pc in next st, ch 1. Rep from * across to within last 2 ch sts, pc next st, dc in last ch st; ch 3, turn.

2nd row: * 4 dc in top of next pc, drop lp from hook, insert hook from **back to front** in first dc of 4-dc group, ch 1 to fasten (**reverse pc made**), ch 1. Rep from * across, dc top of ch-3; ch 3, turn.

3rd row: Rep 2nd row except work pc inserting hook from **front to back.**

Rep 2nd and 3rd rows alternately for pattern.

PICOTS (p)

This is a name given to various kinds of little points. They include chain picots, ring picots, and large picots.

Diagram 53

Simple chain picot (Diagram 53). Work a sc in the foundation st, ch 3, 4, or 5 depending on the length of p desired, and sc in the same sp.

Ring picot (Diagram 54). Work sc in the foundation st, ch 3, 4, or 5 depending on the length of p desired, work a sc in the first ch st.

Diagram 54

Ring picot variation (Diagram 55). Work same as for ring p except work sc or sl st in the root sc.

Diagram 55

Large picot (Diagram 56). Work sl st in foundation st, ch 6, in first ch st from hook work sl st, sc next ch st, hdc next st, dc next st, tr next st, sk 3 sts on foundation, sl st next.

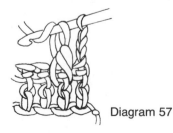

Diagram 56

RAISED DOUBLE CROCHET STITCH
The double crochet stitch is worked in relief (Diagram 57).

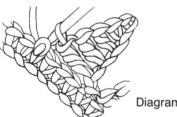

Diagram 57

Make a foundation chain which is a multiple of 2 plus 1.

1st row: Beg in 4th ch st from hook, work dc in each st across; ch 3, turn.

2nd row: Y o working from **front to back** insert hook horizontally, from right to left, around post of next dc, draw lp through, (y o pull through 2 lps) twice (**raised dc made**), dc next st. Rep from * across; ch 3, turn.

3rd row: Y o working from **back to front,** insert hook horizontally, from right to left, around post of next dc, draw lp through, complete as for dc (**raised dc in reverse**), dc next st. Rep from * across, end dc in turning ch-3; ch 3, turn.

Rep 2nd and 3rd rows alternately for pattern.

CROSSED DOUBLE CROCHET STITCH
This stitch, sometimes called the Judith Stitch, is one variation of the crossed double crochet (Diagram 58).

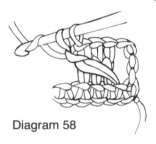

Diagram 58

Make a foundation chain which is a multiple of 4 plus 2.

1st row: Sc in 2nd ch st from hook and in each ch st across; ch 3, turn.

2nd row: * Sk next sc, work dc in each of next 3 sts, y o, insert hook in missed sc, draw up a long lp, (y o pull through 2 lps) twice (crossed dc made). Rep from * across, end dc in turning ch-1; ch 1, turn.

3rd row: Work sc in each st across; ch 1, turn.

Rep 2nd and 3rd rows alternately for pattern.

CROSSED TREBLE CROCHET STITCH
The crossed trebles given here are set one above the other, but they can also be set alternately (Diagram 59).

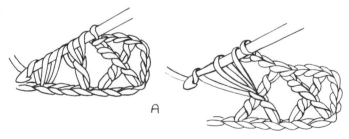

Diagram 59

Make a foundation chain which is a multiple of 4 plus 2.

1st row: Y o twice, insert hook in 6th ch st from hook, draw lp through, * y o pull through 2 lps, y o, sk 2 ch sts, draw lp through next ch st, (y o pull through 2 lps) 4 times, ch 2, work dc in center of crossed sts (**crossed tr made**), y o twice, pull lp through next st. Rep from * across, end tr in last ch st; ch 5, turn.

2nd row: Work cross tr on each cross tr of previous row, tr in top of turning ch; ch 5, turn.

Rep 2nd and 3rd rows alternately for pattern.

KNOT STITCH
This stitch is sometimes called the Love Knot or Solomon's Knot (Diagram 60).

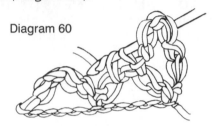

Diagram 60

Make a foundation chain which is a multiple of 5 plus 2.

1st row: Sc in 2nd ch st from hook, * pull up a lp 1 inch long, y o draw through a lp (long ch), insert hook between 1 inch lp and single strand of ch and work sc (**knot st made**), work a second knot st, sk next 4 ch sts, sc in next st (**knot st lp made**). Rep from * across; work 3 knot sts, turn.

2nd row: * Working in long lp of next knot st of previous row sc between long lp and single strand, sc in between long lp and single strand of 2nd knot st, work a knot st lp. Rep from * across, 3 knot sts made, turn.

Rep 2nd row for pattern.

REVERSE SINGLE CROCHET
Used for trims, this stitch is crocheted into the edge of finished piece (Diagram 61).

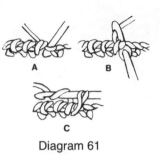

Diagram 61

Work from left to right on foundation. With slip knot on hook, insert hook from front into first st and work a sc, * insert hook in next st to right of hook, work sc. Rep from * around.

PATTERN READING AIDS

Before beginning any design, it is advisable to look over the instructions and get an idea of the general construction. Note the headings in bold type. When you begin to crochet, work instructions in small steps. Reading too far ahead could confuse you, because you may be taking on too much at one time. Each step is set off by commas. Series of steps are set off by semicolons and periods. Learn to work between commas.

If you have trouble keeping your place, use the straight-pin method. Read a phrase; stick a straight pin into the page to show you where your place is. When work is completed to that point, read the next phrase and move the pin. Another method for keeping your place is to place a ruler or giant paper clip on the page just below the row you are working on to keep you from being distracted by subsequent rows.

It is especially important to be patient and to practice. Remember, it is all right to rip out and start again. Think of your mistakes as learning experiences. If you are patient, you will be more open to learning how stitches are formed; you will gain the confidence needed to develop your skill, and eventually your speed, with practice.

Clothing

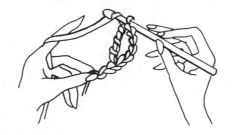

Fanciful Sweaters

TORSO HUGGER

This saucy confection is cooled by shades of blue and green sweetened with pink. Slubby linen/orlon yarn is worked in single and double crochet and in shells. The ribbing is worked vertically.

SIZES: Small (8-10) [medium (12-14)]. Garment measures 15½″ [17½″] across back from underarm to underarm.

MATERIALS: Lightweight bouclé (a nubby-type yarn), 6 (1-oz.) skeins each olive pearl and bright navy, 4 skeins hunter green, 2 skeins mint green, 1 skein bright pink; aluminum crochet hook size H (or English/Canadian hook No. 8) *or the size that will give you the correct gauge.*

GAUGE: 1 shell and 1 sc = 2″; 1 shell row = 1″.

Note: Work with yarn double throughout.

MIDRIFF SECTION: This section is always worked with right side facing you. Front and back are worked in one piece, eliminating side seams. Start around middle of Midriff.

Foundation Strip: With olive pearl (ch 3, dc in 3rd ch from hook) 32 [36] times (a strip of lps made). Strip should measure 30″ [34″] when slightly stretched. Join with sl st to first ch of first ch-3 to form strip into a ring, being careful not to twist strip.

1st rnd: Pull up dc lps on Strips so that Strips will lie flat. With right side facing you, * work 3 dc, ch 2 and 3 dc in base of next dc on Foundation Strip (between 2 lps on strip—shell made), sc in base of next dc (between next 2 lps). Rep from * around, omitting last sc; join with sl st to last sl st (16 [18] shells made along lower edge of strip). Break off. Foundation Strip completed.

2nd rnd: Working along opposite side (upper edge) of Foundation Strip, with mint, sl st in same sp as last sl st, then rep 2nd rnd. Break off. The next 6 rnds will complete lower section of Midriff.

3rd rnd: With green, make lp on hook; sc in ch-2 sp of any olive shell on 1st rnd, * work 5-dc shell in next sc, sc in ch-2 sp of next shell. Rep from * around, omitting last sc; join with sl st to first sc (16 [18] shells). Break off.

4th rnd: Attach bright pink with sl st to any sc on 3rd rnd, ch 3, holding back on hook the last lp of each dc, work 3 dc in same sc, y o hook and draw through all 4 lps on hook (3-dc and ch cl made), * ch 5, sk next shell, in next sc work 4-dc cl. Rep from * 14 [16] times more (16 [18] cl), ch 5; join with sl st to top of first cl. Break off.

5th rnd: With olive pearl, make lp on hook; sc in top of any cl, * keeping ch-5 lp in back of work, work dc in back lp of each of next 5 green dc of 3rd rnd (you will not see bright pink ch-5 lp from right side of work), sc in top of next cl. Rep from * around, omitting last sc; join with sl st to first sc (96 [108] sts). Do not break off.

6th rnd: Ch 1, working in back lp of each st, sc in each st around; join with sl st to first sc (96 [108] sc). Rep 6th rnd twice more. Break off. Lower section of Midriff completed.

To Complete Upper Section of Midriff: Work along opposite side of upper half of Foundation Strip (mint shells on 2nd rnd), as follows:

9th rnd: With green, make lp on hook; with right side facing you, work 3 sc in ch-2 sp of any shell on 2nd rnd, * work 4 dc in next sc (between shells), work 3 sc in next ch-2 sp. Rep from * around, omitting last 3 sc; join with sl st to first sc. Break off.

10th rnd: Attach mint with sl st to center sc of any 3-sc group, make 3-dc and ch cl, * ch 5, sk next shell, in center sc of next 3-sc group work 4-dc cl. Rep from * 14 [16] times more (16 [18] cl made), ch 5; join with sl st to top of first cl. Break off.

11th rnd: With green, make lp on hook; sc in top of any cl, * keeping ch-5 lp in back of work, work 2 dc in back lp of next green dc of 9th rnd, dc in back lp of each of next 2 green dc, 2 dc in back lp of next green dc, sc in top of next cl. Rep from * around, omitting last sc; join with sl st to first sc (112 [126] sts). Do not break off.

12th rnd: Ch 3, working in back lp of each st, dc in next st and in each st around; join with sl st to top of first ch-3 (112 [126] dc, counting ch-3 as 1 dc). Break off. Midriff section completed.

FRONT TOP BODICE: 1st row: Attach olive pearl with sl st to last sl st, work shell of 3 dc, ch 2, and 3 dc in same place, * sk next 3 [2] dc, sc in next dc, sk next 2 dc, work shell in next dc. Rep from * 6 [8] times more (8 [10] shells made); ch 3, turn.

To Shape Armholes and Front Neck: 2nd row: Work shell of 2 dc, ch 2 and 3 dc in same place as turning ch, sc in ch-2 sp of first shell, (work shell of 3 dc, ch 2 and 3 dc in next sc between shells, sc in ch-2 sp of next shell) 3 [4] times (4 [5] shells made); ch 3, turn.

3rd row: Rep 2nd row once more (4 [5] shells made).

4th row: Work shell of 2 dc, ch 2 and 3 dc in same place as turning ch, sc in ch-2 sp of first shell, (work shell in next sc, sc in ch-2 sp of next shell) 2 [3] times (3 [4] shells made); ch 3, turn.

5th row: Work shell in same place as turning ch, sc in ch-2 sp of first shell, (work shell in next sc, sc in ch-2 sp of next shell) 2 [3] times, work shell in top of turning ch of last shell (4 [5] shells); ch 1, turn.

6th row: Sl st in each of next 3 dc of first shell, sc in ch-2 sp of same shell, (work shell in next sc, sc in ch-2 sp of next shell) 3 [4] times (3 [4] shells made); ch 3, turn.

7th through 10th rows: Work shell in same place as turning ch, (sc in ch-2 sp of next shell, work shell in next sc) 3 [4] times (4 [5] shells made); ch 3, turn. Rep 4th row 3 times more (3 [4] shells made on each row).

11th row: Rep 5th row (4 [5] shells).

12th row (shoulder edge): Sl st in each of next 3 dc and ch-2 sp of first shell, (work 5 dc in next sc, sc in ch-2 sp of next shell) 3 [4] times. Break off.

With right side of work facing you, attach olive pearl to top of first dc of first olive pearl shell made on first row, ch

3, and rep 2nd through 12th rows. Front Bodice completed. Neck edging will be added later.

BACK TOP BODICE: 1st row: Sk 2 [5] green dc on Midriff (underarm edge), attach olive pearl to next dc. Ch 3, work shell in same place, * sk next 3 [2] dc, sc in next dc, sk next 2 dc, work shell in next dc. Rep from * 7 [9] times more (9 [11] shells made, leaving 3 [5] dc unworked); ch 3, turn.

To Shape Armholes: 2nd row: Work shell in same place as turning ch, (* sc in ch-2 sp of next shell, work shell in next sc *) 8 [10] times, sc in ch-2 space of last shell, work shell in top of turning ch of last shell (10 [12] shells made); ch 1, turn.

3rd row: Sl st in each of next 3 dc of first shell, sc in ch-2 sp of same shell, (* work shell in next sc, sc in ch-2 sp of next shell *) 9 [11] times (9 [11] shells made); ch 3, turn.

4th row: Rep 2nd row, working last shell in last sc; ch 3, turn.

5th row: Rep 2nd row, repeating from * to * 9 [11] times (11 [13] shells made).

6th row: Rep 3rd row, repeating from * to * 10 [12] times (10 [12] shells made).

7th row: Rep 2nd row, repeating from * to * 9 [11] times, working last shell in last sc (11 [13] shells made); ch 3, turn.

8th row: Rep 2nd row, repeating from * to * 10 [12] times (12 [14] shells made).

9th row: Rep 3rd row, repeating from * to * 11 [13] times (11 [13] shells made).

To Shape Neck: 10th row: Work shell in same place as turning ch, (sc in ch-2 sp of next shell, work shell in next sc) 3 [4] times; sc in ch-2 sp of next shell (4 [5] shells made); ch 1, turn.

11th row: Sl st in each of next 3 dc of first shell, sc in ch-2 sp of same shell, (work shell in next sc, sc in ch-2 sp of next shell) 3 [4] times, work shell in top of turning ch of last shell (4 [5] shells made); ch 1, turn.

12th row (shoulder edge): Sl st in each of next 3 dc and ch-2 sp of first shell, (work 5 dc in next sc, sc in ch-2 sp of next shell) 3 [4] times. Break off.

With right side of work facing you, attach olive pearl to first sc at beg of 9th row; ch 3, then rep 10th through 12th rows. Break off. Back Bodice completed.

Turn piece wrong side out. Sl st shoulder seams together, working through top lps only.

WAISTBAND: Band is worked vertically and separately. When completed, it is joined to Bodice. Using navy, ch 31.

1st row (right side): Dc in 4th ch from hook and in each ch across (29 dc, counting turning ch as 1 dc); ch 1, turn.

2nd row: Working front lps only, sc in first dc and in each dc across, ending with sc in top of turning ch; ch 3, turn.

3rd row: Working in back lp of each st, sk first sc, dc in next and in each sc across. Ch 1, turn.

Repeating 2nd and 3rd rows for pattern, work even in pattern until there are 58 [66] rows in all, or until waistband fits snugly around midriff. End with a 2nd row and omit last ch-3. Break off.

Fold waistband in half crosswise and, with wrong side of work facing you, sl st ends together to form tube.

Top Edging: With navy, make lp on hook and sc in side of any sc row, * work 2 sc over side of dc row, work 1 sc in side of sc row. Rep from * around, omitting last sc. Join with sl st to first sc. Break off.

Hold Bodice and waistband with right sides facing and with top edging of waistband matching lower edge of Bodice. With navy, sl st them together, working through top lps only.

FINISHING: Sleeve Edging: 1st rnd: With navy, make lp on hook; with right sides facing you, sc in each of 2 [5] green dc at underarm, then work along sawtooth edge of Sleeve as follows: sk first shell, work 3 dc in base of next shell, sc in tip of same shell, * work 3 dc in base of V-shape, sc in tip of next shell. Rep from * 6 times more; work 3 dc in base of same shell. Join with sl st to first sc. Turn.

2nd rnd: Working in top lp of each st, sc in each of next 3 dc, * sk next sc, sc in each of next 3 dc. Rep from * around, ending with sc in each of next 2 [5] sc; join with sl st. Break off. Sleeve is slightly puffed.

Neck Edging: 1st rnd: With right side of work facing you, attach green to left shoulder seam, ch 3, work 4 dc in same place, (sc in tip of next shell, work 3 dc in base of same shell) twice; sk next 3 dc, work sc in next sc, sl st in each of 8 sts of next shell, work 3 dc in base of same shell, sc in tip of next shell, work 3 dc in base of same shell, sk next 3 dc, work sc in next sc, sl st in each of 8 sts of next shell, work 3 dc in base of same shell, sk next 3 dc, sc in center front sc, sk next 3 dc, work 3 dc in base of next shell, sl st in each of 8 sts of same shell, sc in next sc, sk next 3 dc, work 3 dc in base of next shell, sc in tip of same shell, work 3 dc in base of next shell, sl st in each of 8 sts of same shell, sc in next sc, sk next 3 dc, (work 3 dc in base of next shell, sc in tip of same shell) twice; work 5 dc in right shoulder seam; continue along back neck as follows: Sk next 3 dc, sc in next ch-2 sp, sl st in each of next 3 dc, (sc in next ch-2 sp, work 4 dc in next sc) 4 times; sk next 3 dc, sc in next ch-2 sp, sl st in each of next 3 dc, sc in next ch-2 sp; join with sl st to top of first ch-3. Break off.

2nd rnd: Attach mint with sl st to last sl st, ch 1, sc in each of next 9 sts, sk next 3 dc, work 3 dc in next sc, sk next 4 sl sts, sc in each of next 8 sts, sk next 3 dc, work 3 dc in next sc, sk next 4 sl sts, sc in each of next 4 sl sts, sk next 3 dc, work 3 dc in center front sc, sk next 3 dc, sc in each of next 4 sl sts, sk next 4 sl sts, work 3 dc in next sc, sk next 3 dc, sc in each of next 8 sts, sk next 4 sl sts, work 3 dc in next sc, sk next 3 dc, sc in each of next 10 sts, sc in each of next 29 sts of back neck edge, decreasing 4 sts as evenly spaced as possible; (to dec: draw up a lp in each of 2 sts, y o hook and draw through all 3 lps on hook); join with sl st to first ch-1. Break off.

3rd rnd: With bright pink, make lp on hook; sc in last sl st, sc in each st around, skipping 3 dc at center front; join with sl st to first sc. Break off.

GRANNY SQUARE PULLOVER

Cotton yarn makes a smocklike top to wear alone or with a turtleneck. Squares of single and double crochet and shells are crocheted together with single crochet and picot stitches.

SIZES: Small (10-12) [medium (14-16)]. Garment measures 18″ [20″] across back from underarm to underarm.

MATERIALS: Medium-weight cotton such as Lily Sugar-'n-Cream cotton yarn, 3 (125-yd.) balls each lavender, sea green, yellow-green, and deep rose (see Note below); aluminum crochet hook size G [H] (or English/Canadian hook No. 9 [8]) *or the size that will give you the correct gauge.*

GAUGE: Each square measures 5½″ [6″].

Note: The garment shown was made of the yarn specified. However, you can substitute knitting worsted (wool or synthetic), if desired, and use size H [I] hook, working loosely. You will need 6 oz. of each color. Be sure to check size of square and block pieces lightly before joining.

Garment is worked in squares which are made separately and then crocheted together. Each square consists

of a Triangle which is squared off in a different color. Mark each completed Square with sticker or tag; this will be helpful in joining.

SQUARE 1 (make 9): Triangle: Starting at center with lavender, ch 6. Join with sl st to form ring.

1st rnd: Work sc in ring, * ch 2, holding back on hook the last lp of each dc, work 2 dc in ring, y o hook, draw through all 3 lps on hook, ch 2, sc in ring. Rep from * 5 times more, omitting last sc; join with sl st to first sc (6 petals made). Break off. Piece should measure 2″ [2¼″] in diameter.

Note: Always work squares with right side facing you.

2nd rnd: With sea green, make lp on hook, sc in tip of any petal, (ch 3, dc in sc between petals, ch 3, sc in tip of next petal) 6 times, omitting last sc; join with sl st to first sc (12 lps made).

3rd rnd: * Work 3 sc in next ch-3 lp, sc in next dc, ch 3, sc in last sc made (p made), work 3 sc in next ch-3 lp. Rep from * 5 times more (6 p made); join with sl st to first sc. Break off.

4th rnd: With yellow-green, make lp on hook, sc in any p, * ch 2, sc in same p, ch 3, sk next 2 sc, sc in next sc (place marker in ch-3 lp just made), ch 2, sc in next sc, ch 3, sk next 2 sc, in next p work sc, ch 2 and sc, sk next 2 sc, work 4 tr in next sc, ch 3, sc in top of last tr made (p made); work 4 tr in next sc, sk next 2 sc, sc in next p. Rep from * twice more, omitting marker. Omit last sc. Join with sl st to first sc. Break off. Triangle completed.

To form square: 5th row: With rose, make lp on hook, in marked ch-3 lp of Triangle 1 work sc, ch 2 and sc, sk next ch-2 sp, in next ch-3 lp work 4 tr, p and 4 tr, sk next ch-2 sp and first tr, in next tr work sc, ch 2 and sc, ch 5; keeping ch-5 in back of work, sk next 2 tr, p and next 2 tr; in next tr work sc, ch 2 and sc, sk next tr and ch-2 sp, in next ch-3 lp work 4 tr, p and 4 tr, sk next ch-2 sp, in next ch-3 lp work sc, ch 2 and sc. Break off. Square completed.

SQUARE 2 (make 9): Triangle: Work in same manner as for Triangle 1 in the following color combination:
1st rnd: Yellow-green.
2nd and 3rd rnds: Sea green.
4th rnd: Lavender.
To form square: With deep rose, work same as 5th row of Square 1.

SQUARE 3 (make 3): Triangle: Work in same manner as Triangle of Square 2.
To form square: With yellow-green, work same as 5th row of Square 1.

SQUARE 4 (make 4): Triangle: Work in same manner as Triangle of Square 1.
To form square: With lavender, work same as 5th row of Square 1.

In addition, make 10 Triangles as for Square 1 and 4 Triangles as for Square 2, omitting 5th rows that form Squares.

BACK: Horizontal Joining Row: Follow Diagram 1 for position, placing each Square with its 5th row corners (see broken lines) pointing in the direction shown. Join Square 2-B to Square 1-A in the direction of the arrow, as follows: With rose, make lp on hook, * sc in corner p on Square 2-B, sc in corner p on Square 1-A (2 corner p joined), ch 3, sc in sc last made (p made), sk 1 tr on Square 2-B, sc in next tr, work p, sc in corresponding tr on Square 1-A, work p, sk next 2 tr on Square 2-B, sc in next ch-2 sp, sc in corresponding ch-2 sp on Square 1-A, work p, sc in center ch-2 sp (or p) on Square 2-B, sc in corresponding center ch-2 sp (or p) on Square 1-A, work p, sc in next ch-2 sp on Square 2-B, sc in corresponding ch-2 sp on Square 1-A, work p, sk 1 tr on Square 2-B, sc in next tr, work p, sc in corresponding tr on Square 1-A, work p, sc in corner p on Square 2-B, sc in corner p on Square 1-A. Do not break off, but continue to join Square 1-D to Square 1-C and Square 2-F to Square 1-E by repeating from * until Row 2 is joined to Row 1. Break off.

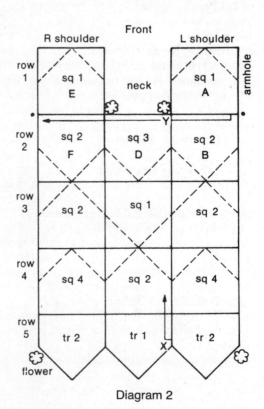

Diagram 1

Diagram 2

Following Diagram 1 for position, join each row to the preceding one in same manner, using sea green to join Triangle Row 5 to Row 4.

Vertical Joining Row: Joining row is worked vertically from bottom to top. With rose, make lp on hook, sc in ch-2 sp before tr corner (X on Triangle 1), sc in corresponding ch-2 on Triangle 2, work p, sk 1 tr on Triangle 1, sc in next tr, work p, sc in corresponding tr on Triangle 2, work p, sc in corner p on Triangle 1, * sk horizontal joining row, sc in corner p on Square 4, work p, sk 1 tr on Square 3, sc in next tr, work p, sc in corresponding tr on Square 4, work p, sc in next ch-2 sp on Square 3, sc in corresponding ch-2 sp on Square 4, work p, sc in next ch-2 sp on Square 3, sc in corresponding ch-2 sp on Square 4, work p, sk 1 tr on Square 3, sc in next tr, work p, sc in corresponding tr on Square 4, work p, sc in corner p on Square 3. Rep from * across, joining each row of squares and ending with sc in corner p on Square 1-A. Break off. Work remaining vertical joining row in same manner.

FRONT: Horizontal Joining Row: Following Diagram 2 for position, join Square 2-B to Square 1-A in same manner as Square 2-B of Back was joined to Square 1-A. Continue to work across Square 3-D (front neck) as follows: Sc in corner p of Square 3-D, work p, ch 3, sc in last sc on p just made (double p made), sk next 2 tr, sc in next tr, work p, (sc in next ch-2 sp, work p) 3 times; sk 1 tr, sc in next tr, work double p, sc in next corner p (8 p's made), continue to join Square 2-F to 1-E as before. Complete as for Back.

Vertical Joining Row: Work same as for Back, ending with sc in corner p of Square 2-B (Y on Diagram), continue along side of Square 1-A (side neck) as follows: Sk horizontal joining row, with wrong side of work facing you, sc in corner p, work p, sk 1 tr, sc in next tr, work double p, sc in next ch-2 sp, work p, sl st in next ch-2 sp. Break off.

Work second vertical joining row in same manner.

UNDERARM INSERT (make 2): Follow Diagram 3 for position. Using rose, join Triangle 1 to Square 2 as before. Break off.

Work along top of Square 2 to make area Z as follows:

1st row: With rose, make lp on hook, sc in first tr on Square 2 (X on Diagram), work p, sc in same tr, sk 1 tr, in next tr work 1 sc, ch 2 and 1 sc (shell made), sk 1 tr, work shell in next ch-2 sp, work shell in next p, work shell in next ch-2 sp, sk 1 tr, work shell in next tr, sk 1 tr, sc in next tr (5 shells made); ch 3, turn.

2nd row: Work 2 sc in last sc made on previous row (p made), work shell in each shell across, sc in next sc; ch 3, turn.

Rep 2nd row twice more, ending last repeat with ch 2, turn.

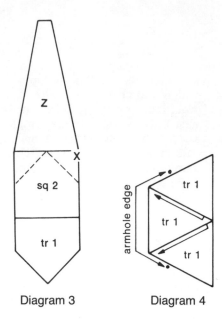

Diagram 3   Diagram 4

5th row: Sc in first shell, work shell in each of next 3 shells, sc in last shell; ch 3, turn.

Rep 2nd row 4 times more, ending last repeat with ch 2, turn.

10th row: Sc in first shell, work shell in next shell, sc in last shell; ch 2, turn.

11th row: Work shell in next shell, sc in next sc; ch 3, turn.

12th row: Work 2 sc in last sc made on previous row (p made), work shell in shell, sc in top of turning ch; ch 3, turn.

13th row: Work 2 sc in last sc made on previous row (p made), shell in shell, sc in next sc; ch 3, turn.

14th and 15th rows: Rep 13th row twice more, ending last rep with ch 2, turn.

16th row: Work shell in next shell, sc in next sc; ch 2, turn.

17th row: Rep 16th row, ending with sc in top of turning ch instead of in sc; ch 2, turn.

18th row: Rep 12th row.

19th through 21st rows: Rep 13th row 3 times more, ending last rep with ch 2, turn.

22nd and 23rd rows: Rep 16th row twice more, ending last rep with sc in top of turning ch; ch 3, turn.

24th row: Rep 12th row.

25th row: Rep 13th row, ending with ch 2, turn.

26th row: Rep 16th row, ending with sl st in next sc. Omit last ch-2. Break off.

To Join Underarm Insert: Using rose and working vertical joining row, join Triangle 1 and Square 2 of insert to Triangle 2 and Square 4 of left side of Back. Continue to join Area Z of insert to Squares 1 and 2-F of Back as follows: Sc in corner p on Square 1, work p, sk first p on Area Z, sc in next p, work p, sk 2 tr on Square 1, sc in next tr, work p, sc in next p on Z, sc in next ch-2 sp on Square 1, work p, sc in next p on Z, sc in next ch-2 sp on Square 1, work p, sc in side of 10th row on Z, work p, sk next 2 tr on Square 1, sc in next tr, work p, sc in next p on Z, sc in corner p on Square 2-F, work p, sc in next p on Z, work p, sk next 2 tr on Square 2-F, sc in next tr, work p, sc in next p on Z, sc in next ch-2 sp on Square 2-F, work p, sc in next p on Z, sc in next ch-2 sp on Square 2-F, work p, sc in side of 23rd row on Z, work p, sk next 2 tr on Square 2-F, sc in next tr, work p, sc in last p on Z, sc in corner p on Square 2-F. Break off.

Join opposite side of Insert to Left Front in same manner, working from top down and reversing order.

Join right Underarm Insert in same manner.

Shoulder Seams: Hold Front and Back together with wrong sides facing, matching shoulder square stitches. With rose, make lp on hook. Working through both layers, sc in right corner p, ch 4, sc in next ch-2 sp, ch 2, sc in center p, ch 2, sc in next ch 2 sp, ch 4, sc in next corner p of back only. Continue along back neck as follows: Sc in next corner p, ch 4, sc in next ch-2 sp, ch 2, sc in next center p, ch 2, sc in next ch-2 sp, ch 4, sc in next corner p, sc in next corner p of back only, ch 4; working through both layers to join other shoulder, sc in next ch-2 sp, ch 2, sc in next center p, ch 2, sc in next ch-2 sp, ch 4, sc in next corner p. Break off.

SLEEVES: Following Diagram 4 for position, using yellow-green and working horizontal joining row, join bottom Triangle in direction of arrow (8 p made). Break off. Join center Triangle to top Triangle in same manner. Holding Sleeve and Armhole with right sides facing, with yellow-green sl st them together between dots (also see dots on Diagrams 1 and 2) through top lps only.

FLOWER MOTIFS (make 6): With rose, rep first rnd of Square 1. Following Diagrams 1 and 2 for position, sew each flower in place by 1 petal at lower edge of pullover and by 4 petals at neck edge.

LONG-SLEEVED PULLOVER

A galaxy of stars is sprinkled across heavenly shades of lavender and blue. Rayon yarn is worked into strips and then joined. Pattern stitches are done in single and double crochet and chain stitches.

SIZES: Small (8-10) [medium (12-14)—large (14-16)]. Garment measures 16″ [18″—20″] across back from underarm to underarm.

MATERIALS: Medium-weight rayon yarn, such as Kentucky All-Purpose Yarn (100% rayon), 6 (100-yd.) skeins sky blue, 5 skeins each orchid and lavender, 1 skein each navy and wine (see Note below); aluminum crochet hook sizes E and G [F and H—G and I] (or English/Canadian hooks No. 11 and 9 [10 and 8—9 and 7]) *or the sizes that* *will give you the correct gauge.*

GAUGE: Star measures 2¼″ [2½″—2¾″] in diameter; 3 shells = 1½″ [1¾″—2″].

Note: The garment shown was made of the yarn specified. However, you can substitute knitting worsted, if desired, which will give you the same gauge. You will need 2 skeins less of each of the 2 main colors and 1 skein each of all other colors.

The sweater is worked in vertical strips which are made separately, and then crocheted together. Always work with the right side facing you, unless otherwise specified.

FRONT: STAR MOTIF 1: Starting at center with navy and size E [F—G] hook, ch 5 [6—6]. Join with sl st to form ring.

1st rnd: Ch 3, work 11 [17—17] dc in ring (12 [18—18] dc, counting ch-3 as 1 dc); join with sl st to top of first ch-3.

2nd rnd: * Ch 4, work hdc in 3rd ch from hook, dc in next ch, sk 1 [2—2] dc on ring, sl st in next dc. Rep from * around (6 points made). Break off.

3rd rnd: With sky blue, make lp on hook, sc in tip of any point, * ch 1, in next sl st between points work tr, ch 1 and tr, ch 2 (mark this ch-2), work sc, ch 1 and sc in same sl st, ch 1, sc in tip of next point, ch 1, in next sl st work sc, ch 1 and sc, ch 2, work tr, ch 1 and tr in same sl st, ch 1, sc in tip of next point, ch 1, in next sl st work sc, ch 1 and sc, ch 1, sc in tip of next point. Rep from * once more, omitting last sc; join with sl st to first sc. Break off.

Make 11 more stars in same colors (12 Star Motifs No. 1).

Make 30 more stars in same manner, using the following colors:

STAR MOTIF 2 (make 6): Navy star, orchid background.

STAR MOTIF 3 (make 4): Navy star, lavender background.

STAR MOTIF 4 (make 8): Wine star, sky blue background.

STAR MOTIF 5 (make 4): Wine star, orchid background.

STAR MOTIF 6 (make 8): Wine star, lavender background.

Mark each completed Motif with a sticker or tag; this will be helpful when making strips.

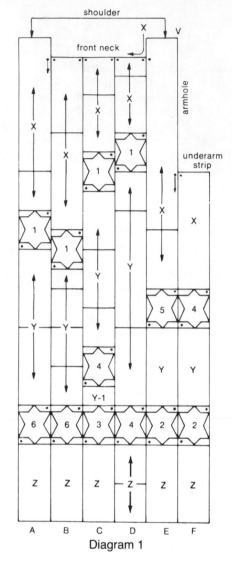

Diagram 1

Diagram 1 shows how the vertical Strips are made and joined.

STRIP A: Section X: 1st row: With right side facing you, using sky blue and size G [H—I] hook, make lp on hook; work 2 sc in marked ch-2 sp of Star Motif 1 (dot on Diagram 1), work sc, ch 2 and sc in same sp (first shell made); in center sc at tip of point work sc, ch 2 and sc (another shell made); work shell in next ch-2 sp, work 2 sc in same sp; ch 1, turn.

2nd row: Sc in each of first 2 sc, work shell in ch-2 sp of each of next 3 shells, sc in each of last 2 sc (3 shells made); ch 2, turn.

Repeating 2nd row for pattern, work even until there are 6 blue rows in all, omitting ch-1 at end of last row.

Note: Always omit ch-1 at end of last row of a number of even rows, unless otherwise specified. Break off.

Attach lavender and work even in pattern as established for 21 rows. Break off.

Section Y: Working along opposite side of Star Motif 1 with sky blue, rep first row. Work even in pattern until there are 12 blue rows in all. Break off.

Attach lavender and work even in pattern for 11 rows. Do not break off, but ch 1, turn.

Horizontal Joining Row: With wrong side of Section X-Y and Star Motif 6 facing you, sc in each of first 2 sc of Section Y, work sc in first shell, sl st in marked ch-2 sp of Star Motif 6 (dot on Diagram 1), sc in same shell of Section Y, sc in next shell, sl st in corresponding sc at tip of point on star, sc in same shell on Section Y, sc in next shell, sl st in corresponding ch-2 sp on star, sc in same shell on Section Y, sc in each of last 2 sc of Section Y (12 orchid rows). Break off.

Section Z: Working along opposite side of Star Motif 6 with lavender, rep first row, then work even in pattern for 11 rows more. Break off. Strip A completed.

STRIP B: Section X: With sky blue, rep first row. Work even in pattern for 14 rows more. Break off.

With wrong side of work facing you, with lavender, work even in pattern for 12 rows. Break off.

Section Y: With sky blue, rep first row. Work even in pattern for 2 rows more. Break off.

With wrong side facing you and with orchid, work in pattern for 6 rows. Break off.

With wrong side facing you and with sky blue, work even in pattern for 6 rows. Break off.

With wrong side facing you and with lavender, work even in pattern for 5 rows; ch 1, turn.

Join Section Y to Star Motif 6 as before (6 lavender rows). Break off.

Section Z: Rep Section Z of Strip A.

STRIP C: Section X: With sky blue, rep first row. Work even in pattern for 8 rows more. Break off.

With wrong side facing you and with lavender, work even in pattern for 6 rows. Break off.

Section Y: With sky blue, rep first row. Work even in pattern for 8 rows more. Break off.

With orchid, work even in pattern for 9 rows. Break off.

With sky blue, work even in pattern for 5 rows; ch 1, turn.

With wrong sides facing you, join Section Y to Star Motif 4 as before (6 sky blue rows).

Section Y-1: With sky blue, rep first and 2nd rows. Join to Star Motif 3 as before (3 sky blue rows).

Section Z: Repeat Section Z of Strip A.

STRIP D: Section X: With sky blue, rep first row. Work even in pattern for 8 rows more. Break off.

With lavender, work even in pattern for 3 rows. Break off.

Section Y: With sky blue, rep first row. Work even in pattern for 5 rows more. Break off.

With orchid, work even in pattern for 18 rows. Break off.

With sky blue, work even in pattern for 11 rows; ch 1, turn.

Join Section Y and Star Motif 4 as before (12 sky blue rows). Break off.

Section Z: Using sky blue, rep first row. Work even in pattern for 5 rows more. Break off.

Using lavender, work even in pattern for 6 rows. Break off.

STRIP E: Section X: With orchid and Star Motif 5, rep first row. Work even in pattern until there are 9 orchid rows in all. Break off.

With sky blue, work even in pattern for 30 rows. Break off.

Section Y: With orchid, rep first row. Work even in pattern for 10 rows more; ch 1, turn.

Join Section Y and Star Motif 2 as before (12 orchid rows). Break off.

Section Z: Rep Section Z of Strip A.

UNDERARM STRIP F: Section X: With sky blue and Star Motif 4, rep first row. Work even in pattern for 17 rows more. Break off.

Section Y: With lavender, rep first row. Work even in pattern for 10 rows more; ch 1, turn.

Join Section Y and Star Motif 2 as before (12 lavender rows). Break off.

Section Z: With orchid, rep Section Z of Strip A.

Vertical Joining Row: Follow Diagram 1 for position. With orchid and size E [F—G] hook and with right side facing you, join Strip B to Strip A, working from top down as follows: Form lp on hook, sc in side of last row of Section X on Strip B (dot on Diagram 1), sc in side of 4th row of Section X on Strip A (dot on Diagram 1); working in direction of arrow, * sc in side of next row on Strip B, sc in side of next row on Strip A. Rep from * to Star Motif 1. To join Star Motifs to sections and to other Star Motifs (Star Motif = 6 rows), continue to join in sc pattern as before, working 1 sc in each ch-1 sp along edge of Star Motif. Complete row in sc pattern. Joining row will form a slight ridge along seam on right side.

Following Diagram 1 for position, join each remaining strip to preceding strip in same manner, joining Strips D and E at neck edge to correspond to Strips A and B, reversing shaping.

BACK: Work in same manner as for Front.

TO JOIN FRONT AND BACK: With wrong sides to-

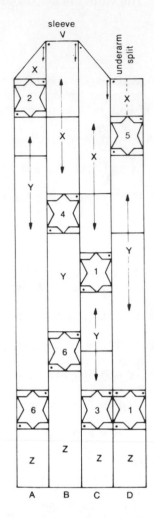

Diagram 2

gether, join Strip A of Back to Underarm Strip F of Front as before. Join opposite side and shoulder seams in same manner.

SLEEVES: See Diagram 2.

Strip A: Section X (armhole shaping): 1st row: With orchid and Star Motif 2, rep first row.

2nd row (dec row): Sc in first 2 sc, work shell in each of next 2 shells, sk next shell, sc in each of last 2 sc; ch 1, turn.

3rd row (dec row): Sc in each of first 2 sc, work shell in next shell, work 2 sc in next shell; ch 1, turn.

4th row (dec row): Sc in each of first 2 sc, work shell in next shell, sc in each of last 2 sc; ch 1, turn.

5th row: Sc in each of first 2 sc, sc in next shell; ch 1, turn.

6th row: Sc in first sc and in each of next 2 sc. Break off.

Section Y: With orchid, rep first row. Work even in pattern as before for 5 rows more, omitting ch-1 at end of last row. Break off.

Using sky blue, work even in pattern for 35 rows; ch 1, turn.

With wrong sides of Section Y and Star Motif 6 facing you, join as before (36 sky blue rows). Break off.

Section Z: With lavender, rep first row. Work even in pattern for 8 rows more. Break off.

STRIP B: Section X: With sky blue and Star Motif 4, rep first row. Work even in pattern for 11 rows more. Break off.

With orchid, work even in pattern for 12 rows. Break off.

Section Y: With sky blue, rep first row. Work in pattern for 13 rows more; ch 1, turn.

Join Section Y and Star Motif 6 as before (15 sky blue rows). Break off.

Section Z: With lavender, rep first row. Work even in pattern for 17 rows more. Break off.

STRIP C: Section X: With sky blue, rep first row. Work even in pattern for 8 rows more. Break off.

With wrong side facing you and with orchid, work even in pattern for 18 rows; ch 1, turn.

19th row (dec row, armhole shaping): With wrong side facing you, sc in each of first 2 sc, work shell in each of next 2 shells, work 2 sc in next shell; ch 1, turn.

20th row (dec row): Sc in each of first 2 sc, work shell in each of next 2 shells, sc in each of last 2 sc; ch 1, turn.

21st through 24th rows: Rep 3rd through 6th rows of Section X on Strip A of Sleeve. Break off.

Section Y: With sky blue, rep first row. Work even in pattern for 8 rows more. Break off.

With lavender, work even in pattern for 5 rows; ch 1, turn.

Join Section Y and Star Motif 3 as before (6 lavender rows). Break off.

Section Z: With lavender, rep first row. Work even in pattern for 8 rows more. Break off.

STRIP D: Section X: To Form Split: 1st row (right side): With orchid, make lp on hook; in marked ch-2 sp of Star Motif 5 work 3 sc, ch 2 and 1 sc; in center sc at point work 2 sc; ch 2, turn.

2nd row: Sk first sc, sc in next sc, work shell in shell, sc in each of last 2 sc; ch 2, turn. Rep 2nd row 4 times more. Break off.

1st row (left side): With orchid, make lp on hook, work 2 sc in center sc at point on Star Motif 5, in next ch-2 sp work 1 sc, ch 2 and 3 sc; ch 2, turn.

2nd row: Sk first sc, sc in next sc, work shell in shell, sc in each of next 2 sc; ch 2, turn. Rep 2nd row 4 times more. Break off. Underarm split completed.

Section Y: With orchid, rep first row. Work even in pattern for 11 rows more. Break off.

28

With sky blue, work even in pattern for 23 rows; ch 1, turn.

With wrong side of Section Y and Star Motif 1 facing you, join as before (24 sky blue rows). Break off.

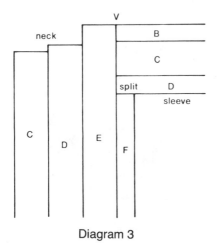

Diagram 3

Section Z: With sky blue, rep first row. Work even in pattern for 8 rows more. Break off.

Following Diagram 2 for position, join Sleeve Strips with vertical joining rows as before. Then join Strip D to Strip A to form tube.

TO JOIN SLEEVES TO BODY: With V's matching (see Diagrams 1, 2, and 3) and wrong sides together, pin Sleeves in place. Working through both layers and using size E [F—G] hook, sc evenly around armhole on right side.

NECK EDGING: 1st rnd: With right side facing you, with orchid and size E [F—G] hook, * work shell in shoulder seam (X on Diagram 1); working in direction of arrow, work shell in side of each of next 3 rows of Strip E; work shell in vertical joining rows and in each shell across Strips D, C, and B; work shell in side of each of next 3 rows of Strip A. Rep from * around; join with sl st to first sc. Break off.

2nd rnd: With double strand of orchid and E [F—G] hook, sc in any shell, * ch 1, sc in next shell. Rep from * around; ch 1, join with sl st to first sc. Break off.

DOLMAN CARDIGAN

Rich tones of gold, jade, and peacock blue invoke the Orient in this sweater with kimono sleeves and obi waist. Suedelike nylon is worked vertically in single and double crochet and shells. The waistband, done horizontally, and the bobble buttons are worked in single crochet.

SIZE: One size will fit 10–14. Garment measures about 31″ across back from sleeve edge to sleeve edge.

MATERIALS: Nylon chenille cord (narrow, suedelike cord), 14 (1-oz.) spools ochre, 4 spools each beige, emerald, apple green, and blue, 2 spools yellow (see Note below); aluminum crochet hook size H (or English/Canadian hook No. 8) *or the size that will give you the correct gauge.*

Note: The garment shown was made of the cord specified. You can get the same gauge and "bulky" look by working with 2 strands of knitting worsted, if desired, and size G hook. You will need the same number of ounces as for the cord.

GAUGE: 3 sc = 1″; 3 sc rows = 1″.

Note: Work with cord double throughout.

DIAMOND PANELS: 1st row: Starting with first diamond on first panel, with ochre * ch 7, turn, working in back lp of each ch st, sc in 4th ch from hook and in each ch across (4 sc); ch 2, turn.

2nd row: Sk first sc, sc in each of next 3 sc, sc in top of turning ch (4 sc); ch 2, turn.

3rd and 4th rows: Rep 2nd row (first Diamond completed). Omit last ch-2 and do not break off or turn, but rep from * on first row 5 times more (6 Diamonds attached point to point and measuring about 12″ in all). Omit last ch-2.

Do not break off or turn, but work along one side of Diamonds as follows, making sure Diamond strip is not twisted.

5th rnd (right side): Ch 1, sc in side of last row made, sc in side of each of next 2 rows; in side of next row work sc, ch 2, and sc, * sc in each of next 3 sts, sk last st on Diamond, sc in side of each of next 3 rows on next Diamond; in side of next row work sc, ch 2 and sc *. Rep

from * to * 4 times more, sc in each of next 3 sts, ch 2, sk last st. Continue to work along opposite side of Diamond strip as follows: Sc in side of each of next 3 rows; in side of next row work sc, ch 2 and sc, then rep from * to * 5 times more, sc in each of next 3 sc, ch 2, sk last sc; join with sl st to first ch-1. Break off.

6th rnd: With apple green, make lp on hook. With wrong side facing you, work sc, ch 2 and sc in ch-2 sp at tip of Diamond strip. Working in front lp only of each st, sc in each of next 4 sc, * in next ch-2 sp work sc, ch 2 and sc, sc in each of next 3 sc, sk next 2 sc, sc in each of next 3 sc on next Diamond *. Rep from * to * 4 times more; in next ch-2 sp work sc, ch 2 and sc, sc in each of next 4 sc, in next ch-2 sp at tip work sc, ch 2 and sc, sc in each of next 4 sc. Rep from * to * 5 times more; work sc, ch 2 and sc in next ch-2 sp, sc in each of next 4 sc; join with sl st to first sc. Break off.

7th row: With beige, make lp on hook. With right side of work facing you, working in back lp of each st, sk first 3 sc after ch-2 sp at tip of Diamond strip, sc in each of next 3 sc, in next ch-2 sp work sc, ch 2, and sc, * sc in each of next 2 sc, sk next 2 sc, work 2 long dc in sp between next 2 skipped sc on 5th rnd, sk next 2 sc, sc in each of next 2 sc, in next ch-2 sp work sc, ch 2 and sc.

Rep from * 4 times more, ending with sc in each of next 3 sc on last Diamond. Break off. The 6-Diamond Panel is completed to measure about 14″. Make 3 more Panels in same manner for Sleeves. Then make 2 more and put aside for Center Back Section.

Work four 5-Diamond Panels in same manner as for 6-Diamond Panel (12″) for Sleeves. Then make one 5-Diamond Panel, omitting 7th row, and put aside for Center Back section.

Work four 4-Diamond Panels (9½″) for Sleeves.

Back: Left Sleeve Section: Joining row: With right side of work facing you, following Diagram 1 for position, fit outside corners of beige edge on a 5-Diamond Panel (A) into inside corners of apple edge on a 6-Diamond Panel (B). Shaded zigzag bands on Diagram are beige 7th rows on Diamonds. Hold Panels together with wrong sides facing. Match first beige sc on 5-Diamond Panel to first apple sc st after corresponding ch-2 sp on 6-Diamond Panel at X. With ochre, make lp on hook. Working in back lp of each st, through both Panels, sc in each st from X to Y. Sc row will form a ridge on right side.

Join 4-Diamond Panel (C) to 5-Diamond Panel in same manner.

Fill-In Rnd: With ochre, make lp on hook. With right side of work facing you, work 3 sc in apple ch-2 sp at bottom of 4-Diamond Panel C (dot on Diagram 1). Work in the direction of arrow as follows: * (Sk next 2 sc, in next sc work 3 dc, ch 2 and 3 dc—shell made—sl st in sc of joining row, work 3 dc in 3rd apple sc before apple ch-2 sp at tip of next Diamond, sl st in ch-2 sp of previous shell made, work 3 dc in same sc—2 shells joined—sk next 2 sc, work 3 sc in next ch-2 sp) twice; sk next 3 sc, work shell in next sc, (**sc in next ch-2 sp, sk next 3 sc, work 3 dc in each of next 2 sts**) 5 times; sk next 3 sc, sc in next ch-2 sp, sk next 3 sc, work shell in next sc, work 3 sc in next ch-2 sp at tip of 6-Diamond Panel *. Rep from * to * once more, working from ** to ** 3 times instead of 5 times. Omit last 3 sc; join with sl st to first sc at bottom of 4-Diamond Panel. Break off.

Right Sleeve Section: Work to correspond to Left Sleeve Section.

Center Back Section: Following Diagram 1 for position, fit outside corners of beige edge on left 6-Diamond Panel (D) into inside corners of apple edge on center 5-Diamond Panel (E). Match 2nd ch st of first ch-2 sp on 6-Diamond Panel (Z on Diagram) to corresponding sc on 5-Diamond Panel and join in same manner as for Sleeve Section. Join right 6-Diamond Panel (F) to Center Panel in same manner, working from top down.

Fill-In Rnd: With ochre, make lp on hook. With right side of work facing you, work 3 sc in ch-2 sp at top of right 6-Diamond Panel (dot on Diagram). Working in direction of arrow, rep from * to * on fill-in rnd of Left Sleeve Sec-

tion. Rep from * to * once more, omitting last 3 sc. Join with sl st to first sc at top of 6-Diamond Panel.

1st shell row (G on Diagram): With blue, make lp on hook. With right side of work facing you, work 1 sc and 2 dc in upper left corner ch-2 sp (shell made). Working in direction of arrow from dot, (sk 2 sts, work shell in next st) 10 times; sk 2 sts, sc in next st (11 shells made). Break off.

2nd shell row (H on Diagram): With emerald, make lp on hook. With wrong side of work facing you, work in direction of arrow from dot on G, as follows: Work shell in 7th st from end of first shell row, (sk 2 dc, work shell in next sc) 8 times; sk next 2 dc, sc in next sc (9 shells made). Break off.

With right side of work facing you, work across opposite side of back to correspond.

Joining Left Sleeve Section to Center Back Section: Following Diagram 1 for placement, hold Sleeve Section and Back Section together with wrong sides facing. Using emerald, sc them together as before (see wavy line), working from bottom up. Join Right Sleeve Section to Center Back Section in same manner.

FRONT: Work Left and Right Sleeve Sections in same manner as for Back.

Right Front Section: With blue, rep first through 5th rnds of 6-Diamond panel.

6th row: With yellow, make lp on hook. With right side of work facing you, sc in ch-2 sp at dot on Diagram 2, * ch 2, holding back on hook the last lp of each dc, work

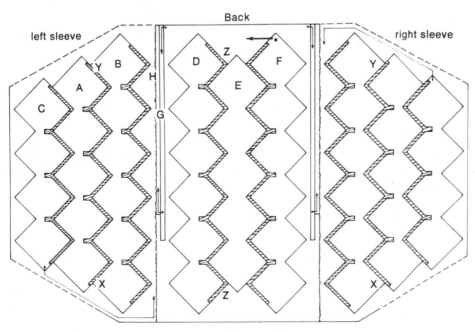

Diagram 1

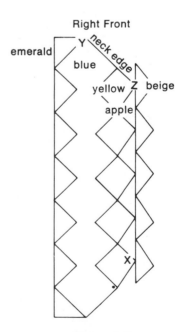

Diagram 2

1 dc in each of next 8 sc, y o hook and draw through all 9 lps on hook, ch 2 loosely, work 2 sc in next ch-2 sp (shell made between 2 Diamonds). Rep from * 4 times more (5 shells made), turn.

7th row: Sk first 2 sc and 1 ch st, in next ch st work 3 dc, ch 2 and 3 dc (shell made), * sk next ch-2, sc in each of next 2 sc, sk 1 ch st, work shell in next ch st. Rep from * 3 times more, sk next ch-2, sc in next sc (5 shells made). Break off.

8th row: With apple, make lp on hook. With right side of work facing you, sc in first ch-2 sp to left of last sc made (X on Diagram 2), then rep from * on 6th row until 4 shells are made, ending with 1 sc in last ch-2 sp. Break off.

9th row: With emerald, make lp on hook. With right side of work facing you, sc in ch-2 sp at top of 6-Diamond Panel (Y on Diagram 2), ch 2, holding back on hook the last lp of each dc, work 1 dc in each of next 4 sc, y o hook, draw through all 5 lps on hook, ch 2 loosely, work 2 sc in next ch-2 sp (top corner half-shell made). Rep from * on 6th row until 5½ shells are made in all. Ch 2, holding back on hook last lp of each dc, work 1 dc in each of next 4 sc, y o hook, draw through all 5 lps on hook, ch 2 loosely, sc in next ch-2 sp at bottom of 6-Diamond Panel (bottom corner half-shell made). Break off.

Buttonhole row: With wrong side of work facing you and using beige, sc in last sc made on 8th row (Z on Diagram 2), ch 2, work 2 dc, ch 2 and 3 dc in same sc (first shell made), sk 1 ch st, sc in next ch st, * sk next ch-2, work 3 dc, ch 2 and 3 dc in next sc (another shell made), sk next sc and ch st, sc in next ch st. Rep from * twice more, sk next ch-2, work 3 dc, ch 2 and 2 dc in last sc, ch 2 and sl st in same sc (5 shells made; buttonloops are formed by the ch-2 on each shell). Break off.

Left Front Section: Work this section in same manner as for Right Front Section, omitting buttonhole row.

Join Right Sleeve Section to Right Front Section in same manner as Right Sleeve Section of Back was joined to Center Back Section.

Join Left Sleeve Section to Left Front in same manner.

Holding Sleeve Sections together with right sides facing, with ochre, sl st them together along broken line (see Diagram 1), working through top lps only.

COLLAR: 1st row (dec row): With emerald, make lp on hook. With right side of work facing you, work 2 sc over ch-2 at top half-shell at beg of 9th row, sc in each st and ch-2 sp around, decreasing 1 st at shoulder seams (to dec, draw up a lp in each of next 2 sts, y o and draw through all 3 lps on hook); end with 2 sc over ch-2 at beg of 9th row on opposite side; ch 1, turn.

2nd row (dec row): Sc in each sc across, decreasing 1 st at shoulder seams and 3 sts evenly spaced along Center Back Section; ch 1, turn.

3rd row (inc row): Sc in each sc across, increasing 1 st at beg and end of row (to inc 1 st: work 2 sc in same st); ch 1, turn.

Rep 3rd row twice more, omitting ch 1 on last row. Break off.

6th row: With wrong side of work facing you, with blue, sc in each sc across. Break off.

7th row: With right side of work facing you, with emerald, sc in each sc across, decreasing 1 st at shoulder seams. Break off.

8th row: With right side of work facing you, with emerald, sc in side of first sc on first row, sc evenly across ends and top edge of collar, ending with sc in side of last sc on first row. Break off.

WAISTBAND: 1st row (dec row): With right side of work facing you, attach emerald to ch-2 sp (same sp in which apple st was worked) of yellow shell at lower edge of Left Front, ch 1, sc in each st and ch-2 sp across lower edge of cardigan, decreasing 1 st at underarm seams and ending with sc in ch-2 sp of yellow shell at opposite side; ch 1, turn.

2nd row (dec row): Sc in each sc across, decreasing 13 sts as evenly spaced as possible; ch 1, turn.

3rd row (dec row): Rep 2nd row once more.

4th row: Sc in each sc across; ch 1, turn.

5th and 6th rows: Rep 4th row twice more, omitting ch 1 on 6th row. Break off.

7th row: With wrong side of work facing you, with blue, sc in each sc across. Break off.

8th row: With right side of work facing you, with emerald, sc in each sc across; ch 1, turn.

Work even in sc for 3 rows more, omitting ch-1 at end of last row. Break off.

12th row: With wrong side of work facing you, with blue, sc in each sc across. Break off.

13th row: With right side of work facing you, with emerald, sc in each sc across; ch 1, turn.

14th row: Sc in each sc across. Break off.

Waistband Shells: With right side of work facing you, with emerald, sc in side of first sc on first row of Waistband, (sk next 2 rows, in side of next row work 5-dc shell, sk next 2 rows, sc in side of next row) twice; sc in side of last row (2 shells made across front edge of Waistband). Break off.

Work across opposite edge of Waistband to correspond, reversing order.

Buttons (make 10): With ochre, ch 4. Join with sl st to form ring. Ch 1, work 6 sc in ring, join to first sc (circle completed). Fold circle in half, working through 2 layers, sl st in next sc and in sc opposite. Break off, leaving 4″ end. Sew a button in center of each yellow diamond.

Lacy Tops

PICOT-EDGED TOP

A picot-edged top in white pearl cotton is made by single-crocheting lace strips together. The strips are formed from shell stitches worked vertically.

SIZES: Small (6-8) [medium (10-12)]. Garment measures 15½″ [17″] across back from underarm to underarm.

MATERIALS: Medium-weight cotton or Coats and Clark's pearl cotton size 5 used **double strand** throughout, 35 [37] (50-yd.) balls white; aluminum crochet hook size E [G] (or Canadian/English No. 11 [9]) *or the size that will give you the correct gauge.*

GAUGE: 1 strip measures 2½″ wide with size E hook; [1 strip measures 2¾″ wide with size G hook].

Note: Top is worked in strips that are crocheted together later. Be careful to get exact gauge because changes in size are determined by changes in hook size.

PATTERN STRIP: Starting at one end, ch 9.

1st row (right side): In 5th ch from hook, work 2 dc, ch 2 and 2 dc; sk next 3 ch, in last ch work dc, ch 3 and sc; ch 4, turn.

2nd row: Work 8 dc in ch-3 sp (shell made); in ch-2 sp work 2 dc, ch 2 and dc; work dc over turning ch-4; ch 4, turn.

3rd row: In ch-2 sp work 2 dc, ch 2 and dc; sk next 2 dc, in next dc work dc, ch 3 and sc; ch 4, turn. Rep 2nd and 3rd rows for pattern until strip measures desired length, ending with 2nd row and omitting ch 4. Do not break off. Mark this side as wrong side. With same side facing you, work along the long edge as follows:

Edging: 1st row: Ch 2, work 3 hdc over lp at end of each row up to last lp. Break off.

With same side (wrong side) of piece facing you, work along the long edge as follows:

1st row: Make lp on hook, sc over turning ch-4 on first shell, * ch 2, sk next 3 dc on same shell, dc in next dc, ch 2, sc over ch-4 on next shell. Rep from * across, ending with ch 2, sk next 3 dc on last shell, dc in next dc; ch 2, turn.

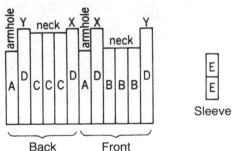

Back   Front   Sleeve

2nd row (right side): Work 3 hdc in each ch-2 sp across. Continuing across short end, work 4 sc over ch-4 sp at end of 8-dc shell, 4 sc over each of next 2 ch sps; join with sl st in next hdc. Break off. Leave opposite short end unworked.

BODY: Using size E [G] hook, work 2 strips with 17 shells each (marked A on Diagram), 3 strips with 18 shells each (B), 3 with 24 shells each (C), 4 with 25 shells each (D).

Picot-Edged Top

Scallop-Edged Top

SLEEVES: Using size E [G] hook, work 4 strips (E) with 8 shells each (2 for each Sleeve).

FINISHING: Following Diagram for placement, join strips of Back, Front, and Sleeves as follows: Placing adjacent strips with right sides together, sc in top lps only of each sc across. Break off. When all Body Strips have been joined as shown on Diagram, join Strip A at left to Strip D at right. Continuing in this manner, join shoulder seams (X to X, Y to Y). Join Sleeve Strips as shown, then join

ends of each strip to form 2 Sleeve rings. Set in Sleeves, easing to fit armholes.

Neck Edging: With right side facing you, sl st in any st at neck edge.

1st rnd: Ch 2, hdc in each st around, decreasing every 4th st to keep work flat; join.

2nd rnd: Rep 1st rnd.

3rd rnd: * Sc in next st, ch 4, sc in 4th ch from hook (p made), sk next st. Rep from * around; join.

Lower Edging: Work sc in any st at lower edge. Rep 3rd rnd of neck edging.

34

SCALLOP-EDGED TOP

A pretty scallop-edged top in ecru cotton crepe is not difficult to make. Strips with rounded ends are composed of double crochet and chain loops and then joined with single crochet.

SIZES: Small (6-8) [medium (10-12)]. Garment measures 15½″ [17″] across back from underarm to underarm.

MATERIALS: Medium-weight cotton such as Unger's Cotton Crepe, 10 [11] (50-gram) balls ecru; aluminum crochet hook size E [F] (or English/Canadian No. 11 [10]) *or the size that will give you the correct gauge.*

GAUGE: 1 strip measures 1⅞″ wide with size E hook; [1 strip measures 2″ wide with size F hook].

Note: Top is worked in strips that are crocheted together later. Be careful to get exact gauge because changes in size are determined by changes in hook size.

PATTERN STRIP: 1st row: Starting at one end, * ch 4, dc in 4th ch from hook. Rep from * until required number of lps have been worked.

1st rnd: Ch 3, work 3 dc over dc of last lp formed, * work 4 dc over dc of next lp. Rep from * up to last lp, place marker in last dc worked; work 12 dc in last lp, working around complete lp to form rounded end of Strip; working along opposite side of Strip, work 4 dc in each ch-3 lp up to last lp, place marker in last dc worked, work 8 dc in last lp to form rounded end; join with sl st in top of ch-3.

2nd rnd: Ch 3, work dc in each dc up to and including marked dc, dc in each of next 4 dc, place marker in last dc worked, work 2 dc in each of next 4 dc, dc in next dc and place marker in dc just worked, dc in each dc up to and including next marked dc, dc in each of next 4 dc, place marker in last dc worked, 2 dc in each of next 4 dc; join with sl st in top of ch-3, place marker in last st worked. Break off.

BODY: Using size E [F] hook, work 6 Pattern Strips with 21 lps each (marked A on Diagram), 4 Strips with 31 lps each (B), 3 Strips with 30 lps each (C), and 3 Strips with 23 lps each (D).

SLEEVES: Using size E [F] hook, work 14 Strips (E) with 5 lps each (7 Strips for each Sleeve).

FINISHING: Following Diagram for placement, join Strips of Back and Front as follows: Place adjacent Strips with right sides together and, working between marked sts at lower edge and marked sts at opposite end, sc in top lp only of each dc across. (If joining Strips of unequal length,

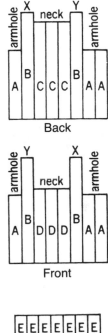

Back

Front

Sleeve

work to marked sts on shorter Strip.) Break off. Continuing in this manner, join underarm seams of Front and Back and join 8 top sts of Front and Back at each shoulder (X to X and Y to Y).

Join 7 strips of each Sleeve, then work Fill-In Row along one long edge of each as follows:

Fill-In Row: With right side facing you and starting at top right corner, sk marked dc, * sk next dc, sc in each of next 6 dc, sk next dc, work shell of 7 dc in next seam. Rep from * 5 times more, sk next dc, sc in each of next 6 dc. Break off.

At beg and end of Fill-In Row, fit sc into corners of Armhole on Body. With right sides together, pin Sleeve to Armhole. Working in top lps only, sc adjacent sts together. Join Sleeve seams in same manner.

Edging: With right side facing you, work 1 row sc around neck edge, working 2 sc in each dc across scallops, working 3-dc shell in each seam along back neck and skipping each seam along front neck. Work 1 row sc around Sleeves and lower edge, working 2 sc in each dc and skipping each seam.

Spring Cotton Sweaters

PANEL MOTIF PULLOVER

Lacy and lyrical, as sweet as a spring breeze, this charming top is composed of strips worked in single and double crochet and shells made with lattice-like centers. It is done in cream, pongee, spice, and peach cotton knit and crochet yarn doubled.

SIZES: Small (8-10) [medium (12-14)]. See Diagram of Front for dimensions.

MATERIALS: Thin-weight knit and crochet cotton used double, such as J. & P. Coats Knit-Cro-Sheen, 8 balls pongee (dark ecru), 6 balls peach, 5 balls spice (light brown), and 3 balls cream (cream comes in 250-yd. balls; colors come in 175-yd. balls); aluminum crochet hook size D [F] (or English/Canadian hook No. 12 [10]) *or the size that will give you the correct gauge.*

GAUGE: 1 strip measures 5¼" wide with size D hook; [1 strip measures 6" wide with size F hook].

Note: Work with 2 strands yarn held together throughout. Back, Front, and Sleeves are worked in strips that are crocheted together later. Be careful to get correct gauge; changes in size are determined by changes in hook size.

PATTERN STRIP: Garment is composed of 3 pattern strips each for Front and Back and 2 for each Sleeve (see Diagrams).

Foundation Chain: With peach, starting at one end of strip, * ch 4, dc in 4th ch from hook (lp made). Rep from * until required number of lps have been worked (as specified under Body and Sleeves directions). Do not break off.

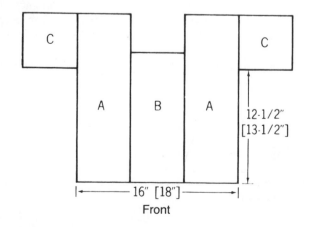

Front

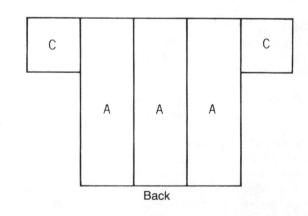

Back

36

1st rnd (wrong side): Ch 3, 3 dc over dc of last lp worked, * 4 dc over dc of next lp. Rep from * to within last lp; in last lp work (4 dc, ch-3 corner sp, 3 dc, ch-3 corner sp and 4 dc) to form end of strip; working along opposite edge of strip, work 4 dc in each ch lp to within last lp; in last lp work (4 dc, ch-3 corner sp, 3 dc and ch-3 corner sp); join with sl st in top of first ch-3 and mark last corner sp. Break off.

2nd rnd (right side): Turn strip over. With cream, make lp on hook and start in marked corner sp. * Work shell of (2 dc, ch 3 and 2 dc) in corner sp; dc in back lp of each of next 3 dc; in next corner sp work shell of (2 dc, ch 3 and 2 dc); dc in back lp of each dc to next ch-3 corner. Rep from * once more; join. Break off.

3rd rnd (right side): With spice, start rnd in next corner sp. * * Work shell of (4 dc, ch 3 and 4 dc) in corner sp, sk 2 dc, sc in each of next 3 dc, work shell in corner sp, sk next dc, sc in each of next 2 dc, * sk 2 dc, 4 dc in next dc, ch 3, 4 dc in next dc, sk 2 dc, sc in each of next 2 dc *. Rep from * to * to within 1 dc of next corner sp, sk dc. Rep from * * once more; join. Break off.

4th rnd: With peach, start rnd in next corner sp. * * Work sc, ch 2 and sc in corner sp; sc in back lp of each of next 11 sts, work sc, ch 2 and sc in next corner sp; sc in back lp of each of next 10 sts, * ch 2, sk ch-3 sp, sc in back lp of next 10 sts *. Rep from * to * to next corner, then repeat from * * once more; join. Break off.

Left Border: With right side facing you, work across one long edge of strip as follows:

1st row: With pongee, start in top right corner sp. Sc in corner sp, sk 5 sc, 3 dc in each of next 2 sc, * sc in next ch-2 sp, sk 4 sc, 3 dc in each of next 2 sc. Rep from * across, ending sk last 5 dc, sc in corner sp; ch 1, turn.

2nd row (wrong side): Sc in first st, * dc in next st, sc in next st. Rep from * across; ch 3, turn.

3rd row: Sk first sc, * sc in next dc, dc in next sc. Rep from * across; ch 1, turn. Rep 2nd and 3rd rows once

more. Break off. Do not turn.

Last row: With peach and with right side facing you, sc in each st across. Break off.

Right Border: Rep Left Border across other long edge of strip.

BODY: Using size D [F] hook, work 5 pattern strips with 26 lps each (marked A on Diagram) and 1 strip with 18 lps (B).

SLEEVES: Using size D [F] hook, work 4 strips (C) with 8 lps each (2 strips for each Sleeve).

FINISHING: Use size D [F] hook for all finishing. Following Diagrams for placement, join strips of Back, Front, and Sleeves as follows: Placing adjacent strips with right sides together, with peach, sc in top lp only of each sc across. Break off. Join Body and Sleeve strips first, then join shoulder, sleeve and underarm seams.

Neck Edging: 1st row: With spice, starting at center back of neck edge, with right side facing you, sc evenly around neck edge, working in back lp of each st; join; ch 1, turn.

2nd row: Sc in each of next 3 sts, dec 1 sc over next 2 sts. Continue in this manner and, at same time, dec 2 sts at shoulder seams and each front corner; join; ch 1, turn.

3rd row: Rep last row.

4th row: Sc in each st around. Break off. Sew back opening.

Sleeve Edging: 1st row: With spice, starting at underarm seam, with right side facing you, working 2 sc over joinings sc in back lp of each st; join; ch 1, turn.

2nd row: Sc in each sc around; join; ch 1, turn. Rep last row 5 times more, omitting ch 1 at end of last row. Break off. Turn last 5 rows to right side and tack in place.

Bottom Edging: Work as for Sleeve Edging for 6 rows.

SQUARE MOTIF PULLOVER

They look like granny squares but they are not. They are marvelous little motifs that start out as flowers, become triangles, then are filled in to form rectangles. Peach, ivory, pink, white, and ecru are the colors; the yarn is a cotton crepe.

SIZES: Small (10-12) [medium (14-16)]. See Diagram for dimensions.

MATERIALS: Medium-weight cotton such as Unger's Cotton Crepe (100% cotton yarn), 1 [2] (1½-oz.) skein each peach and pink, 3 [4] skeins white, 4 [5] skeins ecru, and 5 [6] skeins ivory; aluminum crochet hook size F [G]

(or English/Canadian hook No. 10 [9]) *or the size that will give you the correct gauge.*

GAUGE: Each motif measures 4" [4½"] long, 4½" [5"] wide.

Note: The garment is worked in motifs of various color

combinations, made separately and then crocheted together. Each Motif consists of a flowered center worked in rnds to form a triangle. Then the triangle is squared off with fill-in corners. Tag each completed Motif; this will be helpful in joining.

MOTIF A (make 16): Flower: With peach, starting at center, ch 7. Join with sl st to form ring.

1st rnd: Sc in ring, ch 3; make joined tr as follows: * Y o twice, insert hook in ring, y o and pull lp through (y o and pull through 2 lps on hook) twice. Rep from * once more, then y o and pull through all 3 lps on hook (joined tr made); ch 3, (sc in ring, ch 3, work joined tr, ch 3) 5 times; join with sl st in first sc (6 petals). Break off.

Triangle: 1st rnd: With ecru, make lp on hook, sc in top of any joined tr, ch 3, tr in next sc, ch 3, * sc in next joined tr, ch 3, tr in next sc, ch 3. Rep from * 4 times more; join.

2nd rnd: Ch 3, * (3 dc in next sp) twice; ch 3. Rep from * 5 times more; join to beg ch-3.

3rd rnd: * Sk next 2 dc, 4 tr in next dc, ch 3, 4 tr in next dc, sc in next ch-3 sp, sc in each of next 6 dc, sc in next ch-3 sp. Rep from * twice; join. Break off.

First Fill-In Corner: 1st row: With ivory, work sc, ch 2 and sc in any ch-3 corner sp, sc in each of next 3 tr, 2 hdc in next tr, 2 dc in next sc, sk next 2 sts, work 4 tr, ch 2 and 4 tr in next st, sk next 2 sts, hdc in next sc, sk next 2 sts, work 4 tr, ch 2, and 2 sc in next tr, sk next 2 tr, sc in next ch-3 sp; ch 2 (mark ch st with pin); turn.

2nd row: Sk next sc, sc in each of next 3 sc, sc in ch-2 sp, sk next 4 tr, work 4 tr, ch 2 and 4 tr in next hdc, sk next 4 tr, sl st in next ch-2 sp. Break off.

Second Fill-In Corner: 1st row: With ivory, and wrong side of triangle facing you, starting at unworked corner on triangle, work first row of First Fill-In Corner, omitting last ch 2, sl st in marked st on First Fill-In Corner; turn.

2nd row: Work 2nd row of First Fill-In Corner. Break off.

MOTIF B (make 14): Work in same manner as for Motif A in the following colors:
- **Flower:** pink.
- **Triangle:** ivory.
- **First Fill-In Corner:** white.
- **Second Fill-In Corner:** ecru.

MOTIF C (make 11): Work in same manner as for Motif A in the following colors:
- **Flower:** peach.
- **Triangle:** ivory.
- **First Fill-In Corner:** ecru.
- **Second Fill-In Corner:** white.

MOTIF D (make 11): Work in same manner as for Motif A in the following colors:
- **Flower:** pink.
- **Triangle:** ivory.
- **First Fill-In Corner:** white.
- **Second Fill-In Corner:** white.

TO JOIN MOTIFS: Follow Diagram for position, placing Motifs with triangles pointing in directions shown (see broken lines). Using matching color thread, join Motifs in vertical rows, then in horizontal fill-in rows as follows: With right sides facing, work sc in top lp only of each st on adjacent Motifs. When all Motifs have been joined, fold garment in half at shoulders, wrong side out. Join underarm and Sleeve seams in same manner, leaving sides

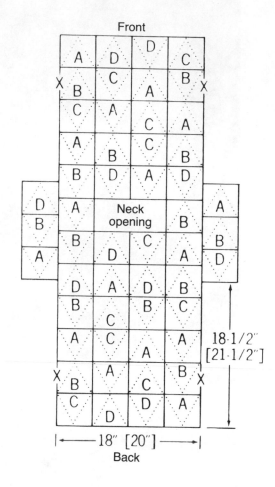

open from X to lower edge for slits.

FINISHING: With ecru, work with right side facing you. Join and break off at end of last rnd on each edging.

Neck Edging: 1st row: Begin at center back, skipping each of the six joinings, sc each st around, join; ch 1. Work 3 more rnds of sc, decreasing 10 sc, spaced evenly, each rnd.

Sleeve Edging: Work 4 rnds sc, decreasing 1 sc at point of each of the three joinings.

Lower Edging: 1st row: Sc along lower edge and slits, decreasing 2 sts at top of each slit and working 3 sc at each outer corner tip. Work 3 more rnds of sc, decreasing 2 sts at top of each slit and working outer corner increases as follows: Work a 2nd rnd increasing 2 sts at 4th st before and after each corner tip. Work a 3rd rnd increasing 2 sts at 8th st before and after corner tip. Working even, work a 4th rnd.

V-STRIPED PULLOVER

This extravaganza of puff stitches and single and double crochet is made with teal, green, and white pearl cotton.

SIZES: Small (8-10) [medium (12-14)]. See Diagram for dimensions.

MATERIALS: Pearl cotton such as D.M.C. Pearl Cotton No. 5, 4 (53-yd.) balls green, 8 balls teal, and 38 balls snow white; aluminum crochet hook size E [G] (or English/Canadian hook No. 11 [9]) *or the size that will give you the correct gauge.*

GAUGE: On size E hook: 5 dc = 1"; 2 rows dc = ¾".

41

On size G hook: 4 dc = 1"; 2 rows dc = ⅞".

Note: Work with 2 strands yarn held together.

BACK: With white, starting at center of back neck (dot on Back Diagram), ch 6. Join with sl st to form ring.

1st rnd (right side): Ch 3, work 11 dc in ring; join with sl st in top of ch 3.

2nd rnd: Ch 3, dc in each of next 2 sts, work 3 dc, ch 3 and 3 dc in next st * dc in each of next 3 sts, work 3 dc, ch 3 and 3 dc in next st. Rep from * once more; join; turn.

Note: From now on, work back and forth in rows, working in back lp of each st (except when working puff st) unless otherwise specified.

1st row: Sl st in each of first 3 dc and 2 ch of ch-3 sp, ch 3, dc in same sp; work dc in each of next 3 sts, work puff st in both lps of next st as follows: Y o, insert hook in same st and pull up ½" lp, (y o, insert hook in same st and pull up ½" lp) 3 times, y o and pull through all 9 lps on hook (puff st made); work dc in each of next 5 sts; in next ch-3 sp work (puff st, dc, ch 3, dc and puff st) for puff-st center; dc in each of next 5 sts, puff st in next st, dc in each of next 3 sts, 2 dc in next ch-3 sp, do not work across remaining sts; ch 3, turn.

2nd row (right side): Dc in first st, 2 dc in next st, dc in each of next 3 sts, puff st in next st, dc in each of next 5 sts, puff st in next st, dc in next st; in next sp work 2 dc, ch 3 and 2 dc for shell-st center; dc in next st, puff st in next st, dc in each of next 5 sts, puff st in next st, dc in each of next 3 sts (2 dc in next st) twice; ch 3, turn. (Turning ch 3 always counts as 1 dc.)

3rd row: Dc in first st, 2 dc in next st, (dc in each of next 5 sts, puff st in next st) twice (2 dc-puff st units made); dc in each of next 3 sts, work shell-st center in next sp, dc in each of next 3 sts, (puff st in next st, dc in each of next 5 sts) twice (2 puff st-dc units made); (2 dc in next st) twice; ch 3, turn.

4th row: Dc in first dc, 2 dc in next dc, dc in next st, make 3 puff st-dc units, work puff-st center in next sp, make 3 dc-puff st units; dc in next st, 2 dc in each of next 2 sts; ch 3, turn.

5th row: Dc in first dc, 2 dc in next dc, dc in each of next 3 dc, 3 puff st-dc units, puff st in next st, dc in next dc, work shell-st center in next sp, dc in next st, 3 puff st-dc units, puff st in next st, dc in each of next 3 sts, 2 dc in each of next 2 sts; ch 3, turn.

6th row: Dc in first st, 2 dc in next st, 4 dc-puff st units, dc in next 3 sts, work shell-st center in next sp, dc in next 3 sts, 4 puff st-dc units, 2 dc in each of next 2 sts; ch 3, turn. Mark first and last sts of this row for back neck (X's on Diagram).

7th row (shoulder shaping): Sk first dc, dec 1 dc as follows: (Y o, insert hook in next st, y o and draw lp

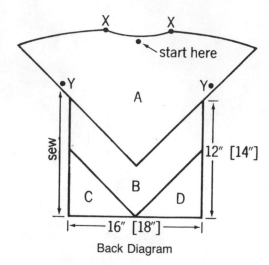

Back Diagram

through, y o and draw through 2 lps on hook) twice, y o and draw through all 3 lps on hook (1 dc dec); 5 puff st-dc units, work puff-st center in next sp, 5 dc-puff st units, dec 1 dc, dc in next st. Break off; turn.

8th row: With green, sc in each st to ch-3 sp, ch 3, sk next ch-3 sp, sc in each st across. Break off; turn.

9th row: With white, working in both lps of each st throughout row, work 2 dc in first st, dc in next st, 5 puff st-dc units, puff st in next st, dc in next st, work shell-st center in next sp, dc in next st, puff st in next st, 5 dc-puff st units, dc in next st, 2 dc in last st. Break off; turn.

10th row: With teal, rep 8th row, but do not break off. At end of row ch 3, turn.

11th row: Working in both lps of each st throughout row, dc in first st, dc in each st to ch-3 sp, work shell-st center in sp, dc in each st to last st, 2 dc in last st. Break off; turn.

12th row: With white, work 2 dc in first st, dc in each of next 3 sts, 6 puff st-dc units, work puff-st center in next sp, 6 dc-puff st units, dc in next 3 sts, 2 dc in last st; ch 3, turn.

13th row: Dc in first st, dc in each of next 4 sts, 6 puff st-dc units, puff st in next st, dc in next st, work shell-st center in next st, dc in next st, 6 puff st-dc units, puff st in next st, dc in each of next 4 sts, 2 dc in last st; ch 3, turn.

14th row: Dc in first st, 7 dc-puff st units, dc in each of next 3 sts, work shell-st center unit in next sp, dc in next 3 dc, 7 puff st-dc units, 2 dc in last st; ch 3, turn.

15th row: Dc in first st, 8 puff st-dc units, work puff-st center in next sp, 8 dc-puff st units, 2 dc in last st. Break off; turn.

16th row: Rep 8th row.

17th row: Rep 9th row, working both puff-st units 8 times instead of 5.

18th row: Rep 10th row.

19th row: Rep 11th row.

20th row: Rep 12th row, working both puff-st units 9 times.

21st row: Rep 13th row, working both puff-st units 9 times.

22nd row: Rep 14th row, working units 10 times.

23rd row: Rep 15th row, working units 11 times.

24th row: Rep 8th row.

25th Row: Rep 9th row, working units 11 times.

26th row: Rep 10th row.

27th row: Rep 11th row.

28th row: Rep 12th row, working units 12 times.

29th row: Rep 13th row, working units 12 times.

30th row: Rep 14th row, working units 13 times.

31st row: Rep 15th row, working units 14 times.

32nd row: Rep 8th row.

33rd row: Rep 9th row, working units 14 times.

34th row: Rep 10th row.

35th row: Rep 11th row (94 dc on each side of center ch-3 sp). Place markers on 33rd st from beg and end of last row (Y's on Diagram). Section A on Diagram 1 completed.

To Shape Cap Sleeves and Section B of Back: 36th row: Sk first 42 sts. With white, (dec 1 dc) twice, 8 puff st-dc units, puff-st center in next sp, 8 dc-puff st units (dec 1 dc) twice; ch 3, turn.

37th row: (Dec 1 dc) twice; dc in next 4 sts, 7 puff st-dc units, puff st in next st, dc in next st, work shell-st center in next sp, 7 puff st-dc units, puff st in next st, dc in next 5 sts, (dec 1 dc) twice; ch 3, turn.

38th row: (Dec 1 dc) twice; dc in next 2 sts, 7 puff st-dc units, puff st in next st, dc in next 3 sts, work shell-st center in next sp, dc in next 3 sts, 7 puff st-dc units, puff st in next st, dc in next 2 sts, (dec 1 dc) twice; ch 3, turn.

39th row: (Dec 1 dc) twice; 8 puff st-dc units, work puff-st center in next sp, 8 dc-puff st units, (dec 1 dc) twice. Break off; turn.

40th row: Rep 8th row; break off; turn.

41st row: With white, (dec 1 dc) twice; dc in next 5 sts, 7 puff st-dc units, puff st in next st, work shell-st center in next sp, 7 puff st-dc units, puff st in next st, dc in next 4 sts, (dec 1 dc) twice. Break off; turn.

42nd row: With teal, rep 8th row, but do not break off; ch 3, turn.

43rd row: Working in both lps of each st throughout row, sk first st, (dec 1 dc) twice; dc in each st to ch-3 sp, work shell-st center, dc in each st to last 4 sts, (dec 1 dc) twice. Break off; turn.

44th row: With white, dec 1 dc, dc in next st, 8 puff st-dc units, work puff-st center, 8 dc-puff st units, dc in next st, dec 1 dc; ch 3, turn.

45th row: Sk first st, (dec 1 dc) twice; dc in next 3 sts, 7 puff st-dc units, puff st in next st, dc in next st, work shell-st center, dc in next dc, 7 puff st-dc units, puff st in next st, dc in next 4 sts, (dec 1 dc) twice; ch 3, turn.

46th row: Sk first st, (dec 1 dc) twice; dc in next dc, 7 puff st-dc units, puff st in next st, dc in next 3 sts, work shell-st center, dc in next 3 sts, 7 puff st-dc units, puff st in next st, dc in next 2 sts, (dec 1 dc) twice; ch 3, turn.

47th row: Rep 44th row, but skip first st and at end of row omit ch 3. Break off; turn. Section B completed.

To Shape Section C: 1st Corner: 1st row: With green, sc in each st in center ch-3 sp, sc in sp (53 sc). Break off; turn.

2nd row: With white, working in both lps of each st throughout, (dec 1 dc) twice; dc in next 4 sts, 6 puff st-dc units, puff st in next st, dc in next 4 sts, (dec 1 dc) twice. Break off; turn.

3rd row: With teal, rep first row (49 sc), ending ch 3, turn.

4th row: Working in both lps of each st throughout row, sk first sc, (dec 1 dc) twice; dc in each st to last 4 sts, (dec 1 dc) twice. Break off; turn.

5th row: With white, (dec 1 dc) twice; 6 puff st-dc units, puff st in next st, (dec 1 dc) twice; ch 3, turn.

6th row: (Dec 1 dc) twice; dc in next 4 sts, 4 puff st-dc units, puff st in next st, dc in next 4 sts, (dec 1 dc) twice; ch 3, turn.

7th row: (Dec 1 dc) twice; dc in next 2 dc, 4 puff st-dc units, puff st in next st, dc in next 2 sts, (dec 1 dc) twice; ch 3, turn.

8th row: (Dec 1 dc) twice; 4 puff st-dc units, puff st in next st, (dec 1 dc) twice. Break off; turn.

9th row: With green, sc in each st across. Break off, turn.

10th row: With white, (dec 1 dc) twice; dc in next 4 sts, 2 puff st-dc units, puff st in next st, dc in next 4 sts, (dec 1 dc) twice. Break off; turn.

11th row: With teal, sc in each st across; ch 3, turn.

12th row: Working in both lps of each st, sk first sc (dec 1 dc) twice; dc in each st to last 4 sts, (dec 1 dc) twice. Break off; turn.

13th row: With white, (dec 1 dc) twice; 2 puff st-dc units, puff st in next st (dec 1 dc) twice; ch 3, turn.

14th row: (Dec 1 dc) twice; dc in next 4 sts, puff st in next st, dc in next 4 sts, (dec 1 dc) twice; ch 3, turn.

15th row: (Dec 1 dc) twice; dc in next 2 dc, puff st in next dc, dc in next 2 dc, (dec 1 dc) twice; ch 3, turn.

16th row: (Dec 1 dc) twice; puff st in next st, (dec 1 dc) twice; ch 3, turn.

17th row: (Dec 1 dc) twice, dc in last st. Break off. Section C completed.

Section D: Starting in ch-3 sp on 40th row, work as for Section C.

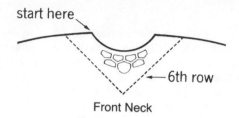

start here

6th row

Front Neck

FRONT: With white, starting along neckline on Diagram 2, ch 75.

1st row (right side): Dc in 4th ch from hook and in each ch across (73 dc, counting ch 3 as 1 dc); ch 3, turn.

2nd row: Ch 3, sk first dc, 4 dc-puff st units, (ch 8, sk next 5 sts, puff st in next st) 4 times; (dc in next 5 sts, puff st in next st) 3 times; dc in next 6 sts; ch 3, turn.

3rd row: Sk first st, 4 dc-puff st units, (work 5 sc, ch 3 and 5 sc in next ch-8 sp) 4 times; puff st in next st, 3 dc-puff st units, dc in next 6 sts; ch 3, turn.

4th row: Dc in first st, 4 dc-puff st units, dc in next 5 sc, puff st in next ch-3 sp, ch 6, sk next 10 sc, puff st in next ch-3 sp, ch 16 for center lp, sk next 10 sc, puff st in next ch-3 sp, ch 6, sk next 10 sc, puff st in next ch-3 sp, 4 dc-puff st units, dc in next 5 sts, 2 dc in last st; ch 3, turn.

5th row: Sk first st, puff st in next st, 5 dc-puff st units, work 5 dc in next ch-6 sp, sk puff st, work over center ch-16 lp as follows: Work puff st in first ch st, then working over ch, work (5 dc, puff st, 5 dc, puff st, 5 dc, puff st, and 5 dc); sk puff st, work puff st in first st of next ch-6 sp, work 5 dc in same sp, puff st in next st, 5 dc-puff st units, dc in last st; ch 3, turn (17 puff sts in row).

6th row: (broken line on Diagram 2): Dc in first dc, 8 puff st-dc units, puff-st center in next st, 8 dc-puff st units, 2 dc in last st. Break off; turn. Starting with 16th row of Back, complete as for Back.

FINISHING: Back Neck Edging: With white and with right side facing you, work 1 row dc evenly across back neck edge between X markers. Sew shoulder seams from markers to sleeve edges. Sew underarm and sleeve seams from Y markers to lower edge.

Arm Edging: With teal, with right side facing you, work 1 row sc in back lp of each st around each arm edge; join. Break off.

Lower Edging: With white, with right side facing you, and starting at 1 side seam, work (sc along edge to next teal stripe, ch 3, sk teal stripe) 8 times, sc to end; join. Break off.

FLORAL BLOUSON

In this distinctive top color changes create different forms from a single hexagonal motif.

SIZES: Free size. The blouson measures 22″ in width across back or front at underarm; 20″ in length from back neck to lower edge. (Using hook one size smaller will give you measurements approximately 1″ less in both width and length.)

MATERIALS: Mercurized knit and crochet "bedspread" cotton such as J. & P. Coats Knit-Cro-Sheen, used **double strand** throughout, 2 (approximately 175-yd.) balls each melon, lilac, cinnamon, and variegated green, 12 (175-yd.) balls or 4 (550-yd.) balls cream; aluminum cro-

HEXAGON COLOR CHART:

A-1:	Rnds 1–4, cinnamon	Rnds 5–6, olive	Rnds 7–8, cream
A-2:	Rnds 1–4, melon	Rnds 5–6, variegated green	Rnds 7–8, cream
A-3:	Rnds 1–4, lilac	Rnds 5–6, olive	Rnds 7–8, cream
A-4:	Rnds 1–4, melon	Rnds 5–6, olive	Rnds 7–8, cream
A-5:	Rnds 1–4, cinnamon	Rnds 5–6, variegated green	Rnds 7–8, cream
A-6:	Rnds 1–4, lilac	Rnds 5–6, variegated green	Rnds 7–8, cream
B-1:	Rnds 1–2, lilac	Rnds 3–4, variegated green	Rnds 5–8, cream
B-2:	Rnds 1–2, melon	Rnds 3–4, olive	Rnds 5–8, cream
B-3:	Rnds 1–2, cinnamon	Rnds 3–4, variegated green	Rnds 5–8, cream
B-4:	Rnds 1–2, cinnamon	Rnds 3–4, olive	Rnds 5–8, cream
B-5:	Rnds 1–2, lilac	Rnds 3–4, olive	Rnds 5–8, cream
B-6:	Rnds 1–2, melon	Rnds 3–4, variegated green	Rnds 5–8, cream
C:	Rnds 1–8, cream		

chet hook sizes F and C (or English/Canadian hook Nos. 10 and 13) *or size that will give you the correct gauge.*

GAUGE: With F hook 5 dc = 1″; 2 rows of dc = 1″; hexagon measures 6″ across at the widest point.

Note: Tag each piece upon completion for easier iden-tification when assembling garment.

HEXAGONS (make 11 of Hexagon C, 1 each of others): Follow the Hexagon Color Chart. Use F hook.

1st rnd: Ch 6, join with sl st to form ring, ch 3, 11 dc in ring, sl st top of ch-3.

2nd rnd: Ch 3, dc same sp, 2 dc each st around, sl st top of beg ch-3. (For B Hexagons fasten off and join new color.)

3rd rnd: * Ch 6, in 4th ch st from hook work sc, dc

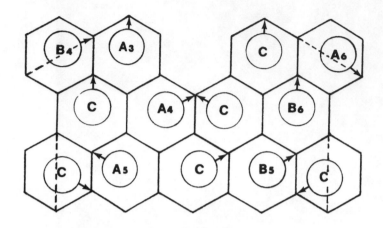

Front

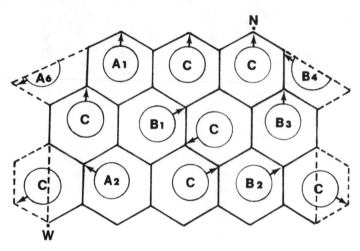

Back

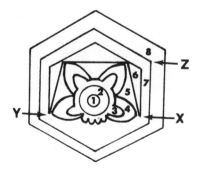

Motif

next ch st, tr next ch st (triangle formed), sk 3 dc, sc next dc, rep from * 3 times, (ch 3, sk 1 dc, sc next dc) 3 times, ch 3, sk dc, sc in sl st.

4th rnd: Working on foundation ch of triangle, * 2 dc in base of tr, 2 dc in base of dc, 2 dc in base of sc, in ch-3 at tip work dc, ch 2 and dc, 2 dc in sc, 2 dc in dc, 2 dc in tr, sc in sc, rep from * for each remaining triangle, end sl st in last sc. Fasten off. **Note:** This is right side.

5th row: (For A and B Hexagons work new color.) Hold piece with right side facing you, and with petals on top. Start at first petal on the right in ch-2 sp at tip. (See Diagram 1, Point X.) Sc in ch-2 sp, * working back lps only dc next 5 sts, holding back last lp on hook, dc in each of next 5 sts, y o pull through all 6 lps on hook (cl), dc next 5 sts, in ch-2 at tip of next petal work sc, ch 2 and sc, rep from * twice, ending last rep with sc in ch-2 sp; ch 2; turn.

6th row: Sc next 2 sts, * sk 3 sts, in next st work 3 dc, ch 2 and 3 dc, sk 3 sts, sc next 3 sts, ** in ch-2 sp work sc, ch 2 and sc, sc next 3 sts, rep from * once, rep from * to ** once. Fasten off. Turn.

7th rnd: (For A Hexagons work new color.) Work back lps only unless specified otherwise. Hold piece with right side facing you and with petals on bottom. Begin in ch-2 sp at tip of first petal on the right. (See Diagram 1, Point Y.) In ch-2 sp work 3 dc, ch 2 and 3 dc, sk 3 dc, dc next 4 dc, 4 dc in each of next 2 ch-3 sps, ch 2, 4 dc in each of next two ch-3 sps, dc next 4 dc, sk 3 dc, in ch-2 sp work 3 dc, ch 2 and 3 dc, sc next 6 sts (in ch-2 sp work sc, ch 2 and sc, sk 3 sts, working both lps, 5 dc in next st, sk 3 sts) 4 times, in ch-2 sp work sc, ch 2 and sc, sc next 6 sts, sl st in beg dc.

8th rnd: Work in back lps only. Work loosely. Sl st next 2 dc, * ch 2, sk ch-2 sp, sl st to within next ch-2 sp, rep from * twice, sc in next ch-2 sp (see Diagram 1, Point Z), sk 2 sts, in next st work 3 dc, ch 2 and 3 dc, dc next 2 sts, sk sc, 2 dc in ch-2 sp, sk sc, dc next 5 dc, sk sc, in ch-2 sp work 3 dc, ch 2 and 3 dc, sk sc, dc next 5 dc, sk sc, 2 dc in ch-2 sp, sk sc, dc next 2 dc, in next dc work 3 dc, ch 2 and 3 dc, sk 2 dc, sc in ch-2 sp, sl st to beg sl st. Fasten off.

JOINING HEXAGONS: See Diagrams 2 and 3 for placement. Note circles (1st and 2nd rnds) should be positioned in the direction of arrows. Dotted lines on Front indicate fold lines of hexagons. Dotted lines on Back indicate position of folded hexagons. **Using C hook** and cream, join hexagons with sc. Work on wrong sides in top lps only. Match sides beginning and ending with a ch st.

NECK FILL-IN: Begin at Point N on Diagram 3. Using cream and F hook, in ch-2 sp after seam joining work sc, * working back lps only sc next 4 sts, dc next 4 sts, tr next

4 sts, sk seam joining, holding back last lp on hook, work dtr in each of next 8 sts (include ch sps, sk seam joining), y o pull through all 9 lps on hook (cl made), tr next 4 sts, dc next 4 sts, sc next 4 sts, sc in ch-2 sp, rep from * once. Do not break off.

NECK EDGING: * Ch 3, sc in 3rd ch st from hook (p), sl st next 4 sts, rep from * around entire neck edge, join to first p. Fasten off.

ARMHOLE EDGING: Attach cream in any seam joining. Work same as for Neck Edging.

CHEVRON WAIST BORDER: Working on Back, hold piece with neck edge on bottom and right side facing. Beg in ch-2 sp at Point W on Diagram 3.

1st rnd: Using cream, attach in ch-2 sp, ch 5, dc same sp, * working back lps only dc each st to within ch-2 sp,

dc in ch-2 sp, sk seam joining, dc next ch-2 sp, dc each st next to ch-2 sp, in ch-2 sp work dc, ch 2 and dc, rep from * around, ending sl st in 3rd ch st of beg ch-5.

2nd rnd: Ch 3, * in ch-2 sp work dc, ch 2 and dc, working back lps only dc next 16 sts, sk next 2 dc, dc next 16 dc, rep from * around, sl st top beg ch-3.

3rd through 11th rnds: Rep 2nd rnd. Fasten off.

NECK TIE: Using cream, ch 2, 5 sc in 2nd ch st from hook, sl st in first sc, chain 36″, 5 sc in 2nd ch st from hook, sl st in first sc. Fasten off. Lace tie through under p sts along neck edge.

BELT: Using cream, ch 7, dc in 4th ch st from hook, dc remaining 3 ch sts, * ch 3, turn, working both lps, dc each st across, rep from * for desired length (suggested: 74 rows). Fasten off. Fringe each end of strip.

STRIPED LONG-SLEEVED JACKET

Yarns of sand, foam, and seashell colors are spun into a versatile spring jacket. It is constructed in strips of single crochet and chain stitches with yarn worked single strand. The strips are then joined with single crochet, using doubled yarn.

SIZES: Free size.

MATERIALS: Thin-weight cotton such as Joseph Galler Parisian Cotton, 16 (120-yd.) balls linen-beige, 8 balls each pale jade and pale rust, 6 balls orchid, and 4 balls of pale pink; aluminum crochet hook size E (or English/Canadian hook No. 11) *or size that will give you the correct gauge.*

GAUGE: 5 rows of pattern stitch = 1″.

STRIPS: 1st row: With beige, work single strand. Ch 11, sc in 5th ch st from hook, sk next st, sc in next st, * ch 1, sk next st, sc in next st, rep from * across; ch 3, turn.

2nd row: Sc next ch sp, * ch 1, sk next sc, sc next ch sp, rep from * across; ch 3, turn.

3rd row: Rep 2nd row until there are 125 rows, fasten off. (Strip should measure approximately 25″.) Make total of 19 strips at this length. Make 18 strips with 95 rows. Make 2 strips with 100 rows. Make 2 strips with 110 rows.

Note: On each strip, mark foundation chain end as bottom of strip. Mark last row as top of strip.

BACK: Work on 125-row strips.

JOINING STRIPS: Use yarn double. Strips are joined right to left. See Diagram for positions.

Joining 1: 1st rnd: Work on Strip 1, with orchid. * Beg at bottom edge (first row), working along one long edge, sc in each end-of-row st, ch 2, turn (mark this end as top edge), working back lps only, sc each st across (side facing you now is right side). Fasten off.

2nd rnd: Work on Strip 2, with jade. * Beg at bottom edge of strip (first row), working along one long edge, sc in each end-of-row st; ch 1, turn. Pick up first strip; have right side facing you with top edge at right; place first strip in front of 2nd strip (wrong sides tog), working top lps only, sc tog the turning ch-2 of Strip 1 and last sc worked on 2nd strip. Continue to sc strips tog joining top lps only of each sc across. Fasten off.

Note: In the remaining joinings, substitute last strip joined for first strip and strip being worked on for 2nd strip.

Joining 2: Work on wrong side of Strip 2, with jade. Rep 1st rnd from *. Work on Strip 3, with rust. Work as for 2nd rnd from *.

Joining 3: Work on wrong side of Strip 3, with orchid. Rep 1st rnd from *. Work on Strip 4, with rust. Rep as for 2nd rnd from *.

Joining 4: Work on wrong side of Strip 4, with rust. Rep 1st rnd from *. Work Strip 5, with pink. Rep 2nd rnd from *.

Joining 5–8: Rep joinings 1–4.

Joining 9: Work on wrong side of Strip 9, with jade. Rep first rnd from *. Work Strip 10, with pink. Rep 2nd rnd from *.

Joining 10: Work wrong side of Strip 10, with orchid. Rep 1st rnd from *. Work Strip 11, with jade. Rep 2nd rnd from *.

Side Edging: Work wrong side of Strip 11, with jade.

Rep 1st rnd. On unworked edge of Strip 1, with pink, work as for 1st rnd from * except after ch 2 turn, work front lps only.

RIGHT FRONT: Join strips from right to left (side to center). Gather four 125-row strips, one 110-row strip, and one 100-row strip. Working with four 125-row strips, rep Joinings 1–3 for Back.

Joining 4: Work wrong side of Strip 4, with rust. Rep 1st rnd from *. Work 110-row strip for Strip 5, with pink. Rep 2nd rnd from * except sk first 15 sts at top of Strip 4

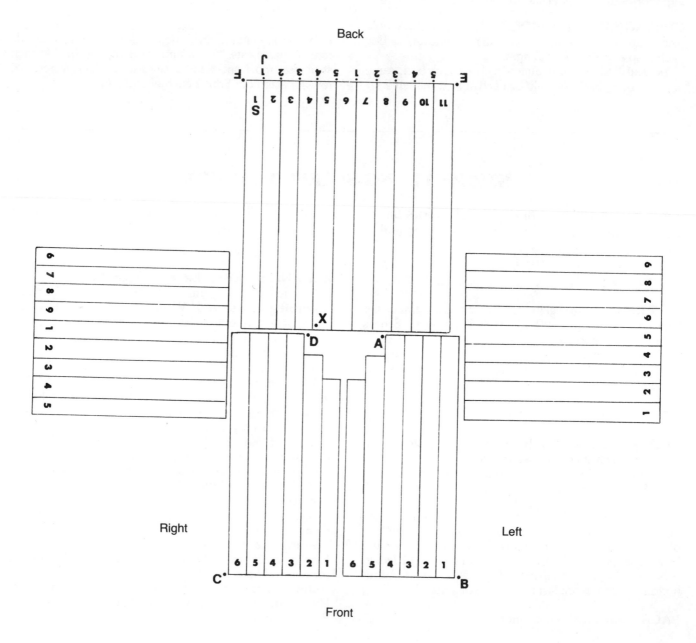

Back

Right

Left

Front

before joining strips tog with sc.

Joining 5: Work wrong side of Strip 5, with orchid. Rep 1st rnd from *. Work 100-row strip as Strip 6, with jade. Rep 2nd rnd from * except sk 10 sts at top of Strip 5 before joining strips tog with sc.

Side Edging: With pink, on unworked edge of Strip 1 work as for 1st rnd from * except after turning ch-2, work front lps only.

LEFT FRONT: Join strips from right to left (center to side).

Joining 1: Work on 100-row strip, with jade. Rep 1st rnd from *. Work on 110-row strip, with rust. Rep 2nd rnd from * except ch 2 turn, work next 9 sts without joining, at 11th st on Strip 2 beg joining.

Joining 2: Work on wrong side of Strip 2, with orchid. Rep 1st rnd from *. Work on 125-row strip, with rust. Rep 2nd rnd except ch 2 turn, work next 14 sts without joining, at 15th st on Strip 3 begin joining to Strip 2.

Joining 3: Work on wrong side of Strip 3. With rust, rep 1st rnd from *. Work on Strip 4. With pink, rep 2nd rnd from *.

Joining 4: Work on wrong side of Strip 4, with jade. Rep 1st rnd from *. Work on Strip 5. With pink, rep 2nd rnd from *.

Joining 5: Work wrong side of Strip 5, with orchid. Rep 1st rnd from *. Work on Strip 6. With jade, rep 2nd rnd from *.

Side Edging: Work on wrong side of Strip 6. With jade, rep 1st rnd.

SLEEVES: Work on 95-row strips. Rep Joinings 1–3 twice.

Joining 7: Work on wrong side of Strip 9, with jade. Rep 1st rnd from *. Work unworked edge of Strip 1, with pink. Rep 2nd rnd from * (cylinder formed). Rep above for 2nd Sleeve.

SHOULDER EDGING: Back: With right side facing you, beg on Strip 1 with orchid. Across top edge, work sc in each joining row (2 sc), * over strip work 4 sc by working in ch sps only, work 4 sc over joining rows, rep from * across, end 2 sc over last joining row; ch 2, turn, sc across, working front lps only. Fasten off.

Left Front: Work 125-row strips only. Beg on Strip 1 with rust. Work as for back shoulder edging.

Right Front: Work 125-row strips only. Begin on Strip 3 with rust. Work as for back shoulder edging.

SLEEVE EDGING: Top: With right side facing you, work across top edge with orchid. Begin at last joining. Work as for back shoulder edging.

Bottom: Using jade, rep top edging; ch 1, turn. * Working back lps, work one rnd of sc even; join in first sc. * Fasten off. Working on right side, using rust, rep from * to *; join; ch 1, turn. Rep from * to *. Fasten off.

FINISHING: Join Shoulders: (See Diagram for placement.) With rust, work on right side, sc tog working inside (bottom) lps only.

Join Sleeves: With orchid, work on right side. For Left Sleeve, place Strip 1 over shoulder seam. (See Diagram for placement.) For Right Sleeve, place Strip 5 over shoulder seam. Sc tog working inside lps only.

Underarm Seams: With jade, work right side. Sc tog working top lps only. Leave 30 sts free at bottom edge.

Final Edging: Note: Always work 3 sc at every corner point.

1st row: Work right side. Start at A on Diagram. With jade, work sc edging to B as follows: Sc in each joining row st, sc ch-sps only on tops and bottoms of strips and sc each end-of-row st on side of front strip. Ch 2, turn.

2nd row: Sc across to A, working back lps only. Fasten off. Start at C on Diagram, work sc edging to D same as for A to B, ch 2, turn; work sc back to A, working back lps only. Start at E, work to F same as for front bottom edgings; ch 2, turn; sc back lps only to E.

3rd row: Begin at X on Diagram, back neck at right shoulder seam. With rust, sc back lps only, decreasing 1 st every 3rd st across neck to next shoulder seam, dec 2 sts at shoulder seam. (Work dec by working 2 sts as 1.) On front neck edging, work * sc to within 5 sts of indentation, sk 4 sts, work shell of 5 dc in next st, sk 5 sts, sc to within next 3 corner sts, work 2 sc in each of 3 corner sts, rep from * once. Continue edging around, working 2 sc in every 3 corner sts and decreasing 2 sts at each side seam. Rep front neck edging for opposite side, dec 2 sts at shoulder seam, sl st beg sc; ch 2, turn.

4th row: Working back lps only, sc around entire piece, except dec 2 sts at shoulder seams, dec every 6th st on front-opening strips, and dec 2 sts at side seams.

Vests and Tunics

LACY VEST

An elegant vest at a price you can afford uses old-fashioned butcher's twine in lovely openwork patterns.

SIZE: One size fits sizes 6-12.

MATERIALS: 24-ply cotton wrapping cord (a soft, loosely twisted butcher's twine sold in hardware and stationery stores), 1 cone (2 lbs., approximately 517 yds.); aluminum crochet hook size H (or English/Canadian hook No. 8) *or the size that will give you the correct gauge.*

GAUGE: 2 V-sts and 1 picot = 3"; 3 rows of V-sts = 5".

Note: Vest is crocheted in 1 piece.

RIGHT FRONT: 1st row (wrong side): Make a foundation strip of 42 lps made to measure about 33" as follows: Starting at lower edge, (ch 3, dc in 3rd ch from hook) 42 times; ch 3, turn.

2nd row (right side): Work 1 dc in last lp made, work 2 dc in each of next 41 lps across (84 dc, counting turning ch as 1 dc); ch 1, turn.

3rd row: Sc in first dc and each of next 5 dc, * ch 12, sc in 6th ch from hook, sc in each remaining ch st (first post formed), sk 2 dc, sc in each of next 8 dc. Rep from * across, ending with sc in each of last 6 dc (8 posts made); ch 3, turn.

4th row: Sk first sc (turning ch counts as first dc), dc in each of next 2 sc, * ch 3, sk next 3 sc and first 3 sc on side of post, sc in next sc on side of post, ch 3, sk next 3 sc, work 9 dc over ch-5 top lp on post, ch 3, sk next 3 sc on opposite side of post, sc in base of next sc, ch 3, sk next 3 sc on side of post and following 3 sc, work dc in

each of next 2 sc. Rep from * across, ending with dc in each of last 3 sc; ch 3, turn.

5th row: Sk first dc, dc in each of next 2 dc, sk next ch-3, next sc and next ch-3, work 2 dc in each of next 9 dc on top of post, (sk next 2 dc between posts, work 2 dc in each of next 9 dc on top of next post) 7 times; sk next ch-3, next sc and next ch-3, work dc in each of last 3 dc (8 half-circles made on tops of posts); ch 12, turn.

6th row (right side): Sc in 9th dc on first half-circle, ch 3, sc in 3rd ch from hook (p made), sc in next dc, (ch 10, sc in 9th dc on next half-circle, p, sc in next dc) 7 times; ch 8, work 1 dtr in top of turning ch; ch 5, turn.

7th row: Sk first 5 ch sts, in next ch st work tr, ch 3 and tr (V-st made), ch 3, sc in 3rd ch from hook (p made), * work V-st in 3rd ch st after p on half-circle, p, sk next 4 ch sts, work V-st in next ch st, p. Rep from * 6 times more; work V-st in ch st after p on last half-circle, sk next 5 ch sts, work dtr in next ch st (16 V-sts made with 15 p's in between); ch 5, turn.

8th row: Work V-st in center of first V-st, * p, work V-st in next V-st. Rep from * across, work dtr in top of turning ch; ch 5, turn.

Rep 8th row 7 times more.

RIGHT FRONT: 16th row: Work V-st in first V-st, (p, work V-st in next V-st) twice; work dtr in next V-st (front armhole edge); ch 5, turn.

17th row: Work V-st in first V-st, (p, work V-st in next V-st) twice; work dtr in top of turning ch; ch 5, turn.

Rep 17th row 4 times more. Omit last ch-5. Break off.

BACK: Work as for Right Front up to 16th row.

16th row: With right side of work facing you, attach twine with sl st to 4th V-st on 15th row (back armhole edge), ch 5, work V-st in next V-st, (p, work V-st in next V-st) 7 times; work dtr in next V-st (opposite armhole edge); ch 5, turn.

17th row: Work V-st in first V-st, (p, work V-st in next V-st) 7 times; work dtr in top of turning ch; ch 5, turn.

Rep 17th row 4 times more. Omit last ch-5. Break off.

LEFT FRONT: Work as for Right Front up to 16th row.

16th row: With right side of work facing you, attach twine with sl st to 13th V-st on 15th row (front armhole edge), ch 5, work V-st in next V-st, (p, work V-st in next V-st) twice; work dtr in top of turning ch; ch 5, turn.

17th row: Work V-st in first V-st, (p, work V-st in next V-st) twice; work dtr in top of ch-5; ch 5, turn.

Rep 17th row 4 times more. Omit last ch-5. Break off.

FINISHING: Sew first two V-sts at top edge of Back to first 2 V-sts at top edge of Front to form each shoulder.

LEFT FRONT EDGING: 1st row: With twine, make lp on hook. With right side of work facing you, work 5 sc over ch-3 lp of unattached V-st next to shoulder joining at left neck edge; working along front edge work 5 sc over each of next 16 lps, work 2 sc over post of each of next 2 dc, work sc over side of next sc, work 2 sc over post of next dc, work sc in foundation lp (lower corner of vest). Break off.

2nd row: With right side of work facing you, attach twine with sl st to 40th sc made on last row, ch 1, sc in next sc, * sk next sc, work 5-dc shell in next sc, sk next sc, sc in each of next 2 sc. Rep from * 8 times more. Sk next

3 sc, work 9-tr shell in next sc, sk next 2 sc, sc in last sc; turn.

3rd row: Sl st in each of next 5 tr of shell, ch 3, holding back on hook the last lp of each dc, work 2 dc in same place as base of ch 3, y o hook, draw through all 3 lps on hook (first 3-dc cl made, counting ch-3 as 1 dc), ch 7, * holding back on hook the last lp of each dc, work 3 dc in 3rd dc of next 5-dc shell, y o hook, draw through all 4 lps on hook, ch 3, sc in 3rd ch from hook (cl made with p on top), ch 5. Rep from * 8 times more; sk next 2 dc on last shell, sc in next sc; ch 1, turn.

4th row: Work 5 sc over first ch-5 lp, * sl st in base of p, work 5 sc over next lp. Rep from * across, ending with sl st in top of ch-3 of first cl made on previous row. Break off.

RIGHT FRONT EDGING: Note: Edging is worked from bottom up.

With twine make lp on hook, with right side of work facing you, sc in foundation lp at corner of lower edge, work to correspond to Left Front edging, reversing order.

FOUR BUTTONS ON CHAIN: Leaving 6″ end, ch 5, join with sl st to form ring. Ch 3, work 6 dc in ring, join with sl st to top of ch-3 (1 button completed); ch 10, sl st in 6th ch from hook (ring formed); ch 3, work 6 dc in ring, join to top of ch-3 (another button formed); ch 7, sl st in 6th ch from hook (ring formed), work button; ch 29, sl st in 6th ch from hook (ring formed), work button. Break off, leaving 6″ end. Turn buttons right side out.

Cut 14 strands twine 7″ long. For a tassel, hold 7 strands together and tie around middle using 6″ end at one end of chain. Tie a tassel at other end of ch. Loop ch through sp at each side of neck and tie.

TUNIC-JUMPER

This fantasy jumper, or tunic, boasts an opulent "breastplate" and scooped-out back. It calls for knitting worsted used doubled; in single and double crochet. The skirt is worked in a shell-stitch variation.

SIZES: Small (8–10) [medium (12–14)].

MATERIALS: Knitting worsted, 4 (4-oz.) skeins purple, 1 skein each dusty pink, russet brown, antique gold, and pistachio green; aluminum crochet hook size J (or English/ Canadian hook No. 6) *or the size that will give you the correct gauge.*

GAUGE: 3 dc = 1″; 3 dc rows = 2″.

Note: Crochet with 2 strands of yarn throughout.

BODICE FRONT: Starting at center (1 on Diagram) with purple, ch 5. Join with sl st to form ring.

1st rnd (right side): Ch 3, work 15 dc in ring (16 dc, counting starting ch as first dc). Join with sl st to top of ch-3. Break off; attach pink.

Note: Always work with right side of work facing you unless otherwise specified.

2nd rnd: Ch 2, sc in place where yarn was attached, work 2 sc in each dc around (32 sc, counting ch-2 as 1 sc). Join to top of ch-2. Break off; attach brown.

3rd rnd: Ch 2, sc in next 19 sc, hdc in next 3 sc, dc in next 6 sc, hdc in next 3 sc (32 sts). Join to top of ch-2.

4th rnd: Ch 2, sk next sc, work 5 dc in next sc (shell made), sk next sc, sc in next 12 sc, sk next sc, work shell in next sc, sk next sc, sc in next sc, hdc in next 3 hdc, work 2 dc in each of next 6 dc, hdc in next 3 hdc. Join to top of ch-2. Break off; attach gold.

5th rnd: Ch 4, sk 2 dc, sc in next dc (center st of shell), ch 3, sk next 2 dc, sc in next 12 sc, ch 3, sk 2 dc, sc in next dc (center of shell), ch 3, sk 2 dc, sc in remaining 19 sts. Join to first ch of ch-4. Break off; attach green.

6th rnd: Ch 2, work 3 sc over lp where yarn was attached, work 4 sc over next ch-3 lp, then sk next sc, work 3 tr, ch 1 and 3 tr all in next sc, sk next sc, sc in next sc, sk next sc, work 3 tr in next sc, ch 1, work 3 tr in next sc; sk next sc, work 3 tr, ch 1 and 3 tr all in next st, then (work 4 sc over next ch-3 lp) twice; sk next sc, dc in next 6 sc, work 2 dc in each of next 6 sc, dc in next 6 sc. Join to top of ch-2. Break off; attach pink.

7th rnd: Ch 2, sc in next 7 sc, ch 3, sk 3 tr, sc in next ch-1 sp, * ch 4, sk 3 tr, work as follows: holding back on hook the last lp of each dc, work 5 dc in next sc, y o draw through all 6 lps on hook (cl made), ch 4, sk 3 tr, sc in next ch-1 sp. Rep from * once more; ch 3, sk 3 tr, sc in next 14 sts, work 2 sc in each of next 12 dc, sc in last 6 dc. Join to top of ch-2. Break off; attach brown.

8th rnd: Ch 3, dc in next 7 sc, work 4 dc over next ch-3 lp, ch 2, work 5 dc over each of next 4 ch-4 lps, ch 2, work 4 dc over next ch-3 lp and mark with pin the first dc of 4-dc group just worked, dc in next 14 sc, ch 2, dc in next 24 sc, ch 2, dc in last 6 sc. Join to top of ch-3. Break off.

With right side of work facing you, attach brown to top of marked st.

9th rnd: Ch 3, dc in next dc and mark it (2 on Diagram), dc in next 16 dc, work 2 dc, ch 2 and 2 dc over next ch-2 lp (first corner made), sk next 3 dc, sc in next 18 dc (waist edge), sk next 3 dc, work 2 dc, ch 2 and 2 dc (2nd corner) in next ch-2 lp, dc in next 18 dc; leave remaining 20 dc unworked for top edge. Break off. Attach gold to ch-2 lp of first corner (3 on Diagram).

10th row: Working along waist edge, ch 3, work 5 dc over same corner lp, ch 1, sk 3 sts, sc in next 16 sc, ch 1, sk 3 sts, work 6 dc over ch-2 lp of 2nd corner. Break off; attach green.

11th row: Ch 3, turn work so that wrong side faces you, dc in place where yarn was attached, working along waist edge dc in next 5 dc, work 4 dc in next ch-1 sp, sk next 3 sc, sc in next 10 sc, sk next 3 sc, work 4 dc in next ch-1 sp, dc in next 5 dc, work 2 dc in top of ch-3. Break off. With right side facing you, attach purple to marked dc on 9th rnd (right underarm—2 on Diagram).

12th row: Ch 3, working along side edge toward waist, dc in next 18 brown dc to gold shell at corner, sl st in top

of gold ch-3, ch 3, sl st in top of green dc above. Turn work.

13th row: Dc in base of ch-3 just made, dc in next 18 dc (omit dc in ch-3). Turn.

14th row: Sl st in first dc, ch 3, dc in each of the 18 dc along side, dc in top of ch-3. [**For medium size only,** ch 3, turn, dc in each purple dc along side edge, omitting starting chain. **Note:** To avoid confusion, extra rows for medium size are not indicated on Diagram.] For both sizes, break off.

Attach purple to top of last dc in gold shell at lower left corner (4 on Diagram), and work purple rows along left side to correspond to right side. Break off.

With right side facing you, turn piece with waist edge up and attach purple to top of right corner purple dc (5 on Diagram).

15th row: Ch 3, working along waist edge, work 3 dc over post of dc where yarn was joined [**For medium size only,** work 4 dc over end dc on next row], dc in next green dc, hdc in next green dc, sc in next 28 green sts, hdc in next green dc, dc in last green dc, work 4 dc over end purple dc on next 1 [2] rows (40 [48] sts). Break off.

Left Shoulder Strap: With right side facing you, turn piece with top edge up and attach purple to ch-2 lp at corner (6 on Diagram).

1st row: Ch 3, working along top edge, dc in place where yarn was attached, dc in next 5 dc. Ch 3, turn.

2nd row: Sk first dc, dc in each dc across and in turning ch (7 dc, counting ch-3 as 1 dc). Ch 3, turn. Rep 2nd row 12 [13] times more. Break off. Broken lines on Diagram indicate top of shoulders.

Right Shoulder Strap: Sk center 10 dc along top edge of Bodice; attach purple to next dc (7 on Diagram).

1st row: Ch 3, dc in next 4 dc, work 2 dc over next ch-2 lp. Ch 3, turn. Work as for other strap.

Note: Purple border will be worked later.

BODICE BACK: The Bodice has a scooped-out back which is worked in semicircular rows as follows:

1st row: Starting at top edge with brown (8 on Diagram), (ch 3, dc in 3rd ch from hook) 18 times (a chain of 18 lps made).

2nd row (right side): Ch 3, 2 dc over post of last dc made, work 3 dc over post of next dc, work 3 hdc over post of each of next 2 dc, work 2 hdc over post of each of next 2 dc, sc over post of each next 6 dc, work 2 hdc over post of each next 2 dc, work 3 hdc over post of next 2 dc, work 3 dc over post of next dc, work 2 dc over post of next dc, ch 2, sl st in same dc.

With same side facing you, turn piece to work along opposite edge of lps as follows:

3rd row: Ch 3, work 2 dc over first ch lp, work 3 dc over each lp to within last lp, work 2 dc over last lp, ch 2,

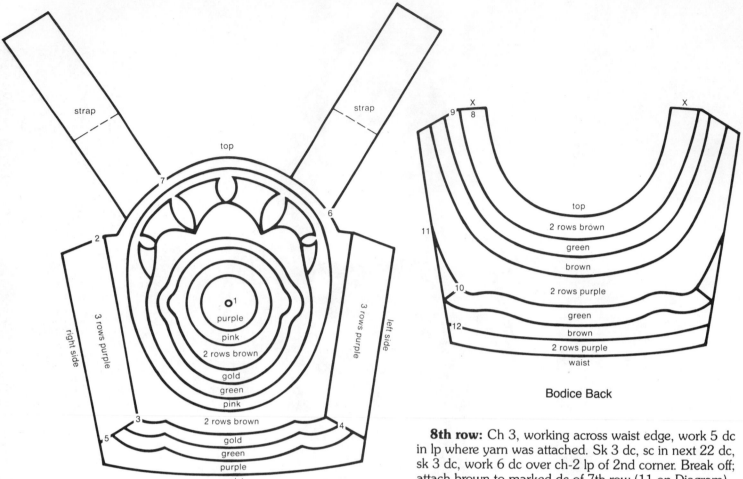

Bodice Front

Bodice Back

sl st in the same lp. Break off; attach green to top of first dc on 3rd row (9 on Diagram).

4th row: Ch 3, dc in each dc across to within last dc and ch-2, then ch 2, sl st in last dc (50 dc, plus ch at beg and end of row). Break off; attach brown to top of first dc on 4th row.

5th row: Work same as for 4th row (48 dc, plus ch at beg and end). Break off; attach purple to top of first dc on 5th row.

6th row: Work same as for 4th row (46 dc, plus ch at beg and end). Break off purple and attach it again to top of 3rd dc on 6th row.

7th row: Ch 2, hdc in next 2 dc, dc in next dc and mark this st, dc in next 4 dc, in next dc work 2 dc, ch 2 and 2 dc (first corner), sk next dc, dc in next 10 dc, work 2 dc in each of next 2 dc (center back), dc in next 10 dc, sk next dc, work 2 dc, ch 2 and 2 dc (2nd corner) in next dc, dc in next 5 dc, hdc in next 2 dc, ch 1, sl st in next dc. Break off; attach green to ch-2 lp of first corner (10 on Diagram).

8th row: Ch 3, working across waist edge, work 5 dc in lp where yarn was attached. Sk 3 dc, sc in next 22 dc, sk 3 dc, work 6 dc over ch-2 lp of 2nd corner. Break off; attach brown to marked dc of 7th row (11 on Diagram).

9th row: Ch 2, sc in next dc, hdc in next 2 dc, dc in next 2 dc, work 2 dc in next dc, in top of green ch-3 work sc, ch 2 and sc (first corner), sc in each st across to within last green dc, work sc, ch 2 and sc all in last green dc (2nd corner), work 2 dc in next purple st, dc in next 2 sts, hdc in next 2 sts, sc in next st, ch 1, sl st in next st. Break off.

[**For medium size only,** attach purple to ch-2 of 2nd corner.

10th row: Ch 3, dc in each st to last purple st of 6th row (underarm edge). Break off purple and attach it to first purple st of 6th row (opposite underarm edge), ch 3, dc in each st to ch-2 lp of first corner. Do not break off, but work across waist edge as follows: Ch 3, work 3 dc over post of last dc worked, work 2 dc over ch-2 lp of first corner, dc in each st across to ch-2 lp of 2nd corner, work 2 dc over ch-2 lp, work 4 dc over post of end dc. Ch 3, turn.]

For small size only, attach purple to ch-2 lp of first corner (12 on Diagram).

10th row: Ch 3, dc in lp where yarn was attached, dc in each st across to ch-2 lp of 2nd corner, work 2 dc over ch-2 lp. Ch 3, turn.

For both sizes: 11th row: Dc in first dc and in each dc across, work 2 dc in top of ch-3 (40 [48] dc, counting ch-3 as 1 dc). Break off.

SKIRT FRONT: Starting at waist edge with purple, ch 49 [55].

1st row: Work 5 dc in 4th ch from hook, sk 2 ch, sc in next ch (first shell made), * sk 2 ch, work 5 dc in next ch, sk 2 ch, sc in next ch (another shell). Rep from * across (8 [9] shells). Ch 3, turn.

2nd row: * Sc in each of center 3 dc on next shell, ch 2. Rep from * across, ending with sc in each of center 3 dc on last shell, ch 2, sc in top of starting ch. Ch 3, turn.

3rd row: Work 2 dc over first ch-2 lp, sc in center sc of next 3-sc group, * work 5 dc over next ch-2 lp, sc in center of next 3-sc group (shell made). Rep from * across, ending with 3 dc over turning ch. Ch 2, turn.

4th row: Sk first dc, sc in next dc, ch 2, * sc in each of center 3 dc on next shell, ch 2. Rep from * across, ending with sc in last dc, sc in top of ch-3. Ch 2, turn.

5th row: Sk first 2 sc, * work 7 dc over next ch-2 lp, sc in center sc of next 3-sc group (shell made). Rep from * across, ending last rep with sc in top of ch-2. Ch 3, turn.

6th row: * Sc in each of center 5 dc of next shell, ch 2. Rep from * across, ending with sc in top of ch-2. Ch 3, turn.

7th row: Work 3 dc over first lp, sc in center sc of next 5-dc group, * work 7 dc over next lp, sc in center sc of next 5-dc group (shell made). Rep from * across, ending with 4 dc over turning ch. Ch 2, turn.

8th row: Sc in each of first 2 dc, ch 2, * sc in each of center 5 dc of next shell, ch 2. Rep from * across, ending with sc in each of last 2 dc, sc in top of ch-3. Ch 2, turn.

9th row: Sk first 3 sc, * work 7 dc over next lp, sc in center sc of next 5-sc group (shell made). Rep from * across, ending with 7 dc over last lp, sc in top of ch-2. Ch 3, turn.

10th through 17th rows: Rep 6th through 9th rows twice.

18th row: Rep 6th row, working ch 3, instead of ch 2, between each 5-sc group.

19th row: Rep 7th row.

20th row: Rep 8th row, working ch 3, instead of ch 2, between each 5-sc group.

21st row: Rep 9th row.

22nd through 24th rows: Rep 18th through 20th rows. Break off.

SKIRT BACK: Work same as Skirt Front. Sew side seams of skirt, matching rows.

SKIRT BORDER: Attach brown at lower edge to 2nd st before one side seam.

1st rnd: Ch 3, work 4 dc over edge before next lp, work 3 hdc over lp, * dc in next 5 sc, work 3 hdc over next ch-3 lp *. Rep from * to * to last lp before next side seam, 3 hdc over lp, work 5 dc over edge before first lp after seam, work 3 hdc over lp. Rep from * to * to end (128 [144] sts), counting ch-3 as 1 st). Join to top of ch-3. Break off; attach pink.

2nd rnd: Ch 2, sc in each st around. Join to top of ch-2. Break off; attach green.

3rd rnd: Ch 2, * sk 2 sc, work 3 dc in next sc, ch 3, holding back on hook the last lp of each dc, work 2 dc in 3rd ch from hook, y o draw through all remaining lps on hook (p cl made), ch 2, sl st in base of p cl just made, work 3 dc in next sc, sk 2 sc, sc in each of next 2 sc. Rep from * around, ending last rep with sc in last sc. Join to top of ch-2 (16 [18] p cl). Break off; attach gold.

4th rnd: Ch 2, sc in next 3 dc, * ch 3, sc in top of next p cl, ch 3, sc in next 8 sts. Rep from * around, ending last rep with sc in last 4 sts. Join to top of ch-2. Break off; attach pink to last sc worked.

5th rnd: Ch 4, holding back on hook the last lp of each tr, work tr in place where yarn was attached, work 2 tr in next sc, y o draw through all 4 lps on hook (tr cl), * ch 3, sc over next ch-3 lp, ch 1, sc over next ch-3 lp, ch 3, sk 3 sc, holding back on hook the last lp of each tr, work 2 tr in each of next 2 sc, y o draw through all 5 lps on hook (another tr cl made). Rep from * around, ending with ch-3. Join to top of ch-4. Break off; attach purple to first ch of first ch-3 lp.

6th rnd: Ch 2, work 3 hdc over same lp, * sk next sc, hdc over next ch-1 lp, sk next sc, work 4 hdc over each of next two ch-3 lps. Rep from * around, ending last rep with 4 hdc over last ch-3 lp. Join to top of ch-2. Break off; attach brown.

7th rnd: Ch 2, hdc in each hdc around. Join to top of ch-2. Break off; attach purple.

8th rnd: Ch 1, sc in each hdc around. Join to ch-1. Break off.

FINISHING: Sew Shoulder Strap ends to Bodice Back at X's, matching inside edges to keep neckline smooth. Sew Bodice side seams. Sew Bodice and Skirt together at waist, easing edges to fit.

With purple, crochet a row of sc around neck edge and armholes, spacing sts to keep edges flat.

Bell-Sleeved Top and Skirt (front) and Three-Color Shell and Skirt

Dresses

BELL-SLEEVED TOP AND SKIRT

This special-occasion dress is made of cotton yarn in two parts, an overblouse plus an A-line skirt with adjustable waistline. The dress has a tunic-length top with lace-work sleeves and skirt hem. It is worked in double crochet, clusters, and shells.

SIZES: Small (10-12) [medium (14-16)]. Tunic Top measures 17½″ [18½″] across back from underarm to underarm, 24″ [24¼″] from shoulder to lower edge. Skirt measures 19″ [20″] wide, 7″ below waistline, and approximately 36″ long.

MATERIALS: Medium-weight cotton such as Lily Sugar-'n-Cream cotton yarn, 22 [25] (125-yd.) balls cream; aluminum crochet hook size H (or English/Canadian hook No. 8) *or the size that will give you the correct gauge.*

GAUGE: 7 dc = 2″; 8 rows (4 dc and 4 sc rows) = 3″.

CARE AND CLEANING: It is best to lay your dress away flat; hanging it up might stretch it out of shape. Dry cleaning rather than washing is advised, although the dress can be washed if special care is taken. Squeeze gently through lukewarm suds, then rinse thoroughly. Press water from garment; do not wring. Spread flat on towels and ease into shape. Allow to dry completely before removing.

TUNIC TOP

FRONT: Starting at lower edge, ch 63 [67] to measure about 17½″ [18½″].

1st row: Dc in 4th ch from hook and in each remaining ch (61 [65] dc, counting turning ch as 1 dc). Ch 1, turn.

2nd row: Work 1 sc in each dc across, sc in top of turning ch (61 [65] sc). Ch 3, turn.

3rd row: Sk first sc (turning ch counts as 1 dc), dc in each sc across (61 [65] dc). Ch 1, turn.

4th and 5th rows: Rep 2nd and 3rd rows.

6th row (dec row): Sl st in first dc, sc in each dc across to within last st. Do not work in last st (2 sts decreased in row). Ch 3, turn.

7th through 22nd rows: Rep 3rd through 6th rows 4 times more.

23rd through 29th rows: Work even in pattern on 51 [55] sts for 7 rows.

30th row (inc row): Work 2 sc in first dc, sc in each dc across, working 2 sc in top of turning ch (2 sc increased in row). Ch 3, turn.

Work even in pattern for 3 rows more; then rep inc row once. Work even in pattern on 55 [59] sts until piece measures 17″ from beg, ending with sc row.

To Shape Armholes: 1st row: Sl st across first 4 [6] sts, ch 3, dc in each dc across to within last 4 [6] sts. Do not work over these 4 [6] sts. Ch 1, turn.

Working in pattern, inc 1 st at beg and end of 4th and 8th rows. Work even on 51 sts until armholes measure 4″ [4¼″] from beg, ending with sc row. Ch 3, turn.

To Shape Neck: 1st short row: Dc in each of next 11 sc (12 sts, counting ch-3 as 1 dc). Ch 1, turn.

2nd row: Sc in each st of last row. Ch 3, turn.

3rd row: Dc in next 8 sts. Ch 1, turn.

4th row: Rep 2nd row.

5th row: Dc in next 6 sts. Ch 1, turn. Rep 2nd row.

Rep last 2 rows once more. Break off.

Leaving center 27 sts free, attach yarn in next st and, reversing shaping, complete as for first side.

BACK: Work same as for Front until armholes measure 5½" [5¾"].

To Shape Neck: Work as for Front, repeating first short row, 2nd row, 5th and 6th rows. Break off. Work other side to correspond.

SLEEVES: Top Section: Starting at lower edge of top section (the 6" lower section is added to sleeve later), ch 60 to measure 15"; join with sl st in first st to form ring. Put a pin in work to be used later as marker for start of lower section.

1st rnd: Ch 6, sk 2 ch, tr in next ch, * ch 2, sk 2 ch, tr in next ch. Rep from * around, ending ch 2, sl st in 4th ch of first ch-6 (20 sps).

2nd rnd: Ch 3, work 2 dc in first ch-2 sp, work 3 dc in each sp around; join with sl st to top of ch-3 (60 dc, counting ch-3 as 1 dc).

3rd rnd: Ch 3, work 3 dc in same st as sl st for first shell, * ch 1, sk 5 dc, work a shell of 4 dc in next dc. Rep from * around, ending ch 1; join with sl st to ch-3 (10 shells).

4th rnd: Ch 3, work 3-dc cl over first shell as follows: (Y o draw up lp in next dc, y o and draw through 2 lps on hook) 3 times; y o and draw through all 4 lps on hook, * ch 5, work 4-dc cl over next shell. Rep from * around, ending ch 5; join with sl st to top of first cl.

5th rnd: Ch 3, * work 5 dc in next ch-5 sp, work 1 dc in top of cl. Rep from * around (60 dc); join.

6th rnd: Ch 6, sk 2 dc, tr in next dc, * ch 2, sk 2 dc, tr in next dc. Rep from * around, ending ch 2, join with sl st in 4th ch of first ch-6 (20 sp).

7th rnd: Rep 2nd rnd (60 dc).

8th rnd: Ch 4, sk 1 dc, dc in next dc, * ch 1, sk 1 dc, dc in next dc. Rep from * around, ending ch 1; join to 3rd st of ch-4 (30 sp).

9th and 10th rnds: Sl st in first sp, ch 4, dc in next sp, * ch 1, dc in next sp. Rep from * around, ending ch 1; join to 3rd st of ch-4 (30 sp).

11th rnd: Ch 3, work 1 dc in each sp and in each dc around (60 dc); join.

12th rnd: Rep 6th rnd.

13th through 16th rnds: Rep 2nd through 5th rnds once. Sleeve should measure 12" from beg.

To Shape Cap: Work in rows from now on.

1st row: Ch 6, sk 2 dc, tr in next dc, * ch 2, sk 2 dc, tr in next dc. Rep from * across until there are 18 sp. Do not work across last 6 sts. Turn.

2nd row: Ch 3, sk sp, dc in next tr, * work 2 dc in next sp, 1 dc in next tr. Rep from * across to last sp, sk 2 ch, dc in next ch of turning ch. Turn.

3rd row: Ch 3, sk 3 dc, dc in next dc, * ch 1, sk 1 dc, dc in next dc. Rep from * across to within last 3 dc, sk last 2 dc, dc in next dc. Turn.

4th row: Sl st in first dc, ch 3, sk sp and next dc, dc in next sp, * ch 1, dc in next sp. Rep from * across to last ch-1 sp, sk last sp, dc in next dc. Turn.

Rep last row 4 [5] times more. Break off.

Lower Section: 1st rnd: Turn Sleeve upside down and, working along opposite edge of foundation ch, attach yarn at marker. Ch 3, work 1 dc in each st of foundation ch (60 dc, counting ch-3 as 1 dc); join with sl st to top of ch-3.

2nd rnd: Ch 3, work 3 dc in same st as sl st for first shell, * sk 3 dc, work 4-dc shell in next dc. Rep from * around; join (15 shells).

3rd rnd: Ch 3, working as for 4th rnd of top section of Sleeve, work 3-dc cl over first shell, then work 2 rice sts as follows: (Ch 4, y o, draw up lp in 4th ch from hook, y o and draw through 2 lps on hook; y o and draw up another lp in same ch as last st, y o and draw through 2 lps on hook; y o and draw through all three lps on hook) twice (2 rice sts completed); * work 4-dc cl over next shell, work 2 rice sts. Rep from * around; join to top of first cl.

4th rnd: Ch 5, sk 1 rice st, sc in sp between this rice st and next one, * ch 5, sc in sp between next 2 rice sts. Rep from * around; join with sl st to first st of ch-5.

5th rnd: Ch 3, work 5 dc in first sp, work 6 dc in each sp around. Join.

6th rnd: Ch 6, sk 2 dc, work tr in sp before next dc, * ch 2, sk 3 dc, tr in sp before next dc. Rep from * around, ending ch 2; join to 4th st of ch-6.

7th rnd: Sl st in first sp, ch 3, work 2 dc in same sp, work 3 dc in each sp around; join.

8th rnd: Ch 3, dc in each dc around; join and break off. This section should measure 6" from first rnd.

FINISHING: Sew side and shoulder seams. Sew Sleeves in place.

Neckband: 1st rnd: With right side of work facing you, attach yarn at right shoulder seam, ch 6, sk about ¾" along neck edge, work tr in next st, * ch 2, sk ¾", tr in next st. Rep from * around; join with sl st in 4th ch of ch-6. Turn.

2nd rnd: Working along wrong side of work, work 2 sc in each ch sp; join. Break off.

SKIRT

Note: Finished length of Skirt is 36". Top part of Skirt is worked in 2 pieces, with side seams. Lace border is added later. Adjust the length of the Skirt, if desired, before border is added.

BACK: Starting at waist edge, ch 55 [59] to measure about 15" [16"]. Work as for first 5 rows of front of Tunic Top, having 53 [57] sts on each row..Work even in pattern for 2 rows more. With 2 pins, mark off center 27 sts, leaving 13 [15] sts on each side of center.

8th row (inc row): Work 2 sc in first dc for first inc, work 1 sc in each dc to first pin, work 2 sc in marked st, work 1 sc in each dc to next pin, work 2 sc in next dc, work 1 sc in each dc to last st, work 2 dc in last st (4 sc inc in row). Ch 3, turn.

Having all increases fall in line with increases of previous inc row, work in pattern and rep inc row every 6th row 4 times more, then every 8th row twice.

Work even on 81 [85] sts until Skirt measures 22½" (or 13½" shorter than finished length), ending with sc row. Break off. If any adjustment in length is needed, work more or fewer rows at this point.

FRONT: Work as for Back. Sew side seams, leaving 4"

opening on left side seam at waistline.

LACE BORDER: Attach yarn at lower edge of Skirt 2 sts from 1 side seam.

1st rnd: Ch 3, work 3-dc shell in same st as ch-3, * sk 3 sc, work 4-dc shell in next sc. Rep from * around (40 [42] shells); join with sl st to top of ch-3.

2nd through 6th rnds: Rep 3rd through 7th rnds of **lower** section of Sleeve.

7th through 10th rnds: Rep 8th through 11th rnds of **top** section of Sleeve.

11th through 17th rnds: Rep 2nd through 8th rnds of **lower** section of Sleeve. Join and break off.

The border should measure 13½" from beg.

TIE: Crochet a ch to tie around waist. Break off. Weave in and out of sts at waistline. Gather to fit and tie ends into bow.

THREE-COLOR SHELL AND SKIRT

This versatile three-colored shell and skirt dress is in coffee, accented with cream and lavender. Strips and panels of double crochet and shell-stitch variation are made and the sections are then crocheted together. If preferred, the overblouse can also be made with cap sleeves.

SIZES: Small (8–10) [medium (12–14)]. Shell measures 15" [17"] across back from underarm to underarm, 19½" [19¾"] from shoulder to lower edge. Skirt measures 17" [19"] wide, 7" below waistline, and approximately 30½" long.

MATERIALS: Medium-weight cotton yarn such as Lily Sugar-'n-Cream, 11 [12] (125-yd.) balls gold, 4 balls light orchid, 1 ball cream; aluminum crochet hook size F [H] (or English/Canadian hook No. 10 [No. 8]) *or the size that will give you the correct gauge.*

GAUGE: 1 star st = ⅞" [1"]. See directions for strip measurements.

SHELL

Note: Shell is worked in vertical strips of different lengths which are made separately and then sewed together.

FRONT: Front Insert: 7-loop Center Strip: 1st row (right side): With orchid, (ch 4, tr in 4th ch from hook) 7 times (7 lps made to measure 6¾" [7"]). Do not break off or turn, but work along one side of lps as follows:

2nd rnd: Ch 3, work 3 dc over post of tr on last lp

Shell

made, work 4 dc over post of tr on each of next 5 lps, work 6 dc over post of tr on first lp made; continue along opposite side of lps as follows: Work 6 dc over ch-4 on same lp, work 4 dc over ch-4 on each of next 5 lps, work 8 dc in last lp; join with sl st to top of ch-3 (7-lp strip completed to measure 1¾″ x 7½″ [2″ x 7¾″]; 64 dc, counting ch-3 as 1 dc). Break off.

3rd row: With right side facing you, attach gold to back lp of last sl st, ch 3, working in back lp only of each st, work dc in next 23 dc, 2 dc in each of next 12 dc, in next 24 dc; leave 4 top dc unworked for center front neck edge (72 dc, counting ch-3 as 1 dc). Break off.

4th row: With right side facing you, attach cream to top of first ch-3 on last row, ch 2, work 2 sc in same sp (3-sc shell made, counting ch-2 as 1 sc), ch 1, sk 3 dc, in sp between dc's work 3 sc (another shell made), (ch 1, sk 4 dc, work shell in next sp between dc's) 16 times; ch 1, sk 3 dc, work shell in top of last dc (19 shells made). Break off.

5th row: With wrong side facing you, attach orchid to last sc made on last row, ch 2, work 2 long dc in same sp (for long dc draw up ½″ lp on hook; first star made), sk next 2 sc, in next ch-1 sp work 1 sc and 2 long dc (another star made), * sk next shell, work star in next ch-1 sp. Rep from * 6 times more; sk next shell, sc in next ch-1 sp (9 stars made); turn.

6th row (dec row): Ch 4, sk 2 long dc, sc in next sc, ch 4, * sk 2 long dc, work star in next sc. Rep from * 6 times more; sc in first ch-2 made on last row (7 stars made); ch 2, turn.

7th row: Work 2 long dc in same sp as turning ch, * sk 2 long dc, work star in next sc. Rep from * 5 times more; sk next 2 long dc, sc in next sc (7 stars made); ch 2, turn.

8th row: Rep 7th row, ending with sc in top of turning ch (7 stars made); ch 4, turn.

9th row (inc row): Work star in 2nd ch from hook, work star in last sc made on last row. Rep 7th row from * across, ending with sc in top of turning ch (8 stars made). Break off. Left side of Front Insert completed. Work along opposite side of Insert as follows: With right side of piece facing you, attach orchid to top of first ch-2 on 4th row, complete in same manner as Left Side. Front Insert completed.

Flower Pendant: Starting at center with orchid, ch 5. Join with sl st to form ring.

1st rnd (right side): Ch 3, work 11 dc in ring (12 dc, counting ch-3 as 1 dc); join with sl st to top of ch-3. Break off.

2nd rnd: With right side facing you, attach gold to back lp of last sl st; ch 3, work dc in same st (counting ch-3 as 1 dc); working in back lp of each st work 2 dc in each dc around; join to top of ch-3 (24 sts made). Break off.

3rd rnd: With right side facing you, attach cream to sp

between any 2 dc sts; ch 1, work 6 dc in same sp (first petal made), * sk next 2 dc sts, in next sp between dc sts work 1 sc and 6 dc (another petal made). Rep from * 4 times more; join to first ch-1 (6 petals made). Break off. Lay completed pendant aside and join to Front later.

Complete front as follows: See Diagram 1 for position of Strips and Insert.

Underarm Strips: 1st row (right side): With gold (ch 3, dc in 3rd ch from hook) 14 times (14 lps made to measure 10¼″ [10½″]). Work along 1 side of lps as follows:

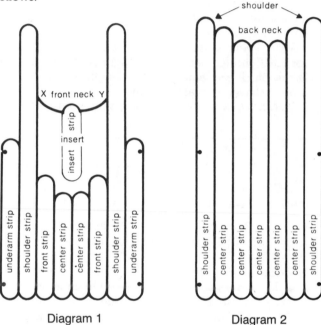

Diagram 1   Diagram 2

2nd rnd (right side): Ch 3, work 2 dc over post of dc on last lp made, work 3 dc over post of dc on each lp to within first lp made, work 5 dc over post of dc on first lp; continue along opposite side of lps as follows: Work 4 dc over ch-3 on same lp, work 3 dc over ch-3 on each lp to within last lp made, work 6 dc in last lp; join to top of ch-3 (Underarm Strip completed to measure 1¾″ x 11″ [2″ x 11¼″]). Break off. Make another Underarm Strip in same manner.

Make two 24-lp Shoulder Strips (1¾″ x 19″ [2″ x 19¼″]); two 9-lp Front Strips (1¾″ x 7″ [2″ x 7¼″]); and two 8-lp Center Strips (1¾″ x 6″ [2″ x 6¼″]).

To Assemble: Following Diagram 1, pin strips together with right sides facing. With gold yarn, working loosely, sl st edges together from wrong side through top lps only, leaving 9-dc scallops at lower edge free. Front lps will form ridges along seam on right side. With orchid, sew Insert in place with whipstitch. Following photograph for placement, sew pendant working between 2 petals with 5 or 6 stitches to lower edge of Insert. Front completed.

BACK: Following Diagram 2, work the following Strips in same manner as for Front: two 24-lp Shoulder Strips (1¾" x 19" [2" x 19¼"]); for Center Strips make two 23-lp strips (1¾" x 18" [2" x 18¼"]) and three 22-lp Strips (1¾" x 17" [2" x 17¼"]).

To Assemble: Following Diagram 2, join Strips as for Front. Back neck edge is slightly scalloped.

To Join Front and Back: With right sides together, pin Underarm Strip to back Shoulder Strip on each side, between dots. Sl st together, working through top lp only of each st. Sew shoulder strap ends together, joining corresponding 3 center sts.

Neck Trim: With right side of Front facing you, attach orchid to last orchid st of Insert at X on Diagram 1; work sc evenly along right shoulder strap, scalloped back neck edge and left shoulder strap; join with sl st at Y. Break off.

Lower Edge Trim: With right side facing you, attach orchid to first dc of a 9-dc scallop, ch 2, sc in same dc, work 2 sc in each of next 8 dc (18 sc, counting ch-2 as 1 sc), * sk seam, work 2 sc in each of next 9 dc. Rep from * around; join with sl st to top of ch-2. Break off.

Armhole Trim: With right side facing you, attach gold to shoulder strap seam, ch 1, working in back lp only of each st, sl st evenly around armhole. Join to first ch-1. Break off.

SLEEVES: 1st rnd: With gold, work 10-lp Strip in same manner as for Underarm Strip.

2nd rnd: With right side facing you, attach orchid to back lp of last sl st worked, ch 3, working in back lps only of each st work dc in next 28 sts, 2 dc in each of next 5 sts, dc in each of next 29 sts, mark last dc made, 2 dc in each of next 3 dc, sl st beg ch-3. Break off.

3rd row: With right side facing, attach gold to st before last sl st made, ch 2, work 2 long dc in same sp (first star made), sk sl st and 1 dc, * work sc and 2 long dc in next st (another star made), sk 2 dc, rep from * 9 times, sc next st (11 stars); ch 2, turn.

4th row: Work 2 long dc in same sp as turning ch, * sk 2 long dc, star in next sc, rep from * across to within last sc, sc in last sc (11 stars); ch 2, turn.

5th row (dec row): Work 2 long dc in same sp as turning ch, * sk 2 long dc, work star in next sc, rep from * 8 times; sk 2 long dc, sc in next sc (10 stars); ch 2, turn.

6th row (dec row): Work same as for 5th row except rep from * to * 7 times (9 stars).

7th row (dec row): Work same as for 5th row except rep from * to * 5 times (7 stars).

8th through 13th rows (dec rows): Work in star st pattern, decreasing one star st at end of each row until only one star st remains. Hold piece with wrong side facing, attach gold at dc before marker. Working along opposite side of Strip, rep 3rd through 13th rows.

Fill-In: With right side facing, work across longest edge. With gold, begin in turning ch-2 at tip of last star st made, work sc, * in sp between star sts work 3 dc shell, work sc tip of next star, rep from * 3 times, work 2 sc over each of next 2 stars, sc next 4 dc at tip of Strip, 2 sc over each of next 2 stars, rep from * to * 4 times. (Seam edge made.) Break off. Make a 2nd Sleeve. Sew Sleeves in place, using gold, working on wrong side in top lps only, with whipstitch. Be sure tip of Strip meets shoulder seam. With orchid, work sc edging around Sleeves and underarm.

SKIRT

Note: Skirt consists of 7 slightly fan-shaped Panels which are made separately and then crocheted together.

CENTER FRONT PANEL: With orchid, work 26-lp Center Strip in same manner as for 7-lp Center Strip on Front Insert of shell (216 dc at end of 2nd rnd, counting ch-3 as 1 dc). Strip should measure 1¾" x 29" [2" x 29¼"].

3rd row: With right side facing you, attach gold to back lp of last sl st, ch 3, working in back lp of each st, dc in next 99 dc, 2 dc in each of next 12 dc, dc in next 100 dc; leave 4 top dc unworked (224 dc, counting ch-3 as 1 dc). Break off.

4th row: With right side facing you, attach cream to top of first ch-3 on last row, ch 1, sk 3 dc, in sp between dc's work 3 sc (first shell made), (ch 1, sk 4 dc, work shell in next sp between dc's) 24 times (25 shells made); ch 1, sk 4 dc, sc in next sp between dc's, (ch 3, sk 4 dc, sc in sp between dc's) 4 times; (ch 1, sk 4 dc, work shell in sp between dc's) 25 times (50 shells made in all); sk 3 dc, sl st in last dc. Break off.

5th row: With wrong side facing you, attach orchid to last sl st made on last row, ch 2, work 2 long dc in same sp (first star made), * sk next 3 sc, in next ch-1 sp work 1 sc and 2 long dc (another star made). Rep from * 24 times more; work star in next sc, sk ch-3 lp, work star in next sc, sk next ch-3 lp, sc in next sc (28 stars made); turn.

6th row (dec row): Ch 4, sk 2 long dc, sc in next sc, ch 4, * sk 2 long dc, work star in next sc. Rep from * 21 times more; sk 2 long dc, sc in next sc (22 stars made); turn.

7th row (dec row): (Ch 3, sk 2 long dc, sc in next sc) 3 times; ch 3, * sk 2 long dc, work star in next sc. Rep from * 17 times more; sk 2 long dc, sc in next sc (18 stars made); ch 2, turn.

8th row (dec row): Work 2 long dc in same sp as turning ch, * sk 2 long dc, work star in next sc. Rep from * 12 times more; sk 2 long dc, sc in next sc (14 stars made); turn.

9th row (dec row): (Ch 3, sk 2 long dc, sc in next sc) 3 times; ch 3, * sk 2 long dc, work star in next sc. Rep from * 9 times more; sk 2 long dc, sc in top of turning ch (10 stars made); ch 2, turn.

10th row (dec row): Work 2 long dc in same sp as turning ch, * sk 2 long dc, work star in next sc. Rep from * 4 times more (6 stars made); sk 2 long dc, sc in next sc. Break off. Left side of Front Panel completed. Work along opposite side of Center Strip as follows: With right side of work facing you, attach orchid to top of first ch-1 on 4th row; complete as for Left Side. Center Front Panel completed.

SIDE AND BACK PANELS (make 6): With gold, work 26-lp Center Strip as before.

3rd row: With orchid, rep 3rd row of Center Front Panel.

4th row: With wrong side facing you, attach gold to top of last dc made on 3rd row, ch 2, work 2 long dc in same sp, sk 3 dc, work star in next sp between dc's, * sk 4 dc, work star in next sp between dc's. Rep from * 25 times more; sk 4 dc, sc in next sp between dc's (28 stars made); turn. Rep 6th row through 10th row of Center Front Panel. Break off. Work along opposite side of Center Strip as follows: With right side facing you, attach gold to top of first ch-3 made on 3rd row; complete as for Left

Side. Panel completed.

TO JOIN PANELS: Hold Center Front Panel and a Side panel, wrong sides together. Working through both layers, attach orchid to st of first star at waist edge, * ch 3, sk 2 long dc along seam, sc in next sc. Rep from * across, ending with sc in top of last st of last star. Break off. With gold, join remaining panels in same manner, following Diagram 3. With orchid, join edge X of Center Front Panel to edge X of last Panel.

WAIST TRIM: With right side facing you, attach orchid to waist edge; ch 1, sc evenly around; join to first ch-1. Break off.

DRAWSTRING: Crochet a ch long enough to tie around waist. Weave under and over sc's around waist edge of skirt.

LOWER EDGE TRIM: With right side facing you, attach orchid at a seam. Work around lower edge of skirt, keeping work smooth and flat, as follows: Work 2 sc over posts of sts, and 5 sc over ch lps, sl st in first sc. Break off.

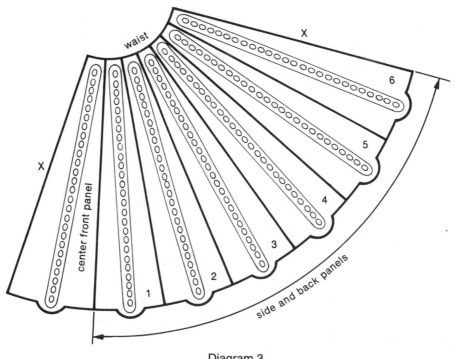

Diagram 3

Shawls

CABBAGE ROSE SHAWL

Lush roses form a bold pattern, dense with color. You make seven large triangles and crochet them together and add a border. Pearl cotton is worked double in single crochet and chain stitches.

SIZE: About 62″ across long edge and 34″ in depth.

MATERIALS: Pearl cotton such as D.M.C. pearl cotton No. 5 (see Note for substitute), 28 (53-yd.) balls blue , 10 balls burgundy, 8 balls dark green, 6 balls each pale green and medium dusty rose, 4 balls pale pink, 2 balls each gold, light dusty rose, and orange; aluminum crochet hook size F (or English/Canadian hook No. 10) *or the size that will give you the correct gauge.*

GAUGE: 3 dc = ½″. Dimensions for various sections of shawl are given in directions.

Note: Use 2 strands of thread held together throughout.

To make the shawl for less cost, cotton thread such as J. & P. Coats Knit-Cro-Sheen can be substituted for the pearl cotton. You will need 9 (175-yd.) balls blue, 4 balls burgundy, 3 balls dark green, 2 balls each pale green,

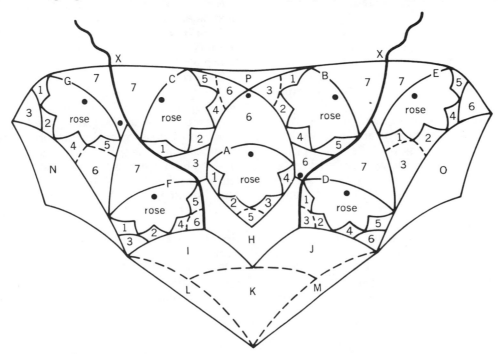

medium rose, and pale pink and 1 ball each gold, light rose, and orange. Work with thread double. Try aluminum hook size E and check gauge.

SECTION A: Rose: Starting at dot on rose (see Diagram), with medium dusty rose, ch 2.

1st rnd: Work 8 sc in 2nd ch from hook, sl st in first sc. Mark beg of each rnd with safety pin.

2nd rnd: Ch 3, * sc in next sc, ch 1. Rep from * 6 times more, sl st in 2nd ch of starting ch-3.

3rd rnd: * In next ch-1 sp work sc, ch 3, and sc; ch 3. Rep from * around; sl st in first sc (16 ch-3 sp).

4th rnd: Ch 1, * sc in next sp, ch 3. Rep from * around; sl st in first sc (16 sp).

5th rnd: Rep 4th rnd. Place pin marker on next to last ch-sp made. Break off. Circle should measure 2½" across.

1st row: With same side facing you and with burgundy, form lp on hook and sc in last ch-3 sp on 5th rnd, (ch 3, sc in next sp) 11 times (4 sp left unworked); place thread marker in next sp; ch 1, turn.

2nd row: Sc in first sp, (ch 3, sc in next sp) 3 times; (ch 3, sc in same sp as last sc worked) 3 times, * (ch 3, sc in next sp) twice; (ch 3, sc in same sp as last sc worked) 3 times. Rep from * once more; (ch 3, sc in next sp) 3 times (19 sp); ch 1, turn.

3rd row: Sc in first sp, * ch 3, sc in next sp. Rep from * across (1 sp decreased); ch 1, turn.

4th through 9th rows: Rep 3rd row 6 times more, omitting ch-1 on last row (12 sp). Break off.

10th row: With same side facing you and with medium dusty rose, sc in same sp as pin marker. Working along outer edge of burgundy sts, (ch 3, sc in next sp) 29 times, ending with sc in sp marked with thread (29 sp); ch 1, turn. Remove markers.

11th row: Sc in first sp, (ch 3, sc in next sp) 6 times; * ch 8, sc in 3rd ch from hook, sc in each of next 2 ch, hdc in each of next 2 ch, dc in each of next 2 ch, sc in same ch-3 sp, (ch 3, sc in next sp) 4 times. Rep from * 4 times more, ending last rep (ch 3, sc in next sp) 6 times. Mark last sp. Break off. Turn.

12th row: With burgundy, sc in marked sp, (ch 3, sc in next sp) 5 times; * ch 3, sk next sc and 2 dc, work sc, ch 3 and sc in next hdc, ch 3, sk next 3 sts, work sc, ch 3, and sc in tip, ch 3, sk next 3 sts, work sc, ch 3 and sc in base of next hdc, ch 3, sk next 2 dc and next sc, sc in next sp, (ch 3, sc in next sp) 3 times. Rep from * 4 times more, ending last rep (ch 3, sc in next sp) 5 times; ch 1, turn.

13th row: Sc in first sp, (ch 3, sc in next sp) 3 times; * ch 3, sk next sp, sc in following sp, (ch 3, sc in next sp) 3 times; ch 3, sc in same sp (tip), (ch 3, sc in next sp) 3 times; ch 3, sk next sp, sc in following sp. Rep from * 4 times more; (ch 3, sc in next sp) 3 times; ch 1, turn. Re-

move marker.

14th row: Sc in first sp, (ch 3, sc in next sp) 7 times; * ch 3, sc in same sp as last sc, (ch 3, sc in next sp) 3 times; ch 3, sk next sp, sc in next sc, ch 3, sk next sp, sc in following sp, (ch 3, sc in next sp) 3 times. Rep from * 3 times more; ch 3, sc in same sp as last sc, (ch 3, sc in next sp) 7 times; ch 1, turn.

15th row: Sc in first sp, ch 3, sk next sp, sc in following sp, (ch 3, sc in next sp) 5 times; * ch 3, sc in same sp as last sc, (ch 3, sc in next sp) 3 times; ch 3, sk next sp, sc in next sc, ch 3, sk next sp, sc in following sp, (ch 3, sc in next sp) 3 times. Rep from * 3 times more; ch 3, sc in same sp as last sc (mark this sp for first petal tip), (ch 3, sc in next sp) 5 times; ch 3, sk next sp, sc in following sp. Break off; turn. Rose is completed.

Area 1: 1st row: Starting at tip of first petal, with orange, work sc in marked sp, (ch 3, sc in next sp) twice; ch 3, dc in next sp, sk next sp, tr in next sc, sk next sp, dc in next sp, (ch 3, sc in next sp) 3 times (last sc made is in tip of next petal); ch 1, turn.

2nd row: Sc in first sp, (ch 3, sc in next sp) twice; sk next dc, tr and dc, (ch 3, sc in next sp) 3 times; ch 1, turn.

3rd row: Sc in first sp, * ch 3, sc in next sp. Rep from * across; ch 1, turn.

4th through 5th rows: Rep 3rd row twice more.

6th row: Sc in first sp, ch 3, sc in next sp. Break off. Turn.

Area 2: Following Diagram, with dark green, work as for Area 1, starting at tip of next petal on Rose. Mark last sp worked.

Area 3: With dark green, work as for Area 1, starting at tip of next petal.

Area 4: With gold, work as for Area 1, starting at tip of next petal.

Area 5: 1st row: With dark green, work sc in marked sp on Area 2, * ch 3, sc in next sp. Rep from * across to last sp worked on Area 3 (11 sp); ch 1, turn.

2nd row: Sc in first sp, * ch 3, sc in next sp. Rep from * across; ch 1, turn. Rep 2nd row 9 times more, ending with 1 sp. Break off.

Area 6: 1st row: With same side facing you and with blue, work across top of Rose as follows: Sc in sp at tip of right petal (in same sp with sc of Area 4), * ch 3, sc in next sp. Rep from * across, ending with last sc in sp at tip of left petal (27 sp). Mark this side as right of piece; ch 1, turn. Rep 2nd row of Area 5, 26 times, ending with 1 sp. Mark sp at each end of 10th row. Break off.

SECTION B: Rose: Work Rose in same colors as for Section A.

Area 1: With dark green, work as for Area 1 on Section A. Mark last sp worked.

Area 2: With dark green, work as for Area 1.

Area 3: 1st row: With dark green, sc in marked sp on Area 1, * ch 3, sc in next sp. Rep from * across to last sp worked on Area 2 (11 sp); ch 1, turn.

2nd row: Sc in first sp, * ch 3, sc in next sp. Rep from * across; ch 1, turn. Rep 2nd row 9 times more. Break off.

Area 4: With orange, work as for Area 1. Mark last sp worked.

Area 5: With gold, work as for Area 1.

Area 6: 1st row: With pale green, sc in marked sp on Area 4, * ch 3, sc in next sp. Rep from * across to last sp worked on Area 5 (11 sp); ch 1, turn.

2nd row: Sc in first sp, * ch 3, sc in next sp. Rep from * across; ch 1, turn. Rep 2nd row 9 times more. Break off.

Area 7: With blue, work as for Area 6 on Section A, starting with sc in same sp as sc of Area 5. Work Sections C through G as for Section B in the following colors:

SECTION C: Rose: 1st through 5th rnds: Light dusty rose.
  1st through 9th rows: Pale pink.
  10th and 11th rows: Light dusty rose.
  12th through 15th rows: Pale pink.
  Area 1: Gold.
  Area 2: Orange.
  Area 3: Dark green.
  Areas 4, 5 and 6: Pale green.
  Area 7: Blue.

SECTION D: Rose: Work Rose in same colors as for Section C.
  Areas 1, 2 and 3: Pale green.
  Area 4: Orange.
  Area 5: Gold.
  Area 6: Dark green.
  Area 7: Blue.

SECTION E: Rose: 1st through 5th rnds: Dark green.
  1st through 9th rows: Pale green.
  10th and 11th rows: Dark green.
  12th through 15th rows: Pale green.
  Areas 1, 2 and 3: Dark green.
  Area 4: Orange.
  Area 5: Gold.
  Area 6: Dark green.
  Area 7: Blue.

SECTION F: Rose: Work Rose in same colors as for Section E.
  Area 1: Orange.
  Area 2: Gold.
  Areas 3 through 6: Dark green.
  Area 7: Blue.

SECTION G: Rose: Work Rose in same colors as for Section A.
  Area 1: Orange.
  Area 2: Gold.
  Area 3: Pale green.
  Areas 4, 5, and 6: Dark green.
  Area 7: Blue.

Note: Work with right sides facing you, for all joinings.

Joining Section A to Section B: With pale green, form lp on hook. Starting at point of Area 4 on Section A (dot on Diagram), sc in sp at point, ch 1, sk sp at point of Area 6 of Section B, sc in next sp along adjacent edge of Section B, * ch 1, sc in next sp on Section A, ch 1, sc in next sp on Section B. Rep from * 32 times, ending with sc in sp at point of Area 6 on Section B (dot on Diagram). Break off.

Joining Section A to Section C: With orange, form lp on hook. Starting at point of Area 6 on Section A, sc in sp at point (dot on Diagram), ch 1, sc in sp at point of Area 6 on Section C, * ch 1, sc in next sp on Section A, ch 1, sc in next sp on Section C. Rep from *, ending last rep with sc in sp before sp at tip of Area 3 on Section C. Break off.

Joining Section F to Section G: With dark green, sc in marked sp on 10th row of Area 7 on Section G (dot), ch 1, sc in sp at point of Area 7 on Section F, * ch 1, sc in next sp on Section G, ch 1, sc in next sp on Section F. Rep from * 26 times, ending last rep with sc in last sp on Area 6 of Section G. Break off.

Joining Sections F and G to Section C: With gold, sc in sp at point on Area 7 of Section G, ch 1, sc in sp at point of Area 7 on Section C, * ch 1, sc in next sp on Section G, ch 1, sc in next sp on Section C. Rep from *, joining the remaining 16 sps of Section G, then join next 27 sps of Section F to Section C, ending last rep with ch 1, sc in point of Area 3 on Section C. Break off. Mark last sc worked on Section F.

Joining Section D to Section E: With dark green, work in same manner as for joining Section F to Section G. Start in marked sp on 10th row of Area 7 on Section E.

Joining Sections D and E to Section B: With gold, work in same manner as for joining Sections F and G to Section C. Mark last sc worked on Section D.

Note: Turn work so that lower edge is facing upward.

SECTION H: 1st row: With blue, sc over marked joining sc on Section F; working towards point of Area 5 on Section A, ch 3, sk about ½″ along edge, sc in next sp (ch-3 sp made). Mark this sp. Work 14 more ch-3 sps evenly spaced across, ending with sc in point of Area 5, ch 3, sc in same sp; work 15 ch-3 sp evenly across, ending sc in marked joining sc on Section D (31 sp). Mark last sp worked. Ch 1, turn.
  2nd row: Sc in first sp, (ch 3, sc in next sp) 15 times; ch 3, sc in same sp as last sc, (ch 3, sc in next sp) 15 times; ch 1, turn. Rep 2nd row 15 times more. Break off.
Joining Section H to Section F: With gold, sc in first marked sp on H, ch 1, sc in next unworked sp on Section F, * ch 1, sc in next sp on H, ch 1, sc in next sp on Section F. Rep from * 15 times, ending sc in last sp on Area 6 of Section F.
Joining Section H to Section D: With gold, work in same manner as for joining Section H to Section F.

SECTION I: 1st row: With blue, sc in sp at point of Area 3 on Section F, ch 6, sk about ½″ along edge, sc in next sp (ch-6 sp made). Work 23 more ch-6 sps evenly spaced across, ending with last sc in sp before sp at point on Section H (24 sp); ch 6, turn.

2nd row: Sc in first sp, * ch 6, sc in next sp. Rep from * to within last 2 sp; ch 6, turn.

3rd through 11th rows: Rep 2nd row 9 times more (4 sp).

12th row: Sc in first sp, place marker in sp just formed, ch 6, sc in next sp. Break off.

SECTION J: 1st row: With blue, working on wrong side, sc in sp at point of Area 6 on Section D and work as for Section I.

SECTION K: 1st row: With blue, sc in marked sp on Section I, ch 6, sc in next sp (ch-6 sp made). Work 10 more ch-6 sp evenly across, ending with sc in sp before point of Section H (11 sp), ch 6; in point work dtr, ch 6 and dtr (mark this sp); work 12 sp evenly across, ending with sc in marked sp on Section J (25 sp); ch 6, turn.

2nd row: Sc in first sp, * ch 6, sc in next sp. Rep from * to within marked sp, ch 6; in marked sp work dtr, ch 6 and dtr (mark sp); * ch 6, sc in next sp. Rep from * to within last 2 sp; ch 6, turn. Rep 2nd row 10 times more (14 sp). Break off. Mark sp at tip of Section K.

SECTION L: 1st row: With blue, sc in first sp along outer edge of Section I, work 29 ch-6 sps evenly spaced across, ending with sc in marked sp on Section K; ch 6, turn.

2nd row: Sc in first sp, * ch 6, sc in next sp. Rep from * to within last 3 sp; ch 6, turn. Rep 2nd row 8 times more (2 sp), omitting ch-6 at end of last row. Break off.

SECTION M: With blue, sc in first sp along outer edge of section J and work as for Section L.

SECTION N: 1st row: With blue, sc in sp at point of Area 3 on Section G, (ch 6, sk next sp, sc in next sp) 16 times, ch 6, sk green joining sps, sc in next sp, (ch 6, sk next sp, sc in next sp) 8 times, ending with last sc in sp before sp at point of Area 3 on Section F (25 sp); ch 6, turn.

2nd through 12th rows: Work as for 2nd through 12th rows of Section I (3 sp). Break off.

SECTION O: With blue, working on wrong side, sc in sp at point of Area 6 on Section E and work as for Section N.

SECTION P: 1st row: With blue, sc in marked sp at end of 10th row along upper edge of Section B, ch 3, sk about ½″ along neck edge, sc in next sp (ch-3 sp made). Work 27 more ch-3 sp evenly across, ending with sc in corresponding sp on Section C (28 sp); ch 3, turn.

2nd row: Sc in first sp, * ch 3, sc in next sp. Rep from * to within last 2 sp; ch 3, turn. Rep 2nd row 10 times more (6 sp). Break off.

EDGING: Working along upper edge with blue, sc in sp at point of Area 6 on Section E, * ch 3, sk next sp, sc in next sp. Rep from * across upper edge, ending with last sc in sp at point of Area 3 on Section G. Break off.

TIES: With gold, ch 2, work 8 sc in 2nd ch from hook, ch 35; sl st in a gold joining (X on Diagram), turn; sl st in each ch across, sl st in first sc. Break off. Make another tie at other X.

CARVED IVORY SHAWL

Clusters of flowers and filigree are hung with heavy tassels. Done in orlon and acrylic yarn, this shawl is composed of triangles worked in shells, clusters, and chain stitches. The border is done in a V-stitch.

SIZE: Approximately 63″ wide and 43″ long, including the 9″ fringe.

MATERIALS: Sport-weight yarn, 9 (2-oz.) skeins ivory; aluminum crochet hook size E (or English/Canadian hook No. 11) *or the size that will give you the correct gauge.*

GAUGE: Each triangle should measure about 6½″ along each side.

FIRST TRIANGLE: Starting at center, ch 6. Join with sl st to form ring.

1st rnd: Ch 4 (counts as 1 tr), work 4 tr in ring, (ch 5, work 5 tr in ring) twice; ch 2, work dc in top of starting ch-4.

2nd rnd: Ch 4, work 4-tr cl as follows over post of last dc: [(Y o hook) twice, insert hook in sp and pull up lp, (y o hook and pull through 2 lps) twice]. Rep directions in brackets 3 times more; y o hook and pull through all 5 lps on hook; * ch 5, sc in center tr of next 5-tr group, ch 5, work 5-tr cl in next ch-5 sp as follows: [(Y o hook) twice, insert hook in sp and pull up lp, (y o hook and pull

through 2 lps) twice]. Rep directions in brackets 4 times more; y o hook and pull through all 6 lps on hook; ch 5, work 5-tr cl in same sp. Rep from * once more; ch 5, sc in center tr of next 5-tr group, ch 5, work 5-tr cl in next ch-2 sp; ch 2, dc in top of starting ch-4.

3rd rnd: Ch 6, over post of last dc work tr, ch 2 and dc; * (ch 5, sc in next ch-5 sp) twice; ch 5, in next ch-5 sp work dc, (ch 2, tr) 3 times, ch 2 and dc. Rep from * once more; (ch 5, sc in next ch-5 sp) twice; ch 5, in next ch-2 sp work dc, ch 2 and tr; ch 2, sl st in 4th ch of starting ch-6.

4th rnd: Ch 4, work 4-tr cl in first ch-2 sp, * ch 5, work 5-dc cl in next ch-2 sp as follows: Holding back last lp on hook, work 5 dc in same sp, y o pull through all 6 lps on hook; ch 7, sk next ch-5 sp, in next (center) ch-5 sp work dc, ch 3 and dc; ch 7, sk next ch-5 sp, work 5-dc cl in next ch-2 sp, ch 5, work 5-tr cl in next ch-2 sp, ch 11, work 5-tr cl in next ch-2 sp. Rep from * twice more, omitting last 5-tr cl on last rep; sl st in top of starting ch-4. Break off.

SECOND TRIANGLE: Work as for first Triangle.

THIRD TRIANGLE: Work through 3rd rnd as for first Triangle.

4th rnd (joining 2 sides): Ch 5, work 4-tr cl in next ch-2 sp, ch 2; with right side facing you, pick up first Triangle and sc in corresponding ch-5 sp on first Triangle, ch 2, work 5-dc cl in next ch-2 sp on 3rd Triangle, ch 3, sc in next ch-7 sp on first Triangle, ch 3, sk next ch-5 sp on 3rd Triangle, work dc and ch 1 in next ch-5 sp on 3rd Triangle, sc in next ch-3 sp on first Triangle, ch 1, dc in same center ch-5 sp as last dc on 3rd Triangle, ch 3, sc in next ch-7 sp on first Triangle, ch 3, sk next ch-5 sp on 3rd Triangle, work 5-dc cl in next ch-2 sp on 3rd Triangle, ch 2, sc in next ch-5 sp on first Triangle, ch 2, work 5-tr cl in next ch-2 sp on 3rd Triangle, ch 5, sc in corner ch-11 sp on first Triangle. With right side facing you, pick up 2nd Triangle and sc in corner ch-11 sp on 2nd Triangle, ch 5, work 5-tr cl in next ch-2 sp on 3rd Triangle, ch 2, sc in next ch-5 sp on 2nd Triangle, ch 2, work 5-dc cl in next ch-2 sp on 3rd Triangle, ch 3, sc in next ch-7 sp on 2nd Triangle, ch 3, sk next ch-5 sp on 3rd Triangle, work dc and ch 1 in next ch-5 sp on 3rd Triangle, sc in next ch-3 sp on 2nd Triangle, ch 1, dc in same sp on 3rd Triangle, ch 3, sc in next ch-7 sp on 2nd Triangle, ch 3, sk next ch-5 sp on 3rd Triangle, work 5-dc cl in next ch-2 sp on 3rd Triangle, ch 2, sc in next ch-5 sp on 2nd Triangle, ch 2, work 5-tr cl in next ch-2 sp on 3rd Triangle, ch 5, sc in corner ch-11 sp on 2nd Triangle. Completing free side of 3rd Triangle, work ch 5, 5-tr cl in next ch-2 sp; ch 5, 5-dc cl in next ch-2 sp; ch 7, sk next ch-5 sp, in next ch-5 sp work dc, ch 3, and dc; ch 7, sk next ch-5 sp, work 5-dc cl in next sp, ch 5; work 5-tr cl in next sp, ch 5; sc in corresponding ch-11 sp on first Triangle, ch 5; sl st in top of starting ch-4. Break off.

FOURTH TRIANGLE: Work through 3rd rnd as for first Triangle.

4th rnd (joining one side): Join to 2nd Triangle in same manner as joining first side on 3rd Triangle to first Triangle. Then, to complete 2 free sides of 4th Triangle, work ch 5, 5-tr cl in next ch-2 sp; ch 5, 5-dc cl in next ch-2 sp; * ch 7, sk next ch-5 sp, in next ch-5 sp work dc, ch 3 and dc, ch 7, sk next ch-5 sp, work 5-dc cl in next ch-2 sp, ch 5, work 5-tr cl in next ch-2 sp, * ch 11, work 5-tr cl in next ch-2 sp, ch 5, work 5-dc cl in next ch-2 sp. Rep from * to * once more. Ch 5, sc in corresponding ch-11 sp on 2nd Triangle, ch 5, sl st in top of starting ch-4. Break off.

Continue in this manner, making 30 more Triangles, joining them as you work and following Diagram for placement.

BORDER: With right side facing you, starting at corner

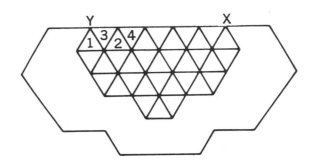

joining sc marked X on Diagram, work along upper straight edge of shawl as follows:

1st rnd: Sc in marked sc, * work 5 sc in each of next 3 ch-sps, work 3 sc in next ch-3 sp, work 5 sc in each of next 3 sp. Rep from * 4 times more; sc in next corner joining sc (Y on Diagram). Continue along side and lower edges as follows: Ch 5, work shell of tr, ch 5 and tr in each of next 7 sp; tr in next joining sc (mark this tr as increase point); work shell in each of next 7 sp, sk next joining sc, ch sp, and joining sc; work shell in each of next 7 sp, tr in next joining sc (mark this tr as increase point); work shell in each of next 7 sp, tr in next joining sc; sk next ch sp, joining sc and ch sp, tr in next joining sc (mark last 2 tr as decrease points); ** work shell in each of next 7 sp, tr in next joining sc (mark this tr as increase point). Rep from ** once more; work shell in each of next 7 sp, tr in next joining sc, sk next ch sp, joining sc and ch sp, tr in next joining sc (mark last 2 tr as decrease points); work shell in each of next 7 sp, tr in next joining sc (mark this tr as increase point); work shell in each of next 7 sp, sk next joining sc, ch sp and joining sc, work shell in each of next 7 sp, tr in next joining sc (mark this tr as inc point); work shell in each of next 7 sp; work dtr in first sc (counts as ch-5 sp); ch 5, turn.

2nd row: Sk first shell, work shell in first tr of each of next 6 shells, work 2 shells in increase point, (mark 2 center tr of these shells as increase points); sk next shell, work shell in first tr of each of next 13 shells, work 2 shells in increase point (mark 2 center tr as increase points); sk next shell, work shell in first tr of each of next 6 shells, tr in each of next 2 tr at decrease point (mark these 2 tr as decrease points); * sk next shell, shell in first tr of each of next 6 shells; work 2 shells in increase point (mark 2 center tr as increase points). Rep from * once more; sk next shell, work shell in first tr of each of next 6 shells; tr in each of next 2 tr at decrease point (mark these 2 tr as decrease points); sk next shell, work shell in first tr of each of next 6 shells; work 2 shells in increase point (mark 2 center tr as increase points); sk next shell, work shell in first tr of each of next 13 shells; work 2 shells in next increase point (mark 2 center tr as increase points); sk next shell, work shell in first tr of each of next 6 shells; dtr in turning ch-5 sp; ch 5, turn.

3rd row: Sk first shell, work shell in first tr of each of next 6 shells; work shell in each of next 2 marked tr (mark center 2-tr of these shells as increase points); work shell in first tr of each shell up to next increase point; work shell in each of next 2 marked tr (mark center 2-tr as increase points); work shell in first tr of each shell up to decrease points; tr in each of next 2 marked tr (mark these 2 tr as decrease points); sk next shell, work shell in first tr of each shell up to next increase point; work shell in each of next 2 marked tr (mark center 2-tr as increase points); work shell in first tr of each shell up to next increase point; work shell in each of next 2 marked tr (mark center 2 tr as increase points); work shell in first tr of each shell up to next decrease points; tr in each of next 2 marked tr (mark these 2 tr as decrease points); sk next shell, work shell in first tr of each shell up to next increase point; work shell in each of next 2 marked tr (mark center 2-tr as increase points); work shell in first tr of each shell up to next increase point, work shell in each of next 2 marked tr (mark center 2 tr as increase points); work shell in first tr of each of next 6 shells; dtr in turning ch-5 sp; ch 5, turn.

4th through 11th rows: Rep 3rd row 8 times more, working ch 1 instead of ch 5 at end of last row. Break off.

12th row: Start at beginning of the 11th row; sc in top of turning ch-5, sk first shell, * ch 5, sc in first tr of next shell, ch 6, sl st in sc to form ring, ch 4, in this ring work 4-tr cl and (ch 5, 5-tr cl) twice to form shamrock; sc in first tr of next shell. Rep from * across, ending ch 5, sc in last tr; turn.

13th row: Sk last ch-5 made, * work 5-tr cl in next ch-5 sp over shamrock, ch 4, sc in same sp, ch 5, in next ch-5 sp work sc, ch 5 and sc; sk next ch-5 sp between shamrocks. Rep from * across, ending ch 4, work 4-tr cl in same sp, sc in last sc. Break off. Turn.

Start at the beginning of 13th row; sc in first cl. Continuing along upper straight edge of shawl with right side facing you, work 5 sc over each end st across end of border; sl st in sc at X. Working back lps, sl st in each sc to Y and work 5 sc over each end st across other end of border. Sl st in top of dtr. Break off.

FRINGE: To make one tassel, cut six 24″ lengths of yarn. Hold lengths together and fold in half. Draw folded end through a ch-5 sp at outer edge of border, draw ends through fold, and pull to tighten. Make a tassel in each ch-5 sp across border.

Take first 2 tassels and form single overhand knot 2″ below first row of knots, * take next 2 tassels and form single knot 2″ below first row of knots. Rep from * across.

TIES: Sl st in st at top edge (X on Diagram), ch 40, sc in 5th ch from hook (picot made), sk next 4 ch, work 5-tr cl in next ch, sl st in each remaining ch across; sl st in X. Break off. Rep for other Tie starting at Y.

MEDALLION SHAWL

Sculpted flowers and leaves set in meshwork are done in shades of peach and green. Two tones of rust liven the dancing fringe. Orlon acrylic and nylon yarn are worked in three panels with a variety of stitches that are reminiscent of Irish crochet.

SIZE: Approximately 86″ wide and 36″ long, including the 12″ fringe.

MATERIALS: Fingering-weight yarn, 4 (1-oz.) skeins rust, (color A), 3 skeins each pink (B), orange (C), and green (D), 2 skeins gray (E), 1 skein each peach (F) and teal (G); aluminum crochet hook size E (or English/Canadian No. 11) *or the size that will give you the correct gauge.*

GAUGE: Dimensions are given at end of directions for each section of shawl.

FIRST MEDALLION: LARGE ROSE (make 3): Starting at center with color F, ch 2.

1st rnd: Work 6 sc in 2nd ch from hook; sl st in first sc.

2nd rnd: (Ch 4, sc in next sc) 6 times, ending with last

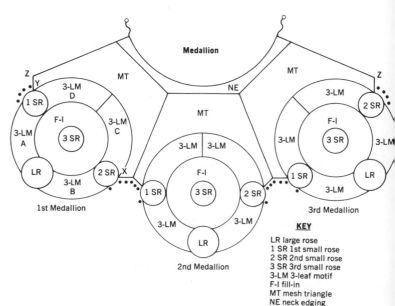

KEY
LR large rose
1 SR 1st small rose
2 SR 2nd small rose
3 SR 3rd small rose
3-LM 3-leaf motif
F-I fill-in
MT mesh triangle
NE neck edging

sc in sl st.

3rd rnd: In each lp work sc, 5 dc and sc (6 petals made); sl st in first sc. Break off F.

4th rnd: With B, sl st in back of work between any 2 petals, ch 5, (sl st in back of work between next 2 petals, ch 5) 5 times; sl st in first sl st (6 ch across backs of petals).

5th rnd: In each lp work sc, 7 dc and sc (6 petals made); sl st in first sc.

6th rnd: (Sl st in back of work between petals, ch 6) 6 times; sl st in first sl st.

7th rnd: In each lp work sc, 9 dc and sc (6 petals made).

8th rnd: * Working along edge of next petal, work (sc in each of next 2 sts, 3 dc in next st) 3 times; sc in each of last 2 sts on petal. Rep from * 5 times more; sl st in first sc. Break off. Ruffled flower should measure about 4″ in diameter.

LEAF MOTIF (make 36): Starting along center with D, (ch 4, dc in 4th ch from hook) 4 times (4 lps made). Do not turn.

1st rnd (right side): Working along dc edge of lps, * in first lp work sc, 5 dc and sc (first shell made), work shell of 5 dc and 1 sc in each of next 3 lps *; ch 3, working along opposite side of lps, rep from * to * once more, marking with safety pin the center dc of the first shell worked on this side; ch 3, sl st in first sc (chain of 4 lps completed with shells worked along both sides and ch-3 at each end). Work next 2 rows across 1 edge of leaf only.

2nd row: Ch 2, sk next 2 dc of first shell, sc in next dc, (sk next 2 dc, work 5 dc in next sc, sk next 2 dc, sc in next dc) 3 times; ch 2, turn.

3rd row (wrong side): Sk first sc and 2 dc, sc in next dc, (sk next 2 dc, 5 dc in next sc, sk next 2 dc, sc in next dc) twice. Break off. Leaf should measure about 1¾″ x 3½″.

TO JOIN LEAVES: Hold first leaf with right sides of first 3 rows facing you and marked edge at top.

1st row: Working along upper edge of first rnd (marked with safety pin), with E, in marked dc, work sc, ch 3 and sc (move marker to ch-3 sp), (ch 3, work sc, ch 3 and sc in center dc of next 5-dc shell) 3 times; ch 5, sc in 3rd ch from hook (p made), ch 2, sc in ch-3 sp at tip of Leaf; continuing along outer edge of Leaf, (ch 5, make p, ch 2, sk next 2 sts, sc in next st) 7 times (do not work across end of leaf); ch 3, turn.

2nd row: Hold 2nd Leaf with right side facing you, and work sc in marked dc, ch 1, sc in next p on first Leaf, ch 1, sc in same dc on 2nd Leaf; * ch 3, sc in center dc of next shell on 2nd Leaf, ch 1, sc in next p on first Leaf, ch 1, sc in same dc on 2nd Leaf. Rep from * twice more, ending in center of 4th shell on 2nd Leaf. Working around 2nd Leaf, ch 5, make p, ch 2, sc in ch-3 sp at tip of 2nd Leaf, (ch 5, make p, ch 2, sk next 2 sts, sc in next st) 7 times (do not work across end of leaf); ch 3, turn.

Join 3rd Leaf to 2nd in same manner as joining 2nd Leaf to first, working as for 2nd row and omitting turning ch-3 at end; ch 5, sc in ch-3 sp at tip of 3rd Leaf, ch 5, sc in ch-3 joining sp between 3rd and 2nd Leaves, ch 5, sc in ch-3 sp at tip of 2nd Leaf, ch 5, sc in ch-3 joining sp between 2nd and first leaves, ch 5, sc in ch-3 sp at tip of first Leaf, ch 5, sc in first sc of first joining row. Break off.

Work 11 more sets of 3-Leaf motifs in same manner.

1st SMALL ROSE (make 3): Working with C throughout, work as for large rose through 5th rnd. Break off. Rose should measure about 2½" in diameter.

2nd SMALL ROSE (make 3): Work in same manner as first Small Rose in the following colors:
1st through 3rd rnds: B
4th and 5th rnds: C

3rd SMALL ROSE (make 3): Work as for first Small Rose in the following colors.
1st through 3rd rnds: A
4th and 5th rnds: C

JOINING LARGE ROSE TO LEAF MOTIFS: 1st rnd: With right side of Rose facing you, with E, (sl st in back of work between 2 petals on last rnd, ch 7) 6 times; sl st in first sl st (ch lps made behind petals).

2nd rnd: (Ch 5, in next ch-7 lp, work dc, ch 5 and dc; ch 5, sc in next sl st) 6 times.

3rd rnd: Work 2 sc in first ch-5 lp; ch 3, sc in 3rd ch from hook (p made), 2 sc in same ch-5 lp. Pick up first 3-Leaf motif with wrong side facing you and hold it so that it is above Large Rose and marked ch-3 sp is above last sc worked on Large Rose (see relationship of Large Rose to 3-Leaf Motif marked A on Diagram). Work 2 sc in next ch-5 lp of Large Rose, ch 1, sc in marked ch-3 sp on Leaf to join, ch 1, work 2 sc in same lp on Rose, (work 2 sc in next ch-5 lp on Rose, ch 1, sc in next ch-3 sp on Leaf, ch 1, work 2 sc in same lp on Rose) 3 times (Rose joined to end of Leaf Motif). (Work 2 sc, p and 2 sc in next lp on Rose) 8 times. Pick up 2nd 3-Leaf Motif (B on Diagram) with right side facing you and hold it above Large Rose. Work 2 sc in next ch-5 lp of Large Rose, ch 1, join to 3rd ch-3 lp from marked lp on Leaf, ch 1, work 2 sc in same lp on Rose. Continue joining as before, ending in marked ch-3 lp on Leaf. Work 2 sc, p and 2 sc in last lp on Rose; sl st in first sc. Break off. Semicircle made with Large Rose in center.

JOINING 2nd SMALL ROSE TO LEAF MOTIFS: 1st rnd: With right side of a 2nd Small Rose facing you, with E, (sl st in back of work between petals on last rnd, ch 6) 6 times; sl st in first sl st (ch lps made behind petals).

2nd rnd: Rep 2nd rnd of Joining Large Rose to Leaf Motifs, working into ch-6 lps.

3rd rnd: Work 2 sc, p and 2 sc in first ch-5 lp. Pick up semicircle with right side of Large Rose facing you and hold it so that first 4 p's from edge of 3-Leaf Motif (B) are adjacent to Small Rose. Work 2 sc in next ch-5 lp on Small Rose, ch 1, sc in first p on Leaf, ch 1, work 2 sc in same lp on Rose, (work 2 sc in next lp on Rose, ch 1, sc in next p on Leaf, ch 1, work 2 sc in same lp on Rose) 3 times; (work 2 sc, p and 2 sc in next lp on Rose) 8 times. Pick up 3rd 3-Leaf Motif (C) with wrong side facing you and hold it above Rose, continuing curve of semicircle. Work 2 sc in next lp on Rose, ch 1, sc in 4th p from left on Leaf Motif, ch 1, work 2 sc in same lp on Rose, (work 2 sc in next lp on Rose, ch 1, sc in next p on Leaf, ch 1, work 2 sc in same lp on Rose) 3 times; work 2 sc, p and 2 sc in last lp on Rose; sl st in first sc. Break off.

JOINING 1st SMALL ROSE TO LEAF MOTIFS: 1st and 2nd rnds: Using a first Small Rose, rep first and 2nd rnds of joining 2nd Small Rose.

3rd rnd: Work 2 sc, p and 2 sc in first ch-5 lp. Pick up 4th 3-Leaf Motif (D), with right side facing you, and hold it above Rose. Join as before to first 4 p's at lower edge of Leaf. Work over next 8 lps of Rose as before. Now join to last 4 p's on free end of Motif A to form circle. Work 2 sc, p and 2 sc in last lp on Rose; join and break off.

JOINING LEAF MOTIFS C AND D TO COMPLETE CIRCLE: With right side facing you and Large Rose at right, with E, start at inner edge of circle and sc in marked ch-3 sp on shell of lower Leaf, ch 1, sc in corresponding ch-3 sp on upper Leaf, (ch 1, sc in next ch-3 sp on lower Leaf, ch 1, sc in next ch-3 sp on upper Leaf) 3 times.

Break off. Circle completed.

FILL-IN SECTION: With right side facing you, hold circle so that Large Rose is at bottom. Work over ch-5 lps and p's of inner edge as follows:

1st rnd: With B, sl st in first ch-5 lp of Leaf Motif A, ch 3, work 4 dc in same lp, (work 5 dc in next ch-5 lp) 5 times; * ch 3, dc in next picot at joining of Leaf Motif and Small Rose, (ch 3, sc in next p) twice; ch 3, dc in next p at next Leaf and Rose joining, ch 3 *; (work 5 dc in next ch-5 lp) 12 times. Rep from * to * once more; (work 5 dc in next ch-5 lp) 6 times; (ch 3, sc in next p) twice; ch 3, sl st in top of ch-3.

2nd rnd: (Ch 4, sc between next two 5-dc groups) 5 times; (ch 4, sc in next ch-3 lp) 5 times; (ch 4, sc between next two 5-dc groups) 11 times; (ch 4, sc in next ch-3 lp) 5 times; (ch 4, sc between next two 5-dc groups) 5 times; (ch 4, sc in next ch-3 lp) 3 times; sl st in beg sl st.

3rd rnd: Ch 3, work 3 dc in first lp, work 4 dc in each lp around; sl st in top of ch-3.

4th rnd: * Ch 3, sc between next two 4-dc groups. Rep from * around; sl st in sl st.

5th rnd: Ch 3, work 2 dc in first lp, work 3 dc in each lp around; sl st in top of ch-3. Break off B.

6th rnd: With E, work sc in sl st, * ch 2, sc between next two 3-dc groups. Rep from * around; sl st in first sc.

7th rnd: Ch 3, * work 2 dc in next lp, work 3 dc in next lp. Rep from * around, ending with 2 dc in last lp; sl st in top of ch-3. Break off.

8th rnd: With G, work sc between ch-3 and first 2-dc group, * ch 4, sk 5 dc, sc between last dc skipped and next dc. Rep from * around, ending ch 4, sk next 4 dc and ch-3, sl st in first sc (17 lps).

9th rnd: Ch 3, work 2 dc in next lp, work 3 dc in each lp around; sl st in top of ch-3.

10th rnd: Ch 1, sc in each dc around, decreasing 3 sc evenly spaced as follows: Draw up a lp in each of 2 sc, y o hook and draw through all 3 lps on hook. Sl st in ch-1 (48 sc on rnd).

11th rnd: Pick up a 3rd Small Rose with right side facing you, ch 3, sl st between any 2 petals, ch 3, sk next 7 sc on 10th rnd of fill-in, sc in next sc, (ch 3, sl st between next 2 petals, ch 3, sk next 7 sc on 10th rnd, sc in next sc) 5 times; sl st in sl st. Break off. Fill-in completed.

MESH TRIANGLE: Hold circle with right side facing you and Large Rose at bottom. Counting from left to right and starting with 2nd Small Rose, place marker on 5th free p (X on Diagram). Counting from right to left, mark corresponding 5th free p on first Small Rose (Y on Diagram).

1st row: With B, sc in X p, * (ch 4, sc in next p) 3 times; ch 4, tr in p at joining, ch 4, sc in next p. Rep from * 6 times more; (ch 4, sc in next p) 3 times (working last sc in Y p—38 lps); ch 5, turn.

2nd row: * (In next ch-4 lp work shell of sc, ch 3 and sc; ch 5) 3 times; holding back the last lp of each st on hook, work 2 tr in each of next 2 lps, y o hook and pull through all 5 lps on hook (4-tr cl made); ch 5. Rep from * 6 times more; shell in next lp, ch 5, shell in next lp, tr in last lp (tr counts as ch-5 lp); ch 5, turn.

3rd row: Sk first shell, * shell in next ch-5 lp, ch 5. Rep from * up to last ch-5 lp, tr in last ch-5 lp; ch 5, turn.

4th row: Rep 3rd row, omitting last ch-5 (28 shells). Break off; turn.

5th row: Counting last tr made as 1 lp, sk first 5 ch-5 lps; with C, sc in 6th lp, * ch 5, shell in next lp. Rep from * up to last 6 ch-5 lps, tr in next lp; ch 5, turn.

6th through 16th rows: Rep 3rd row, omitting last ch-5 on last row. Break off. One Medallion completed.

Make 2 more Medallions in same manner.

JOINING MEDALLIONS: Following Diagram for placement, with right side facing you, match 12 adjacent C lps and 6 adjacent B lps of first and 2nd Medallions. Starting at upper edge with C, sc in first lp of first Medallion, sc in first lp of 2nd Medallion, (ch 4, sc in next lp of first Medallion, sc in next lp of 2nd Medallion) 17 times. Break off.

Join 3rd Medallion to 2nd in same manner.

NECK EDGING: Work along upper edge of 3 joined Medallions as follows:

1st row: With right side facing you, with C, sc in first ch-5 lp, ch 5, sk first shell, * work 5 dc in next ch-5 lp, work shell in next ch-5 lp. Rep from * 8 times more across top of all Medallions; work 5 dc in next ch-5 lp, tr in last ch-5 lp; ch 5, turn.

2nd row: (Work shell in center st of next 5-dc group, ch 5) 10 times; tr in last dc of last group; ch 5, turn.

3rd row: Work 7 dc in each of next 9 ch-5 lps, tr in last ch-5 lp. Break off.

FINISHING: Ties (make 2): With C, ch 5. Join with sl st to form ring. Work 8 sc in ring, ch 35, join with sl st to one end of last row of neck edging. Break off. Make 2nd tie in same manner and join to other end of neck shaping.

Fringe: To make one tassel, cut six 24″ lengths of one color. Hold lengths together and fold in half. Draw folded end through p or ch-3 lp along lower edge, draw ends through fold, and pull to tighten. Space tassels about ½″ apart along lower edge of shawl from Z to Z, making F tassels at dots and A tassels along remainder of edge.

Coat and Poncho

JOSEPH'S COAT

Crocheted with a warm, soft combination of mohair and knitting worsted in a variety of pattern stitches, the coat is a one-of-a-kind tour de force. Its motifs are inspired by Persian art and rendered in brilliant colors.

SIZES: One size will fit sizes 12-16. Sleeve length is adjustable. Coat measures 21″ across back from underarm to underarm; length from back of neck to lower edge is 50″.

MATERIALS: Knitting worsted (100% wool), 8 (4-oz.) skeins navy, 7 skeins brown, 3 skeins each sea green and scarlet, 2 skeins each lavender and turquoise, 1 skein pink; 100% mohair, 9 (40-gr.—about 1½-oz.) balls navy, 8 balls brown, 4 balls red, 3 balls each light purple and sea green, 2 balls oriental blue, and 1 ball pink; aluminum crochet hook size J (or English/Canadian hook No. 6) *or the size that will give you the correct gauge.*

GAUGE: 3 dc = 1″; 1 dc row = 1″.

Note: Use 2 strands of knitting worsted and 1 strand of mohair held together throughout. Match worsted with mohair (for instance, scarlet worsted with red mohair). The color changes are designated by the worsted color only.

All rows of Section A are worked with right side of work facing you.

BACK: SECTION A (BACK MEDALLION): AREA 1: (See Diagram 1). Starting at center with pink, ch 6. Join with sl st to form ring.

1st rnd: Ch 3, work 11 dc in ring (12 dc, counting ch-3 as 1 dc); join with sl st to top of first ch-3. Break off.

2nd rnd: Attach lavender with sl st to back lp of any dc on circle; * ch 4, work hdc in 3rd ch from hook, dc in next ch; working in back lp only of each st, work sl st in

Section A (Back Medallion)

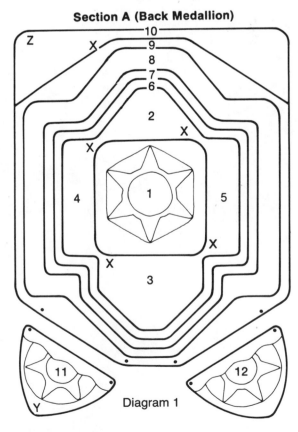

Diagram 1

each of next 2 dc on circle. Rep from * around, working last sl st in first sl st (6 triangles made). Break off.

3rd rnd: Attach green with sl st to tip of any triangle; * work 2 dc in back lp of each of next 2 sl st, sl st in tip of next triangle. Rep from * around; 2 dc in each of last 2 sl sts; sl st in first sl st. Break off.

4th rnd: With brown, make lp on hook, work 2 sc in last sl st made, * sk next dc, work 3 dc in next dc, ch 2, work 3 dc in next dc, sk next dc, sc in each of next 6 sts, sk next dc, work 3 dc in next dc, ch 2, 3 dc in next dc, sk next dc, work 2 sc in next sl st. Rep from * around omitting last 2 sc on last rep. Join to first sc. Break off. Area 1 completed. Piece should measure 4½″ x 5″.

AREA 2: 1st Row: Attach lavender with sl st to ch-2 sp (X on Area 2); ch 1, working in back lp of each st, sc in each of next 8 sts, sc in next ch-2 sp (10 sc, counting ch-1 as 1 sc); ch 1, turn.

2nd (dec) row: Draw up lp in each of next 2 sts, y o draw through all 3 lps on hook (1 st dec), sc in each sc across decreasing 1 st at end of row (8 sc); ch 1, turn.

3rd (dec) row: Working in both lps of each st, rep 2nd (dec) row (6 sc).

4th (dec) row: Rep 2nd (dec) row (4 sc).

5th (dec) row: Dec 1 sc at beg of row, sc in each sc across (3 sc). Break off.

AREA 3: 1st row: With lavender, rep first row of Area 2.

2nd row: Working in top lp of each st, sc in each sc across (10 sc); ch 1, turn.

3rd row: Working in both lps, rep 2nd row (10 sc).

4th row: Rep 2nd row.

5th (dec) row: Working in both lps of each st and decreasing 1 sc at beg and end of row, sc in each sc across (8 sc); ch 1, turn.

6th (dec) row: Working in top lp of each st, rep 5th (dec) row (6 sc).

7th (dec) row: Rep 5th (dec) row (4 sc).

8th (dec) row: Working in top lp of each st, dec 1 st at beg of row, sc in each sc across (3 sc.) Break off.

AREA 4: 1st row: Attach lavender to ch-2 sp (X on Area 4); ch 1, working in back lp of each st, sc in each of next 12 sts, sc in next ch-2 sp (14 sc, counting ch-1 as 1 sc); ch 1, turn.

2nd row: Working in top lp of each st, sc in each sc across; ch 1, turn.

3rd row: Working in both lps of each st, rep 2nd row.

4th row: Rep 2nd row, omitting last ch-1 (14 sc). Break off.

AREA 5: Work as for Area 4.

AREA 6: 1st rnd: Attach turquoise to center sc of Area 2 (6 on Diagram), ch 1, work 1 sc, ch 2 and 1 sc in next sc, sc in side of each of next 4 sc, sk next 2 sc in ch-2 sp, sc in side of each of next 2 sc of Area 4, work sc, ch 2 and sc in first sc on last row of Area 4, sc in each of next 12 sc, work sc, ch 2 and sc in next sc, sc in side of each of next 2 sc, sk next 2 sc in ch-2 sp, sc in side of each of next 3 sc of Area 3, ch 2, sc in side of each of next 3 sc, work sc, ch 2 and sc in first sc on last row of Area 3, sc in next sc, work sc, ch 2 and sc in next sc, sc in side of each of next 3 sc, ch 2, sc in side of each of next 3 sc, sk 2 sc in ch-2 sp, sc in side of each of next 2 sc on Area 5, work sc, ch 2 and sc in first sc on last row of Area 5, sc in each of next 12 sc, work sc, ch 2 and sc in next sc, sc in side of each of next 2 sc, sk 2 sc in ch-2 sp, sc in side of each of next 4 sc, work sc, ch 2 and sc in first sc on last row of Area 2; join to first ch-1 (69 sc). Break off.

AREA 7: 1st rnd: Attach scarlet to back lp of last sl st, ch 1, working in back lp of each st, sc in next sc, work 1 sc, ch 2 and 1 sc in next ch-2 corner sp (corner made), sc in each of next 8 sc, work corner in next ch-2 sp, sc in each of next 14 sc, work corner in next ch-2 sp, sc in each of next 6 sc, work corner in next ch-2 sp, sc in each of next 4 sc, work corner in next ch-2 sp, sc in each of next 3 sc, work corner in next ch-2 sp, sc in each of next 4 sc, work corner in next ch-2 sp, sc in each of next 6 sc, work corner in next ch-2 sp, sc in each of next 14 sc, work corner in next ch-2 sp, sc in each of next 8 sc, work corner in next ch-2 sp, sc in next sc, join to first ch-1 (89 sc). Break off.

AREA 8: 1st rnd: Attach green to last sl st, ch 3, working in back lp of each st, dc in each of next 2 sc, work 4 dc in next corner sp, dc in each of next 4 sc, * holding back on hook the last lp of each dc, work dc in each of next 2 sc, y o, draw through all 3 lps on hook (1 dc dec), dec 1 more dc, dc in each of next 2 sc, work 4 dc in next corner sp, dc in each of next 16 sc, work 4 dc in next corner sp, dc in each of next 3 sc, sk next 5 sc, sc in next corner sp, sc in each of next 6 sc, work sc, ch 2 and sc in next corner sp, sc in each of next 5 sc, work sc, ch 2 and sc in next corner sp, sc in each of next 6 sc, sc in next corner sp, sk next 5 sc, dc in each of next 3 sc, work 4 dc in next corner sp, dc in each of next 16 sc, work 4 dc in next corner sp, dc in each of next 2 sc, dec 2 dc, dc in each of next 4 sc, work 4 dc in next corner sp, dc in each of next 2 sc; join to top of first ch-3 (83 dc, 23 sc). Break off.

AREA 9: Attach navy to back lp of last sl st, ch 1, working in back lp of each st, sc in each of next 4 dc, ch 2, sc in each of next 4 dc, sk next 2 dc, work 2 dc in each of next 2 dc, sk next 2 dc, sc in each of next 2 dc, ch 2, sc in each of next 20 dc, ch 2, sc in each of next 3 dc, sk next 2 dc, work 3 dc in next sc, sk next 2 sc, sc in each of next 5 sc, work sc, ch 2 and sc in next corner sp (corner made), sc in each of next 7 sc, work corner in next corner sp, sc in each of next 5 sc, sk next 2 sc, work 3 dc in next sc, sk next 2 dc, sc in each of next 3 dc, ch 2, sc in each of next 20 dc, ch 2, sc in each of next 2 dc, sk next 2 dc, work 2 dc in each of next 2 dc, sk 2 dc, sc in each of next 4 dc, ch 2, sc in each of next 4 sc; join to first ch-1. Break off.

AREA 10: 1st row: With brown, make lp on hook, sc in ch-2 sp to left of last sl st made (X on Area 10); working in back lp of each st, sc in each of next 4 sc, sk next dc, work 3 dc in each of next 2 dc, sk next dc, sc in each of next 2 sc, sc in next ch-2 sp; ch 1, turn.

2nd row: Sk first sc, sc in each of next 4 sts, work 3 dc in each of next 2 dc, sk next 2 dc, sc in each of next 4 sc, working in top lp of each st, sc in next sc then in next 8 navy sc, sc in next ch-2 sp, sc in each of next 4 sc, sk next dc, work 3 dc in each of next 2 dc, sk next dc, sc in each of next 2 sc, sc in next ch-2 sp; ch 1, turn.

3rd row: Sk first sc, sc in each of next 4 sts, work 3 dc in each of next 2 dc, sk next 2 dc, sc in each of next 3 sc, sl st in next sc. Break off.

AREA 11: Starting at center with green, ch 6. Join with sl st to form ring.

1st rnd: Ch 3 (place marker in 3rd ch st), work 6 dc in ring (7 dc, counting ch-3 as 1 dc); ch 3 (place another marker in first ch st); join with sl st to first sl st on ring. Break off.

2nd row: Sk first ch-3, attach scarlet to back lp of next dc, * ch 4, work hdc in 3rd ch from hook, dc in next ch; working in back lp of each st, sl st in each of next 2 dc. Rep from * twice more, omitting last sl st on last rep. Break off (3 triangles made).

3rd row: Attach turquoise to first marked ch st, ch 3, work 1 dc in same ch st, * sl st in tip of next triangle, working in back of each st, work 2 dc in each of next 2 sl st. Rep from * once more; sl st in tip of last triangle, work 2 dc in next marked st. Break off. Piece is roughly the shape of a semicircle.

4th rnd: Attach navy to top of last dc made, working along straight edge of semicircle, work 3 sc over side of same dc, work 3 sc over next ch-3 sp, sk sl st, (work 3 sc over next ch-3 sp) twice; ch 2, continue along curved edge and, working in back lp of each st, sc in each of next 6 sts to point of center of triangle, work sc, ch 2 and sc in next sl st at point of triangle, sc in each of next 6 sts, ch 2; join to first sc. Break off.

AREA 12: Work as for Area 11.

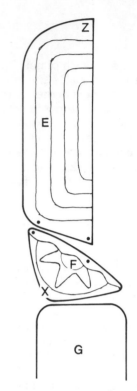

Diagram 2

JOINING AREAS 11 AND 12 TO SECTION A: Following Diagram 2 for placement, hold Area 11 and main section with right sides facing; using navy, sl st them together between dots, joining 14 matching sts through top

Layout Diagram

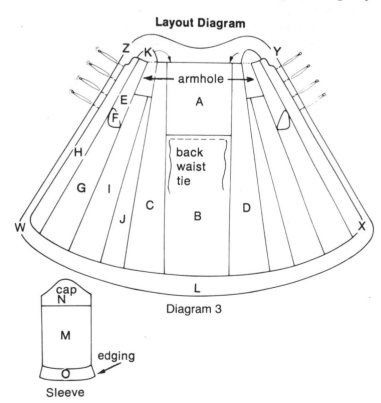

Diagram 3

lps only. (Front lps will form a slight ridge along each edge on right side.) Join Area 12 in same manner. Back Medallion completed. It should measure 12″ x 15″.

SECTION B: This section extends down the back from lower edge of Medallion as shown on Diagram 3.

1st row: With right side of work facing you, attach brown to ch-2 sp on Area 11 (Y on Diagram 1), sc in same sp, working in back lp of each st, sc in each of next 7 sts, work 3 hdc in next ch-2 sp of Area 11, work 1 hdc in next ch-2 sp of main Section A, 1 hdc in each of next 9 sc, work 1 hdc in next ch-2 sp of Section A, work 3 hdc in next ch-2 sp of Area 12, sc in each of next 7 sc, sc in next ch-2 sp of Area 12 (point of triangle—33 sts); ch 1, turn. Place marker in turning ch.

2nd row: Working in top lp of each st, sc in each of next 11 sts, dc in each of next 11 sts, sc in each of remaining 11 sts, pull up a long lp in last sc, drop yarn; do not turn (33 sts).

3rd row: With scarlet, make lp on hook, with same side (wrong side) of work facing you, working in back lp of each st, sc in first sc made on previous row, * ch 3, sk 3 sts, sc in next st. Rep from * across; ch 5, pull up a long lp in last ch st and drop yarn. Turn.

4th row: Pick up dropped brown lp. Keeping ch-5 in back of work ch 2, * working in top lp of each st, sc in next scarlet sc, working over and covering ch-3 lp of last row work dc in each of next 3 brown sts of row before. Rep from * across; sc in last scarlet sc; ch 3, turn.

5th row: Sk first sc, working in top lp of each st, dc in each st across (33 dc, counting ch-3 as 1 dc); pull up a long lp in last dc, drop yarn; turn.

6th row: Pick up dropped scarlet lp, holding ch-5 at back of work, sk first 2 dc of previous row, working in top lp of each st, sc in next dc, * ch 3, sk 3 dc, sc in next dc. Rep from * across, leaving last 2 sts (dc and turning ch) unworked; ch 5, pull up a long lp in last ch and drop yarn. Do not turn.

7th row: Pick up dropped brown lp, ch 3, sk first brown dc, dc in top lp of next brown dc, * sc in back lp of next scarlet sc, working over and covering scarlet ch-3 lp, working in top lp of each st, work dc in each of next 3 brown dc. Rep from * across, ending with sc in last scarlet sc, dc in last dc and in top of turning ch-3; ch 3, turn.

8th row: Sk first dc, working in top lp of each st, dc in each st across (33 dc); pull up long lp in last dc, drop yarn. Do not turn.

9th row: With same side of work facing you, holding ch-5 in front of work, pick up dropped scarlet lp, working in back lp of each st, sc in top of turning ch, then rep 3rd row from *.

10th row: Pick up dropped brown lp, keeping ch-5 in back of work, ch 2, rep 4th row from *.

Rep 5th through 10th rows 7 times more, then rep 5th through 7th rows once more, omitting last ch-3. Break off. Section B completed. It should measure 11″ x 32″ (18 rows of scarlet.)

EDGING: With right side of work facing you, attach navy to first brown dc of upper left 6-dc corner on Section A (Z on Diagram 1); ch 1, sc in each of next 6 sts (mark last st made), sc in next 25 sts, work 3 dc in next ch-2 sp of Section A, sc in each of next 7 sc on Area 11, sc in next ch-2 sp of Area 11, continuing along edge of Section B, work 2 sc in side of each of next 2 rows, * sk next row (9 scarlet-dot row), (ch 1, work 2 sc in side of next row) 3 times. Rep from * 7 times more, ch 1, sk next row, work 2 sc in side of next row, ch 1, work 4 sc in side of last row, ch 2, sc in side of same row, sc in each of next 32 sts across bottom, ch 2, work 4 sc in side of next row. Complete edging along side of Section B and A to correspond to other side. (Edging is not continued across top of Section A.) Break off.

SECTION C: Note: Section is worked vertically from top of coat down and always with right side facing you.

1st row: With right side of work facing you, attach green to marked st of edging at upper left edge of Section A, ch 1, working in back lp of each st, sc in each of next 2 sc, sl st in next sc, (ch 6, * dc in 4th ch from hook, dc in each remaining ch st, sk 2 sts, sl st in next st—post formed—sc in each of next 3 sts, sl st in next st *) 5 times; (ch 7, rep from * to *) 3 times; (ch 8, rep from * to *) 3 times; (ch 9, rep from * to *) 3 times; (ch 10, rep from * to *) 3 times, omitting last sl st (17 posts made). Break off.

2nd row: With scarlet, make lp on hook, working in back lp of each st, work sc in each of first 3 sts made on previous row, * sk next 2 sts (sl st and ch st), sc in base of each remaining dc on side of post, ch 2, work 2 sc over ch-3 top lp, ch 2, sc in each dc on opposite side of post to within last dc of post, sk last dc and next sl st, sc in each of next 3 sc. Rep from * across. Break off.

3rd row: With turquoise, make lp on hook, working in back lp of each st work sc in each of first 2 sc made on previous row, * sk next 2 sc, sc in each sc to within next ch-2 sp, in ch-2 sp work sc, ch 2 and sc, work sc in each of next 2 sc at top of post, in next ch-2 sp work sc, ch 2 and sc; working down opposite side of post work sc in each sc to within last sc on left side of post, sk next 2 sc, sc in next center sc between posts. Rep from * across, ending with sc in each of last 2 sc. Break off.

4th row: With lavender, make lp on hook, working in back lp of each st, work sc in first sc made on 3rd row, sk next 2 sc, sc in next sc, in next corner ch-2 sp work sc, ch 2 and sc, * sc in each of next 4 top sc, sc in next ch-2 sp, sk sts on left side of post, dc in center sc between posts,

sk sts on right side of next post, sc in next ch-2 sp of same post. Rep from * 4 times more, * * sc in each of next 4 top sc, sc in next ch-2 sp, y o hook, pull up lp in 3rd sc from top on left side of same post, pull up lp in 3rd sc from top on right side of next post, (y o hook, pull through 2 lps on hook) 3 times; sc in next ch-2 sp. Rep from * * 10 times more; sc in each of next 4 sc on top of last post, work sc, ch 2 and sc in next ch-2 sp, sc in each of next 5 sc on left side of last post, sk next 2 sc, sc in last sc. Break off.

5th row: With pink, make lp on hook, work 2 sc in right ch-2 sp on first post at top of back, * ch 6, sk 6 sc, working in both lps, work 2 sc in next st (st between posts). Rep from * across, ending with 2 sc in left ch-2 sp on last post. Break off.

6th row: With lavender, make lp on hook, work sc in first lavender ch-2 sp made on 4th row, * ch 1, sk next 2 sc on 5th row, working over and covering ch-6 lp and working in back lp of each st work sc in each of next 6 sc on 4th row. Rep from * across, ending with ch 1, sk 2 sc, sc in last ch-2 sp on 4th row. Break off. Section C completed.

SECTION D: Note: Section is worked vertically from bottom of coat to top and always with right side facing you.

1st row: With green, make lp on hook, working in back lp of each st, sc in each of first 3 navy sc of the 4-sc group at lower corner of Section B, sl st in next sc, (ch 10, * dc in 4th ch from hook, dc in each remaining ch st, sk 2 sts, sl st in next st—post formed—sc in each of next 3 sts, sl st in next st *) 3 times; (ch 9, rep from * to *) 3 times; (ch 8, rep from * to *) 3 times; (ch 7, rep from * to *) 3 times; (ch 6, rep from * to *) 5 times (17 posts). Break off.

2nd row: Rep 2nd row of Section C.

3rd row: Rep 3rd row of Section C.

4th row: With lavender, make lp on hook, working in back lp of each st work sc in first sc made on previous row, sk next 2 sc, sc in each of next 5 sc on right side of first post, in next ch-2 sp work sc, ch 2 and sc, * sc in each of next 4 sc on top of post, sc in next ch-2 sp, y o hook, pull up lp in 3rd sc from top on left side of post, pull up lp in 3rd sc from top on right side of next post, (y o hook, pull through 2 lps) 3 times; sc in next ch-2 sp. Rep from * 10 times more; * * sc in each of next 4 sc on top of post, sc in next ch-2 sp, sk sts on left side of post, dc in center sc at base between posts, sk sts on right side of next post, sc in next ch-2 sp. Rep from * * 4 times more; sc in each of next 4 top sc, work sc, ch 2 and sc in last ch-2 sp, sc in next sc, sk 2 sc, sc in last sc. Break off.

5th row: Rep 5th row of Section C.

6th row: Rep 6th row of Section C. Back completed.

LEFT FRONT: SECTION E: Note: Work this section

always with right side of work facing you.

1st row: With lavender, ch 21, dc in 4th ch from hook and each ch across (19 dc, counting turning ch as 1 dc). Break off.

2nd row: With turquoise, make lp on hook, work 3 sc over turning ch-3, ch 2, working in back lp of each st, work sc in each of next 17 dc, ch 2, work 3 sc in side of last dc. Break off.

3rd row: With scarlet, make lp on hook, working in back lp of each st, sc in each of first 3 sc made on previous row, in next ch-2 sp work sc, ch 2 and sc, sc in each of next 17 sc, in next ch-2 sp work sc, ch 2 and sc, sc in each of next 3 sc. Break off.

4th row: With green, make lp on hook, working in back lp of each st work dc in each of first 4 sc made on previous row, in ch-2 sp work 2 dc, ch 1 and 2 dc, dc in each of next 19 sc, in next ch-2 sp work 2 dc, ch 1 and 2 dc, dc in each of next 4 sc. Break off.

5th row: With navy, make lp on hook, working in back lp of each st work dc in each of first 6 dc, work 2 sc in next ch-2 sp, sc in each of next 23 sc, work 2 sc in next ch-2 sp, dc in each of next 6 dc. Break off.

SECTION F: Work as for Area 11 on Section A.

Following Diagram 2 for position, hold Sections E and F with right sides together; using navy, sl st them together between dots, joining last 6 dc on Section E with 6 sc on Section F, working through top lps only.

SECTION G: 1st row: With brown, make lp on hook; with right side of work facing you, work 3 hdc in corner ch-2 sp on Section F (X on Diagram 2), working in back lp of each st, sc in each of next 7 sts, work 3 hdc in next ch-2 sp of Section F (13 sts); ch 1, turn.

2nd row: Working in top lp of each st, sc in each st across (13 sc); pull up a long lp in last sc and drop yarn. Do not turn.

Rep 3rd through 10th rows of Section B once; then rep 5th through 10th rows of Section B, 6 times more; then rep 5th row once more. Break off. Section G should measure 4½" x 26½".

EDGING: With right side facing you, attach navy to first dc made on 5th row of Section E (Z on Diagram 2), ch 1, sc in each of next 5 sts, in next sc work sc, ch 2 and sc (mark last sc made), sc in each of next 25 sc, work 3 dc in last sc on Section E, sc in next ch-2 sp on Section F, sc in each of next 7 sc, work 2 sc in side of each of next 2 rows of Section G, * sk next row, (ch 1, work 2 sc in side of next row) 3 times. Rep from * 6 times more; ch 1, sk next row, work 4 sc in side of last row, ch 2, sc in side of same row, sc in each of next 12 dc, ch 2, work 4 sc in side of next row (mark first of these 4 sc), * * sk next row, (ch

1, work 2 sc in side of next row) 3 times. Rep from * * 6 times more; ch 1, sk next row, work 2 sc in side of each of next 2 rows, sc in each of next 5 sc on Section F, work 3 dc in next sc, work 2 sc each in side of 5th and 4th rows of Section E, work 1 sc each in side of 3rd and 2nd rows of Section E, sc in base of each of next 10 dc, work 1 sc each in side of 3rd and 2nd rows of Section E, 2 sc each in side of 5th and 4th rows of Section E, sl st in beg ch-1. Break off.

SECTION H: Note: Section is worked vertically from top down and always with right side facing you.

1st row: Attach green to first marked sc at left corner of Section E, then continue in same manner as first row of Section C, ending by working (ch 10, rep from * to *) once instead of 3 times for last post; omit last sl st (15 posts made). Break off.

2nd row: Rep 2nd row of Section C.

3rd row: Rep 3rd row of Section C.

4th row: Rep 4th row of Section C, but rep from * * 8 times more instead of 10 times more.

5th row: Rep 5th row of Section C.

6th row: Rep 6th row of Section C.

SECTION I: Note: Section is worked vertically from bottom up and always with right side facing you.

1st row: With navy, make lp on hook, working in back lp of each st and starting with 2nd marked st on edging of Section G, sc in each of first 3 sc, sl st in next sc, ch 10, * dc in 4th ch from hook, dc in each remaining ch st, sk 2 sts, sl st in next st, sc in each of next 3 sts, sl st in next st *; (ch 9, rep from * to *) 3 times; (ch 8, rep from * to *) 3 times; (ch 7, rep from * to *) 3 times; (ch 6, rep from * to *) 3 times (13 posts made). Break off.

2nd row: With brown, rep 2nd row of Section C.

3rd row: With scarlet, rep 3rd row of Section C.

4th row: With brown, rep 4th row of Section C, repeating from * to * twice more instead of 4 times more, and repeating from * * to * * 8 times more instead of 10 times more.

5th row: With scarlet, rep 5th row of Section C.

6th row: With brown, rep 6th row of Section C.

SECTION J (underarm insert): Note: Section is worked vertically from top down.

1st row: With navy, make lp on hook, with wrong side of Section I facing you, work 1 sc and 2 dc in last sc made on last row of Section I (star made); * sk 2 sts, work 1 sc and 2 dc in next st (another star made). Rep from * across to within last 3 sts, sk next 2 sts, sc in last st (31 stars made); ch 2, turn.

2nd row: Work 2 dc in last sc made on previous row, * sk next 2 dc, work star in next sc. Rep from * across to within last 7 stars, sk next 2 dc, sl st in next sc (25 stars made); turn.

3rd row: Sl st across first 5 stars, * sk next 2 dc, work star in next sc. Rep from * across to within last star, sk next 2 dc, sc in turning ch (19 stars made); ch 2, turn.

4th row: Rep 2nd row (13 stars made); turn.

5th row: Sl st across first 4 stars, then rep 3rd row from * across (8 stars made). Break off. Left Front completed.

RIGHT FRONT: Work to correspond to Left Front.

LEFT SHOULDER INSERT: SECTION K: Work as for Area 11 on Section A. Following Diagram 4 for position, hold Section K and Sections H-E with right sides facing, using navy, sl st them together between dots, working through top lps only. Then join Section K to Sections C-A in same manner. (Arrow on K area on Diagram 3 indicates joining to C-A.)

RIGHT SHOULDER INSERT: Work same as for Left Shoulder.

BORDER: SECTION L: 1st rnd: With navy, make lp on hook, with right side of work facing you, sc in first lavender sc at bottom edge of Section H on right front (X on Diagram 3); * ch 5, sc in 5th ch from hook (p made), sk ½" of edge, sc in edge. Rep from * evenly along right front edge for 52 p's in all, work in same manner for 26 p's along neck edge, 52 p's along left front edge and 86 p's along bottom edge; join with sl st to first sc.

2nd rnd: Ch 6, dc in 6th ch from hook (lp made), sc in joining sc (corner lp made), (make lp, sk 2 p's, sc in next sc) 26 times; make lp, sc in same sc (another corner lp made), (make lp, sk 2 p's, sc in next sc) 13 times; work corner lp, (make lp, sk 2 p's, sc in next sc) 26 times; work corner lp, (make lp, sk 2 p's, sc in next sc) 43 times; join with sl st to first sc (112 lps made).

3rd rnd: Ch 5, sc in 5th ch from hook (p made), sc in joining sc, ch 5, sc in 5th ch from hook (another p made), sk corner lp, sc in next sc, * work p, sc in same sc of 2nd row, p, sk next lp, sc in next sc of 2nd row. Rep from * around (224 p's made).

4th rnd: Ch 6, dc in 6th ch from hook (lp made), sc in same sc (corner lp made); (make lp, sk 2 p's, sc in next sc) 27 times; work another corner lp (mark lp), (work lp, sk 2 p's, sc in next sc) 14 times; work corner lp (mark lp), (make lp, sk 2 p's, sc in next sc) 27 times; work corner lp, (make lp, skip 2 p's, sc in next sc) 44 times; join (116 lps). Break off.

COLLAR EDGING: 1st row: With right side of work facing you, attach navy to sc before marked corner lp at right neck edge (Y on Diagram 3); rep 3rd row of edging

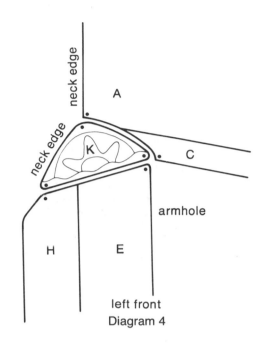

across neck edge ending with sc in sc after second marked corner lp at left neck edge (Z on Diagram 3); turn.

2nd row: Ch 6, dc in 6th ch from hook, sk 1 p, sc in next sc. Rep from * across neck edge. Break off.

LOWER EDGING: Note: If coat is correct length, omit this row.

With right side of work facing you, attach navy to first sc at left front lower edge (W on Diagram 3); ch 5, sc in 5th ch from hook (p made), sc in same sc, ch 5, sc in 5th ch from hook, sk next lp, sc in next sc, * p, sc in same sc, p, sk next lp, sc in next sc. Rep from * across. Break off if coat is correct length. If longer coat is desired, add extra lp and p rows.

SLEEVES: Section M: Starting with brown at lower edge above cuff, ch 39.

1st row (wrong side): Dc in 4th ch from hook and each ch across (37 dc, counting turning ch as 1 dc), pull up long lp in last dc and drop yarn; turn.

2nd row: With scarlet, make lp on hook; with right side of work facing you, working in top lp of each st, sc in last dc made on previous row, * ch 3, sk 3 dc, sc in next dc. Rep from * across ending with sc in top of turning ch, ch 5, pull up a long lp in last ch and drop yarn. Do not turn.

3rd row: With right side facing you, pick up dropped

brown lp, ch 2, * working in top lp of each st, sc in next scarlet sc, working over and covering ch-3 lp of last row, dc in each of next 3 brown dc of first row. Rep from * across, ending with sc in last scarlet sc; ch 3, turn.

4th row: Working in top lp of each st, sk first st, dc in each st across, ending with dc in top of ch-2 (37 dc, counting turning ch as 1 dc), pull up a long lp in last dc, drop yarn. Do not turn.

5th row: Pick up dropped scarlet lp, keeping ch-5 in front of work sk first 2 dc, working in back lp of each st, sc in next dc, * ch 3, sk 3 dc, sc in next dc. Rep from * across leaving last 2 dc unworked; ch 5, pull up a long lp in last ch, drop yarn, turn.

6th row: Pick up dropped brown lp, ch 3, dc in next dc, * working in top of each st, sc in next sc, working over and covering ch-3 lp, dc in each of next 3 dc. Rep from * across, ending with sc in next sc, dc in next dc and in top of turning ch; ch 3, turn.

7th row: Rep 4th row, ending with dc in top of ch-3; turn.

8th row: Pick up dropped scarlet lp, keeping ch-5 in back of work, working in top lp of each st, sc in last dc made on previous row. Rep 2nd row from * across.

9th row: Rep 3rd row.

Rep 4th through 9th rows twice more, then rep 4th row once more (37 dc), or work to within 6″ of desired length to underarm. Break off.

SECTION N (cap): Note: All rows are worked with right side facing you and in back lp of each st.

1st row: Attach navy to last dc made on last row, ch 3, dc in each dc across, increasing 10 dc evenly spaced (47 dc).

2nd row: Attach green to top of turning ch on previous row, ch 1, sc in each of next 3 dc, sl st in next sc, ch 6, * dc in 4th ch from hook, dc in each remaining ch st, sk 2 dc, sl st in next dc, sc in each of next 3 dc, sl st in next dc *, ch 8. Rep from * to * once, (ch 10, rep from * to *) twice; ch 8, rep from * to * once, ch 6, rep from * to * once (6 posts made). Break off.

3rd row: With scarlet, make lp on hook, sc in each of first 4 sts made on previous row, rep 2nd row of Section C from * across, ending with 1 sc in each of last 4 sts.

4th row: With turquoise, make lp on hook, sc in each of first 3 sc made on previous row, rep 3rd row of Section C from * across, ending with sc in each of last 3 sc.

5th row: With lavender, make lp on hook, sc in each of first 2 sc on previous row, sk next 2 sc, sc in next sc, in next ch-2 sp work sc, ch 2 and sc, sc in each of next 4 top sc, sc in next ch-2 sp, sk sts on left side of post, dc in center sc at base between posts, sk sts on right side of next post, sc in next ch-2 sp of same post, * sc in each of

next 4 top sc, sc in next ch-2 sp, y o hook, pull up lp in 3rd sc from top on left side of post, pull up lp in 3rd sc from top on right side of next post, (y o hook, pull through 2 lps) 3 times; sc in next ch-2 sp. Rep from * twice more; sc in each of next 4 top sc, sc in next ch-2 sp, dc in center sc at base between posts, sk sts on right side of last post, sc in next ch-2 sp, sc in each of next 4 top sc, in next ch-2 sp work sc, ch 2 and sc, sc in next sc, sk next 2 sc, sc in each of last 2 sc. Break off.

6th row: With pink, make lp on hook, work 2 sc in first ch-2 sp made on previous row, rep 5th row of Section C from * across.

7th row: With lavender, make lp on hook, sc in first ch-2 made on 5th row, * ch 2, sk next 2 sc of 6th row, working over and covering ch-6 lps of previous row and working in back lp of each st, sc in each of next 6 sc on 5th row. Rep from * across, ch 2, sk last 2 sc, sc in last ch-2 sp on 5th row. Break off.

8th row: With navy, make lp on hook, sc in first sc and each st across. Break off.

SECTION O: Edging: 1st row: With navy, make lp on hook, with right side of work facing you, sc in top of turning ch on first row of Section M, * ch 5, sc in 5th ch from hook (p made), sc in next dc. Rep from * across (36 p's made); turn.

2nd row: * Ch 6, dc in 6th ch from hook (lp made), sk 2 p's, sc in next sc. Rep from * across (18 lps made); turn.

3rd row: Make p, sc in last sc made on previous row, * p, sk next lp, sc in next sc, p, sc in same sc. Rep from * across; p, sk last lp, sc in last sc (36 p's made). Break off if Sleeve is correct length. If longer Sleeve is desired, add extra lp and p rows.

Sew Sleeve seam. Hold Sleeve and armhole with right sides facing. Using navy, sl st them together, working through top lps only.

BACK WAIST TIE: With brown, * ch 2, sc in 2nd ch from hook. Rep from * until piece measures 60″. Break off.

Weave tie through 2nd row of Section B over and under about 3 sts at a time (see Diagram 3); draw ends to inside of coat and tie at front around Waist. This will hold Back of coat close to Body.

FRONT TIES (make 8): With navy, crochet a chain 10″ long. In last ch pull up a 5″ lp, pull up a 5″ lp in 2nd, 3rd, and 4th ch from hook, remove hook, make knot at base of lps. Cut ends of lps to form tassel.

Starting just below Collar, sew 4 ties to wrong side of lavender edge of each front of coat, about 5″ apart. Weave to right side through edging.

PONCHO-SKIRT

A practical, versatile, yet exciting addition to a fall wardrobe, this poncho, which can double as a skirt, features elegant vertical banding and heavy fringe. It calls for knitting worsted used double, and is done in single and double crochet and shell-stitch variations.

SIZE: One size fits all. Waist is adjustable with elastic. Length of center panel is 28″, plus fringe.

MATERIALS: Knitting worsted, 10 (4-oz.) skeins dark royal blue, 1 skein each light royal blue, sky blue, avocado, dusty pink, tobacco gold, olive, and cardinal, 3 skeins rust; aluminum crochet hook size I (or English/Canadian hook No. 7) *or the size that will give you the correct gauge;* strip of narrow elastic to fit waist.

GAUGE: 3 side shells = 4″; 4 rows = 1″.

Note: Use yarn double throughout.

CENTER PANEL: Row of Circles: Starting at center of first circle with avocado, ch 4. Join with sl st to form ring.

1st row: Ch 4, work 7 tr in ring (half-circle made), * ch 10, sl st in 6th ch from hook (another ring made), ch 3, sl st in first ch of ch-10; with same side of piece facing you, turn your work so that the half-circle is to your right, and swing your hook around in position to work in new ring; work 6 tr in the new ring (8 tr, counting the two ch-3 as 2 tr—another half-circle made). Rep from * 8 times more (string of 10 joined half-circles made). Break off.

2nd row: Work along other side of each ring to complete circles as follows: Attach olive to last dc made, work 8 tr in last ring worked into (16 tr, half avocado and half olive—2½" circle completed); * work sc **over** the joining of 2 half-circles, work 8 tr in next ring. Rep from * across; join with sl st in top of ch-3 (10 circles completed). Break off.

3rd row: Work stripe along center of circles as follows: Attach gold in sl st. * Ch 3, sl st over ring between olive and avocado sts, ch 3, sl st in joining of rings. Rep from * across circles, ending by working across last circle; join. Break off.

4th rnd: Work around edges of circles as follows: Attach pink to sl st. Work 2 sc in each of next 5 tr in circle, * ch 1, sk 2 tr on circle and 2 tr on next circle, work 2 sc in each of next 4 tr. Rep from * 8 times more; work 2 sc in each of next 2 tr to top of last circle, sc in top of circle; work along opposite edge of circles to correspond to other side; join. Break off.

5th rnd: Attach cardinal to sl st and work in back lps of sts. Ch 2, sc in each of next 4 sc, ch 2 (corner), sc in each of next 5 sc, * sk next 3 sc, over next ch-1 work 4 long dc (draw up lp ½" for each dc), sk next 3 sc, sc in each of next 2 sc. Rep from * 8 times more; sc in next 3 sc on last circle, ch 2 (corner), sc in next 9 sc (across top of circle), ch 2 (corner), sc in next 5 sc. Finish working across edge of circles to correspond to other side; join. Break off.

6th row: Attach light royal blue to a corner of last rnd and work across long edge of panel as follows: Ch 3, dc in same place. Work in back lps only. * Dc in next 5 sts, 2 dc in next dc. Rep from * 8 times more; dc in next 8 sts, 2 dc in corner (75 dc). Break off. Work along opposite edge in same manner.

7th row: Attach sky blue to top of ch-3 at beg of last row. Work in back lps only. Ch 2, sc in next dc, * ch 1, sk 2 dc, work 3 sc in next dc. Rep from * 22 times more; ch 1, sk 2 dc, sc in next dc, ch 1, sl st in last st. Break off. Work along opposite edge in same manner.

8th row: Attach dark royal blue to ch-2 at beg of last row. Ch 3, dc in next sc, * over next ch-1 work a long dc in back lp of each of next 2 dc of **6th row** (light royal blue sts), ch 1. Rep from * 23 times more; do not ch 1 at end of last rep, dc in each of last 2 sts. Ch 3, turn.

9th row: Sk first dc, dc in each dc and over each ch-1 across (76 dc, counting ch-3 as 1 dc). Break off. Work 8th and 9th rows across opposite edge in same manner.

10th row: Work along side of panel with the avocado half-circles. With right side facing you, attach rust in last st made at end of last row. Ch 3, sk first dc where yarn was attached, dc in each dc across (76 dc). Break off.

11th row: Attach cardinal to top of ch-3 at beg of last row. Ch 3, dc in each dc across (76 dc). Break off.

12th row: Attach sky blue to top of ch-3 at beg of last row. Ch 2, sc in each dc across (76 sc). Mark last sc. Break off.

Now work along side of Panel with the olive half-circles. With right side facing you, work 1 row sc each, rust, gold, and pink and 1 dc row avocado, having 76 sts on each row. Center Panel completed.

Make another Panel in same manner for other side of poncho-skirt.

SIDE SECTION A: With right side facing you, attach dark royal blue to marked sky blue sc on last panel (X on Diagram). Ch 2, turn.

1st row (wrong side): Work sc in each sc across (lower edge—76 sc). Ch 2, turn.

2nd row: Work 2 dc in first sc (first side shell made), * sk next 2 sc, work sc and 2 dc in next sc (another side

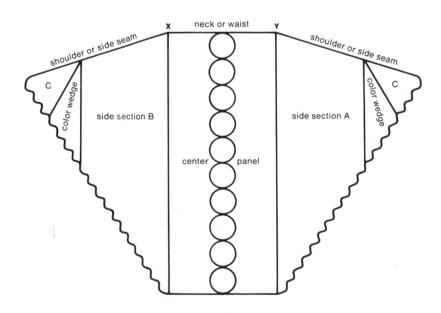

shell made). Rep from * to within last 3 sc (25 side shells), sk 2 sc, sc in ch-2 (shoulder or side), ch 2 (mark this chain), turn.

3rd row: Work 2 dc in first sc, * sk next 2 dc, work side shell in next sc. Rep from * to within last 2 side shells, sc in last sc (lower edge—24 side shells). Ch 2, turn.

4th row: Rep 3rd row (23 side shells). Ch 2, turn.

5th row: Rep 3rd row (22 side shells). Ch 2, turn.

6th row: Work 22 side shells, sc in top of ch-2 of last shell. Ch 2, turn.

7th row: Rep 3rd row (21 shells). Ch 2, turn.

8th row: Rep 3rd row (20 shells). Ch 2, turn.

9th row: Rep 3rd row (19 shells). Ch 2, turn.

10th row: Work 19 shells, sc in top of ch-2 of last shell. Ch 2, turn.

11th row: Rep 3rd row (18 shells). Ch 2, turn.

12th row: Rep 3rd row (17 shells). Ch 2, turn.

13th row: Rep 3rd row (16 shells). Ch 2, turn.

14th row: Work 16 shells, sc in top of ch-2 of last shell. Ch 2, turn.

15th row: Rep 3rd row (15 shells). Ch 2, turn.

16th row: Rep 3rd row (14 shells). Ch 2, turn.

17th row: Rep 3rd row (13 shells). Ch 2, turn.

18th row: Work 13 shells, sc in top of last ch-2. Ch 2, turn.

19th row: Rep 3rd row (12 shells). Ch 2, turn.

20th row: Rep 3rd row (11 shells). Ch 2, turn.

21st row: Rep 3rd row (10 shells—lower edge). Break off.

Color Wedge: There is a color wedge at each end of poncho-skirt, front and back (see Diagram). Work each row with right side facing you and in back lp of sts.

1st row: With right side facing you, attach cardinal between last 2 shells made. Ch 3, dc in each dc and sc of next 3 shells, hdc in each dc and sc of next 3 shells, sc in each dc and sc of remaining 3 shells (27 sts). Break off.

2nd row: Sk ch-3 and first 3 dc made on last row, attach rust to next dc. Ch 3, dc in next 9 sts, hdc in next 6 sts, sc in next 4 sts, sl st in next st. Break off.

3rd row: Skip ch-3 and first 2 dc of last row, attach light royal blue to next dc. Ch 3, dc in next 4 sts, hdc in next 5 sts, sc in next 4 sts, sl st in next st. Break off.

4th row: Skip ch-3 and first 2 dc of last row, attach sky blue to next dc. Ch 3, dc in next 2 sts, hdc in next 2 sts, sc in next 3 sts, sl st in next st. Break off. Wedge completed.

Now complete side with 4 more rows of side shells (C on Diagram) as follows:

1st row: Sk ch-3 and first 2 dc of last row, attach dark royal blue to next st. Ch 3, 2 dc in same st (side shell), sk 2 sts, work sc and 2 dc in next st (side shell), sk next 2 sky blue sts, side shell in next light royal blue st, sk next 2 sky blue sts, side shell in next rust st, sk next 2 rust sts, side shell in next cardinal st, sc in last cardinal st. Ch 1, turn.

2nd row: Sl st in first 2 dc and in sc of first shell, ch 2, 2 dc in same place. Work 2 more side shells, sc in top of last ch-2. Ch 2, turn.

3rd row: Work 3 side shells, sc in last ch-2. Ch 1, turn.

4th row: Sl st in first 2 dc and in sc of first shell, ch 2, 2 dc in same place, sc in next sc. Break off.

Shoulder or Side Edge: Now work along shoulder (side), filling in saw-tooth edge so it will be even. With wrong side facing you, attach dark royal blue to marked ch at shoulder (side) edge on 2nd row of Section A, * work 4 dc in next V of saw-tooth edge, work 2 sc in next point of saw-tooth. Rep from * across. Break off. Side Section A completed.

SIDE SECTION B: Work side along opposite edge of center panel as follows: With wrong side facing you, attach dark royal blue to avocado st at neck edge of panel (Y on Diagram). Ch 2, turn.

1st row (right side): Work sc in each dc across (lower edge—76 sc). Ch 2, turn. Starting with 2nd row of dark royal blue, work as for other side, working color wedge in olive, avocado, pink and gold.

Work side sections on other Center Panel in same manner.

FINISHING: Sew shoulder or side seams.

Fringe: Cut twelve 12″ strands rust for tassel. Fold in half and draw folded end, from right side of garment, through a point on edge. Draw ends through folded end and pull tight. Knot a tassel in each point around.

With dark royal blue work a row of sc evenly around neck (or waist) edge. Sl st in first sc. Break off. Run elastic through sc's, draw up to desired waist size, tie ends, and hide them in edging.

Beachwear

RACY RIBBED BIKINI AND CAPE-SKIRT

This exotic cover-up also can be worn as a hip-hugger skirt or cape. You crochet five panels and join them together. Worked in single and double crochet, the cape-skirt has a grape leaf motif. The bikini utilizes the same motif. The ribbed texture is achieved by working in the back loop of each stitch.

CAPE-SKIRT

SIZES: One size fits all.

MATERIALS: Quick-weight cotton such as Lily Double Quick crochet cotton, 14 (115-yd.) skeins gold (Color G), 6 skeins black (B), and 4 skeins each red (R) and cream (C); aluminum crochet hook size H (or English/Canadian hook No. 8) *or the size that will give you the correct gauge.*

GAUGE: 4 sc = 1″ on leaves.

Note: Use cotton double throughout. After changing colors, work over ends as you crochet. Tag each piece upon completion for easier identification when assembling garment.

PANEL 1: Leaves: See Diagram 1.
  Note: Work in back lp only of each st throughout.
  Leaf 1: With R, ch 20 to measure about 5″.
  1st row: Work sc in 3rd ch from hook and in each ch across (18 sc); ch 2, turn.
  2nd row: Sc in first sc and in each of next 17 sc; in turning ch-2 sp, work sc, ch 1 and sc (mark ch-1 sp); working along other edge of foundation ch, work sc in each of next 15 sts (last 3 sts omitted); ch 2, turn.
  3rd row: Sc in each sc to within marked sp; in sp, work sc, ch 1 and sc (mark ch-1 sp); sc in each sc across to within last 3 sts (17 sc on each side of Leaf, ch-1 sp at end); ch 2, turn.

4th through 7th rows: Rep 3rd row (on 8th row there are 15 sc on each side of Leaf, ch-1 sp at end).
  8th row (short row): Work sc in each sc across to within ch-1 sp, sl st in sp. Break off. Leaf should measure about 3¾″ x 6″.
  Leaf 2: Section 1: With C, ch 30 to measure about 7½″.
  1st row: Work sc in 3rd ch from hook and in each ch across (28 sc); ch 2, turn.
  2nd row: Sc in first sc and in each of next 27 sc; in turning ch-2 sp, work sc, ch 1 and sc (mark ch-1 sp); work sc in each of next 25 sts of foundation ch (last 3 sts omitted); ch 2, turn. Work 3rd through 8th rows as for Leaf 1 (27 sc on each side of ch-1 sp on 3rd row, 25 on each side of 8th row). Break off C; turn. Leaf should measure about 3¼″ x 8½″.
  Section 2: Attach B with sl st in last sl st worked.
  9th row: Working along 8th (short) row, work 1 sc in each of next 23 sc (last 2 sts omitted); ch 2, turn.
  10th through 19th rows: (dec rows): Draw up lp in each of next 2 sts, y o, draw through all 3 lps on hook (1 sc dec), sc in each sc across to within last sc (1 sc dec at beg and end of row—21 sc); ch 2, turn. Rep dec row 9 times more (3 sc).
  20th row: Dec 1 sc. Break off. Completed Leaf should measure 5½″ at widest point x 8½″.
  Leaf 3: With G only, work Sections 1 and 2 as for Leaf 2 without breaking off between sections.
  Assembling Leaves: Join through back lps only when working on Leaf 1, through both lps on Leaves 2 and 3.
  Follow direction of arrows on Diagram 1. Starting at

Above left: Long-Sleeved Pullover
Above right: Granny Square Pullover

Right: Floral Blouson

Right: Striped Long-Sleeved Jacket
Far right: Lacy Vest

Below left: Dolman Cardigan
Below right: Torso Hugger

Above left: Panel Motif Pullover
Above right: Square Motif Pullover

Above: Joseph's Coat, front view
Left: Joseph's Coat, back view

Left: Carved Ivory Shawl
Above: Cabbage Rose Shawl

Above: Cloche with Matching Clutch

Right: Sunset Bathing Suit and Cover-Up
Far right: Racy Ribbed Bikini
and Cape-Skirt

Above: Medallion Shawl

Left: Summer hats *(left to right):* San Remo; St. Tropez; Majorca

Below: Winter hats *(top to bottom):* Petal Cloche; Twining Vine Cap; Helmet

Above: Belts *(clockwise from top left):* Florentine; Sweetheart; Medallion; Serpentine; Trefoil

Left (left to right): Garlands of Roses Pectoral; Flower Ornament; Egyptian Gold Body Ornament

Above: Baby Afghan
Left (clockwise from top left): Granny Square
Slippers; Men's Slipper-Socks; Elfin Slippers

Above (clockwise from top left): Shirvan Shoulder Bag;
Golden Mandala Purse; Diminutive Purse; Flower Pocket
Shoulder Bag
Above right: Pillows *(clockwise from top left):* Greek Key;
Aubusson; Arrowhead; Intarsia
Right: Christmas Tree and Snowflakes

Left: Shirvan Afghan
Above: Bokhara Afghan

Above: Mihrab Afghan
Right: Shiraz Afghan

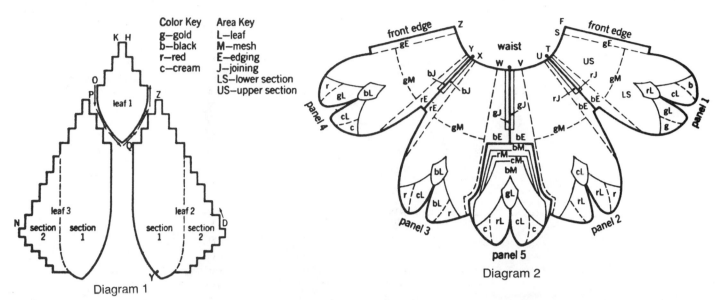

Color Key
g—gold
b—black
r—red
c—cream

Area Key
L—leaf
M—mesh
E—edging
J—joining
LS—lower section
US—upper section

Diagram 1

Diagram 2

Corner O on Leaf 1 with R, sl st in first 3 sts on curved edge, insert hook in next st, then insert hook from front (top) to back, in Corner P on Leaf 3, y o, draw up through the 2 sts and lp on hook (1 st each on Leaves 1 and 3 worked tog); (sl st in next 3 sts on Leaf 1, work next st on Leaf 1 and next corner on Leaf 3 tog) twice; sl st in next 3 sts on Leaf 1, insert hook in sl st at upper point of Leaf 1, then insert hook in last corner on Leaf 3, y o, draw through all 3 lps on hook, insert hook in Corner Q on Leaf 2, y o, draw through both lps on hook (sl st in next 3 sts on Leaf 1 and next corner on Leaf 2 tog) 3 times; sl st in last 3 sts on Leaf 1. Break off. (Letters Y and Z on Diagram 1 are for Bikini only.)

Note: Assembled leaves will cup slightly.

Mesh: See Diagrams 1 and 2.

Note: Work in both lps of each st throughout. Sides of mesh will not be identical.

Lower Section: Following Diagram 1, attach G with sl st at Corner D on Leaf 2 and follow direction of arrow.

1st row: Sc in same st as last sl st made; * ch 3, dc in 3rd ch from hook (lp st made), sc in next corner on Leaf 2 *. Rep from * to * 12 times more, ending at Corner H; work lp st, sc in Corner K. Working along edge of Leaves 1 and 3, rep from * to * 13 times, ending in Corner N (27 lps); turn.

2nd row: Work lp st, sc in ch-3 of first lp st, * work lp st, sc in next ch-3 lp *. Rep from * to * 11 times more; work lp st, sc in same ch-3 lp (1 lp st inc made). Rep from * to * twice more; inc 1 lp st, then rep from * to * 11 times more (last lp st omitted—28 lps); turn.

3rd row: Work lp st, sc in first ch-3 lp, * work lp st, sc in next ch-3 lp *. (Rep from * to * to next inc lp of last row, inc 1 lp st in inc lp) twice; then rep from * to * to within last lp (29 lps); turn.

4th row: Rep 3rd row (30 lps).

5th and 6th rows: Rep 3rd row, working to within last 3 lps on each row (28 lps).

7th, 8th, and 9th rows: Rep 3rd row, breaking off at end of last row (31 lps).

Note: Mark 2nd inc lp on last row.

Upper section (short rows): With wrong side facing you, attach G to marked inc lp.

1st row: Sc in same st, working across top edge of mesh, * work lp st, sc in next ch-3 lp. Rep from * 9 times more (10 lps); turn.

2nd row: Work lp st, sc in first ch-3 lp, * work lp st, sc in next ch-3 lp. Rep from * across 8 times more (10 lps); turn. Rep 2nd row 16 times more. Break off. Mesh should measure about 13½" from tip of Leaf 1 to waist edge.

Work the remaining Panels as for Panel 1 as follows:

PANEL 2: With C, work Leaf 1. With R, work both sections of Leaf 2. With R, work Section 1 of Leaf 3; with B, work Section 2. With C, assemble Leaves. With G, work mesh.

PANEL 3: With B, work Leaf 1. With B, work Section 1 of Leaf 2; with R, work Section 2. With C, work Section 1 of Leaf 3; with R, work Section 2. With B, assemble Leaves. With G, work mesh.

PANEL 4: With B, work Leaf 1. With C, work both sections of Leaf 2. With G, work Section 1 of Leaf 3; with R, work Section 2. With B, assemble Leaves. With G, work mesh.

PANEL 5 (Center Back): With G, work Leaf 1. With C, work both sections of Leaf 2. With R, work Section 1 of

Leaf 3; with C, work Section 2. With G, assemble Leaves. Work mesh as follows:

With B, work first through 4th rows as for mesh on Panel 1. Break off. With right side facing you and Leaf 1 at top, sk first 6 lps of last row; attach C in next ch-3.

5th row: Work sc in same lp, * work lp st, sc in next ch-3 sp *. (Rep from * to * to next inc lp, inc 1 lp st) twice; rep from * to * to within last 9 lps (16 lps); turn.

6th row: Work even in lp st pattern, working incs over incs of previous row (18 lps). Break off; turn.

7th row: Sk 2 lps, attach R in next ch-3, sc in same sp, work even in lp st pattern, working incs over incs to within last 2 lps (15 lps); turn.

8th row: Work even in lp st pattern, working incs over incs (17 lps). Break off; turn.

9th row: Attach B to first lp (B lp) of 4th row of mesh, sc in same place and work even in lp st pattern, working incs over incs to within last 3 lps of 4th row (35 lps). There should be 12 lps on each side of piece, an inc lp at each top corner and 9 lps across top. Break off; reattach B to end lp of first row of mesh.

10th row: Work 3 sc in each ch-3 sp of each B lp st. Break off.

EDGINGS: Panel 1: Front edging: With wrong side facing you, attach G at corner S on Diagram 2.

1st row: Working along front edge, work sc in same st, then work in pattern of lp st and sc 16 times evenly spaced along side of mesh to within last 3 lps on side; turn.

2nd row: Work lp st, sc in first ch-3 lp, * work lp st, sc in next lp. Rep from * to within last 2 lps; turn.

3rd row: Rep 2nd row, working to within last 3 lps.

4th row: Rep 2nd row, working to within last 2 lps (9 lps). Break off.

Panel 1: Side edging: Attach B in corner st at T on Diagram 2.

1st row: With right side facing you, work 70 sc evenly spaced along smooth side edge of mesh, to within jagged edge; ch 2, turn. Work in back lps only for remainder of edging.

2nd row: Sc in each st across to within last 6 sts; ch 2, turn.

3rd through 6th rows: Sc in each st across to within last 8 sts; ch 2, turn. Rep 2nd row 3 times more.

7th row: Work 1 sc in each of next 18 sts (20 sts unworked). Break off.

Panel 2: Side edging: Attach B at U on Diagram 2. With wrong side facing you, work first through 7th rows as for Panel 1 side edging.

Panel 2: Center Back edging: Attach B at V on Diagram 2.

1st row: With right side facing you, working in both lps, work 84 sc evenly spaced along side of mesh and across 5 free lps at lower edge of mesh. **Note:** This will cause lower edge to curve slightly. Break off. Reattach B at waist edge in first sc of last row and work in back lps only for remainder of edging.

2nd row: Work 1 sc in each of next 42 sc; ch 2, turn.

3rd row: Work 1 sc in each sc across to within last 6 sc; ch 2, turn.

4th row: Sc in each sc across; ch 2, turn. Rep 3rd and 4th rows 4 times more, omitting ch-2 at end of last row (12 sc). Break off.

Panel 3: Center Back edging: Attach B at W on Diagram 2. With wrong side facing you on first row, work edging to correspond to Panel 2 Center Back edging. Break off.

Panel 3: Side edging: Attach R at X on Diagram 2. Work first through 7th rows as for Panel 1 side edging.

Panel 4: Side edging: Attach R at Y on Diagram 2. With wrong side facing you, work first through 7th rows as for Panel 1 side edging.

Panel 4: Front edging: Attach G at Z on Diagram 2. With right side facing you, work first through 4th rows as for Panel 1 front edging.

FINISHING: Joining Panels 2 and 3: (See gJ area on Diagram 2.) Starting at waist edge of Center Back edging on Panel 2, attach G at dot. Working in both lps, sc in each of first 3 sc, sk 2 sc, work 3 hdc in next sc; (working on next corner, work 1 sc in each of first 3 sts, sk 2 sc, work 3 hdc in next sc) 4 times; sc in first sc on next corner; then on B sts of Panel 3, work sc in corresponding st on Center Back edging, (work 3 hdc in next st, sk 2 sc, sc in each of next 3 sts) 5 times, ending at waist edge. Do not break off.

With right sides together, join Panels by working 1 row sc in top lps of corresponding sts of last row. Break off. Attach B and join remaining 12 sts of Center Back edging. Break off.

With right sides together, pin Panel 5 between Panels 2 and 3; with B, whipstitch in place. Break off.

Joining Panels 1 and 2: (See Area rJ on Diagram 2.) Starting at waist edge (dot) of side edging on Panel 1, attach R. Working in both lps, sc in each of first 3 sc, sk 2 sc, work 3 hdc in next sc, (working on next corner, work 1 sc in each of first 3 sc, sk 2 sc, work 3 hdc in next sc) twice; sc in first sc on next corner; then on Panel 2, sc in corresponding st on side edging, (work 3 hdc in next sc, sk 2 sc, sc in each of next 3 sts) 3 times. Do not break off.

With right sides together, join Panels by working 1 row sc in top lps of corresponding sts of last row. Break off. Attach B and join remaining 17 sts of side edging. Break off.

Joining Panels 3 and 4: (See Area bJ on Diagram 2.) With B, join same as for Panels 1 and 2. With R, work remaining 17 sts together.

Waist edging: Attach G at F on Diagram 2.

1st row: With right side facing you, work sc evenly spaced across waist edge, decreasing 1 sc at each panel seam (to dec, insert hook in each of next 2 sts, y o, draw through all 3 lps on hook); ch 2, turn.

2nd row: Working in back lps only, sc in each sc across; ch 2, turn.

3rd row: Rep 2nd row once more.

4th row: Working in back lps only, work 1 sc in each sc across, decreasing 1 sc at center of each panel and at seams; ch 2, turn.

5th row: Rep 4th row once more, working ch 3 at end of last row.

6th row: Working in both lps, work hdc in next st, * ch 2, sk 2 sts, hdc in each of next 2 sts. Rep from * across. Break off.

Tie: With G, * ch 3, dc in 3rd ch from hook. Rep from * for desired length; (ch 3, sc in 3rd ch from hook) 4 times for Tie trim; sl st in end of tie. Break off; attach G to other end of Tie and make Tie trim. Weave Tie through last row of waist edging.

RACY RIBBED BIKINI

SIZE: Bra will stretch to fit 32″ to 36″ bust. Pants will stretch to fit 33″ to 37″ hips.

MATERIALS: Quick-weight cotton such as Lily Double Quick crochet cotton, 6 (115-yd.) skeins black (color B), 2 skeins gold (G), and 1 skein each red (R) and cream (C); aluminum crochet hook size H (or English/Canadian hook No. 8) *or the size that will give you the correct gauge;* 7 yards round nylon elastic.

GAUGE: 4 sc = 1″.

Note: Use cotton double throughout.

Bra

Left Cup: Work Leaf 2 of Skirt/Cape Cover-Up, working Section 1 with G and Section 2 with B. Mark last st for side edge.

Section 3: Attach R with sl st to dot at Y on Diagram 1 for Skirt/Cape Cover-Up. Work as for Section 2, until 9 sts remain. Mark last row for center edge. Break off.

Right Cup: Work as for Left Cup, working Section 1 with C, Section 2 with R, and Section 3 with B.

With R, join with sl st through both lps of the corresponding 9 sts along center edge. Break off.

Neck Ties: Attach B to Leaf at Z on Diagram 1. To make p lp, ch 7, join to form ring, ch 1, work 2 sc in ring, ch 3, work 3 sc in ring. Do not break off, but continue to work p lps until strap measures about 17″. Then make bobble as follows: (Ch 3, sc in 3rd ch from hook) twice; join with sl st to last sc worked in ring to complete bobble. Break off. Work other Tie in same manner.

Side Ties: Attach B to side edge of Bra and work p lps as for Neck Ties to measure about 18″; work bobble. Break off. Work other Side Tie in same manner. Thread 4 strands elastic through wrong side of lower edge of Bra. Draw in ends to fit, knotting them to hold. Tack ends in place.

Pants

Left Back: 1st Row: Starting at side edge with B, * ch 3, dc in 3rd ch from hook (lp made). Rep from * 6 times more (7 lps); mark ch-3 of first lp, (sk next lp, work next lp) 3 times (marked lps to be used for joining sides later); ch 2, turn.

2nd row: Work 3 sc over post of dc of last lp made, work 3 sc over post of each of next 6 dc (21 sc); ch 2, turn. Work in back lps only for remainder of back.

To Shape Leg Opening: 3rd row: Sc in each sc across to within last sc (leg edge), work 2 sc in next sc (1 sc inc, mark leg edge); ch 2, turn.

4th row: Work 1 sc in each sc across; ch 2, turn. Rep last 2 rows once more (23 sc).

Continue in pattern, increasing 1 sc at leg edge every row 15 times (38 sc at end of 21st row); then inc 1 sc at lower edge every other row twice (40 sc). Work 1 row even. Piece should measure 7″ from beg.

Crotch Shaping: 27th row: Work sc in each sc across; ch 6, turn.

28th row: Sc in 3rd ch from hook and in each of next 3 ch, sc in each sc across (44 sc); ch 2, turn. Work 10 rows even. Break off.

Right Back: With R, work same as for Left Back until there are 33 sc. Break off R; attach C. With C, continue as for Left Back until there are 37 sc. Break off C; attach G. With G, work as for Left Back to Crotch Shaping (40 sc). Break off.

With right sides tog, matching top edges, with B, work sl st through both lps on B edge and 1 lp on G edge of corresponding sts (4 sts remain on left edge of crotch). Break off.

Right Front: Starting at side edge with B, work same as for Left Back through 2nd row. Work in back lps only for remainder of front.

3rd row: Marking last st for lower edge, work 1 sc in each sc across; ch 2, turn. Work even in pattern for 17 more rows; then inc 1 sc at lower edge of next 4 rows (25 sc at end of 24th row).

Crotch Shaping: 25th row: Sc in each sc across; ch 12, turn.

26th row: Work 1 sc in 3rd ch from hook and in each of next 9 ch, sc in each sc across (35 sc); ch 2, turn. Work 10 rows even. Break off.

Left Front: With R, work same as for Right Front through 16th row. Break off R; attach C. With C, continue as for Right Front until there are 22 sts. Break off R; attach G. With G, continue as for Right Front until there are 25 sts. Break off.

Join Fronts as for Back sections (10 sts remain on left edge of Crotch). Break off.

Right Side Joining Panel: With R, ch 7. Join with sl st to form ring.

1st row: Ch 1, work 2 sc in ring, ch 1, with right side of pants front facing you, starting at right lower edge, sl st in first marked lp, ch 1, work 3 sc in ring, do not break off; * ch 7, join to form ring, ch 1, work 3 sc in ring, ch 1, sl st in next marked lp, ch 1, work 3 sc in ring, do not break off *. Rep from * to * twice more, ending at top edge. Now work along other side of rings and join to back as follows:

2nd row: Ch 3, work 3 sc in last ring worked, ch 1, starting at top edge of pants back, sl st in first marked lp, ch 1, 3 sc in ring; do not break off. Rep from * to * on first row 3 times, ending last rep with sl st in first sl st; break off. With B, work left Panel to correspond.

Sew crotch edges together. Thread 4 strands elastic through top and leg edges and fasten as for Bra.

SUNSET BATHING SUIT AND COVER-UP

A dazzling palette of island pastels mixed with a variety of intricate stitches creates a smashing set for the sun.

SIZES: One size fits all. Bra will stretch to fit 32″ to 36″ bust. Pants will stretch to fit 33″ to 37″ hips.

MATERIALS: Medium-weight rayon such as Kentucky All-Purpose #301 yarn, 12 (100-yd.) skeins orchid, 6 skeins sea green, 2 skeins each sky blue, peach, and ecru, 1 skein bright turquoise; aluminum hooks sizes G and F (or English/Canadian hooks Nos. 9 and 10) *or the sizes that will give you the correct gauge.*

GAUGE: 6 dc = 1½″ with G hook; 2 rows of dc = 1¼″.

Note: Tag each Motif upon completion for easier identification when assembling motifs.

COVER-UP

DECORATIVE STRIP: MOTIF A (make 2): Use G hook.

1st rnd: Use orchid. Ch 5, join to form ring with sl st in first ch st, ch 3, * work 2-dc cl in ring as follows: (Y o, pull thread through, y o pull through 2 lps) twice, y o, pull through all 3 lps on hook. Rep from * 10 times; sl st top beg ch-3 (total 12 sts); ch 3, turn.

2nd rnd: Work 2-dc cl same sp, work dc and 2-dc cl in each st around, sl st top beg ch-3 (total 24 sts); ch 3, turn.

3rd rnd: Dc same sp, work 2-dc cl next st, * work 2 dc next st, work 2-dc cl next st, rep from * around, end sl st in top of beg ch-3 (total 36 sts). Fasten off. Turn.

4th rnd: Use peach. Beg in any st, * work shell of 2 dc, ch 2 and 2 dc; in each of next 5 sts work 2-dc cl, rep from * around, sl st beg dc. Fasten off. Turn.

5th rnd: Use green. Beg in any ch-2 sp, * in ch-2 sp work ch 3, sc in 3rd ch st from hook (p), and sc, work sc in each of next 9 sts, in ch-2 sp work sc, p and sc, sk 4 sts, in next st work shell of 4 tr, p and 4 tr, sk 4 sts, rep from * twice ending sl st in beg sc. Fasten off. **Note:** This side is right side.

MOTIF B (make 2): Work same as for Motif A, substituting blue for rnd 4.

MOTIF C: 1st rnd: Use turquoise. Ch 4, join with sl st to form ring, ch 3, 11 dc in ring, sl st top of ch-3.

2nd rnd: Ch 4, * dc next st, ch 1, rep from * around, sl st in 3rd ch st of beg ch-4. Fasten off.

3rd rnd: Use peach. Work 3 sc over each ch-1 sp, sl st beg sc. Fasten off.

4th rnd: Use green. Beg in center sc of any 3-sc group, * work sc, ch 2, sk 2 sc, in next st work shell of 2-dc cl, ch 2 and 2-dc cl, ch 2, sk 2 sc, rep from * around, sl st in beg sc. Fasten off.

5th rnd: Use blue. Beg in any * ch-2 sp, at center of cl shells, work sc, p, and sc, in next ch-2 sp work 4 sc, sc in next sc, 4 sc in next ch-2 sp, in ch-2 sp at center of next shell work sc, p and sc, sk ch-2 sp, in sc work shell of 3 dc, p and 3 dc, sk ch-2 sp, rep from * twice; sl st beg sc.

Fasten off. **Note:** This side is right side.

MOTIF D: Work as for Motif C, substituting blue in 3rd rnd and orchid in 5th rnd.

MOTIF E: Work as for Motif C, substituting green in 1st and 2nd rnds, turquoise in 3rd rnd, peach in 4th rnd, and orchid in 5th rnd.

MOTIF F (make 2): 1st rnd: Use turquoise. Ch 4, join with sl st to form ring, ch 3, 5 dc in ring; ch 4, turn.

2nd rnd: (Dc next st, ch 1) 4 times, dc in top ch-3. Fasten off.

3rd rnd: Use blue. Go back to beg ch-4 of last rnd, work 3 sc over top of ch, work 3 sc in each of next 4 ch-1 sps, ch 1, work 3 sc over side of end dc, 3 sc over next ch-3, sc in next ch sp, 3 dc over side of next dc, 3 sc over next ch sp, sl st beg sc. Fasten off.

4th rnd: Use green. Beg in sc after sl st just made, work sc, * ch 2, sk 2 sc, in next st work shell of 2-dc cl, ch 2 and 2-dc cl, ch 2, sk 2 sc, sc next st, rep from * once. Fasten off.

5th rnd: Use orchid. Beg in first sc of last rnd, work shell of 3 dc, p and 3 dc, sk to ch-2 sp at center of cl shell, work sc, p and sc, over next ch-2 sp work 4 sc, sc next sc, 4 sc over next ch-2 sp, in ch-2 sp at center of next cl shell, work sc, p and sc, in next sc work shell of 3 dc, p and 3 dc, continue around working sc back lps only in each remaining st, and sl st beg dc. Fasten off. **Note:** This side is right side.

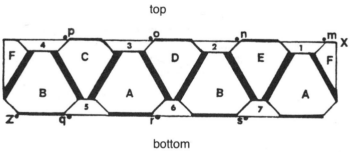

top

bottom

Diagram 1

Connecting Motifs: Place Motifs in position shown in Diagram 1. Be sure Motifs have right side facing. Be sure to match up the 11 sc sts between p sts on each of the Motifs to be joined. Dots indicate where Motifs are joined. Pin Motifs tog where they are to be joined. Turn strip to wrong side; join, where pinned, with sl st or overcast st. Use green, working top lps only.

Note: Keep identification tags on Motifs.

Top Fill-In: Area 1: Place strip with right side facing in position of Diagram 1. Use ecru. Begin at M on Diagram 1. Sk p at tip of Motif F, sc down next 4 sts (3 dc and sc) on Motif F, work p, sk p, seam joining and p, sc in next 5

sts on Motif A, work 2 p, sk p, sc in next 5 sts on same Motif, sk p, seam joining and p, sc up next 4 sts on Motif E, ch 3, turn. Work 3-dc cl same sp as turning ch (3-dc cl worked 3 dc same sp holding back last lp on hook, y o, pull through all 4 lps on hook), ch 1, work 4-dc cl in next p, ch 1, sc next p, ch 3, sc next p, 4-dc cl next p, ch 1, 4-dc cl in end sc (beg st of Fill-In). Fasten off. Using ecru, work remaining Fill-In Areas in same manner as for Fill-In Area 1. See Diagram 1 for positions. Begin in Area 2 at N, Area 3 at O, and Area 4 at P.

Bottom Fill-In: Area 5: Turn strip so that bottom is at top. Have right side facing. Begin at Q. Use ecru. Sk p at corner tr shell of Motif B, work sc in next 5 sts on Motif B, work p, sk p, seam joining and p, sc in next 4 sts on Motif C, work 2 p, sk p, sc in next 4 sts, work p, sk p, seam joining and p, sc in next 5 sts of Motif A, ch 3, turn. Work 3-dc cl in same sp as turning ch, ch 1, work 4-dc cl in next p, ch 1, sc in each of next 2 p, 4-dc cl in next p, ch 1, 4-dc cl in end sc, sl st top of first cl. Fasten off. Work remaining Fill-In Areas in same manner as Area 5. Begin Area 6 at R, substituting blue for ecru. Begin Area 7 at S using ecru.

Edging Top Of Strip: Use orchid. Hold Decorative Strip right side facing in position of Diagram 1. Begin working at X on Diagram 1. Starting in 3rd dc to right of p st at tip of Motif F, * work dc in each of next 3 dc, sk p, (work 2-dc cl) twice in each of next 2-cl sts (sk ch-1 between cl), work 5 hdc in next ch-3 sp, (work 2-dc cl) twice in each of next 2 cl, sk p, work dc in each of next 3 dc, ** ch 2, sk sc and p, sl st next st (ch 2, sk next 4 sts, sl st next st) twice, ch 2, sk p and sc, rep from * twice, rep from * to ** once. Fasten off.

BODICE TOP: Pattern st for this section is seed st, which is worked sc, dc alternately on first row and then worked dc in sc sts and sc in dc sts on next row. Always work ch-2 for turning ch and begin working in next st. Hold strip right side facing in position of Diagram 1. Counting from right to left, mark 2nd ch-2 sp on edging over Motif E. Counting from left to right, mark 2nd ch-2 sp on edging over Motif C. Turn piece so that wrong side is facing you.

Right Front: 1st row: Use orchid. (Ch 3, dc in 3rd ch st from hook) five times (5-lp foundation ch formed), begin at marker over Motif E (do not remove marker), work sc and dc in each of next ch-2 sps, * sc next st, dc next st, rep from * across; ch 2, turn.

2nd row: Work dc in next sc, sc next dc, continue across to within foundation ch lp in pattern st (should end in dc), now work in the 5 ch-lps in seed st pattern as follows: 4 sts first lp, 2 sts 2nd lp, 4 sts 3rd lp, 2 sts 4th lp, 4 sts 5th lp; ch 2, turn.

3rd through 20th rows: Work 18 rows even in seed st pattern. Fasten off.

Left Front: Hold piece wrong side facing.

1st row: Use orchid. Begin in end dc of Strip edging. With sc, work in pattern across to marker (do not remove marker) in ch-2 sp over Motif C, now work 5-lp foundation ch as follows: (Ch 3, dc in 3rd ch st from hook) 5 times; ch 2, turn.

2nd row: Working in seed st pattern, starting with dc, work 4 sts in first lp, 2 sts in 2nd lp, 4 sts in 3rd lp, 2 sts in 4th lp, and 4 sts in 5th lp. Continue working in pattern to end of row; ch 2, turn.

3rd through 20th rows: Work 18 rows even in seed st pattern. Fasten off.

Back: Have wrong side facing.

1st row: Use orchid. * Work (ch 3, dc in 3rd ch st from hook) 5 times, * beg at marker over Motif C, work across Strip edging to marker over Motif E, rep from * to *; ch 2, turn.

2nd row: In first lp work dc, sc and dc, continue working in pattern st, * work 2 sts in 2nd lp, 4 sts in 3rd lp, 2 sts in 4th lp, and 4 sts in 5th lp, * work in pattern st across to within next lp foundation ch, work 4 sts in first lp, rep from * to *; ch 2, turn.

3rd through 20th rows: Work 18 rows even in pattern st. Fasten off.

Shoulder Seams: Join on wrong side with sc, working top lps only.

Underarm Seams: Join on wrong side. Match up lps of foundation chains. Work 3 sc over each set of lps.

BODY: Hold piece so that Decorative Strip is on top. Have right side facing. You will be working on bottom edge of strip. Refer to Diagram 1, begin at point marked Z.

1st row: Use green. * Omit p at corner of Motif B, begin in next dc, work both lps, dc next 5 sts, ch 2, sk p, sl st next 11 sts, ch 2, sk p, dc next 5 sts,** sk p, in base of cl on Fill-In Area (work 2-tr cl) twice, in stitch between cls work one 2-tr cl, in base of next cl (work 2-tr cl) twice, rep from * across strip ending at ** on last rep, ch 3, turn.

2nd row: * (In next dc work 4-dc cl, sk 2 sts, in next st work dc, ch 3 and dc, sk 2 sts) 3 times, in next dc work 4-dc cl,** sk 2 sts, work dc, ch 3 and dc in next tr cl, (4-dc cl in next tr cl, dc, ch 3 and dc in next tr cl) twice, sk 2 dc, rep from * across ending at ** on last rep, end dc in turning ch (22 cls); ch 3, turn.

3rd row: Work dc, ch 3 and dc in cl, * in ch-3 sp work sc, ch 2 and sc, work dc, ch 3 and dc in cl, rep from * across, end dc in turning ch; ch 3, turn.

4th row: In ch-3 sp work dc, ch 3 and dc, * in ch-2 sp work 4-dc cl, work dc, ch 3 and dc in next ch-3 sp, rep from * across, end dc in turning ch; ch 3, turn.

5th row: Work sc, ch 2 and sc in ch-3 sp, * work dc, ch 3 and dc in cl, work sc, ch 2 and sc in next ch-3 sp, rep

from * across, end dc in turning ch. Fasten off. Turn.

6th row: (inc row): Use ecru. Begin in break-off st, dc, (work 4-dc cl in ch-2 sp, dc, ch 3 and dc in ch-3 sp) 4 times, * work 4-dc cl, ch 3 and 4-dc cl in next ch-2 sp, work dc, ch 3 and dc in next ch-3 sp *, rep ( ) 3 times, rep from * to *, rep ( ) 4 times, rep from * to *, rep ( ) 3 times, rep from * to *, rep ( ) 4 times, end 4-dc cl in last ch-2 sp, dc in turning ch; ch 3, turn.

7th row: Rep 3rd row. Fasten off. Turn.

8th row: Use blue. Dc in break-off st, rep 4th row.

9th row: Rep 5th row, do not fasten off, ch 3, turn.

10th row: In ch-2 sp work 4-dc cl, work dc, ch 3 and dc in next ch-3 sp, rep from * across, ending 4-dc cl in last ch-2 sp, dc turning ch; ch 3, turn.

11th row: Rep 3rd row. Fasten off, turn.

12th row: (inc row): Use turquoise. In break-off st work dc, (in ch-3 sp work dc, ch 3 and dc, in ch-2 sp work 4-dc cl) 7 times, * work dc, ch 3 and dc in next ch-3 sp, work 4-dc cl, ch 3 and 4-dc cl in ch-2 sp, * rep ( ) 9 times, rep from * to *, rep ( ) 7 times, end dc, ch 3 and dc in last ch-3 sp, dc in turning ch. Fasten off.

13th row: Use lilac. Dc in break-off st, * work sc, ch 2 and sc in ch-3 sp, work dc, ch 4 and dc in cl, rep from * across, end sc, ch 2 and sc in last ch-3 sp, dc in end dc; ch 3, turn.

14th row: * Work 4-dc cl in ch-2 sp, work dc, ch 4 and dc in ch-4 sp, rep from * across, ending 4-dc cl in last ch-2 sp, dc in turning ch; ch 3, turn.

15th row: Work dc, ch 4, and dc in cl, * work sc, ch 2 and sc in ch-4 sp, work dc, ch 4 and dc in cl, rep from * across, dc in turning ch; ch 3, turn.

16th row: Work dc, ch 4 and dc in ch-4 sp, * in ch-2 sp work 4-dc cl, work dc, ch 4 and dc in next ch-4 sp, rep from * across, dc in turning ch, ch 3, turn.

17th row: * Work sc, ch 2 and sc in ch-4 sp, work dc, ch 4 and dc in cl, rep from * across, end sc, ch 2 and sc in last ch-4 sp, dc in turning ch. Fasten off.

18th row: Use peach. Rep 14th row.

19th row: Rep 15th row.

20th row: (inc row): Mark off 8th ch-2 sp from right and 8th ch-2 sp from left. Work dc, ch 4 and dc in ch-4 sp, (in ch-2 sp work 4-dc cl, in next ch-4 sp work dc, ch 4 and dc) 7 times. * In marked ch-2 sp work 4-dc cl, ch 4 and 4-dc cl, * rep ( ) to within next marker, rep from * to *, rep ( ) 7 times, dc in turning ch. Fasten off.

21st row: Use green. Dc in break-off st, * work sc, ch 2 and sc in ch-4 sp, work d, ch 5 and dc in cl, rep from * across, end sc, ch 2 and sc in last ch-4 sp, dc in turning ch; ch 3, turn.

22nd row: * Work 4-dc cl in ch-2 sp, work dc, ch 5 and dc in ch-5 sp, rep from * across ending 4-dc cl in last ch-2 sp, dc in turning ch; ch 3, turn.

23rd row: Work dc, ch 5 and dc in cl, * work sc, ch 2

and sc in ch-5 sp, work dc, ch 5 and dc in cl, rep from * across, end dc in turning ch; ch 3, turn.

24th through 33rd rows: Work dc, ch 5 and dc in ch-5 sp, * in ch-2 sp work 4-dc cl, work dc, ch 5 and dc in next ch-5 sp, rep from * across, end dc in turning ch; ch 3, turn. Rep 21st row from * through 24th row twice, rep 21st row from *. Fasten off. Do not turn.

34th row: Use lilac. Sc in turning ch, * 4-dc cl in ch-2 sp, ch 2, sc, ch 2 and sc in next ch-5 sp, ch 2, rep from * across, end 4-dc cl in last ch-2 sp, sc in end dc. Mark this end dc and fasten off.

EDGING: Right Front: 1st row: Use orchid. Have right side facing. Beg at last marker. Over side of marked dc work * sc, dc and sc (remove marker), over next end-of-row st work dc and sc, over next end-of-row st work dc, sc and dc, over next end-of-row st work sc and dc, rep from * up to corner p on Motif A, sk p, work in pattern alternating dc and sc sts over next 5 sts on Motif A, (mark last st made), sk 2 p's, work in pattern alternating dc and sc sts over next 4 sts on Motif F, ch 2, sk p, sl st each st around Motif F.

Neck Edging: Work sc edging around neck opening as follows: * work 2 sc in next end-of-row st, 1 sc in next end-of-row st, rep from * around to 2nd Motif F.

Left Front: Sl st each st around Motif F to p, sk p, work in pattern alternating dc and sc sts over next 4 sts on Motif F, sk 2 p sts, work in pattern alternating dc and sc on next 5 sts on Motif A, (mark the first of these 5 sts), sk p, * working in pattern alternating dc and sc sts, work 3 sts over next end-of-row st, 2 sts over next end-of-row sts, rep from * across through last end-of-row st; ch 2, turn.

2nd row: Use F hook. Work in seed st pattern across to within st before marker, work this st and marked st as 1 (dec), remove marker, work next 2 sts as 1, (mark last st made); turn.

3rd row: Work in pattern st to within last 2 sts of 2nd row, work last 2 sts as 1 (dec); ch 2, turn.

4th row: Work next 2 sts as 1 (dec), work to within marked st, work this st and next st as 1 (dec); remove marker, turn.

5th row: Sl st across to beg of 4th row. Fasten off.

Right Front: Use F hook and orchid. Have right side facing. Beg at hem edge in first st of edging. Rep 2nd through 5th rows.

BUTTONS AND LOOPS: Use lilac and G Hook.

Buttons: Have right side of garment facing. Work on Left Front. Beg at Motif F, counting from top down, sl st in 12th sl st, * ch 4, sl st in 4th ch st from hook to form ring, ch 1, work 6 sc in ring, sl st in beg ch-1, ch 1, (work next 2 sc as 1) 3 times, sl st in ch-1, (Button) sl st next 6 sts, rep from * 4 times omitting 6 sl sts on last rep. Fasten off.

Loops: Have right side facing. Work on Right Front. Count from top down 12 sts on Motif F (mark 12th st), count down next 24 sts on edge, sl st in 24th st, ch 5, (sl st next 6 sts, ch 5) 4 times, sl st next st. You should be at marker. Fasten off.

BATHING SUIT

Bra

(See Diagram 2). See directions for Cover-Up. Make one each of Motifs A, B, C, D, and E.

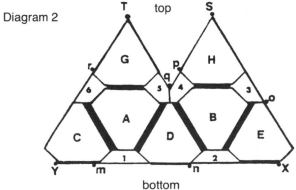

Diagram 2

Motif G: Work as for Motif C, substituting blue in first and 2nd rows, green in 3rd row, turquoise in 4th row, and orchid in 5th row.

Motif H: Work as for Motif C, substituting peach in first and 2nd rows, turquoise in 3rd row, blue in 4th row, and green in 5th row.

Joining Motifs: Place Motifs, right side facing, as positioned in Diagram 2. Dots indicate where Motifs are joined. Match up the 11 sc sts between p's on the Motif edges to be joined. Pin Motifs tog in place. Turn piece to wrong side. With green, sl st Motifs tog working top lps only.

Fill-In Areas: With right side facing, begin holding piece so that bottom is on top. Work Fill-In Areas in same manner as for Fill-In Area 1 on Cover-Up decorative strip. Use ecru for Areas 1, 2, 3, and 6; blue for Areas 4 and 5. Begin Area 1 at M; Area 2 at N; Area 3 at O; Area 4 at P; Area 5 at Q; and Area 6 at R.

Neck Ties: Have right side facing. Use orchid. Begin at S on Diagram 2. Sc in p at tip of Motif H, * work p 21 times, sc in base of 3rd p from hook. Fasten off. * Begin at T on Diagram 2. Sc in p at tip of Motif G. Rep from * to *.

Side Ties: Use orchid. Beg at X on Diagram 2. Sc in p's at corner of Motif E. * Work 24 p's, sc in base of 3rd p from hook. Fasten off. * Beg at Y, sc in p at corner of Motif C. Rep from * to *. Working on wrong side, thread 4 strands of elastic through sts at lower edge of Bra. Draw ends to fit, knotting them to hold. Tack ends in place.

Pants

Pattern st for pants is seed st. Work dc and sc alternately 1st row. Work sc in dc sts and dc in sc sts on subsequent rows. Always make ch-2 for turning ch, and begin working in next st.

Back: 1st row: Use lilac. (Ch 3, dc in 3rd ch st from hook) 18 times. (Foundation ch-lp formed).

2nd row: Ch 2 (ch 2 counts as first sc), over side of last dc made work dc and sc, over side of next dc, work dc, sc and dc, * over side of next dc work sc, dc and sc, over side of next dc work dc, sc and dc, rep from * across, ch 2, turn.

3rd through 8th rows: Work 6 rows even in seed st pattern. Fasten off.

9th and 10th rows: Use peach. Work 2 rows even. Fasten off.

11th row: Use turquoise. Work 1 row even. Fasten off.

12th row: Use blue. Work 1 row even, ch 2, turn.

13th row: (inc row): Work, increasing 1 st at beg and end of row.

14th row: Use green. Work 1 row even.

15th through 19th rows: Use orchid. Work 5 rows even.

20th row: Rep 13th row.

21st through 23rd rows: Work 3 rows even. (Mark each end st of 23rd row.)

24th through 39th rows: Work 16 rows, dec 1 st at beg and end of row. Work dec by working 2 sts as 1. If next st should be a dc, work as follows: pull thread through next st, y o, pull thread through next st, y o, pull through 3 lps on hook, y o, pull through 2 lps on hook; if next st should be a sc (pull thread through next st) twice, y o, pull through all 3 lps on hook.

40th through 43rd rows: Dec 2 sts at beg and end of row.

44th row: Work decreasing 1 st at beg and end of row.

45th through 47th rows: Work 3 rows even. Fasten off.

Front: Rep 1st through 23rd row of Back. Fasten off. Turn.

24th row: Use orchid. Sk last 12 sts made on 23rd row. Beg in next st. Work in pattern st to within end 12 sts, ch 2, turn.

25th through 30th rows: Work 6 rows, decreasing 2 sts at beg and end of row.

31st row: Dec 1 st at beg and end of row.

32nd through 37th rows: Work 6 rows even. Fasten off. Working on wrong side, sew Front and Back tog with orchid. On each side, begin at waist edge, sew to marker. Sew crotch seam. Thread 4 strands of elastic through waist and leg edges as for Bra.

Summer Hats

ST. TROPEZ HAT

In lime, lavender, and blue, this hat features a cupola–shaped crown and a curvy brim. Both are made in sections and then joined. Triangle, square, and circle motifs are worked in single and double crochet.

SIZE: One size fits all.

MATERIALS: Synthetic straw yarn (100% viscose rayon), 6 (24-yd.) skeins each pearl gray, olive green, and orchid, 4 skeins medium blue, 2 skeins lime; aluminum crochet hook size H (or English/Canadian hook No. 8) *or the size that will give you the correct gauge;* tapestry needle.

GAUGE: 5 dc = 2″.

Note: Use 2 strands of straw yarn throughout. Work loosely for best results, pulling up loops ½″. When joining or breaking off straw, leave 4″ end. Weave end halfway through crochet, then double it back so that it cannot pull out.

Crown of hat is made in 4 separate sections that are then joined. The brim is composed of 4 Squares and 4 Circles. You crochet the Circles separately, then crochet the Squares right from the edge of the Crown; finally, you join the Circles to the Squares.

CROWN: First Section: 1st row: (right side) Starting in center with medium blue, ch 9, dc in 4th ch from hook and in each of next 4 ch; in last ch work 3 dc, ch 2 and 3 dc; continuing along opposite side of foundation ch, and working in single lps only, work dc in each ch across (last dc is made in base of ch-3 to make 18 dc in all, counting ch-3 as 1 dc). Break off. Turn.

2nd row: Working back lps only, attach pearl gray with sl st to last dc worked, ch 3, dc in each of next 8 dc, work 3 dc, ch 2 and 3 dc in ch-2 sp, dc in remaining 9 dc (24 dc). Break off. Turn.

3rd row: Attach olive green in same place, ch 3 and attach marker; working in back lps only, work dc in each of next 11 dc, work 3 dc, ch 2 and 3 dc in ch-2 sp, dc in remaining 12 dc (30 dc). Break off. Mark this side as right side.

Make 3 more sections in same manner. Mark Sections A through D.

JOINING CROWN SECTIONS: Hold A and B Sec-

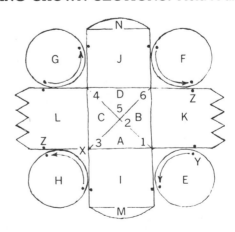

tions together with wrong sides facing. Attach orchid in a marked ch-3, working in top lps, sc tog same ch-3 and corresponding dc on Section B. Working through both sections, sc in each of next 14 dc from 1 to 2 on Diagram.

Note: Crown on Diagram is shown flat to make drawing easier to follow. Ch 3, then join Sections A and C, working from 2 to 3 on Diagram as follows: Sk ch-sps, working top lps, sc next 15 dc (3 Sections joined). Break off. Hold Sections C and D together, attach orchid, and join as before from 4 to 5, ch 1, drop lp from hook, insert hook in orchid ch-3 lp on top of Crown, draw dropped lp through, ch 2, holding Sections D and B together, join as before from 5 to 6 (all 4 Sections joined). Do not break off. Ch 1, work 2 sc in side of each dc and 2 sc in each joining around lower edge of Crown, making sure Crown does not cup in; join with sl st to first sc. Break off.

BRIM CIRCLE: Starting at center with medium blue, ch 5, join with sl st to form ring.

1st rnd: Ch 3, work 11 dc in ring; join with sl st to top of first ch-3. Break off.

2nd rnd: Attach pearl gray to any dc, ch 3, dc in same dc, working in top lps only, work 2 dc in each dc around; join to top of first ch-3 (24 dc). Break off.

3rd rnd: Attach olive green to any dc, * ch 4, sk 3 dc, sc in next dc. Rep from * 4 times more; ch 4, sc at beg of first ch-4 (6 lps made).

4th rnd: Over each ch-4 lp, work (sc, ch 2, sc) 3 times; join to first sc (6 petals made). Break off. Place marker in 3rd ch-2 of a petal, sk 2 petals and put a 2nd marker in first ch-2 sp on next petal.

Work 3 more Circles in same manner. Mark Circles E through H.

SQUARE: 1st row: Join olive green to 2nd sc in joining on Crown at X on Diagram, ch 2, sk 1 sc, work sc, ch 1, and sc in next sc (V-st made), * sk next 2 sc, V-st in next sc. Rep from * twice; sk next sc, sc in next sc in joining (4 V-sts). Ch 2, turn.

2nd row: Work V-st in ch-1 sp of each V-st across, sl st in top of ch-2. Ch 2, turn.

Rep 2nd row 7 times more for a total of 9 rows of V-sts. Break off. Square I completed. Put marker at beg and end of 7th row. Join olive green to Section D and make Square J. With orchid, make Squares K and L, adding 1 more row of V-sts to each. Put a marker at beg and end of 7th row.

Joining Circles to Squares: Join Circle E to Squares I and K between markers (dots on Diagram) in the direction of arrow, as follows: Attach lime to ch-2 sp at first marker (dot Y) on Circle, ch 1, drop lp from hook, insert hook from right side in sp at marker on Square K, draw dropped lp through, ch 1, sc in next ch-2 sp on Circle, (ch

1, drop lp from hook, sk 1 row on Square K, insert hook in side of next row on Square K, draw dropped lp through, ch 1, sc in next ch-2 sp on Circle) 3 times (1 side joined); ch 1, join in first row on Square I, continue to join in same manner to markers.

Join remaining Circles and Squares in same manner.

Finishing row: With right side facing you, attach orchid to dot Z on Square L (row above marker), * ch 2, sc in next free ch-2 on Circle H. Rep from * along free edge of Circle, ch 2, work sc in ch-2 of last row of Square I, V-st in each of next 4 V-sts, sc in end sc, ch 2, sc in corresponding ch-2 sp on Circle E, ch 2, turn; work sc in next sc, work dc, ch 1 and dc in each of next 4 V-sts, ch 2, sc in end sc, sk 2 ch sts, sc in joining sc on Circle H, ch 2, turn; sc in next sc, work dc, ch 2, and dc in each of next 4 V-sts (Section M completed), ch 2, sc in joining sc on Circle E; * ch 2, sc in next ch-2 sp on Circle. Rep from * along edge of Circle, ch 2, sc in side of corresponding row on Square K. Break off.

Attach orchid at Z on Square K and work another finishing row in same manner along opposite side of Brim, making Section N on Square J (do not work along edges of orchid Squares K and L).

With lime, embroider or sl st row of ch sts over 1 olive dc border on each Crown section and under first row of each orchid Square.

SAN REMO HAT

With citrus and berry shades dominating, clusters and shells form the round crown and scalloped brim of this straw beauty.

SIZE: One size fits all.

MATERIALS: Synthetic straw yarn (100% viscose rayon), 6 (24-yd.) skeins royal blue, 4 skeins each yellow, pumpkin, olive green, and purple, 2 skeins orchid; aluminum crochet hook size H (or English/Canadian hook No. 8) *or the size that will give you the correct gauge;* tapestry needle.

GAUGE: 5 dc = 2″.

Note: Use double strand of straw throughout. Work loosely for best results, pulling up loops ½″. When joining or breaking off straw, leave 4″ end. Weave end halfway through crochet, then double it back so that it cannot pull out.

The crown is composed of top and side sections worked separately. The side section is worked up from a crocheted band and joined to top, then worked down from the band to brim. The brim is worked right from the crown and is made in one piece with an insert along front edge.

CROWN: Starting at top with yellow, ch 5 loosely; join with sl st to form ring.

1st rnd: Ch 3, work 11 dc in ring, join with sl st to top of first ch-3. Break off. Turn.

2nd rnd: Attach pumpkin with sl st to last sl st, ch 2, work hdc in same place, work 2 hdc in each dc around (24 hdc, counting ch-2 as 1 hdc); join to top of first ch-2. Break off. Turn.

3rd rnd: Attach olive green to last sl st, ch 3, dc in same place, dc in back lp of each of next 5 hdc, * 2 dc in back lp of next hdc, dc in back lp of each of next 5 hdc. Rep from * twice more; join to top of first ch-3 (28 dc). Break off.

4th rnd: Attach royal blue to last sl st, ch 1, sc in same place, * working in back lps only, work sc in next dc, 2 sc in next dc. Rep from * around, ending last rep with sc in last dc (42 sc). Break off. Top of Crown completed.

SIDE SECTION: The next 4 rnds are worked as a separate Band and sewed to top of Crown.

1st rnd: With yellow, ch 4, * work 4 dc in 4th ch from

hook (first cl made). Ch 3, turn. Sk first dc, holding back on hook last lp of each dc, work dc in each of next 3 dc and in top of turning ch, y o, draw straw through all 5 lps on hook (2nd cl made), ch 9. Rep from * 4 times more, ending last rep with ch 5 instead of ch 9; join to base of first cl to form ring. Break off.

2nd rnd: Attach pumpkin to center ch of a yellow ch-5, ch 1, * 4 dc over side of dc of next cl (remember, each yellow unit is composed of 2 cl), ch 2, 4 dc over side of dc of next cl, sc in center ch of next ch-5. Rep from * around, ending with sl st in first ch-1. Break off.

3rd rnd: Attach purple to any sc on previous rnd, ch 3, work dc in same sc, * ch 2, 2 dc in same sc, ch 2, work sc, ch 2 and sc in next ch-2 sp, ch 2, 2 dc in next sc. Rep from * around, ending last rep with sl st in top of ch-3. Break off.

4th rnd: Attach royal blue to a ch-2 sp between 2 sc, ch 1, * work 3 dc in next ch-2 sp, sc in next ch-2 sp. Rep from * around, ending last rep with 3 dc; join to first ch-1 (40 sts). Break off.

With needle and double strand royal blue straw, working on wrong side, in top lps, sc top of Crown to last rnd of Side Section, omitting 2 sc spaced evenly on Crown edge.

Working downward, complete Side Section as follows:

5th rnd: Attach olive green to first ch of a yellow ch-5, ch 3, dc in each of next 4 ch, * work 4 dc over side of dc of next cl, work 4 dc over side of dc of following cl, dc in each ch of next ch-5. Rep from * around; join to top of ch-3. Break off.

6th rnd: Attach orchid to first dc of a 5-dc group, ch 3, dc in each of next 4 dc, * ch 2, sk 3 dc, 2 sc in each of next 2 dc, ch 2, sk 3 dc, dc in each of next 5 dc. Rep from * around, omitting 5 dc on last rep; join to top of ch-3. Break off.

7th rnd: Attach royal blue to ch-2 sp before a 5-dc group, ch 3, work 3 dc in same sp, * holding back on hook last loop of each dc, work 3 dc in center dc of next 5-dc group, y o, draw straw through all 4 lps on hook (cl made), ch 1, 4 dc in next ch-2 sp, ch 1, 4 dc in following ch-2 sp. Rep from * around, omitting last 4-dc group on last rep, ch 1; join to top of ch-3. Break off.

8th rnd: Attach purple to ch-1 sp between any two 4-dc groups, ch 3, 5 dc in same sp, * ch 1, sc in sp before next cl, ch 2, sc in next ch-1 sp, ch 1, 6 dc in next ch-1 sp. Rep from * around, ending with ch 1; join to top of ch-3. Break off. Crown completed.

BRIM: 1st rnd: Attach olive green to ch-1 before any 6-dc group, * ch 5, sk 6-dc group, (sc in next sp, ch 2, holding back on hook last lp of each tr, work 2 tr in same sp, y o, draw straw through all 3 lps on hook, ch 3, sc in same sp) 3 times (1 petal made in each of the 3 sps be-

tween two 6-dc groups, making a 3-petal group). Rep from * around, ending with sc in first sl st. Break off.

2nd rnd: Attach yellow to first sc of first petal of a 3-petal group, * ch 2, sc in top of same petal, work 3 dc in first sc of next petal, sc in top of same petal, work 3 dc in first sc of 3rd petal, sc in top of same petal, ch 2, sc in last sc of same petal, ch 5, sc in first sc of next petal. Rep from * around, ending with sc where yellow was attached. Do not break off.

3rd rnd: Ch 1, * sc in next ch-2 sp, sc in next sc, (ch 2, holding back on hook last lp of each dc, work dc in each of next 3 dc, y o, draw straw through all 4 lps on hook, ch 2, sc in next sc) twice; sc in next ch-2 sp, work 2 sc over next ch-5 lp. Rep from * around; join to first sc. Break off.

4th rnd: Attach pumpkin to first sc of any 2 sc over ch-5 lp, ch 1, sc in next sc, * 4 dc over next ch-2 lp, ch 1, (3 dc over next ch-2 lp) twice; ch 1, 4 dc over next ch-2 lp, sc in each of next 2 sc. Rep from * around; join to first ch-1. Break off.

5th rnd: Attach purple to first sc of any 2-sc group, ch 3, dc in same sc, * 2 dc in next sc, ch 1, sk 4 dc, 6 dc in next ch-1 sp, dc in sp between next two 3-dc groups, 6 dc in next ch-1 sp, 2 dc in next sc. Rep from * around; join to top of ch-3. Break off.

6th rnd: Attach royal blue to first ch-3 of first 6-dc group made on last rnd, ch 3, work dc in each of next 5 dc, * 2 dc in next sp before single dc, 2 dc in sp after single dc, dc in each of next 6 dc, 3 dc in sp before next 4-dc group, 3 dc in sp after 4-dc group, dc in each of next 6 dc. Rep from * around; join to top of first ch-3. Break off.

FRONT INSERT: Attach pumpkin in sp between two 3-dc groups, ch 4, 5 dc in same sp (6-dc shell made). Break off. Work another 6-dc shell in sp between next two 3-dc groups. Break off. Attach yellow to 6th blue dc before first pumpkin 6-dc shell, * 2 dc in first pumpkin dc, 2 sc in each of next 4 dc, 2 dc in last dc, (sk 5 blue sts, sc in next dc) 3 times; work over next pumpkin shell as before, sk next 5 blue sts, sc in next dc. Break off. Front Insert completed.

7th rnd: Attach orchid to first yellow dc, ch 1, sc in next dc, sc in next 8 sc, sc in next 2 dc, 3 dc in next sc (shell made), sc over ch-5 lp, 4 dc in next sc (shell made), sc over next ch-5 lp, 3 dc in next sc (shell made), * sc in each st to within next two 3-dc groups, work 3 dc in sp between groups, rep from * 3 times, sc remaining sts; sl st in first ch-1. Break off.

8th rnd: Attach royal blue to sc between first and 2nd shells, ch 3, 2 dc in same sc, sk 1 dc, sc in each of next 2 dc, 3 dc in next sc, sk next dc, sc in each st around; join to top of ch-3. Break off.

MAJORCA HAT

This sun-shader is done in jewel tones. It has a high, round crown and a wide slit brim. The hat is worked in clusters and a shell-stitch variation.

SIZE: One size fits all.

MATERIALS: Synthetic straw yarn (100% viscose rayon), 6 (24-yd.) skeins each hot pink and emerald green, 4 skeins each gold, lime, and pale turquoise; aluminum crochet hook size H (or English/Canadian hook No. 8) *or the size that will give you the correct gauge;* tapestry needle.

GAUGE: 5 dc = 2".

Note: Use 2 strands of straw yarn throughout. Work loosely for best results, pulling up loops ½". When joining or breaking off straw, leave 4" end. Weave end halfway through crochet, then double it back so that it cannot pull out.

Crown of hat is made in one piece. The Brim is composed of Triangles and Fans, all made separately. These motifs are then crocheted together, leaving a split on one side, and then sewn to Crown.

CROWN: Starting at top with gold, ch 5 loosely; join with sl st to form ring.

1st rnd: Ch 3, work 11 dc in ring; join with sl st to top of ch-3 (12 dc, counting ch-3 as 1 dc).

2nd rnd: Ch 3, dc in same place as last sl st, 2 dc in each dc around; join to top of ch-3 (24 dc).

3rd rnd: Ch 3, dc in same place as last sl st, * dc in next dc, 2 dc in next dc. Rep from * around; join to top of ch-3 (36 dc). Break off.

4th rnd: Attach emerald green with sl st to a dc, sc in same place, * 2 sc in next dc, sc in next dc. Rep from * around; join to first sc (54 sc). Break off. Piece should measure 6" in diameter.

5th rnd: Join hot pink to a sc, ch 3, dc in next sc and in each sc around; join to top of ch-3.

6th rnd: Ch 3, dc in next dc and in each dc around; join to top of ch-3. Break off.

7th rnd: Attach lime to sp between any 2 dc, sc and 2 dc in same sp (first shell made), * sk 3 dc, work sc and 2 dc in next sp between dc (another shell made). Rep from * around (18 shells); join to first sc. Break off.

8th rnd: Attach turquoise to sp between any 2 shells, shell in same place, * work shell in next sp between shells. Rep from * around (18 shells); join to first sc. Break off.

9th rnd: With lime, rep 8th rnd.

10th rnd: Attach emerald green in sp between any 2 shells, ch 1, * ch 3, sc in next sp between shells. (Make sure you are working loosely enough to keep Crown from cupping in.) Rep from * around; join to ch-1. Break off.

11th rnd: Attach hot pink to a ch-3 lp, ch 3, 2 dc over same lp, work 3 dc over lp around; join to first ch-3. Break off.

12th rnd: With emerald green, attach in any sp between 3-dc group, ch 1, * ch 3, sc in sp between next 3-dc group. Rep from * around; join to ch-1. Break off. Crown is completed.

BRIM SHELL TRIANGLE: 1st row: With emerald green, ch 15 (place first marker in first ch st made), work 2 dc in 3rd ch from hook (place 2nd marker in ch-2 lp just formed), * sk next 2 ch, work shell in next ch. Rep from * twice more; sc in last ch (4 shells made). Ch 2, turn.

2nd row: Work 2 dc in last sc of previous row, work shell in sc of each of next 2 shells, sc in next sc. Ch 2, turn. Rep 2nd row once more.

4th row: Work 2 dc in last sc of previous row. Work shell in sc of next shell, sc in next sc. Ch 2, turn.

5th Row: Rep 4th row once more.

6th row: Work 2 dc in last sc of previous row, sc in next sc. Break off. Finished piece is triangular, with 2 straight edges and 1 scalloped edge.

Trim: Work loosely to keep work flat. Attach gold in ch st at first marker, work 3 sc over each ch-2 lp across base ch, 3 sc in lp at 2nd marker (five 3-sc groups), continue along scalloped side as follows: * 3 dc in next sc between points, sc in next ch-2 lp at tip of point. Rep from * twice more. Break off. One straight edge of Triangle is not trimmed.

Work 5 more Triangles in same manner.

FAN MOTIF: Starting at center base of Fan with lime, ch 5, join with sl st to form ring.

1st row: Ch 3, work 7 dc in half of ring; do not join. Break off.

2nd row: Attach turquoise to top of first ch-3, ch 3, dc in same st, 2 dc in each dc across (16 dc, counting ch-3 as 1 dc). Ch 3, turn.

3rd row: Sk first dc, dc in each dc across, ending with dc in top of turning ch (16 dc). Break off. Turn.

4th row: Attach lime to last dc made on 3rd row, ch 3, 2 dc in same dc, sk next 2 dc, 2 sc in each of next 3 dc, sk next dc, 3 dc in next dc, place marker in last dc made, 3 dc in next dc, sk next dc, 2 sc in each of next 3 dc, sk next 2 dc, 3 dc in top of turning ch (24 sts). Break off. Work 2 more Fans in same manner.

SINGLE-CROCHET TRIANGLE: 1st row: Starting at point with lime, ch 2, sc in 2nd ch from hook. Ch 1, turn.

2nd row: Work 2 sc in sc. Ch 1, turn.

3rd row: Work 2 sc in first sc, sc in next sc. Ch 1, turn.

4th row: Work 2 sc in first sc, sc in each sc across. Ch 1, turn. Rep 4th row 8 times more (12 sc). Break off. Work another Triangle in same manner.

JOINING BRIM TO CROWN: Following Diagram, Shell Triangles are lettered A through F, Fan Motifs G, H, and I, and the single crochet Triangles J and K. Crown is shown flat to make drawing easier to follow.

Joining Shell Triangles: Join Sections A through F to edge of Crown as shown in Diagram as follows: Working on A, over untrimmed edge, attach emerald green in first end-of-row sc, ch 1, sl st in any sc on Crown, 2 sc in same sp on A, 2 sc over next ch-2 on A, (sl st in next sc on Crown, 2 sc in next sc on A, 2 sc over next ch-2 on A) twice; sl st in next sc on Crown. Continue joining Triangles B through F in same manner. Sl st in beg ch-1. Break off.

Joining Fans and Sc Triangles: Pin Fan Motif G in place. Attach hot pink at 1. Working through both layers of G and A, sc evenly across to 2 as far as marker on Fan (row of sc will form a ridge), ch 4, sc in edge of Crown between A and B Sections, ch 4, starting at marker at 3, sc evenly to 4, joining G and B. Pin remaining Fans in place, then join them as before. Pin and join Triangles in same manner.

When hat is assembled, work a row of sc in emerald green evenly along edge of Brim from 1 around to 5, leaving split in Brim free.

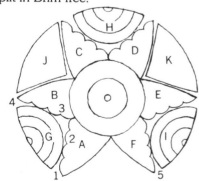

Winter Hats

TWINING VINE CAP

Medallion motifs are used here with a ball-fringe addition. Knitting worsted is worked double in single and double crochet and chain loop stitches.

SIZES: One size fits all.

MATERIALS: Knitting worsted, 1 oz. each moss green, bright pink, lavender, and taupe; aluminum crochet hook size K (or English/Canadian hook No. 4) *or the size that will give you the correct gauge.*

GAUGE: 5 dc = 2".

Note: Use 2 strands of knitting worsted throughout. Work loosely for best results, pulling up first lp of each dc ½", except where longer lps are directed.

CROWN: Starting at top, with 2 strands of moss green, ch 5. Join with sl st to form ring.

1st rnd (right side): Ch 3, work 11 dc in ring; join with sl st to top of first ch-3 (12 dc, counting ch-3 as 1 dc). Break off.

2nd rnd: With bright pink, make lp on hook and working in back lps only, work 2 sc in each dc around; join (24 sc). Break off.

3rd rnd: With moss green and working through both lps, work 1 sc in each sc around; join. Break off.

4th rnd: With lavender, work 2 sc in each sc around; join (48 sc). Break off. Piece now measures 4½" in diameter.

5th rnd: Attach taupe, ch 3; working in back lps only, work dc in each sc around; join (48 dc). Break off.

6th rnd: Attach moss green, ch 3; working in back lps only, work dc in each dc around; join. Break off. Put piece aside.

MEDALLIONS: Starting at center, with moss green, ch 5. Join with sl st to form ring. Ch 3, work 11 dc in ring; join with sl st (12 dc). Break off. Right side is facing you.

Work 5 more Medallions in same manner. Join Medallions as follows, always having right sides facing you: With lavender make lp on hook, work 2 sc in any dc on 1 Medallion, 2 sc in each of next 5 dc (12 sc). * Work 2 sc in any sc on another Medallion, 2 sc in each of next 5 dc on same Medallion. Rep from * until all 6 Medallions are joined. Break off.

With bright pink, make lp on hook, work 2 sc in each of next 6 dc on last Medallion, sl st in joining between Medallions. Work 2 sc in each dc across each of next 5 Medallions and sl st in each joining; join strip into circle with sl st in first lavender sc. Break off.

Next rnd: On pink side of Medallions and counting from any joining, sk 6 sc, make lp on hook with taupe, and sc in sp before next sc (center), * ch 4, sk next 6 sc, y o hook, insert hook in sl st of joining between Medallions, draw up 1" lp, (y o, draw through 2 lps) twice—long dc made; ch 4, sc in center sp on next Medallion. Rep from * around, ending with ch 4, long dc in next joining, ch 4, sk 6 sc, sl st in first sc. Do not break off.

Following rnd: Sl st in next ch-4 lp, ch 3, work 3 dc

over same lp, work 4 dc over each lp around, ending with sl st in top of first ch-3. Break off.

Next rnd: Attach lavender to any taupe dc of last rnd, ch 1, sc in same sp, sc in each sc around; join with sl st. Break off. This is lower edge of cap.

Working around lavender edge of Medallions and using moss green, rep the 2 rnds worked with taupe, but do not break off.

Next rnd: Ch 3, dc in each dc around; join (48 dc). Break off. Mark last dc worked.

To Join Pieces: Hold Crown with right side facing you. Make lp on hook with bright pink, then sc in any dc on last rnd of Crown, sc in each of next 3 dc; then pick up the other piece at marked moss green edge. Hold this edge behind Crown (wrong sides together), insert hook toward you in marked dc from right side of Medallions and work a sl st; * work 1 sc in each of next 4 moss green dc of Crown, sk 3 moss green dc following last sl st on Medallion piece, insert hook as before in next dc of Medallion piece and work sl st. Rep from * around. Break off. With

Crown facing you, on last rnd mark 1 bright pink sc directly below any long dc on Medallion piece.

VINES: With lavender, make lp on hook and, working in back lps of pink joining rnd, work 1 sc in marked st, * ch 12, sl st in 4th ch from hook to form ring, work 5 sc in ring, ch 8, sc in next pink sc, 1 sc in each of next 7 pink sc. Rep from * around. Join. Break off.

On 4th rnd of Crown, mark 1 lavender sc approximately above center between any 2 lavender vines. Make lp on hook with bright pink and, working in front lps only, work 1 sc in marked st, * ch 12, sl st in 4th ch from hook to form ring, work 5 sc in ring, ch 8, sc in next lavender sc, sc in each of next 7 sc. Rep from * around. Join. Break off.

Make lp on hook with lavender and work 1 sc in a green sc on first rnd of Crown, * ch 12, sl st in 4th ch from hook to form ring, work 5 sc in ring, ch 8, sc in each of next 2 moss green sc. Rep from * around. Last rep will have only 1 sc. Join. Break off.

HELMET OR CAP

Designed with a curved edge to cover the ears, this head-warmer can be made into a simple cap by leaving off the earflaps. Knitting worsted is worked doubled in single and double crochet and cluster variations.

SIZES: One size fits all.

MATERIALS: Knitting worsted, 1 oz. each pale antique gold, yellow, rust, red brown, and chocolate brown; aluminum crochet hook size J (or English/Canadian hook No. 6) *or the size that will give you the correct gauge.*

GAUGE: 3 dc = 1″; 2 dc rows = 1½″.

Note: Use 2 strands of knitting worsted throughout. On some rnds 2 different colors are held together. Work loosely for best results, pulling up first lp ½″ of each dc.

CAP: Starting at top of crown, with 1 strand each of gold and yellow, ch 5. Join with sl st to form ring.

1st rnd: Ch 3, work 11 dc in ring, join with sl st to top of first ch-3.

2nd rnd: Ch 3, work dc in same place as sl st, work 2 dc in each dc around. Join with sl st to top of first ch-3 (24 dc, counting turning ch as 1 dc).

3rd rnd: Ch 3, dc in same place as sl st, * dc in next dc, 2 dc in next dc. Rep from * around, ending with dc in last dc. Join with sl st to top of first ch-3 (36 dc). Break off. Piece should measure 4½″ in diameter.

4th rnd: Attach chocolate brown and red brown to last sl st, ch 3, dc in each dc around. Join with sl st to top of first ch-3 (36 dc).

5th rnd: Ch 3, 3 dc in same place as sl st, * ch 1, sk 3 dc, 4 dc in next dc (shell made). Rep from * around,

Cap

Helmet

ending with ch 1, sl st to top of first ch-3 (9 shells made). Break off.

6th rnd: Attach gold and yellow to sl st. * Sc in each of next 4 dc, working over ch-1 of last rnd and into dc's of 4th rnd, work as follows: (y o, insert hook in back lp of next dc, draw up a lp ½″, y o, draw through 2 lps) 3 times; y o, draw through all 4 lps on hook (3-joined long dc made), work sc in each of next 4 dc of last rnd. Rep from * around, ending with 3-joined long dc in back lps of dc's of 4th rnd. Sl st in first sc. Break off.

7th rnd: Attach 2 strands rust to last sl st. Ch 3, dc in each st around, sl st to top of first ch-3 (45 dc).

8th rnd: Attach gold and yellow to sl st. Sc in each sc around. Join. Break off (45 sc). Attach red brown and chocolate brown.

9th and 10th rnds: Ch 3, dc in each sc around. Join.

11th rnd: Sc in each dc around. Join. Break off (45 sc).

12th rnd: Attach 2 strands of rust. Sc in each sc around. Join. Break off (45 sc). For cap variation only work 3 more rows of sc.

EARFLAPS: 1st row: Attach yellow and gold in any sc. Ch 3, 2 dc in same place (first shell made), 3 dc in next sc. Break off both colors.

2nd row: Attach red brown and chocolate brown in 4th sc to right of first shell, sl st in same sc, sl st in next sc, sk next sc, 2 dc in next sc, 2 dc in each dc of shell and in next sc (16 dc), sk next sc, sl st in each of next 2 sc. Turn.

3rd row: Sk first sl st, sc in next sl st and in each dc, sc in next sl st. Break off.

Sk 16 sc, attach yellow and gold to next sc, then complete as for first Earflap.

Last rnd: Attach 2 strands of rust. Ch 3, dc in each st around. Join. Break off.

OPENWORKED CAP

Ringed with medallions, this cap is worked into a strip and the crown is added last. Single and double crochet stitches are done in doubled knitting worsted.

SIZES: One size fits all.

MATERIALS: Knitting worsted, 1 oz. each bright coral, hot pink, bright yellow, and gray-blue heather; aluminum

crochet hook Size J (or English/Canadian hook No. 6) *or the size that will give you the correct gauge.*

GAUGE: 3 dc = 1″; 2 dc rows = 1½″.

Note: Use 2 strands of knitting worsted throughout. Work loosely for best results, pulling up first lp of each dc ½″, except where longer lps are directed.

CROWN: Starting at top, with 2 strands of bright coral, ch 5. Join with sl st to form ring.

1st rnd (right side): Ch 3, work 11 dc in ring, join with sl st to top of first ch-3 (12 dc, counting ch-3 as 1 dc). Break off.

2nd rnd: Attach hot pink to last sl st; ch 1, work 2 sc in same place, work 2 sc in each dc around; join with sl st (24 sc). Break off.

3rd rnd: Attach bright yellow to last sl st; ch 1, work 1 sc in back lp of each sc around. Join. Break off.

4th rnd: Attach heather to any sc. Working in back lps only, ch 3, dc in same sp, * dc in next sc, 2 dc in next sc. Rep from * around, ending with dc in last sc. Join with sl st (36 dc). Break off. Piece now measures 5″ in diameter. Put piece aside.

MEDALLION: Starting at center, with heather, ch 5; join with sl st to form ring. Ch 3, work 11 dc in ring; join with sl st (12 dc). Break off. Right side of work is facing you.

Work 5 more Medallions in same manner. Join Medallions as follows, always having right side facing you: With bright coral, make lp on hook, work 2 sc in any dc on 1 Medallion, 2 sc in each of next 5 dc (12 sc). * Work 2 sc in any dc on another Medallion, 2 sc in each of next 5 dc on same Medallion. Rep from * until all 6 Medallions are joined. Break off.

With bright yellow, make lp on hook, work 2 sc in each of next 6 dc on same Medallion, sl st in joining between Medallions. Work 2 sc in each dc across each of next 5 Medallions and sl st in each joining; join strip into circle with sl st in first bright coral sc. Break off.

Next rnd: On bright coral side of Medallions and counting from any joining, sk 6 sc, make lp on hook with hot pink, and sc in sp before next sc (center), * ch 4, sk next 6 sc, y o hook, insert hook in sl st of joining between Medallions, draw up 1″ lp, (y o, draw through 2 lps) twice—long dc made; ch 4, sc in center sp on next Medallion. Rep from * around, ending with ch 4, long dc in next joining, ch 4, sk 6 sc, sl st in first sc. Do not break off.

Following rnd: Sl st in next ch-4 lp, ch 3, work 3 dc over same lp (mark last dc worked), work 4 dc over each lp around, ending with sl st in top of first ch-3. Break off.

Working around yellow edge of Medallions and using heather, rep last 2 rnds. Break off.

Next rnd: Attach bright coral to any heather dc of last rnd, ch 1, sc in same sp, sc in each sc around; join with sl st. Break off. This is lower edge of cap.

To Join Pieces: Hold Crown with right side facing you and attach heather to any dc on last rnd of Crown, ch 3, dc in each of next 2 dc, ch 1; then pick up other piece at marker. Hold hot pink edge behind Crown (wrong sides together), * insert hook toward you in sp before next dc from right side of Medallion at marker, then work a sl st; ch 1, work 1 dc in each of next 3 blue dc of Crown, ch 1, sk next 4 hot pink dc. Rep from * around, ending with sl st in sp before next dc, ch 1, sl st in top of first ch-3. Break off.

PETAL CLOCHE

The illusion of a ribboned band is set off by a three-layered brim. Knitting worsted doubled is worked in double crochet and shell stitches.

SIZES: One size fits all.

MATERIALS: Knitting worsted, 2 oz. navy, 1 oz. each wine, pale blue, and natural; aluminum crochet hook size K (or English/Canadian hook No. 4) *or the size that will give you the correct gauge.*

GAUGE: 5 dc = 2″.

Note: Use 2 strands of knitting worsted throughout. Work loosely for best results, pulling up first lp of each dc ½″.

Starting at center of crown, with 2 strands of navy, ch 5; join with sl st to form ring.

1st rnd: Ch 3, work 11 dc in ring, join with sl st to top of first ch-3 (12 dc, counting ch-3 as 1 dc).

Work in back lps only for next 3 rnds.

2nd rnd: Work 2 sc in each sc around. Join (24 sc).

3rd rnd: Ch 3, dc in same sp, * dc in next sc, 2 dc in next sc. Rep from * around, ending with dc in last sc. Join (36 dc).

4th rnd: Ch 3, dc in each dc around. Join (36 dc). Work in both lps for next 5 rnds.

5th rnd: Ch 3, dc in same sp, dc in each of next 2 dc, * 2 dc in next dc, dc in each of next 2 dc. Rep from * around. Join.

6th rnd: Ch 3, dc in each dc around. Join (48 dc).

7th rnd: Rep 6th rnd. Break off. Piece should measure 5½″ from beg.

8th rnd: With natural, make lp on hook, work sc in

each dc around. Join (48 sc). Break off.

9th rnd: Attach wine with sl st to any sc, ch 3, work 3 dc in same sp, * sk 3 sc, work 4 dc in next sc. Rep from * around, ending with sl st in top of first ch-3. Break off.

10th rnd: Work in back lps only. With natural, make lp on hook, sc in last sl st made, sc in each of next 3 wine dc, work as follows over sts of 8th rnd: * (y o, insert hook in back lp of next natural sc on 8th rnd, y o and draw through lp, y o and draw through 2 lps, leaving remaining lps on hook) 3 times; y o and draw through all 4 lps on hook—3-joined-dc made, work sc in each of next 4 wine dc of 9th rnd. Rep from * around, ending with 3-joined-dc. Join with sl st to first sc. Break off.

11th rnd: With navy, make lp on hook, work sc in same sc as last sl st, sc in each of next 3 sc, * sc in top of 3-joined-dc, sc in each of next 4 sc. Rep from * around, ending with sc in top of joined dc. Join (60 sc). Break off.

For scalloped brim work as follows:

12th rnd: Push navy rnd toward you. With wine make lp on hook, work sc in the top of joined dc, ch 4, * sc in next joined dc, ch 4. Rep from * around. Join with sl st in

first sc. Do not break off.

13th rnd: Over each ch lp work 1 sc, 1 hdc, 2 dc, 2 tr, 2 dc, 1 hdc, and 1 sc. Join (12 petals made). Break off.

14th rnd: Push petal rnd toward you. With pale blue, make lp on hook, work sc in sp between sc's of any 2 petals, * ch 5, sk petal, sc between next 2 sc. Rep from * around, ending with ch 5, sl st in first sc. Join. Do not break off.

15th rnd: With pale blue, rep 13th rnd.

16th rnd: With wine, make lp on hook, sk first sc of any petal, sc in hdc and in each of next 7 sts of same petal, * sk last sc of same petal and first sc of next petal, sc in each of next 8 sts. Rep from * around, ending by skipping last 2 sc, sl st in first sc. Break off.

17th rnd: Push last petal rnd toward you. With natural make lp on hook, work as for 14th rnd, but work ch 6 lps instead of ch 5.

18th rnd: With natural, over each lp work 1 sc, 1 hdc, 2 dc, 1 tr, 1 dtr (y o hook 3 times for dtr), 1 tr, 2 dc, 1 hdc and 1 sc. Join. Break off.

19th rnd: With navy, work 1 sc in each st around. Join. Break off.

SCALLOP-EDGED CAP

Two colors of knitting worsted are combined for a tweedy effect. Single and double crochet stitches are used in this pretty cap.

SIZES: One size fits all.

MATERIALS: Knitting worsted, 1 oz. each apple green, flaming pink, and rust; aluminum crochet hook size J (or English/Canadian hook No. 6) *or the size that will give you the correct gauge.*

GAUGE: 3 dc = 1"; 2 dc rows = 1½".

Note: Use 2 strands of knitting worsted throughout. On some rounds 2 different colors are held together. Work loosely for best results, pulling up first lp ½" of each dc.

Starting at top of crown with 1 strand each of green and rust, ch 5. Join with sl st to form ring.

1st rnd: Ch 3, work 11 dc in ring. Join with sl st to top of first ch-3.

2nd rnd: Ch 3, work dc in same place as sl st, work 2 dc in each dc around. Join with sl st to top of first ch-3 (24 dc, counting turning ch as 1 dc).

3rd rnd: Ch 3, dc in same place as sl st, * dc in next

dc, 2 dc in next dc. Rep from * around, ending with dc in last dc. Join with sl st to top of first ch-3 (36 dc). Break off green only. Piece should measure 4½" in diameter.

4th rnd: Attach pink to last sl st, with rust and pink ch 3, dc in each dc around. Join (36 dc).

5th rnd: Ch 3, 2 dc in next dc, 3 dc in next dc, sk next dc, * sc in each of next 2 dc, sk next dc, 3 dc in each of next 2 dc, sk next dc. Rep from * around, ending with sc in each of next 2 dc, sk next dc, sl st in top of ch-3. Break off both colors.

6th rnd: Attach 2 strands of green in first of last 2 sc; ch 3, working in back lp only, dc in same sc, 2 dc in next sc, * ch 1, sk 2 dc, sc in back lp of each of next 2 dc, ch 1, sk 2 dc, 2 dc in each of next 2 sc. Rep from * around, ending with ch 1, sk 2 dc, 2 sc in each of next 2 dc, ch 1, sk 2 dc, sl st in top of ch-3. Break off green.

7th rnd: Attach 2 strands of rust to last sl st. Ch 3, dc in each of next 3 dc, dc in ch-1 sp, * dc in each of next 2 sc, dc in ch-1 sp, dc in each of next 4 dc, dc in ch-1 sp. Rep from * around, ending with dc in each of next 2 sc, dc in ch-1 sp (48 dc). Join with sl st. Break off 1 strand rust. Attach green.

8th and 9th rnds: With green and rust, ch 3, dc in each dc around. Join.

10th rnd: Sc in each dc around. Join. Break off green only (48 sc). Attach pink.

11th and 12th rnds: With rust and pink, sc in each sc around. Join.

13th rnd: Ch 3, dc in each sc around. Join.

14th rnd: Sc in each dc around. Break off both colors.

15th rnd: Attach 2 strands of green with a sl st, sl st in next sc, * 3 sc in next sc, sl st in each of next 2 sc. Rep from * around, ending with 3 sc in last sc, sl st in first sl st. Break off.

CLOCHE WITH MATCHING CLUTCH

There is a nice, thick, cushiony edge on this hat, and the flat clutch, which has a big fat zipper closing, is a generous 9″ x 14″. The clutch is mostly double-crocheted with shells in doubled needlepoint and crewel yarn.

CLOCHE

SIZES: One size fits all.

MATERIALS: Needlepoint and crewel wool, 160 yds. black (color A), 120 yds. pink (B), 80 yds. heather (C), 40 yds. each peach (D), light orange (E), lime (F), and bright orange (G); aluminum crochet hook size H (or English/Canadian hook No. 8) *or the size that will give you the correct gauge.*

GAUGE: 4 sc = 1″.

Note: Yarn comes in 3-strand lengths. Use yarn double (6 strands) throughout.

Starting at top of crown with B, ch 6. Join with sl st to form ring.

1st rnd (right side): Ch 3, work 11 dc in ring (12 dc, counting ch-3 as 1 dc); join with sl st to top of ch-3; ch 1, turn.

2nd rnd (wrong side): Ch 1, working in back lps only, work 2 sc in sl st and 2 sc in each sc around (24 sc); join with sl st in first sc, ch 1, turn.

3rd rnd: Working in back lps only, work sc in sl st and in each sc around (24 sc); join; ch 1, turn.

4th rnd: Working back lps only, work sc in sl st, * 2 sc in next sc, sc in next sc, rep from * around, ending 2 sc in last sc (36 sc); join. Break off B; attach D.

5th rnd: With wrong side of work facing you, ch 4, sc in 2nd ch from hook, hdc in next ch, dc in next ch (triangle made), sk 3 sc, * sl st in next sc, work triangle, sk 3 sc. Rep from * 7 times more (9 triangles); join to base of ch-4. Break off D; attach C with sl st in last sl st worked between triangles. Turn.

6th rnd: Ch 3, work 3 dc in sl st, * sc in top of next triangle, 4 dc in next sl st between triangles. Rep from * 7 times more; sc in top of next triangle; join. Break off C; attach D. Turn.

7th rnd: With wrong side of work facing you, ch 1, sc in each st around, increasing 1 sc every 5th st (54 sc); join. Break off D; attach F. Turn. Cup-shaped piece should measure about 6½" in diameter.

8th rnd: With right side facing you, ch 3, work dc in each st around, increasing 1 dc every 6th st (63 dc); join. Break off F; attach A.

9th rnd: With wrong side facing you, ch 3, working in front lps only, work dc in each st around, increasing 1 dc every 7th st (72 dc); join. Break off A; attach B. Turn.

10th rnd: With right side facing you, ch 1, working in back lps only, work sc in each st around; join. Break off B; attach E. Turn.

11th rnd: With wrong side facing you, work triangle, * sk 3 sc, sl st in next sc, work triangle. Rep from * 16 times more; sk 3 sc; join (18 triangles). Break off E; attach C to last sl st worked. Turn.

12th rnd: With right side facing you, ch 3, work 2 dc in sl st, * sc in top of next triangle, 3 dc in next sl st between triangles. Rep from * 16 times more; sc in top of next triangle; join. Break off C; attach E. Turn.

13th through 20th rnds: With wrong side facing you, ch 1, work sc in each st around (72 sc); join. Break off E; attach F. Turn. With F, work 1 rnd sc in front lps with right side facing you. With A, work 1 rnd in front lps with wrong side facing you. With B, work 1 rnd sc in back lps with right side facing you. With B, work 1 rnd sc in front lps with wrong side facing you. Rep 11th rnd with G, 12th rnd with C, and 13th rnd with G. Break off G; attach A.

21st rnd: With right side facing you, ch 1, working in back lps, work sc around, increasing 1 sc every 12th st (78 sc); join. Turn.

22nd rnd: Ch 1, working in back lps, sc around, increasing 1 sc every 12th and 13th st (90 sc); join. Turn.

23rd through 28th rnds: Ch 1, working in back lps, sc evenly around; join and turn. Rep 23rd rnd 5 times more. Break off.

CLUTCH

SIZE: About 8½" x 13½".

MATERIALS: Needlepoint and crewel wool, 180 yds. black (color A), 140 yds. pink (B), 100 yds. heather (C), 60 yds. each peach (D), light orange (E), lime (F), and bright orange (G); aluminum crochet hook size H (or English/Canadian hook No. 8) *or the size that will give you the correct gauge;* ⅝ yard felt; heavy cardboard, two 8½" x 13½" pieces, two 1" x 8½" pieces, and one 1½" x 13½" piece; 12" jumbo plastic zipper.

GAUGE: 4 sc = 1"; 7 dc = 1".

Note: Front, Back, and Sides are made in 1 piece without seams. Bottom is made separately and sewn in place.

Yarn comes in 3-strand lengths. Use yarn double (6 strands) throughout.

BAG FRONT, BACK, AND SIDES: Starting at top edge with B, ch 104. Join with sl st to form ring.

1st rnd (wrong side): Sc in same place as sl st and in each ch around (104 sc); join with sl st in first sc. Ch 1, turn.

2nd rnd (right side): Sc in sl st, working in front lps only, work sc in each sc around; join. Break off B; attach D. Turn.

3rd rnd: With wrong side facing you, ch 4, sc in 2nd ch from hook, hdc in next ch, dc in next ch (triangle made), sk 3 sc, * sl st in next sc, work triangle, sk 3 sc. Rep from * 24 times more (26 triangles); join to base of ch-4. Break off D; attach C with sl st to last sl st worked. Turn.

4th rnd: With right side facing you, ch 3, work 2 dc in same sl st, * sc in top of next triangle, 3 dc in next sl st between triangles. Rep from * 24 times more; sc in top of next triangle; join. Break off C; attach D.

5th rnd: With wrong side facing you, ch 1, sc in each st around (104 sc); join. Break off D; attach F.

6th rnd: With right side facing you, ch 3, working in front lps, dc in each sc around; join. Break off F; attach A.

7th rnd: With wrong side facing you, ch 3, working in front lps, dc in each dc around; join. Break off A; attach B.

8th through 11th rnds: With right side facing you, ch 1, working in back lps only, sc in each dc around; join. Break off B; attach E. With E rep 3rd rnd. With C rep 4th rnd. With E rep 5th rnd. Break off E; attach F.

12th rnd: With right side facing you, working in front lps, sc in each st around; join. Break off F; attach A.

13th rnd: With wrong side facing you, ch 1, working in front lps, sc in each st around; join. Break off A; attach B.

14th rnd: With right side facing you, ch 3, working in back lps, dc in each st around; join. Ch 1, turn.

15th rnd: Working in back lps, sc in each st around; join. Ch 1, turn.

16th through 19th rnds: Rep last rnd. Break off B; attach G. With G rep 3rd rnd. With C rep 4th rnd. With G rep 5th rnd. Break off G; attach A.

20th rnd: With right side facing you, ch 1, working in back lps, sc in each st around; join. Ch 3, turn.

21st through 24th rnds: Working in back lps, dc in each sc around; join and turn. Rep 20th and 21st rnds once more, then 20th rnd again. Break off A.

BAG BOTTOM: With A, ch 48.

1st rnd: Sc in 3rd ch from hook and in each of next 45 ch, ch 2, working along opposite edge of ch, sc in each of next 46 ch.

2nd rnd: Ch 1, turn; * working back lps, sc in each of next 46 sc, in ch-2 sp work 6 dc. Rep from * once more; join with sl st in turning ch-1. Break off.

With right sides facing you, sc Bottom of bag to last rnd of Front, Back and Sides, working top lps only.

LINING: For Front and Back cut 2 pieces felt 14½" x 18"; for sides, cut 2 pieces 3" x 9½"; for Bottom cut 1 piece 4" x 14½". Fold felt pieces in half over matching cardboard pieces and pin all open sides. Stitch around pinned sides as close to cardboard as possible, forming sealed envelopes. Whipstitch sections together to form bag, keeping all seams to outside and folded edge of front and back at top.

Slip completed lining in crocheted bag and whipstitch together around top edge. Sew zipper in place about ½" from top edge.

Bags

PINWHEEL PILLOW BAG

Ebullient colors and textures spin around in this circular shoulder bag. You start at the center and keep going round and round, adding popcorn and spiral stitches here and there. A zipper closing may be added if you wish.

SIZE: Approximately 14″ in diameter.

MATERIALS: Heavyweight yarn such as Aunt Lydia's rug yarn, 4 (70-yd.) skeins cork or flax (color A), 1 skein each forest green (B), light orchid or pink (C), dark red or brick (D), light blue (E), medium blue (F), old rose or orchid (G), navy (H) and turquoise (I); aluminum crochet hook size H (or English/Canadian hook No. 8) *or the size that will give you the correct gauge.*

GAUGE: 7 sc = 2″; 3 rnds = 1″.

FLAP: Starting at center with A, ch 5. Join with sl st to form ring.

1st rnd (wrong side): Ch 3, work 11 dc in ring (12 dc, counting ch-3 as 1 dc); join with sl st to ch-3.

2nd rnd: Work in back lps only. Work 2 sc in same place as sl st, work 2 sc in each st around (24 sc); join with sl st to first sc.

3rd rnd: Work in back lps only. Sc in sl st, * sk next sc, in next sc work 2 dc, 1 tr and 2 dc, sk next sc, sc in next sc. Rep from * 4 times more; sk next sc, in next sc work 2 dc, 1 tr and 2 dc; join. Piece should measure approximately 4″ in diameter. Break off A. Turn. Attach E to any tr.

4th rnd (right side): Work in back lps. Ch 3, work 2 dc, ch 1 and 2 dc in same sp as sl st (first corner made), * sc in each of next 5 sts, work 2 dc, ch 1 and 2 dc in next tr (another corner made). Rep from * 4 times more; sc in each of next 5 sts; join (6 corners made); ch 1.

5th rnd: Work in back lps. Sc in each of next 2 sts, * work corner in next ch-1 sp, sc in each of next 9 sts. Rep from * 4 times more; work corner in next ch-1 sp, sc in each of next 7 sts; join with sl st in first sc. Break off E. Attach D to sc before any corner.

6th rnd: Ch 2; in 2nd ch from hook, work 5 sc, drop lp from hook, insert hook in first sc of 5-sc and in dropped lp, y o and draw through both lps on hook (popcorn made), sc in same place as sl st, * ch 7, work popcorn in 2nd ch from hook, sc in next sc after corner, ch 7, work popcorn, sc in first sc before next corner. Rep from * 4 times more; ch 7, work popcorn, sc in sc after corner; ch 5, sl st in first sc. Break off E. Attach F to ch-1 sp on any corner of 5th rnd.

7th rnd: Ch 3; working over ch separating popcorns, work first corner in same ch-1 sp, * working in back lps, sc in each of next 2 E dc, sk popcorn and push it forward, sk popcorn-sc, sc in each of next 7 E sts, sk popcorn and its sc and push them forward, sc in each of next 2 E sts, work corner in next ch-1 sp. Rep from * 5 times more, omitting corner on last rep; join. Break off E. Turn. Attach H to any corner ch-1 sp.

8th rnd (wrong side): Work in front lps only. * In ch-1 sp work sc, ch 2 and sc (sc-corner made), sc in each of next 6 sts, hdc in next st, dc in each of next 2 sts, 3 tr in each of next 2 sts, dc in each of next 2 sts, hdc in next st, sc in next st. Rep from * 5 times more, join. Break off H. Turn. Attach C to any ch-2 sp.

9th rnd (right side): Work in front lps only. * Work sc-corner in ch-2 sp, sc in each of next 6 sts, work sc-

corner in next st, sc in each of next 4 sts, sk next 2 sts, work 4 dc in next st, remove hook from lp, insert hook in first dc of 4-dc and in dropped lp, y o and draw through both lps on hook (popcorn made). Sk next 2 sts, sc in each of next 4 sts. Rep from * 5 times more; join. Break off C. Turn. Attach A to first ch-2 sp on last rnd.

10th rnd (wrong side): Work in back lps only. * Work sc-corner in ch-2 sp, sc in each of next 2 sts, (y o hook, insert in next st, y o and draw through, y o and draw through 2 lps on hook) 3 times (4 lps remain on hook); sk popcorn and push it to front of piece. Rep directions in ( ) 3 times (3 more lps on hook), y o and draw through all lps on hook, ch 1 (fan made), sc in each of next 2 sts, work sc-corner in next ch-2 sp, sc in each of next 8 sts.

Rep from * 5 times more; join. Break off A. Turn. Attach I to first ch-2 made on last rnd.

11th rnd (right side): Work in back lps only. In ch-2 sp work ch 3 and 3 dc, finish as for popcorn (first popcorn made), * sc in each of next 10 sts, work sc-corner in next ch-2 sp, sc in each of next 3 sts, popcorn in next st (center of fan), sc in each of next 3 sts, work popcorn in next ch-2 sp. Rep from * 5 times more, omitting final popcorn in last rep. Break off I. Attach B to first popcorn made on last rnd.

12th rnd: Work in back lps only. Ch 3 and with B, work 7 dc in popcorn (8-dc shell made, counting ch-3 as 1 dc), * sk next st, 8 dc in next st (shell made), sc in each of next 4 sts, (sk next st, shell in next st) twice; sk next st, work sc-corner in next ch-2 sp, sc in each of next 4 sts, sk popcorn, sc in each of next 2 sts, sk next st, shell in next popcorn. Rep from * 5 times more, omitting final shell in last rep; join. Break off B. Attach G to any sc-corner ch-2 sp.

13th rnd: * Work sc-corner in ch-2 sp, (y o hook, draw up lp in next st, y o and draw through 2 lps on hook) 5 times; y o and draw through all 6 lps on hook, ch 1 (cl made); ch 6 and starting in 2nd ch from hook, work 4 dc in each of next 5 ch, sc in cl (rose center completed), (ch 4, in 4th ch from hook work 3 dc and 1 sc) 4 times (4 petals made); wrap petals around rose counterclockwise, sc in end sc of center (petals completed), 2 sc in each of next 2 sts, * * work 2 sc in each of next 2 skipped I sts on 11th rnd * *; 2 sc in next st, sc in next st, work rose and petals (second rose and petals made), sc in each of next 2 sts. Rep from * * to * * once more; sc in next st. Rep from * 5 times more; join. Break off G. Attach C to any corner ch-2 sp.

14th rnd: * Work corner in ch-2 sp, sc in next st, ch 6, starting in 2nd ch from hook, work 4 dc in each of next 5 ch sts, sc in last ch st (bud made), sc in next (cl) st, push rose to front, sc in each of next 4 sts, work bud, sc in each of next 6 sts, push rose to front, sc in each of next 9 sts. Rep from * 5 times more. Break off C.

BAG FRONT: Starting at center with A, ch 5. Join with sl st to form ring.

1st rnd (right side): Ch 3, work 11 dc in ring (12 dc, counting ch-3 as 1 dc); join with sl st in top of ch-3.

Note: For the next 4 rnds work in back lps only.

2nd rnd: Work 2 sc in each st around (24 sc); join with sl st in first sc.

3rd rnd: Sc in sl st and in each st around (24 sc); join.

4th and 5th rnds: Rep 2nd and 3rd rnds (48 sc); join. Break off A. Turn. Attach E to any st.

6th rnd (wrong side): With E, work in front lps only. * Sc in each of next 5 sc, 2 sc in next sc (inc made). Rep from * around (56 sc); join.

Note: Work with wrong side facing you and in back lps only for all remaining rnds of front.

7th through 17th rnds: Work 1 rnd sc, working inc over 2nd st of each inc on last rnd (64 sc); join. Rep 7th rnd 3 times more (88 sc). Break off E, attach F to any st, and rep 7th rnd 3 times (112 sc). Break off F. Attach A to any st and repeat 7th rnd 4 times (144 sc). Break off A. Turn. Attach A to 8th sc between any two inc points.

SIDE: 1st row (right side): Working in back lps only, sc in same place as sl st, sc in each st to next inc, draw up lp in each of next 2 sc, y o and draw through 2 lps on hook (dec made), sc in each st around, working dec at each of next 5 inc points, sc to within 8th st of next inc point (leave remaining sts unworked for top of bag); ch 1, turn.

2nd row: Working in back lps only, work sc in each st around, working dec over each dec on last row; ch 1, turn.

3rd row: Rep 2nd row. Break off A.

Make bag Back and Side in same manner.

To Join: With right sides of Back and Front facing, using A, sc sides together. Break off.

With A, work corner in any ch-2 sp on flap, sc in each st to next corner, work corner in ch-2 sp. Break off. With right sides facing, center this edge along top edge of Bag back and sc the 2 pieces together along top edge. Break off.

STRAP: With right side facing you, attach D to right end of bag back at point where Flap joins Back, sc in same place. Working toward bag side, sc in next st, (draw up lp in each of next 2 sts, y o and draw through all 3 lps on hook) 8 times, working across top edge of bag side and onto top edge of bag front to next dec point; for Strap (ch 3, dc in 3rd ch from hook for cl) 25 times; then work along top edge of left side of bag to correspond to right side. Rep directions in parentheses 25 times for another Strap. Work sc in each D st along bag Side to beg of first Strap, ch 2, hdc in 2nd ch from hook, sk first cl on Strap, * (sc in first ch of next cl, ch 2, hdc in 2nd ch from hook) * 24 times; sc in each D st along other side of bag, ch 2, hdc in 2nd ch from hook, sk first cl of 2nd Strap; rep from * to * 24 times; join. Break off.

DIMINUTIVE PURSE

This evening bag is a charming reminder of the reticules great grandmother carried, and it's perfect for today's fashions. You start with a circle and single crochet a little pouch, incorporating a border of dimensional yellow rosebuds as you go.

SIZE: Measures 7½″ in width at widest point; 7″ in height.

MATERIALS: Thin-weight cotton such as Coats &

Clark's Metallic Knit-Cro-Sheen, 2 (100-yd.) balls each gold (color A), ecru (B), canary yellow (C), chartreuse green (D); aluminum crochet hook size F (or English/Canadian hook No. 10) *or the size that will give you the correct gauge.*

GAUGE: 9 sc = 2″; 5 rows = 1″.

Note: Work with double yarn throughout.

UPPER CIRCULAR SECTION (top of bag): Starting at center with 2 strands of A, ch 5. Join with sl st to form ring.

Note: In this pattern, turning ch-2 counts as sc and is counted as first sc of the new row or rnd.

1st rnd: Ch 2, work 11 sc in ring (12 sc, counting ch-2 as 1 sc); join with sl st in top of ch-2.
2nd rnd: Ch 2, sc same sp, work 2 sc in each st around (24 sc); join with sl st in top of ch-2; ch 2, turn.
3rd rnd: Sc in each sc around (24 sc); join.
4th rnd: Ch 2, * 2 sc in next sc (inc made), sc in next sc. Rep from * around, ending with 2 sc in last sc (36 sc); join.
5th rnd: Ch 2, sc in each sc around (36 sc); join.
6th and 7th rnds: Rep 4th and 5th rnds (54 sc); join. Break off A. (Piece should measure about 3½″ in diameter). Attach B with sl st to any sc, ch 2.

LOWER SECTION: 1st row: Sc in next sc, * inc in next sc, sc in each of next 2 sc. Rep from * 7 times more; inc in next sc (36 sc worked over portion of circle); ch 2, turn.
2nd row: Work sc in each sc across last row, leaving last 2 sc unworked (34 sc); ch 2, turn.
3rd row: Sc next sc, * inc in next sc, sc in each of next 2 sc. Rep from * 9 times more. Sk last 2 sc (42 sc); ch 2, turn.
4th and 5th rows: Rep 2nd row (38 sc). Break off B. Turn. Attach D to last st worked, ch 2.
6th row: Sc in each of next 36 sc, sk last sc (37 sc); ch 2, turn.
7th row: Sc in each of next 35 sc, sk last sc (36 sc); ch 2, turn.

FLOWER TRIM: 8th row: Sc in each of next 3 sc, * ch 3, sc in each of next 4 sc. Rep from * 7 times more (8 ch-3 lps made—36 sc); turn.
9th row: Sl st in each of first 3 sc (mark 2nd sl st made), sk next sc, * working over ch-3 lp, work sc, ch 3 and 7 dc; ch 3, sc in 3rd ch from hook (p made), work 4 more dc in lp (p shell made); sk next 4 sc, rep from * 7 times more (8 shells made). Break off D. With same side facing

you, attach C to marked st at beg of row, ch 2.
10th row: Sc in next sl st; working in sc's on 8th row, **behind** shells, work sc in each of 4 sc between first 2 shells, * sc in each of next 4 sc between shells. Rep from * 5 times more; sc in next sc after last shell (32 sc); ch 2, turn.
11th row: Sc in each sc across row (32 sc); ch 2, turn.
12th row: Sc in each of next 3 sts, * ch 9, work 4 dc in 4th ch from hook, work 4 dc in each of next 5 ch (rosebud made), sc in each of next 4 sc. Rep from * 6 times more; sc in each of last 4 sc (7 rosebuds made). Break off C. Turn. Attach D to last sc made, ch 2.
13th row: Sc in each of next 3 sc, * ch 4, work 5 dc and 1 sc in 4th ch from hook (cup shell made), sc in same

(C) sc; working in front of rosebud, sc in each of next 4 sc. Rep from * 6 times more (7 cup shells made); ch 2, turn.

14th row: Sc in each of next 3 sc, working behind cup shell. * Sc in each of the 2 sc at base of next cup shell and in each of next 2 sc, insert hook in p of p shell on 9th row, y o and draw lp through, insert hook in next sc on last row, y o and draw lp through, y o and draw through all 3 lps on hook. Rep from * 5 times more (6 p shells attached), sc in each sc to end of row. Break off D. Turn. Sk last sc worked and attach B to next sc, ch 2.

BOTTOM: 15th row: Sc in each sc across row to within last 3 sc, pull up a lp in each of next 2 sc, y o, pull through all lps on hook (dec made—36 sc); ch 2, turn.

16th through 21st rows: Work 6 more rows sc, decreasing 1 st at beg and end of each row (24 sts). Break off B.

EDGING: With A, work 1 rnd sc around entire piece. Break off.

BACK: Work in same manner as for Front.

FINISHING: With right sides facing, using A and beginning at Section 2 side edge, sl st or whipstitch sides and lower edges together; turn.

STRAP: Attach A at top of seam on 1 side, sc in same sp, ch 3, (y o, insert hook in 3rd ch from hook, y o and draw up a lp, y o and draw through 2 lps on hook) 3 times; y o and draw through all 4 lps on hook (3-dc cl made), * ch 3, sc in 3rd ch from hook, ch 3, sc in same ch, ch 3, work 3-dc cl over side of last sc made. Rep from * for desired Strap length, sc to opposite seam edge, sl st in same sp. Break off.

FLOWER POCKET SHOULDER BAG

Here is a decorative and durable shoulder bag made from macrame cords. The body of the bag is worked in single crochet. The motifs which form pockets and flaps are attached later.

SIZE: Measures 12½″ in width; 11″ in height.

MATERIALS: Macrame braided cord (fine), 12 (20-yd.) spools each dark olive and antique gold, 2 spools each red and orange, rattail (heavy), 1 (20-yd.) spool each red and orange; aluminum crochet hook size I (or English/Canadian hook No. 7) *or size that will give you the correct gauge;* fabric glue (dry-cleanable and clear drying).

GAUGE: 3 sc = 1″.

Note: The nature of these cords requires special attention to the fastening off and tucking in of ends. Be sure to leave ends of at least 2″ when making beg lp on hook and when fastening off. Next to each fasten-off ch st make a knot. When bag is completed tuck in ends of at least 1″ in length. Place glue under stitches through which the end has been pulled. Press and let dry.

BACK: Work back lps only throughout.

1st row: Use dark olive. Ch 29, beg in 3rd ch st from hook, sc in each st across, tag this row; ch 2, turn. (Ch-2 counts as sc.)

2nd row: Sc each st across, ch 2, turn.

3rd through 6th rows: Rep 2nd row 4 times. Mark this side as right side. Fasten off. Turn.

7th through 12th rows: Use antique gold. Rep 2nd row 6 times. Fasten off. Turn.

13th through 24th rows: Use dark olive. Rep 2nd row 12 times. Fasten off. Turn.

25th through 30th rows: Use antique gold. Rep 2nd row 6 times. Fasten off. Turn.

31st through 36th rows: Use dark olive. Rep 2nd row 6 times; ch 2, turn. Do not break off.

Sides and Bottom: Formed by edging Back section. Work back lps only. **1st row:** (Side 1) Sc in each st across last row of Back section. (Bottom) Working on next edge sc in each end-of-row st. (Side 2) Working on next edge, sc in each of foundation ch sts, ch 2, turn.

2nd row: Working dec of 1 sc at each corner, sc in each st around to beg of 1st row. Fasten off. Turn.

3rd and 4th rows: Use antique gold. Work 2 rows of sc even. Fasten off.

FRONT: Work as for Back.

LEFT POCKET: Work back lps only.

1st row: Use red macrame cord. Ch 12, sc in 3rd ch st from hook, sc in each st across; ch 2, turn.

2nd through 12th rows: Work 11 rows of sc even. Fasten off.

Pocket Flap: 1st rnd: Use red macrame cord. Ch 5, join in first ch st to form ring, ch 3, 11 dc in ring, sl st top of beg ch-3. Fasten off. Do not turn.

2nd rnd: Use orange rattail. Start in any dc. Work both lps. Work 2 sc in each st around; sl st in beg sc.

3rd rnd: * Ch 4, hdc in 3rd ch st from hook, 2 dc next ch st, sk 2 sts on circle, working back lps, sl st in each of next 2 sts, rep from * around. Fasten off. (6 triangle petals formed.)

4th rnd: Use antique gold macrame cord. Start in ch st at tip of any triangle. Sl st in each st to tip of 4th triangle, sc in same ch st at tip of triangle, mark this st, dc and tr in first sl st between triangles, tr and dc in next sl st, sc in tip of next triangle, 2 hdc in each of 2 sl sts between triangles, sc in tip of next triangle, dc and tr in next sl st, tr and dc in next sl st, sc in same sp as beg sl st. Do not break off.

Attaching Flap to Pocket: Pick up pocket. Hold piece so that foundation ch is on your right and side edges are on top and bottom. Begin working on top edge at foundation-ch end. Continuing with lp on hook from Flap, sc in each end-of-row st across this edge, sc in back lps only across next edge, sc in each end-of-row st across next edge, sl st in marked st on Flap. Do not break off. Remove marker.

Attaching Pocket to Bag: Pick up Front section. Hold piece, right sides facing, with tagged end on your left and top edge on top. Find the 3rd row on this section. (Do not include side rows.) From top edge, count down 12 sts on this row and mark the 12th st. Mark the 12th st down, from top edge, on every other row through 15th row.

Joining Rnd: On 15th row, count down 2 sts from marked st, continuing with lp on hook from flap attachment, sl st in 2nd st from marker, work back lps, sc tog dc on Flap and next st on 15th row, sc tog tr on Flap and marked st on 15th row, * sc tog next st on Flap to top lp of next marked st, sc tog next st on Flap to bottom lp of same marked st, rep from * 4 times, sc tog next st on Flap to marked st on 3rd row, working over next edge of pocket sc tog each st on edge of pocket to corresponding st on 3rd row, work joining for bottom edge in same manner as for top edge, work joining for right side to 15th row in same manner as opposite side, sl st in beg sl st of joining rnd. Fasten off.

RIGHT POCKET: Work as for Left Pocket, using orange macrame cord.

Flap: Work as for Left Pocket Flap, using orange macrame cord for 1st rnd and red rattail for 2nd and 3rd rnds.

Attaching Flap to Pocket: Work same as for Left Pocket.

Attaching Pocket to Bag: Working over 21st through 34th rows on Front section, attach in same manner as for Left Pocket.

JOINING FRONT AND BACK SECTIONS: Place

sections tog, right sides facing. Use antique gold cord. Begin at top edge of bag. Work top lps only. Sc sections tog, working around side, bottom and side. Do not break off.

Edging: Turn bag to right side. Work sc edging around top edge by working sc in every other end-of-row st. Fasten off.

BAG FLAP: Flower Motif A: 1st rnd: Use orange macrame cord. Ch 5, join with sl st to form ring, ch 3, 11 dc through ring. Fasten off.

2nd rnd: Use red rattail. Work 2 sc in each st around, sl st beg sc.

3rd rnd: * Ch 4, hdc in 3rd ch st from hook, 2 dc in next ch st, sk 2 sts on circle, working back lps, sl st in each of next 2 sts, rep from * 3 times. Mark last sl st worked. Fasten off.

Flower Motif B: Rep Flower Motif A.

Flower Motif C: Work as for Flower Motif A. On 1st rnd use red macrame cord and on 2nd and 3rd rnds use orange rattail.

Attaching Flower Motifs: 1st row: Use antique gold macrame cord. Pick up Motif A. Hold piece so that triangles are on the right. Begin in ch st at tip of top triangle, work back lps only, sc next 16 sts, pick up Motif C, hold Motif with triangles on the bottom, begin in marked sl st, sc in next 12 sts, pick up Motif B, hold piece so that triangles are on the left, begin in marked sl st, sc next 17 sts around; ch 2, turn.

2nd row: Work back lps only. Sc next 12 sts, leaving last 4 sts on this Motif and first 4 sts on next Motif free, work 4 sc in each of next 4 sts, sk next 4 sts and the first 4 sts on the last Motif, sc remaining 13 sts; ch 2, turn.

3rd rnd: Work back lps. Sl st next 9 sts, sk 3 sts, dc next 4 sts on center Motif, sk 3 sts, sl st remaining 10 sts, sc in each of the next 2 end-of-row sts, * (work sc in each st up to tip of next triangle, work sc, ch 1 and sc in tip of triangle) twice; ** sc up to joining, sc over posts of next 2 sts, sc in each st up to tip of next triangle, in tip work sc, sl st in ch-1 sp at tip of last triangle, sc same sp as last sc made, rep from * once; rep from * to **, sc in each of next 2 end-of-row sts. Do not break off.

Attaching Flap to Bag: Place Flap against Back section, wrong sides facing tog with tagged edge of Back at right. Be sure Flap is centered. Sl st Flap and Back section tog, working on right side. Fasten off.

STRAP: Use dark olive. Ch 7, sc in 2nd ch from hook, sc in each ch st across; * ch 2, turn. Working back lps only, sc each st across, rep from * 62 times or for desired length. Fasten off.

Strap Fastening: Circle: Use orange macrame cord. Ch 5, join with sl st to form ring, ch 3, 11 dc in ring, sl st top beg ch-3. Fasten off. Use antique gold macrame cord. Sc in each st around Circle (cup formed), sl st beg sc. Fasten off.

Tie: Use dark olive. Leave 6" ends, ch 3, sc in 3rd ch st from hook (p), work a 2nd p, leave 6" end. Fasten off. Pull ends through center of cupped Circle leaving p's in center. Continue to pull ends through side of Bag, placing 1 end to left of seam and one end to right of seam. Pull ends through 6th row of Strap, placing 1 end through first 2 sts of row and one end through last 2 sts on row. Tie secure knots. Fasten off. Rep strap fastening for opposite side.

SHIRVAN SHOULDER BAG

A totem from the Shirvan Afghan (see page 00), framed by single crochet and double crochet stitches with slip stitch accents, covers a roomy tote bag.

SIZE: Approximately 15" in length and 12" in width.

MATERIALS: Knitting worsted 12 oz. navy, 4 oz. camel, 2 oz. each cardinal, scarlet, light blue, and royal blue; aluminum crochet hook H (or English/Canadian hook No. 8) *or size that will give you the correct gauge.*

GAUGE: 3 sc = 1"; 3 rows of sc = 1".

Note: Work with yarn double strand throughout.

BAG: Use navy. Form foundation ch lps as follows: (Ch 4, dc in 4th ch st from hook) 17 times.

1st rnd: Ch 2, work sc over post of last dc made, * 2 sc over post of each dc across; ch 2, turn (ch-2 counts as sc.)

2nd row: Work sc in each st across (34 sts); ch 2, turn. Rep 2nd row until piece measures approximately 30". Do not break off.

Joining: Fold piece in half, matching up first and last rows; working along side edges, sc edges tog working sc over post of each end-of-row st. Fasten off. Begin at fold edge, join opposite side edges in same manner. Do not break off.

Edging: Working over ch-sps of foundation lps, work 2 sc in each lp, sl st in beg sc of side edging. Fasten off. Mark this edge.

FLAP: Rectangle Motif: See instructions for Shirvan Afghan on page 00. Make rectangle from instructions for Rectangle No. 1, substituting colors as follows:

1st rnd: light blue.
2nd rnd: camel.
3rd rnd: scarlet.
4th rnd: light blue.
5th rnd: cardinal.
6th rnd: scarlet.
7th rnd: Use light blue. Right side facing, begin in any corner ch-sp, * work sc, ch 2 and sc in ch-sp, working back lps, sc in each st across to within next ch-sp, rep from * around, end sl st in beg sc. Fasten off.

Fill-In: 1st row: Use camel. Working on long edge of Rectangle, with right side facing, begin in right corner ch-sp, working back lps, sc in each st across to within ch-sp;

ch 2, turn (ch 2 counts as sc).

2nd row: Work next 2 sc as 1 (dec), sc in each st across; ch 2, turn.

3rd row: Sc in each st across to within last 2 sts, work last 2 sc as 1 (dec); ch 2, turn.

4th and 5th rows: Rep 2nd and 3rd rows. Fasten off. (Decrease edge will be bottom edge of Flap.) Work fill-in for opposite edge in same manner, starting at bottom edge of Flap in first sc after ch-sp and reversing shaping by working dec's at end of 2nd row and beg of 3rd row.

FLAP EDGING: 1st row: Use royal blue. Hold piece with right side facing and bottom edge at your right. Work on fill-in last made. Starting at bottom edge on last row, sk first 7 sts on row, sc next 3 sts, hdc next 3 sts, dc to within last sc on row, in last sc work dc, ch 2 and sc (mark the ch-2 sp), sc next 4 end-of-row sts, working back lps sc in each st across Rectangle, sc next 4 end-of-row sts, in next end-of-row st work sc, ch 2 and sc, work dc to within last 13 sts on row, hdc next 3 sts, sc next 3 sts, leave 7 sts free. Fasten off.

2nd row: Use scarlet. With right side facing, begin in marked ch-2 corner. Work sc edging around Flap, working 3 sc in each of the 6 corner sts and in beg and end sts of royal blue edging, and working back lps only across bottom edge of Rectangle; sl st beg sc. Fasten off.

SLIP STITCH ACCENT: Hold Flap with bottom edge on bottom, working over 3rd row of fill-in on the right, with scarlet, sk 1 st after edging, sl st over next 9 sts on 3rd row, working a diagonal line to the left sl st over next st on 2nd row, sl st over next st on first row. Fasten off. Work accent for opposite side in same manner, working diagonal to the right.

BOBBLES: Hold Flap right side facing, with bottom edge on top. Use royal blue. Working at left Rectangle corner, in center dc work sc and 3 dc (shell made), (ch 6, sl st in 6th ch st from hook, ch 2, work 7 dc in ring, sl st beg ch 2) twice, sc over post of end dc of shell. Fasten off. Turn Flap to wrong side. Work Bobble for opposite corner in same manner.

ATTACHING FLAP TO BAG: Use navy. With wrong sides tog, sl st Flap top edge and marked edge on bag tog, working back lps only. Fasten off.

STRAP: Using scarlet and cardinal together (4 strands) work a ch 10" longer than desired length, turn; sl st in each st across chain. Fasten off. Tie ch in a knot at each end. Insert knotted ends through foundation lp sps at each side edge of bag and tie.

GOLDEN MANDALA PURSE

This small, but striking, purse creates an impact by evolving from a central motif. The combination of fibers and unique stitch variations heightens the effect.

SIZE: Approximately 8½″ in width and 9½″ in length.

MATERIALS: Rayon macrame braided cord (fine), 100 yds. navy; rattail (lightweight), 40 yds. gold, 20 yds. pale lime green; aluminum crochet hook H (or English/Canadian hook No. 8) *or size that will give you the correct gauge;* fabric glue (dry-cleanable and clear drying).

GAUGE: 3 dc = 1″; 2 rows dc = 1½″.

Note: Cords used here require special attention to fastening off and tucking in of ends. Leave ends of at least 2″ when making beg lp on hook and when fastening off.

Next to each fasten-off st make an extra knot. When bag is completed tuck in ends of at least 1″ in length. Place glue under stitches through which ends have been drawn.

FRONT: 1st rnd: Use navy. Ch 6, join with sl st to form ring, ch 3, work 11 dc in ring, sl st top of beg ch-3. Fasten off.

2nd rnd: Work with right side facing throughout. Use gold. Work 2 hdc in each st around, sl st beg hdc. Fasten off.

3rd rnd: Use navy. Begin in any st, * work dc, work 2 dc in next st, rep from * around, sl st beg dc (36 sts). Fasten off.

4th rnd: Use gold. Begin in any st. Make a lp on hook, draw up a lp, y o, pull through 1 lp on hook, pull up a lp in same sp, y o, pull through 1 lp on hook, y o, pull through all 3 lps on hook (cl made), work cl in each of next 3 sts, working in base of next dc (draw up lp about 1″, y o, pull through one lp on hook) three times, y o, pull through all 4 lps on hook (long-cl made), ch 1, * work cl in each of next 4 sts, work long-cl in next st, ch 1, rep from * 4 times; sl st beg st. Fasten off.

5th rnd: Use green. Begin in any ch-1 sp after long-cl st. Work cl in each st around, sl st in beg st (42 sts). Fasten off.

6th rnd: Use navy. Starting in any st, * work sc in next 7 sts, (2 hdc in each of next 2 sts, 2 dc next st, 2 tr next st, 2 dc next st, 2 hdc in each of next 2 sts) twice, rep from * once, sl st in beg sc. Fasten off.

7th rnd: Ch 2, working back lps, hdc in next 6 sts, ** dc in next 6 sts, * working both lps 2 tr in each of next 2 tr, * working back lps, dc in next 12 sts, rep from * to *, dc in next 6 sts, hdc in next 7 sts, rep from **, sl st in top of beg ch-2. Fasten off.

BACK: Work as for Front.

JOINING: Put 2 pieces tog, wrong sides facing, with short edges on top. Begin at left corner, working back lps, sc pieces tog around 3 sides; do not break off.

STRAP: Ch for desired length, making sure ch is straight, work sc in beg sc of joining, turn; work sl st in each st across ch. Fasten off.

Gifts

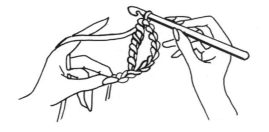

Neckpieces

ROSETTE COLLAR

Add a bright note to any outfit with this gaily colored accessory composed primarily of shells and clusters.

SIZE: Neck opening measures 23″; front panel measures 9″ in length and 6″ in width at widest point.

MATERIALS: Pearl cotton such as D.M.C. no. 5, 3 (50-yd.) spools each pastel green, baby blue, pale pink, rose, salmon and rust; aluminum crochet hook size F (or English/Canadian hook No. 10) *or the size that will give you the correct gauge.*

GAUGE: 5 dc = 1″; 2 rows of dc = 1″.

Note: Use 3 strands throughout.

COLLAR: Note: See General Instructions for how to start row with sc or dc.
   1st rnd: With green, * ch 4, work 3 dc in 4th ch st from hook (shell made), ch 3, turn; (y o, draw up a lp in next st, y o, draw through 2 lps) 3 times, y o, draw through all 4 lps on hook (cl made); turn piece with right side of shell facing you; rep from * 19 times (20 cl-shells made). Fasten off.
   2nd row: With blue, work sc in top of last cl made, work along side edge of cl's, * over post of dc work sc and 3 dc, ch 2, over ch-4 of shell work 3 dc and sc, rep from * across, end sc in base of first shell. Fasten off. Do not turn.
   3rd row: With pink, sc in first sc of 2nd row, ch 4, sk next 3 sts, * work sc, ch 3 and sc in ch-2 sp, sk 3 dc, dc in sc, ch 3, dc in next sc, sk 3 dc, rep from * across to

within last cl, end sc, ch 3 and sc in last ch-2 sp, ch 4, sc in end sc, ch 3, turn.
   4th row: *** In ch-4 sp, work 3-dc cl (3-dc cl worked as follows: Work 3 dc holding back last lp on hook, y o, pull through all 4 lps on hook), ch 4, work 3-dc cl in 4th ch st from hook, mark this cl, in same ch-4 sp work 3-dc cl, * in next ch-3 sp (between sc sts) work dc, ch 3 and dc, ** in next ch-3 sp (between dc sts) work sc, ch 3 and sc, rep from * across ending last rep at **, working over end ch-4 sp rep from *** to *, ch 3, sl st in end sc. Fasten off. Do not turn. Tag this side as right side of piece.
   5th row: With rose, sk cl group at beg of 4th row, * in next ch-3 sp between dc sts work dc, ch 3 and dc, ch 6, sc over post of last dc made, in same ch-3 sp continue dc, ch 3 and dc (lp-shell made), sc next ch-3 sp between sc sts, rep from * across to within end cl group, omitting end sc in last rep. Fasten off. Do not turn.
   6th row: With rust, sk first lp-shell on 5th row, * sc in next sc, 3 dc in first ch-3 sp of next lp-shell, work 3 dc, ch 2 and 3 dc in ch-6 lp, 3 dc in next ch-3 sp, * rep from * to * twice more, sc in next sc. Fasten off; sk next 4 lp-shells, rep from * to * 4 times, sc next sc. Fasten off; sk next 4 lp-shells, rep from * to * 3 times, sc next sc. Fasten off.

ROSETTE STRINGS: Rosettes: With salmon, * ch 6, beg in 2nd ch st from hook, work 4 dc in each of next 4 ch sts, sc last ch st (Rosette made)*, ch 10, rep from * to * twice. Fasten off.

Leaves: With green, sc in end sc st of first Rosette made, * ch 5, hdc in 2nd ch st from hook, dc next st, tr next st, sc in same sc,* rep from * to * once (2 leaves made), ch 4, sc in end sc of 2nd Rosette made, rep from * to *, sc in end sc of last Rosette, rep from * to *. Fasten off. Make 2 more sets of Rosette and Leaf strings in same manner. Make one more Rosette and Leaf string substituting blue for salmon.

Attaching Rosettes: Hold Collar with right side facing. Counting from neck opening edge, sk 2 lp-shells, pick up 1 string of Rosettes, working in ch-6 lp of next lp-shell, pull 3rd Rosette through front to back, working above lp in ch-2 sp of rust row, pull same Rosette through from back to front. Working on opposite side of collar, attach

2nd Rosette string in same manner. Working at center of collar, attach 3rd Rosette string around center rust sc by drawing 3rd Rosette through front to back around post of sc st.

NECK FASTENING: Work in sps under marked cl; pull 3rd Rosette of 4th (blue) Rosette string through both sps.

FRONT SEAM: Fold collar at center, with wrong side facing. Hold piece so that neck opening is on your right and fold on your left with green cl-shells in pairs on top edge. Count off 5 pairs of cl-shells; with green * sc tog the corresponding posts on next pair of cl-shells, ch 3, rep from * 4 times omitting ch-3 on last rep. Fasten off.

GARLANDS OF ROSES PECTORAL-COLLAR

Adorn yourself with enchanting picot rosebuds placed in cascading rows for a spectacular effect. There is an added attraction: The pectoral can be made simply as a collar.

SIZE: Collar measures 19″ in length and 2″ in width. Pectoral measures 14″ in length and 5″ in width.

MATERIALS: Rattail (lightweight) 100 yds. pearl gray, 70 yds. each orchid, rose, and seal brown; aluminum crochet hook size G (or English/Canadian hook No. 9) *or the size that will give you the correct gauge;* fabric glue (dry-cleanable and clear drying).

GAUGE: 4 dc = 1″; 2 rows of dc = 1¼″.

Note: Rattail requires special attention to fastening off and the tucking in of ends. Be sure to leave ends of at least 2″ when making beginning loop on hook and when fastening off. Next to each fasten-off chain stitch make a knot. When piece is completed tuck in ends of at least 1″ in length. Place glue under stitches through which ends have been drawn.

COLLAR: Using gray, form foundation ch lps, (ch 4, dc in 4th ch st from hook) 16 times.

1st rnd: Ch 2 (ch 2 counts as sc), working over post of last dc made, work 3 dc, over each dc post across work 4 sc; ch 2, turn.

2nd row: Work sc next st, ch 3, sc in 3rd ch st (p made), * work sc in next 4 sts, p, rep from * across ending sc in last 2 sts. Fasten off. Turn.

3rd row: Use orchid. Starting in last sc made work sc, p, work sc in next st, * ch 4, sk p, sc in next 2 sts, p, sc in next 2 sts, rep from * across to within last p, ch 4, sk last p, sc next st, p, work sc last st. Fasten off. Do not turn.

4th row: Use rose. Begin in first ch-4 sp on 3rd row. * In ch-4 sp work sc, ch 4, hdc in 3rd ch st from hook, dc next ch st (bud p formed) and sc, ch 4, sk p, rep from * across, omitting ch-4 on last rep. Fasten off. Do not turn.

5th row: Use brown. Starting in the first sc on 3rd row, work sc, ch 4 and sc in first sc on 4th row, (mark ch-4 sp just made), ch 4, sk bud p, * in next ch-4 sp work 2 sc, bud p and 2 sc, ch 4, rep from * across through last ch-4 sp, ch 4, sk bud p on 4th row, sc in last sc on 4th row, ch 4, sc in last sc on 3rd row (mark this last ch-4 sp made). Fasten off.

PECTORAL: 1st rnd: Use gray. Sk first 6 bud p's made on 5th row. Starting in 2nd sc after 6th bud p, work sc, * ch 9, starting in 3rd ch st from hook work sc next st, hdc next 2 sts, 2 dc next st, 2 tr next st (leaf made), sk ch-4 sp, sc next sc,** sk sc, bud p and sc, sc next st, rep from

* twice; rep from * to **. Fasten off.

2nd row: Use brown. Starting in ch-2 tip of first leaf made on 1st row, work sc, bud p and sc, * ch 7, work sc, bud p and sc in ch-2 tip of next leaf, rep from * twice. Fasten off.

3rd row: Use rose. Begin in first ch-7 sp of 2nd row. * In ch-7 sp work 2 sc, bud p, 4 sc, bud p and 2 sc; sk bud p, rep from * twice. Fasten off.

4th row: Use orchid. Starting in next sc after first bud p on 3rd row, * work sc in next 2 sts, bud p, sc in next 2 sts, ch 1, sk bud p, rep from * 4 times omitting ch-1 on last rep. Fasten off.

5th through 16th rows: Use gray. Starting in next sc after first bud p on 4th row, work sc, * work leaf, sk sc, ch 1 and sc, sc in next st, ** ch 1, sk bud p, sc in next st, rep from * twice, rep from * to **. Fasten off. Rep 2nd through 5th rows twice. Rep 2nd through 4th rows once.

17th row: Using brown, rep 5th row.

NECK FASTENING: Use gray.

Buttons: Ch 5, join with sl st to form ring, ** ch 3, work 11 dc in ring, sl st beg ch-3; ch 1, * (draw up a lp in next st) twice, y o, pull through all 3 lps on hook, rep from * 3 times, sl st beg ch 1, ** ch 9, join with sl st in 5th ch st from hook, rep from ** to **. Fasten off. Put glue inside buttons and stuff ends in. Place one button through each marked ch sp.

EGYPTIAN GOLD BODY ORNAMENT

Regal hues transform simple stitches into a body ornament that recalls the mysteries of Egypt and the lure of gold.

SIZE: Neckpiece measures 13½" in length around neck edge and bib measures approximately 14".

MATERIALS: Rattail (lightweight), 30 yds. each of light blue and orange, 50 yds. royal blue, 70 yds. gold; aluminum crochet hook size H (or English/Canadian hook No. 8) *or the size that will give you the correct gauge;* fabric glue (dry-cleanable and clear drying), 3 dozen beads, 1 dozen each orange, light blue, and royal blue, approximately ⅜" in diameter with ⅛" hole.

GAUGE: 4 dc = 1"; 2 rows = 1¼".

Note: Rattail requires special attention to the tucking in of ends. Leave ends of at least 2" when making beg lp on hook and when fastening off. Next to each fasten-off st make a knot. When piece is complete tuck in ends of at least 1" in length. Place glue under stitches through which ends have been drawn.

BIB: With royal blue, leaving 14" ends when making beg lp on hook and when fastening off, work ch 46 for foundation ch. Fasten off.

1st row: Starting in first ch st with gold, work 2 sc, (ch 5, sk 4 ch sts, 2 sc next st) 9 times, ch 3, working along opposite edge of foundation ch, work dc in each st across, ch 2, sl st in same sp as last dc made. Fasten off.

2nd row: Use royal blue. With right side facing, working along edge with ch-5 sps, sk first sc on edge, dc next sc, sk 2 ch sts, holding back last lps on hook work 2 dc in

next ch st, y o, pull through all 3 lps on hook (2-dc cl made), in same sp work (ch 2, cl) twice (3-cl shell made); * ch 2, sk to center ch st of next ch-5 sp, work 3-cl shell, rep from * across ending dc in first sc of 2 end sc sts. Fasten off. Turn.

3rd row: Use gold. Sc in last dc made, * work 2 sc in next ch-2 sp, ch 3, sc in 3rd ch st from hook (p made), 2 sc in next ch-2 sp, p, sk next ch-2 sp, rep from * across omitting last p on last rep, sc in end dc. Fasten off.

4th row: Use light blue. With right side facing, sk first 5 p sts made on 3rd row, (work 2 dc in each of next 2 sc, sk p st) 8 times (32 dc sts). Fasten off. Turn.

5th row: Work back lps only on following rows. Use gold. Work sc each st across. Fasten off. Turn.

6th row: Use royal blue. Sk first 5 sts, dc each st across to within last 5 sts (22 dc sts). Fasten off. Turn.

7th row: Rep 5th row.

8th row: Use orange. Sk first 3 sc, dc each st across to within last 3 sts (16 dc sts). Fasten off. Turn.

9th row: Use gold. Work dc each st across. Ch 1, turn.

10th row: Work sc each st across. Ch 3, turn.

11th row: Work dc each st across. Fasten off. Do not turn.

12th row: Rep 8th row (10 sts). Fasten off. Turn.

13th row: Rep 5th row.

14th row: Use light blue. Work hdc each st across. Fasten off. Turn.

15th row: Use gold. Work sc next 5 sts, ch 6, sc next 5 sts. Fasten off. Do not turn.

16th row: Use royal blue. In ch-6 lp work 9 sc (ring made); ch 3, turn.

17th row: * 3-dc cl next sc (3-dc cl made as follows: Holding back last lps on hook, work 3 dc same sp, y o, pull through all 4 lps on hook), ch 3, 2-dc cl in 3rd ch st from hook, sk 1 sc on ring, rep from * twice, work 3-dc cl in next st, ch 2, sl st in end sc (cl-flower made). Fasten off.

EDGING: Use gold. Hold piece with right side facing, and neck opening edge at your right. Begin in 4th row in end-of-row st, * work 2 sc over post of dc, over post of next sc work 3 sc, sl st each st to next end-of-row dc st, rep from * once, continue working sc edging to within next corner tip, work 3 sc in corner tip, work sc edging to within cl-flower, work sc between ch sp and cl, work sc between cl's (ch 1, p, ch 1, sk horizontal cl, sc in top of next cl) twice, ch 1, p, ch 1, sc between cl's, sc between cl and ch-sp, continue working edging for opposite side in same manner as for first side, reversing order.

BEADING: Fringe: Cut 3 strands of gold 16″ in length. Hold lengths together, fold in half. Work in 2nd p of edging around cl-flower. Draw folded end through ch-sp of p, draw ends through lp and tighten. Make a 2nd knot, directly under first knot. Work fringe of 20″ lengths in next p; work fringes of 24″ lengths in next 2 p; work 20″ lengths in 5th p and 16″ lengths in 6th p. String beads on fringe ends. Vary the color placement of the beads.

CLUSTER NECKLACE

Create your own antique simply with shells and picots.

SIZE: Necklace measures 18″ in length.

MATERIALS: Cotton embroidery twist No. 4, mat finish, 2 (11-yd.) skeins each rose and beige; aluminum crochet hook size F (or English/Canadian hook No. 10) *or the size that will give you the correct gauge;* one ½″ snap fastener.

GAUGE: 4 dc = ¾″.

Note: Leave ends of at least 6″ when making beginning lps on hooks and when fastening off.

1st row: With rose, * ch 4, work 3 dc in 4th ch from hook (shell made, right side), ch 3; turn shell with wrong side facing you, (y o, draw up lp in next st of shell, y o, draw through 2 lps on hook) 3 times, y o, draw through all 4 lps on hook (1 cl made); turn shell with right side facing you. Rep from * 13 times more (14 cl-shells made). Piece should measure about 18″ from beg. Break off.

2nd row: With tan, sc in tip of last cl-shell made, * ch 3, sc in 3rd ch st from hook (ring p), (ch 3, sc same ch st) twice (2 p's), * working along edge of cl-shells, ** ch 3, work sc in center of next cl-shell, rep from * to * (p group); ch 3, sc in sp between next 2 cl's. Rep from ** 13 times more, ending with ch 3, sc in center of last cl-shell, work p, ch 3, sc in top of last cl. Break off. Place snap on wrong side under end p groups. Sew on snaps with ends.

SILKEN RIBBON CHOKER-BELT

Encircle your neck or waist with ribbon clusters in stained-glass tones that evoke an elegance of days gone by.

SIZE: Measures 12″ in length and 1½″ in width. (Pattern can be adjusted to belt length if desired.)

MATERIALS: Three-line cord or grosgrain ribbon ⅛″ wide, 20 yds. gold and 10 yds. each teal and wine; aluminum crochet hook size F (or English/Canadian hook No. 10) *or size that will give you the correct gauge.*

GAUGE: 1 cl-shell = 1¼″.

Note: Leave ends of at least 10″ when making a beg lp on hook or when fastening off. Ends can serve as streamer ties.

1st row: Use gold. * Ch 4, work 3 dc in 4th ch st from hook (shell made), ch 3; turn shell with wrong side facing, (y o, draw up a lp in next st) 3 times, y o, pull through all 4 lps on hook (cl made), rep from * 8 times (9 cl-shells), or for desired length if making belt. Fasten off.
2nd row: Use teal. In top of last cl made work sc; working along side edges of cl-shells, ** ch 3, sc in center of same cl-shell, * ch 3, sc in center of next cl-shell, rep from * across to last cl-shell, ch 3, sc in base of same cl-shell, rep from ** across opposite side, ending sl st in beg sc. Fasten off.
3rd row: Use wine. In last sl st made, work sc, ** ch 3, in next sc work 3 sc, ch 1, * working over ch-3 sp, dc in st between cl-shells, ch 1, 3 sc in next sc, rep from * across to last cl-shell, ch 3, sc in next sc at tip of band, rep from ** across opposite side to end cl-shell, ending sl st in beg sc. Fasten off.

FLOWER ORNAMENT

With cotton yarn and fancy stitches, you can sculpt an ornament to be worn as your whimsy takes you.

SIZE: 7″ in length and 5″ in width.

MATERIALS: Cotton embroidery twist No. 4, mat finish, 11 yds. pale yellow, 22 yds. each pale lilac and dark lilac, 33 yds. pale blue. Pearl cotton, size 5, 4 (50-yd.) spools hunter green; aluminum crochet hook size E (or English/

Canadian hook No. 11) *or the size that will give you correct gauge.*

GAUGE: For mat cotton 4 dc = 7/8" and 2 rows dc = 1⅛"; for pearl cotton 5 dc = 1" and 2 rows of dc = 1".

Note: Use yarn double throughout.

LARGE FLOWER: 1st rnd: With dark lilac, ch 5, join with sl st to form ring, ch 3, 11 dc in ring, sl st top beg ch-3.

2nd rnd: Ch 1, * working back lps, 4 dc in next st, sl st next st, rep from * 5 times, ending last rep sl st in beg ch-1 (6 small petals formed).

3rd rnd: * Ch 3, placing ch in front of petal, work sl st in next sl st, rep from * 5 times.

4th rnd: * Work 6 dc over next ch-3 sp, sl st in next sl st, rep from * 5 times (6 large petals formed). Fasten off.

Turn piece to wrong side. Mark this side as right side of flower.

5th rnd: Hold flower with right side facing. With pale lilac, working behind large petals, sc in any sl st between ch lps of 4th row, * ch 4, sk petal, sc in next sl st between ch lps of 4th row, rep from * 5 times, end sl st in beg sc.

6th rnd: * Work 8 tr over ch-4 sp, sl st in next sc, * rep from * to * twice, sl st in each of next 4 ch st, sl st in sc, rep from * to *; leave last lp free. Fasten off.

SMALL FLOWERS (make 4): 1st rnd: With pale blue, ch 5, join to form ring, ch 1, 9 sc in ring, sl st beg ch-1.

2nd rnd: * Ch 3, work 3 dc in 3rd ch st from hook, sk 1 sc, work sl st in next sc, rep from * 4 times (5 petals formed). Fasten off.

BUDS (make 2): With pale lilac, ch 3, work 9 dc in 3rd ch st from hook, sl st top of ch-3. Fasten off.

LEAVES: On first Small Flower: Work with green. Pick up 1 Small Flower, working back lp, sc in any sl st between petals (mark this sc),* ch 8, beg in 3rd ch st from hook, work hdc in each of next 2 ch sts, dc in next 2 ch sts, tr in next 2 ch sts (Leaf formed), sc in back lp of next sl st between petals, rep from * twice; (ch 1, turn, working edging over 3 leaves, sl st in each st around) twice. Do not break off.

On Bud: Pick up Bud, work with wrong side facing, working back lps only, sc in each st around, working on first Small Flower sc in back lp of last free sl st between petals. Do not break off.

On 2nd Small Flower: Pick up 2nd Small Flower, (sc in back lp of any sl st between petals, work Leaf) twice; sc in back lp of next sl st between Petals. Do not break off.

Joining Large Flower: Pick up Large Flower, with right side facing, hold flower so that ch lps are on the left and 3 petals are on the right, in bottom ch lp work sc, working on 2nd Small Flower sc in next sl st between petals; working on Large Flower sc in same ch-lp sp, sl st in marked st. Fasten off. (Flower group formed).

For 2nd flower group, rep Leaves to within joining Large Flower. Holding Large Flower with free ch-lp on bottom right, join 2nd flower group same as for first.

SMALL FLOWER CENTERS (make 2): With yellow, * work ch 3, sc in 3rd ch st from hook (p made), rep from * once, sl st in beg ch st of first p, ch 10, sc in 3rd ch st from hook (3rd p), work p, sl st in beg ch of 3rd p. Fasten off. Keeping chain on wrong side, draw one p-group through center of each Small Flower on first flower group. Attach Centers for 2nd flower group. Chains can serve as points to fasten ornament.

Belts

TREFOIL BELT

Picots highlight this multistitch belt of satin cord. The length of the belt is adjustable.

SIZE: Decorative front piece 6″ wide; sides 3¾″ wide, and length 32″.

MATERIALS: Rattail (lightweight), 100 yds. dark brown, 50 yds. each light blue, olive, red, and silver; aluminum crochet hook G (or English/Canadian hook No. 9) *or size that will give you the correct gauge;* fabric glue (dry-cleanable and clear drying).

GAUGE: 4 dc = 1″; 2 rows of dc = 1¼″.

Note: Rattail requires special attention to the tucking in of ends. Leave ends of at least 2″ when making beg lp on hook and when fastening off. Next to each fasten-off ch st make a knot. When belt is complete tuck in ends of at least 1″ in length. Place glue under stitches through which ends have been drawn.

RIGHT MOTIF: Circles: (make 3): Use light blue. Ch 5, join to form ring, ch 3, 11 dc in ring, sl st beg ch-3. Fasten off.

Note: See General Instructions for how to start row with sc or dc.

Joining Circles: Use olive. Pick up 1 Circle, * work 2 sc in each st around, sl st in beg sc, do not break off *; pick up 2nd Circle, rep from * to *; pick up 3rd Circle, work 2 dc in each st around, sl st in beg dc. Fasten off.

Picot Edging: Use red. Work back lps only. Hold piece so that 2 small Circles are on top. Counting from sl st joining between small Circles, sk 4 sc, on left small Circle, sc next st, * work ch 3, sc in 3rd ch st from hook (p made), sl st next 3 sts *, rep from * to * 4 times; sk remaining sts on Circle; counting from joining sts, sk 3 sts on large Circle, sl st next 3 sts, rep from * to * 5 times; sk remaining sts on Circle, counting from joining sts, sk 4 sts on next small Circle, sl st next 3 sts, rep from * to * 4 times, p, sc in next st. Fasten off.

Fill-In: 1st rnd: Use dark brown. Work back lps only. In sl st before last p made, work sc, sk p and sc, sc in next green sc on Circle; work sc in corresponding st on next Circle, sk sc and p, * (sc in next sl st, 2 sc in center sl st, sc in next sl st, sk p) 4 times, sk next 2 sl sts, work 2 tr in each of next 2 sl sts, sk 2 sl sts and p, rep from * once, rep ( ) 3 times, sc next sl st, 2 sc next sl st, sl st in beg sc.

2nd rnd: Working back lps only, ch 1, sk 2 sc, * sc next 8 sts, ch 2, and sc next 8 sts, working both lps hdc next tr, 3 tr next tr, ch 2, 3 tr next tr, hdc next tr, rep from * once; sc next 8 sts, ch 2 and sc next 7 sts, sl st in beg ch-1. Fasten off.

3rd rnd: Use silver. Work back lps only. Begin in any corner ch-2 sp. * Work sc, ch 2 and sc in ch-2 sp, sc in each st to within next ch-2 sp, rep from * around, end sl st in beg sc. Fasten off.

4th rnd: Use dark brown. Hold piece so that small Circles are on the right and large Circle at left. Begin at top right ch-2 corner in 2nd ch st. Work back lps only. Sl st in each st (including ch sts) around, sl st beg sl st; do not break off.

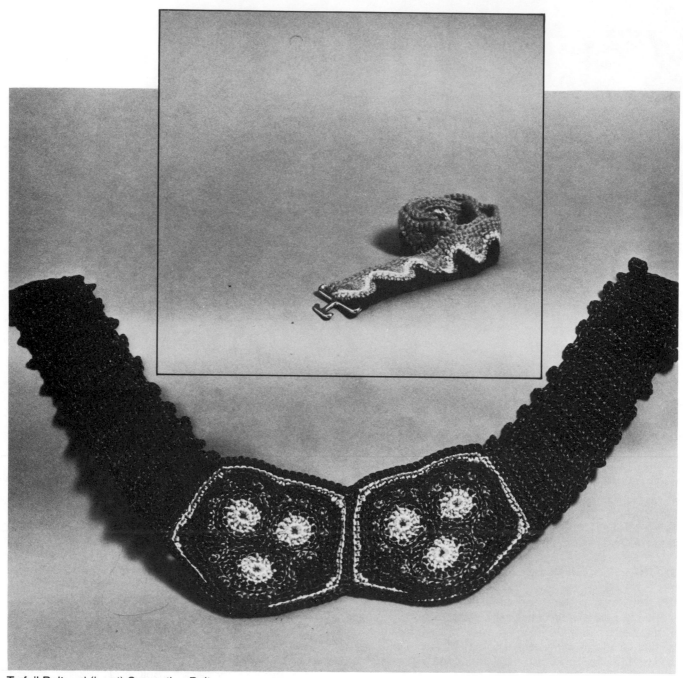

Trefoil Belt and (inset) Serpentine Belt

RIGHT BAND: 1st row: Ch 2 (ch 2 counts as sc); working back lps, sc in each st across next edge (14 sts); ch 3, turn.

2nd row: Working back lps, dc in each st across; ch 2, turn.

3rd row: (dec row): Working back lps, sc in each st across to within last 2 sts, work last 2 sts as 1 as follows: (Pull lp through next st) twice, y o, pull through all 3 lps on hook; ch 3, turn.

4th through 7th rows: Rep 2nd and 3rd rows twice.
8th row: Rep 2nd row.

9th row: Work back lps. Sc each st across (11 sts); ch 3, turn.

10th through 21st rows: Rep 8th and 9th rows 6 times, or for desired length. Fasten off.

LEFT MOTIF: Work as for Right Motif through 3rd rnd of Fill-In.

4th rnd: Use dark brown. Hold piece so that small Circles are on left and large Circle at right. Begin at top right ch-2 sp in 2nd ch st. Working back lps only, sl st each st (including ch sts) around, sl st in beg sl st; do not break off.

LEFT BAND: 1st row: Ch 2 (ch 2 counts as sc), working back lps only, sc in each st across next edge (14 sts), ch 3, turn.

2nd row: Working back lps, dc in each st across; ch 2, turn.

3rd row: (dec row): Work next 2 sts as 1 sc, sc in each remaining st across, ch 3, turn.

4th through 21st rows: Work as for Right Band. Do not fasten off.

JOINING MOTIFS: Use silver. Place Motifs, right sides tog, on top and Bands at bottom. Working on top edge, join Motifs with sl st in back lps of silver sts.

EDGING: Pick up dark brown lp, ** ch 2, * sk end st of next dc row, in end st of next sc row work sc, ch 3 and sc, ch 1, rep from * to within Motif edge, sl st in each st across Motif edges, in end st of next row, work sc, ch 3 and sc, ch 1, rep from * to * through end row of Band, ch 2, sl st in each st across end row, rep from **, sl st beg ch st of edging. Fasten off.

FASTENINGS (make 2): Ch 5, join with sl st to form ring, * ch 1, 6 sc in ring, sl st in beg ch-1; turn. Sk next 3 sc on ring, folding ring, sl st in next st, * (cup button formed), ch 15, sl st in 5th ch st from hook, rep from * to *. Fasten off.

Attach Fastenings: On Left Band, working from back to front, insert 1 button of first Fastening through last dc row between 2 end sts, sk next dc row, insert 2nd button in next dc row between end sts. On same Band at opposite edge, insert 1 button of 2nd Fastening through last dc row, sk next dc row, insert 2nd button in next dc row. Place end of Right Band over end of Left Band. Work buttons through corresponding spaces on Right Band.

SERPENTINE BELT

The wavy pattern in this belt is created with triangles and shells of single and double crochet. The belt hooks with a brass catch.

SIZE: 1¾″ wide; length will fit up to 32″ waist.

MATERIALS: Needlepoint and crewel wool, 30 yds. dynamo red (color A), 20 yds. bronze (B), and 10 yds. each antique gold (C) and light antique gold (D); aluminum crochet hook size E (or English/Canadian hook No. 11) *or the size that will give you the correct gauge;* 2″-wide brass T-bar catch.

GAUGE: 4 sc = 1″.

1st row (right side): Starting at lower edge with B, ch 6, * sc in 3rd ch from hook, hdc in next ch, dc in next ch, tr in next ch (triangle made), ch 10. Rep from * 16 times more, omitting ch-10 on last rep (17 triangles made with 4 ch sts between). This length includes adjustable overlap for hem at ends of belt. Break off B; turn. Attach C with sl st to last st worked.

2nd row: With wrong side facing you, using C and working in back lps only, sc in same st as sl st, sc in each of next 3 sts along triangle side, * 2 sc in top of triangle; working along opposite side of triangle work 1 sc in base of each of next 4 sts, sk 1 ch, sc in each of next 2 ch between triangles, sk 1 ch, sc in each of next 4 sts along side of next triangle. Rep from * 15 times more, ending with 2 sc in top of triangle, 1 sc in each of next 4 sts. Break off C; turn. Attach D with sl st to 3rd sc from last sc worked.

3rd row: With right side facing you, using D and working in front lps only, work sc in same place as sl st, work sc in next sc, * 2 sc in each of next 2 sc at tip of triangle, sc in each of next 4 sc, sk 2 sc, sc in each of next 4 sc on side of next triangle. Rep from * 16 times more, ending with 2 sc in each of next 2 sc, 1 sc in each of next 2 sc, leaving last 2 sc unworked. Break off D; do not turn. Attach A with sl st to last C sc of 2nd row.

4th row: With right side facing you, using A and working in back lps only, ch 1, work 2 sc in next sc of 2nd row; working on 3rd row, sc in each of next 2 sc, * 2 sc in next sc, sc in each of next 2 sc, 2 sc in next sc, (y o hook, pull up a lp in next sc, y o and pull through 2 lps on hook) 3 times; sk 2 sc; rep directions within parentheses 3 times more, y o and pull through all 7 lps on hook (cl made). Rep from * 16 times more, ending with (2 sc in next sc, sc in each of next 2 sc) twice; 2 sc in next sc on 2nd row, sl st in last sc. Break off A; do not turn. Reattach A with sl st to beg of last row.

5th row: With right side facing you, using A and working in back lps only, sl st in each of next 6 sts, work sc in each st to within last 6 sts, sl st in remaining 6 sts. Break off A.

Fold desired amount at each end of belt over catch bars and sew on wrong side.

MEDALLION BELT

This gleaming gold and green belt may become a timeless addition to your wardrobe. It is actually more of a jewelry item than it is a piece of clothing!

SIZE: 2½" wide and 32" long; length is adjustable.

MATERIALS: Rattail (lightweight), 50 yds. each olive, pale lime green, and gold; aluminum crochet hook size G (or English/Canadian hook No. 9) *or size that will give you the correct gauge;* fabric glue (dry-cleanable and clear drying).

GAUGE: 4 dc = 1"; 2 rows dc = 1¼".

Note: Rattail requires special attention to the tucking in of ends. Leave ends of at least 2" when making a beg lp on hook and when fastening off. Next to each fasten-off stitch make a knot. When belt is complete, tuck in ends of at least 1" in length. Place glue under stitches through which ends have been drawn.

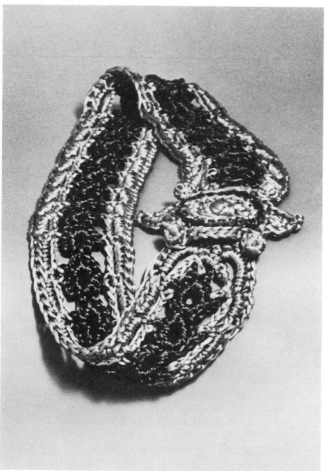

BAND: 1st rnd: Use olive. * Ch 6, join with sl st to form ring, ch 2 (ch 2 counts as sc), 2 sc in ring, ch 3, 3 sc in ring, rep from * 22 times, ch 3, working opposite side of rings, work 3 sc, ch 3 and 3 sc in each ring across; end ch 3, sl st in beg ch-2. Fasten off.

2nd rnd: Use green. With right side of ring-strip facing you, starting in last ch-3 lp made, work sc, ch 5, sk 3 sc, sc in next ch-3 lp, * ch 3, sk 6 sc, sc in next ch-3 lp, rep from * through first ch-3 lp on last ring, ** (ch 5, sc next ch-3 lp on same circle) twice; working opposite side of strip, rep from * to **, ch 5, sl st in beg sc. Fasten off.

3rd rnd: Use gold. With right side facing, begin in last sl st made, work 2 sc, ch 6, sk ch-5 sp, sc in next sc, (ch 3, sk ch-3 sp, sc in next sc) 21 times, ch 6, sk ch-5 sp, 2 sc in next sc, ch 6, sk ch-5 sp, sc in next sc, rep ( ) 21 times, ch 6, sl st in beg sc.

4th rnd: Ch 2, hdc in next sc, * over next ch-6 lp work 2 hdc, ch 3 and 4 hdc, work 4 hdc over each ch-3 sp across to within next ch-6 lp, over ch 6-lp work 4 hdc, ch 3 and 2 hdc *, work hdc in each of next 2 sc, rep from * to *, sl st top of beg ch-2. Fasten off.

MEDALLION: Leave ends of at least 6" when making beg lp on hook and when fastening off on all rnds for Medallion.

1st rnd: Use gold. Ch 5, join with sl st to form ring, ch 3, 11 dc in ring, sl st top of beg ch-3. Fasten off.

2nd rnd: Use olive. Work back lps only on remaining rnds. Work 2 sc in each st around (24 sts), sl st beg sc. Fasten off.

3rd rnd: Use green. Work sc in each st around; sl st in beg sc. Fasten off.

4th rnd: Use gold. Starting in any st * sl st in next 6 sts, ch 6, sl st same sp, rep from * around.

5th rnd: Sl st next st, * sk 1 sl st, in next sl st work 3 dc, ch 3, sc in 3rd ch st from hook (p) and 3 dc, sk next sl st, sl st next sl st, working behind ch-6 lp, sl st next 10 sl sts, rep from *. Fasten off. Gather up all the ends, pull them to right side, through hole at center of Medallion; with all the ends tog make 2 knots, now pull ends back through center hole to wrong side of Medallion, leaving knots on right side of Medallion. Tuck in and glue all ends in place on both Band and Medallion.

FASTENINGS (make 2): Use lime. Ch 5, join with sl st to form ring, * ch 1, 6 sc in ring, sl st in beg ch-1, fold ring in half with wrong side facing you, sk 2 sc, sl st next sc (button formed), * ch 15, rep from * to *. Fasten off. Put glue inside buttons, stuff ends in. Fold Band, right side facing, so that ends meet. Have ch-3 sps at corners of Band meeting. Pick up one Fastening, draw 1 button through both ch-3 sps at top corners of Band; work 2nd Fastening through bottom corner ch-3 sps on Band in same manner. Open Band so that opening is at center, folds on each side. Take up Medallion; position shells at top and bottom; put buttons through the ch-6 lps. Belt can be adjusted to size by placing buttons through sps between dc groups.

ROSETTE BELT

Bulky-weight yarn, beautifully worked in single and double crochet and shell-stitch variations, creates a unique belt in any color.

SIZE: 3″ x 27″; length adjustable.

MATERIALS: Heavy rug yarn (100% wool), 1 (4-oz.) skein rust; aluminum crochet hook size H (or English/Canadian hook No. 8) *or the size that will give you the correct gauge.*

GAUGE: 3 sc = 1″.

FLOWER: Starting at center, ch 5. Join with sl st to form ring.

   1st rnd: Ch 3, work 11 dc in ring. Join with sl st to top of ch-3 (12 dc, counting ch-3 as 1 dc).

2nd rnd: Ch 7, sk next dc, hdc in next dc, (ch 6, sk next dc, hdc in next dc) 4 times; ch 6, sk next dc. Join to first ch of ch-7 (6 lps completed).

3rd rnd: Sl st in ch-6 lp, work 6 sc in each lp around. Join. Do not break off. (Flower Motif should measure 3″ in diameter.)

RIGHT BAND: 1st row: Sl st in each of next 3 sc of first lp, ch 3, * working back lps, dc in next sc, sk 2 sc, in next sc work 1 dc, ch 2 and 1 dc (V-st made), sk 2 sc, dc in each of next 2 sc. Ch 3, turn (ch-3 counts as dc).

2nd row: Sk first dc, dc in next dc, work V-st in ch-2 lp of V-st, sk 2nd dc of V-st, dc in next dc, dc in top of turning ch. Ch 3, turn. Rep 2nd row until Band measures the desired length, sk 2 dc, 3 sc in ch-2 sp of V-st, ch 3, sk 2 dc, sl st in end dc. Break off.

LEFT BAND: With right side facing you, sk 9 sc along lower edge of Flower Motif, attach yarn with sl st to next sc, ch 3, complete Band as before, repeating from * on first row of Right Band.

EDGING: With right side of Right Band facing you, attach yarn with sl st in first ch-3 sp, * 3 sc in ch-3 sp, sl st in each of next 3 sc, 3 sc in next ch-3 sp, ch 2, continuing to work around long edge of Band, work 2 hdc over post of each dc, sc in each sc along edge of Flower Motif, work 2 hdc over post of each dc. Ch 2. Rep from * around, ch 2, join in first sc. Break off.

BUTTONS ON CHAIN: With rust, ch 4, join to form ring. Ch 1, work 8 sc in ring; join to first sc (circle completed). Fold circle in half, working through 2 layers, sl st in next sc (1 button completed), ch 14, sl st in 4th ch from hook (ring formed); work 8 sc in ring, join to first sc (circle completed). Fold circle in half, complete as for first button. Break off. Work another ch with 2 buttons in same manner. Weave in all ends.

Pull buttons at end of ch through holes formed on last rnd at both ends of Left Band. Sk next row, pull buttons on 2nd ch through holes at both ends of next row. Place Right Band over Left Band. Button clasp through corresponding lps on Right Band.

SHAMROCK BELT

A shamrock motif in rayon cord is worked in single and double crochet and picot stitches.

SIZE: Width of band is 3½″; length is adjustable.

MATERIALS: Rattail (lightweight), 140 yds. pale teal; aluminum crochet hook size G (or English/Canadian hook No. 9) *or the size that will give you the correct gauge;* fabric glue (dry cleanable and clear drying).

GAUGE: 4 dc = 1″.

Note: Rattail requires special attention to the tucking in of ends. Leave ends of at least 2″ when making beg lp on hook and when fastening off. Next to each fasten-off ch st make a knot. When belt is complete tuck in ends of at least 1″ in length. Place glue under stitches through which ends have been drawn.

MEDALLION: Starting with blue, at center, ch 5. Join with sl st to form ring.

1st rnd: Ch 1, work 3 sc in ring, (ch 3, work 4 sc in ring) twice; ch 3. Join with sl st to first ch-1.

2nd rnd: Sl st in each of next 3 sc, work 5 dc in next ch-3 lp (petal made), (sl st in each of next 4 sc, work 5 dc in next ch-3 lp) twice (3 petals made). Join to first sl st. Break off.

3rd rnd: Sc in center dc of a petal, ch 4, in center st of next 3-sl st group, work 1 dc, ch 2, and 1 dc (V-st made), ch 8, sc in center dc of 2nd petal, ch 8, in center st of next 3-sl st group work 1 V-st, ch 4, sc in center dc of 3rd petal, ch 6, sc in center sl st of next 3-sl st group, ch 6. Join to first sc.

4th rnd: Ch 2, work 3 sc in next ch-4 lp, 2 sc in ch-2 lp of V-st, (4 sc, ch 2, and 4 sc in next ch-8 lp) twice; 2 sc in ch-2 lp of next V-st, 4 sc in next ch-4 lp, ch 3, (6 sc in next ch-6 lp) twice, ch 3. Join with sl st to top of beg ch of ch-2 (50 sts).

5th rnd: Ch 2, sc in each of next 9 sc, 3 sc in next ch-2 sp, ch 5, sk 2 sc, sc in next sc, ch 7, sk 2 sc, sc in next sc, ch 5, sk 2 sc, work 3 sc in next ch-2 sp (lower edge formed), sc in each of next 10 sc, 3 sc in next ch-3 sp, sc in each of next 12 sc, 3 sc over next ch-3 sp. Join to top of beg ch-2. Do not break off (Medallion completed).

RIGHT BAND: 1st row: * Ch 4, sk next sc, dc in next sc, (ch 1, sk next sc, dc in next sc) 4 times. Ch 3, turn.

2nd row: (Dc in ch-1 sp, dc in next dc) 4 times; dc in each of next 2 ch sts of turning ch (11 dc, counting ch-3 as 1 dc). Ch 3, turn.

3rd row: Work dc in each st across. Ch 4, turn.

4th row: Sk first 2 dc, dc in next dc, * ch 1, sk next dc, dc in next dc. Rep from * 3 times, ending with dc in top

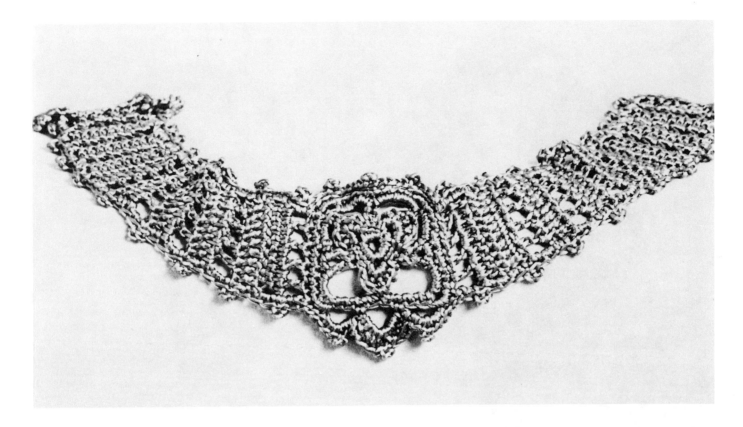

of turning ch (5 sps made). Ch 3, turn.

5th row: Rep 2nd row; ending ch 4, turn.

6th through 9th rows: Rep 4th and 5th rows twice.

10th row: Rep 4th row.

11th through 14th rows: Rep 2nd through 5th rows. Rep 4th and 5th rows until Band measures desired length, ending with a 4th row. Break off (Right Band completed).

LEFT BAND: With right side facing you, sk lps along lower edge of Medallion, attach cord to 3rd sc after ch-5 lp on right side; complete Band as before, repeating from * on first row of Right Band. Break off.

EDGING: Note: Edging is worked completely around the belt. With right side of Right Band facing you, attach cord to 3rd ch st of turning ch on last row.

Working in back lps only, sl st in each of next 10 sts of short end of Band; continue to work along lower edge of Band, * work sc over post of next dc, ch 3, sc in 3rd ch st from hook (p), 2 sc over post of next dc, rep from * to Medallion. Working back lps only, sl st in each of next 3 sc, over ch-5 lp work 4 sc, p and 4 sc, in next ch-7 lp work 4 dc, p and 4 dc, in next ch-5 lp work 4 sc, p and 4 sc, sl st in back lps only of next 3 sts, rep from * to *. Working in back lps only, sl st next 11 sts across short end of Band, continue working along upper edge of Band, rep from * to * to Medallion. Working back lps only, sl st next 3 sts, (work p, sl st next 6 sc) twice, work p, sl st next 3 sts, rep from * to * across. Join to first sl st. Break off.

BUTTONS ON CHAIN: Work same as for Rosette Belt (see page 143).

FLORENTINE BELT

Satin cord, crocheted in shells and clusters, illuminates Renaissance colors to create a jewellike quality.

SIZE: 2″ wide and 32″ long; length is adjustable.

MATERIALS: Rattail (lightweight), 50 yds. each of dark brown, olive, gold, cardinal red, and turquoise blue; aluminum crochet hook size G (or English/Canadian hook No. 9) *or size that will give you the correct gauge;* fabric

Florentine Belt (left) and Sweetheart Belt

glue (dry-cleanable and clear drying).

GAUGE: 4 dc = 1″; 2 rows dc = 1¼″.

Note: Rattail requires special attention to the tucking in of ends. Leave ends of at least 2″ when making a beg lp on hook and when fastening off. Next to each fasten-off ch st make a knot. When belt is complete tuck in ends of at least 1″ in length. Place glue under stitches through which ends have been drawn.

BAND: 1st rnd: Use brown. (Ch 4, dc in 4th ch st from hook) 37 times. (Foundation ch lps formed.) Over post of last dc made, work 3 sc, work 3 sc over next 35 dc posts, in end lp, work 9 sc (mark 7th sc), working over opposite side, work 3 sc over each of next 35 ch-4 sps, work 6 sc in last lp, sl st in beg sc. Fasten off.

2nd row: Use olive. With right side facing, begin in marked st (remove marker), sl st, * sk 2 sc, in next sc work shell of 6 dc, sk 2 sc, sc in next st, rep from * 17 times, ending last rep with sl st. Fasten off.

3rd row: Use gold. Work sl sts in back lps only. Sl st in first sl st of 2nd row. * Sl st next 3 sts, ch 2, sl st next 3 sts, sc in both lps of next sc, rep from * across, ending last rep with sl st in sl st. Fasten off.

4th row: Use red. Sl st in back lp of first sl st of 3rd row, ch 4, * sk 3 sl sts, work 3 sc in ch-2 sp, ** ch 2, sk 3 sl sts, work 3-dc cl in next sc as follows: Holding back last lps on hook work 4 dc in same sp, y o, pull through all 5 lps on hook, ch 2, rep from * 16 times, rep from * to **, ch 4, sk 3 sl sts, sl st in back lp of end sl st. Fasten off.

5th row: Use blue. Sl st in back lp of first sl st of 4th row, ch 5, sk 4 ch sts, sc in center sc of 3-sc group, (work 3 sc in next ch-2 sp) 34 times, sc in center sc of 3-sc group, ch 5, sk 4 ch sts, sl st in back lp of end sl st. Fasten off. Tuck in and glue ends.

TIE: 1st Bobble: Use olive. (Ch 4, sc in 4th ch st from hook—p made) 3 times, sc in sc of first p, mark this last sc made, rep ( ) 5 times, sc in sc of 3rd p from hook. Fasten off.

2nd Bobble: Use red. * Ch 5, join with sl st to form ring, work 6 sc in ring, sl st in beg sc, rep from * once, ch 8, join with sl st in 5th ch st from hook to form ring, work 6 sc in ring, sl st in beg sc, mark this sl st.

3rd Bobble: Use blue. Ch 4, work 4-dc cl in 4th ch st from hook, work p. Fasten off. (Mark base of cl.)

4th Bobble: Use gold. Work as for blue.

Joining: With brown, make a lp on hook, pull through a lp at marked st on olive bobble, and pull through lp at marked st on red bobble, y o, pull through all 3 lps on hook, ch 32, pull through lp at marked st on blue bobble, pull through lp at marked st on gold bobble, work 3 p sts, sc in sc of 3rd p from hook. Fasten off. Tuck in and glue ends.

FASTENING: Fold belt right side facing, opening at center with unworked loop at center left. Fold tie ch in half, insert ch in unworked lp from back to front; pull ch through back to front of first lp at center right opening. Bring ch around front to back through lp to left of unworked lp. Pull bobble ends through ch lp. Pull tight.

SWEETHEART BELT

Silver hearts fasten this belt, which is composed of interlocking shells done in needlepoint and crewel yarn.

SIZE: 2″ wide and 30″ long; length is adjustable.

MATERIALS: Needlepoint and crewel wool, 40 yds. light rose (color A), 20 yds. each medium rose (B), dark gray (C), dark wisteria (D), and purple (E); aluminum crochet hook size H (or English/Canadian hook No. 8) *or the size that will give you the correct gauge;* one 2″ x 2¼″ heart-shaped "sew-on" buckle.

GAUGE: 3 dc = 1″.

Note: Yarn comes in 3-strand lengths. Use yarn double (6 strands) throughout.

1st row: Starting at one end of center pattern, with A ch 4, work 2 dc in 4th ch from hook (shell made), * ch 4, turn (wrong side of shell is now facing you), work 2 dc in 4th ch from hook (base of shell). Rep from * 31 times more (33 shells in zigzag pattern completed). Piece should measure about 30″.

Note: To lengthen or shorten belt by 1½″, add or subtract 2 shells.

Do not turn piece, always work with same side facing you. Break off A; attach B with sl st to last st worked.

2nd row: With right side of last shell worked facing you, using B, sc in same st as sl st, work 3 dc in base of same shell, * sc in top of ch-4 on next shell, ch 3, sc in 3rd ch from hook (p made), sc in base of same shell, 3 dc in base of next shell. Rep from * 15 times more. Break off B; attach C with sl st to post of last dc worked on last shell.

3rd row: With C, work 3 sc over same post as sl st, then working along opposite side of A shells, work 3 sc over post of ch-4 on first A shell, * 3 dc in base of next shell, sc in base of next shell, 2 sc over post of next ch-4. Rep from * 15 times more; (mark last sc made), 3 sc in first B sc. Break off C; attach D with sl st to marked C sc.

4th row: With D, work sc in same place as sl st (mark this sc), sc in next 3 sc, then working into B row, * work 3 dc in next sc, sk 3 dc, sc in next sc, ch 3, sk p. Rep from * 15 times more, ending with 3 dc in next sc, sk 3 dc, then work sc in each of next 4 C sc. Break off D; turn; attach E to marked D sc.

5th row (top edge of belt): Working in front lps only, on wrong side, work hdc, ch 3 and hdc in same place as sl st, then working into 3rd (C) row, hdc in next 3 sts, * work hdc in each of next 2 sc, hdc in each of next 3 dc, sk 1 sc. Rep from * across, ending with hdc in each of next 2 sc, hdc, ch 3 and hdc in next D sc; sl st in same sp. Break off.

Sew buckle in place at each end of belt.

Slippers

GRANNY SQUARE SLIPPERS

An old favorite becomes fanciful footwear. Using a clever variation on the granny square, make squares and join on right side with single crochet for a special textured effect. Cluster and shell stitches lend additional texture.

SIZE: Fits 7–10.

MATERIALS: Rug or bulky yarn weight, 2 oz. each of eggplant purple, emerald green, orange, lavender, and rust; aluminum crochet hook size F (or English/Canadian hook No. 10) or *the size that will give you the correct gauge.*

GAUGE: 4 sc = 1″; 1 square = 3½″ x 3½″.

Note: See General Instructions for how to start row with sc or dc.

SQUARE (Make 16): With eggplant, ch 5, join with sl st in first ch st to form ring.

1st rnd: Ch 3, 11 dc in ring, sl st in top of ch-3; ch 2, turn.

2nd rnd: Sc in next dc, sc, ch 2 and sc in next dc, * sc in each of next 2 dc, sc, ch 2 and sc in next dc, rep from * twice, sl st in beg ch-2. Fasten off. Do not turn.

3rd rnd: With emerald, begin in any ch-2 sp, * work 3 dc, ch 2 and 3 dc in ch-2 sp, sk next sc, sl st in back lps of next 2 sts, sk next st, rep from * 3 times; sl st in beg dc. Fasten off.

4th rnd: With orange, begin in any ch-2 sp, * sc, ch 2 and sc in ch-2 sp, sl st in back lps of next 3 dc, work 2 dc, holding back last lp of each dc on hook, in next sl st, y o, pull through all 3 lps on hook (cl made); work another cl in same sl st; sl st in each of next 3 dc. Rep from * 3 times,

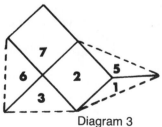

Diagram 1

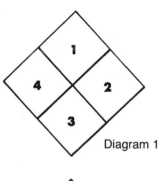

Diagram 2

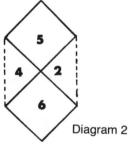

Diagram 3

Granny Square Slippers (clockwise from top left), Men's Slipper-Socks, and Elfin Slippers

sl st in beg sc. Fasten off. Turn piece to other side, and mark as right side.

5th rnd: With lavender, working on right side, begin in any ch-2 sp, * sc, ch 2 and sc in ch-2 sp, sk next sc, work back lps only, sc in each of next 3 sl sts, sl st in next 2 cl sts, sc in next 3 sl sts, sk next sc st, rep from * 3 times, sl st beg sc. Fasten off. Do not turn.

JOININGS: See Diagram 1 for position. With rust, work-ing on right sides, sc tog 4 squares to form large square. Hold piece, with wrong sides facing, in diamond position; label top Square 1, right Square 2, bottom Square 3, and left Square 4. See Diagram 2. Fold small Squares 2 and 4 in half so that their tips are meeting. Sc a 5th Square to Squares 4, 1 and 2 in position over Square 1. Sc a 6th Square to free edges of Square 3. See Diagram 3. Sc a 7th Square to Squares 2 and 6. Sc 8th Square in corre-sponding position to Square 7.

ELFIN SLIPPERS

Whimsical and warm, these charming slippers cheer the heart, comfort the feet, and delight the eye. Take a simple square made with slanting shell stitch, fold, and sew to form a slipper. Shells and picots become flowers and leaves for the ankle trim.

SIZE: Directions are for small, foot length 8½″ [Medium, foot length 9½″; large, foot length 10½″.]

MATERIALS: Knitting worsted weight acrylic, 6 oz. lav-ender, 2 oz. each pale rose, orange, pantile brown, and olive green; aluminum crochet hook size H (or English/Canadian hook No. 8) or *the size that will give you the correct gauge;* large-eyed tapestry needle.

GAUGE: 1 slanting shell st = ⅞″; 2 rows of slanting shells = 1″.

SQUARE: With lavender ch 36 [39–42].
1st row: Beg in 3rd ch st from hook, work 2 dc, * sk 2 ch sts, in next ch st work sc and 2 dc (slanting shell made) rep from * across, ending sk 2 ch sts, sc in last ch st, 11 [12–13] slanting shells, mark this side as wrong side, ch 2, turn.
2nd row: Work 2 dc in same sp as turning ch-2, * sk 2 dc, in sc work shell, rep from * across, ending sc in top of end ch-2, ch 2, turn. Rep 2nd row until there are 25 [27–29] rows. Sl st each st across last row. Fasten off. Hold piece so that foundation ch edge is at bottom and wrong side is facing you. Mark foundation ch edge as Side A, right side edge as B; end-row edge as C, and left side edge as D.

ANKLE TRIM: On Side B, counting up from foundation ch edge, mark the end-shell of the 11th (9th–11th) row.
1st row: Working along Side B, with olive green, in base of marked end-shell work sc, ch 4, work 2 dc in 4th ch st from hook, ch 3 and sc in 3rd ch st from hook (p made), 3 dc in same sp as 2 dc (leaf made), * sk next row, sc in base of end-shell on next row, work leaf, rep from * through end row, sc in top of ch-2 at tip, 8 [10–10] leaves made; working along side C ** work a leaf, sk 2 dc, sc next sc, rep from ** 6 [8–8] times. Fasten off.
2nd row: With orange, sc in sc between first 2 leaves on 1st row, ch 4, starting in 2nd ch st from hook work 4 sc in each of next 3 ch sts (flower made), * sk next leaf, sc in sc between leaves, work a flower, rep from * around, end with sc in sc between last 2 leaves, work flower, sl st same sp (16 [18–18] flowers made). Fasten off.
3rd row: With pink, sc in sc between first and 2nd flow-ers of 2nd row, * work a flower, pick up leaf below next flower (3rd leaf), sk next flower, pulling leaf up around skipped flower sc in tip of leaf, ch 2, sk next flower on 2nd row and leaf below it, sc in sc between flowers, rep from * across, work flower in same sp as last sc between flowers, end sl st in same sp. Fasten off.
4th row: With pantile brown, begin in first ch-2 sp of 3rd row, * sc, work flower, sc same sp, ch 4, sk to next ch-2 sp, rep from * across. Fasten off.

FINISHING: With wrong side facing you (trim is worked on wrong side), fold square on the diagonal so that Side D is tog with Side A. Beg at diagonal fold point (toe); whipstitch edges A and D tog with lavender and tapestry needle (sole formed). Continue sewing Sides B and C tog about 4″ [4″–5″] placing fringe to right side (heel formed). Turn piece to right side; fold flower fringe edge down.

MEN'S SLIPPER-SOCKS

Warm and cozy slipper-socks are simple to make. They are worked in plain and long single crochet with two strands of knitting worsted.

SIZE: Large (sole measures 11″ before stretching).

MATERIALS: Knitting worsted, 4 oz. royal blue, 3 oz. red, 2 oz. each beige, sky blue, and lavender; aluminum crochet hook size G (or English/Canadian hook No. 9) *or size that will give you the correct gauge.*

GAUGE: 5 sc = 1½″; 3 rows of sc = 1″.

Note: Use yarn double strand throughout.

SOLE: Work back lps only throughout. Use royal blue.
1st row: Ch 8, beg in 3rd ch st from hook, * sc in each st across, ch 1, turn (ch-1 counts as sc).
2nd row: Sc same sp as turning ch (inc), sc in each st across to within last st, 2 sc last st (inc).
3rd through 6th rows: (Rep 1st row from * and 2nd row) twice. (Total 13 sts on last row.)
7th through 12th rows: Work 6 rows sc even.
13th through 15th rows: Work 3 rows of sc, dec at end of each row; dec by working 2 sc as 1 as follows: (Pull through lp in next st) twice, y o, pull through all 3 lps on hook. (Total 10 sts).
16th through 35th rows: Work 20 rows of sc even.
36th and 37th rows: Work 2 rows of sc decreasing 1 sc at beg and end of each row. Fasten off.

UPPER: Work back lps only throughout.
1st row: Use royal blue. Ch 7, begin in 3rd ch st from hook, sc in each st across, ch 1, turn.
2nd through 5th rows: Work 4 rows of sc increasing 1 sc at beg and end of each row (total 14 sts).
6th row: Use red. * Sc in next 2 sts, work in st on previous row (5th row) corresponding to next st, pull through a long lp, y o, pull through both lps on hook (long sc made), rep from * across, end sc in last 2 sts. Fasten off. Do not turn.
7th through 9th rows: Use beige. Work 3 rows sc even. Fasten off. Do not turn.
10th row: Use sky blue. Work as for 6th row. Do not turn.
11th row: Use lavender. Work 1 row sc even. Do not turn.
12th row: Use red. Work as for 6th row. Do not turn.

13th row: Use lavender. Sc in next 7 sts, ch 1, sc in remaining 7 sts; ch 1, turn.
14th row: Sc in each st to within ch-1 sp, in ch-1 sp work sc, ch 1 and sc, sc in each remaining st; ch 1, turn.
15th row: Work as for 14th row. Fasten off. Do not turn.
16th row: Use sky blue. Sc in each st to within ch-1 sp, sc in ch-1 sp, sc in each remaining st. Fasten off. Do not turn.
17th row: Use red. Sc in each st to within center st of row, working both lps of center sc work sc, ch 1 and sc, sc remaining sts, ch 1, turn. Rep 14th row 6 times.
24th row: Sc in each st to within st before ch-1 sp, work next st and st after ch-1 sp as 1 sc, ch 8, beg in 2nd ch st from hook, sc each ch st (spoke formed), sc in same sp as last st made on row, sc in each of the remaining sts, ch 1, turn.
25th row: Sc in each st to end st on spoke, ch 1, 2 sc in ch-2 at tip of spoke, ch 1, (mark both ch sps), sc in each foundation ch st of spoke, sc in each of the remaining sts on row. Fasten off. Turn.

SIDES: Right Side: 1st row: Use royal blue. Begin in break-off st. Working to within first marker on this side, work as for 6th row on Upper, remove marker, ch 1, turn. Work 2 rows sc even. Fasten off. Do not turn.
4th row: Use beige. Work as for 6th row of Upper, ch 1, turn. Work 1 row sc even. Fasten off. Turn.
6th row: Use sky blue. Work as for 6th row of Upper. Fasten off. Do not turn.
7th row: Use lavender. Work 1 row sc even. Fasten off. Do not turn.
8th row: Use red. Work as for 6th row of Upper. Fasten off. Do not turn.
9th through 11th rows: Use royal blue. Work 3 rows of sc even. Fasten off.
Left Side: Start at spoke tip in sc after 2nd marker. Rep 1st through 11th rows of Right Side.

FINISHING: Heel Seam: Use royal blue. Right side facing, sc tog end rows of Sides, working back lps only. Fit Upper to Sole, matching toes and heels, pin in place. Use royal blue. Sc tog, working reverse sc. Use royal blue. Work reverse sc edging around ankle edge.

Children's Hat, Scarf, and Mitten Sets

NEWSBOY CAP SET

A Victorian cap with picot detailing and a Newsboy cap crowned with a unique star pattern are coordinated with scarves and mittens. Hats and mittens are worked in single and double crochet. The Newsboy scarf is worked in a chevron pattern; the Victorian scarf is done in a cluster variation.

SIZE: Boy's medium.

MATERIALS: Knitting worsted, 6 oz. rust, 5 oz. navy, small amounts red and lime green; for cap only, 2 oz. rust, 1 oz. navy, small amounts red and lime green; for scarf, 4 oz. rust, 2 oz. navy, small amounts of red and lime green; for mittens, 2 oz. navy, small amounts red, lime green, and rust; aluminum crochet hook size H (or English/Canadian hook No. 9) *or the size that will give you the correct gauge.*

CAP

GAUGE: 3 sc = 1″.

Note: Use 2 strands of knitting worsted throughout.

CROWN: Star: Starting at center with red, ch 5; join with sl st to form ring.

1st rnd (right side): Ch 3, work 11 dc in ring; join to top of first ch-3 (12 dc, counting ch-3 as 1 dc). Break off.

2nd rnd: With navy, make lp on hook, work 2 sc in each dc around; join (24 sc). Circle should measure 2¼″ in diameter.

3rd rnd: * Ch 11, sl st in 5th ch from hook (top lp made), (ch 2, sk next 2 ch sts, sl st in next ch st) twice (first spoke made); sc in each of next 4 sc. Rep from * 5 times more (6 spokes made); join to base of ch-11.

4th rnd: * Work 3 dc in first ch-2 lp, work 3 hdc in next ch-2 lp, in top lp work 3 sc, ch 2 and 3 sc; working along opposite side of spoke, work 3 hdc in next ch-2 lp, 3 dc in last ch-2 lp, sk first sc, sc in each of next 2 sc, sk next sc. Rep from * around. Join to top of first dc (6 points made). Break off.

5th rnd: Attach red to back lp of last sl st, ch 1, sc in same place; working in back lps only, work sc in each of next 8 sts, * in ch-2 lp work 1 sc, ch 2 and 1 sc, sc in each of next 9 sts, sk next 2 sc, sc in each of next 9 sts of next point. Rep from * 4 times more; in ch-2 lp work 1 sc, ch 2 and 1 sc, sc in each of next 9 sts. Join to first ch-1. Break off.

6th rnd: With lime, make lp on hook, * in ch-2 lp of any point work 1 sc, ch 2 and 1 sc; sc in each of next 9 sc, sk next 2 sc, sc in each of next 9 sc of next point. Rep from * around. Join to first sc. Break off. Star should measure 9¾″ in diameter.

WEDGE TRIANGLE: 1st row (right side): Attach rust to ch-2 lp of any point; working in back lps only, work sc in each of next 9 sc, sk next 2 sc (base of point), sc in each of next 9 sc; ch 1, turn.

2nd row: Sk first sc, sc in each of next 7 sc, sk next 2 sc, sc in each of next 7 sc; ch 1, turn.

3rd row: Sk first sc, sc in each of next 5 sc, sk next 2 sc, sc in each of next 5 sc; ch 1, turn.

4th row: Sk first sc, sc in each of next 3 sc, sk next 2 sc, sc in each of next 3 sc; ch 1, turn.

5th row: Sk first sc, sc in next sc, sk next 2 sc, sc in next sc. Break off.

Work 5 more wedge triangles in same manner between points of Star. Crown completed.

BAND: 1st rnd: Attach rust to lime ch-2 lp at tip of any point; ch 1, sc in same place, work as follows to fill in saw-toothed edges of triangle: * (Work 2 sc in center of next V-shape, sc in tip of V) twice; work 2 sc in break-off st, work sc in tip of next V, 2 sc in next V, sc in next tip of V, sc in next lime ch-2 lp (13 sc). Rep from * around (piece will cup), ending with sl st in first ch-1 (78 sc).

Work in back lps only of 2nd through 7th rnds.

2nd rnd: * Dec 1 st (to dec, draw up lp in each of next 2 sts, y o, pull yarn through all 3 lps on hook), sc in each of next 11 sc. Rep from * around; sl st in next st (72 sc.)

3rd rnd: * Dec 1 st, sc in each of next 10 sc. Rep from * around; sl st in next st (66 sc).

4th rnd: * Dec 1 st, sc in each of next 9 sc. Rep from * around; sl st in next st (60 sc).

5th rnd: * Dec 1 st, sc in each of next 8 sc. Rep from * around; sl st in next st (54 sc).

6th and 7th rows: Work 2 rows of sc even.

VISOR: 1st row: Sk next sc, (dc in each of next 8 sc, work 3 dc in next sc) twice; dc in each of next 8 sc, sk next sc, sl st in following sc; turn.

2nd row: Sc in first dc, dc in each of next 8 dc, 2 dc in each of next 2 dc, (dc in each of next 3 dc, 2 dc in each of next 2 dc) twice; dc in each of next 9 dc; sl st in last sl st. Break off.

3rd row: With right side facing you, attach navy to last sl st, ch 1, sc in each of next 3 dc, work 2 hdc in next dc, hdc in each of next 5 dc, 2 hdc in each of next 2 dc, hdc in each of next 5 dc, 2 hdc in each of next 4 dc, hdc in each of next 5 dc, 2 hdc in each of next 2 dc, hdc in each of next 5 dc, 2 hdc in next dc, sc in each of next 3 dc; sl st in last sl st. Break off.

4th row: With right side facing you, attach red to back lp to first st; working in back lps only, work sl st in each st across, ending with sl st in last sl st. Break off.

5th row: With lime, rep 4th row.

FINISHING: With rust, sl st a ring over 2nd navy band of Crown.

SCARF

GAUGE: 7 sc = 2″; 4 rows = 1″.

Note: Work loosely for best results. Use single strand of rust throughout. Sc pattern is reversible.

1st (loop) row: With single strand of rust, work foundation ch lp as follows: Ch 3, dc in 3rd ch from hook (first lp made), (ch 3, turn, dc in 3rd ch st of previous ch 3) 15 times (16 lps made); ch 1. Do not turn.

2nd row: Work along one side of lps as follows: work 1 sc in first lp (last lp made), work 2 sc in next lp, work 3 sc in next lp, ch 2, work 3 sc in next lp, work 2 sc in each of next 3 lps, work sc in each of next 2 lps, work 2 sc in each of next 3 lps, work 3 sc in next lp, ch 2, work 3 sc in next lp, work 2 sc in next lp, sc in last lp; ch 1, turn.

3rd row: Sc in each of next 6 sc, in ch-2 lp work sc, ch 2 and sc, sc in each of next 9 sc, sk 2 sc, sc in each of next 9 sc, in ch-2 lp work sc, ch 2 and sc; sc in each of next 6 sc; ch 1, turn.

4th row (dec row): Dec 1 st (to dec, pull up lp in each of next 2 sts, yo, draw yarn through all 3 lps on hook), sc in each of next 5 sc, in ch-2 lp work sc, ch 2 and sc; sc in each of next 9 sc, sk 2 sc, sc in each of next 9 sc, in ch-2 lp work sc, ch 2 and sc; sc in each of next 5 sc, dec 1 st; ch 1, turn.

Rep 4th row until piece measures 33″, or to length desired, ending with ch 3; turn.

Last (loop) row: Sk next 2 sc, sc in next sc, ch 2, sk sc, sc in next sc, ch 2, sk next 2 sc, sc in ch-2 lp, (ch 2, sk sc, sc in next sc) 9 times; ch 2, sk 2 sc, sc in ch-2 lp, (ch 2, sk sc, sc in next sc) twice; ch 2, sk 2 sc, sc in next sc (16 lps made). Break off.

Edging For Last Row Completed: 1st row: Attach double strand of lime to first lp on last row, ch 1, sc in same lp, 2 sc in each of next 2 lps, ch 2, 2 sc in each of next 4 lps, 1 sc in each of next 2 lps, 2 sc in each of next 4 lps, ch 2, 2 sc in each of next 3 lps. Break off.

2nd row: Attach double strand of red to first ch-1 of last row, ch 1, sc in each of next 4 sc, ch 2, sk next ch-2, sc in each of next 8 sc, sk 2 sc, sc next 8 sc, ch 2, sk ch-2, sc in each of next 5 sc, sl st in last sc. Break off.

Edging For First Row Completed: 1st row: Attach double strand of lime to first lp on foundation ch lp row, ch 1, sc in same lp, 2 sc in next lp, sc in each of next 2 lps, 2 sc in each of next 4 lps, ch 2, 2 sc in each of next 4 lps, sc in each of next 2 lps, 2 sc in each of next 2 lps. Break off.

2nd row: Attach double strand of red to first ch-1, ch 1, sc in each of next 3 sc, sk next 2 sc, sc in each of next 8 sc, ch 2, sk ch-2, sc in each of next 8 sc, sk next 2 sc, sc in each of next 4 sc. Break off.

Fringe: Cut eight 14″ lengths of navy for each tassel. Knot 12 tassels across each end of scarf, spacing evenly. Hold length together, fold in half. Draw folded end through stitch, draw ends through loop and tighten.

MITTENS

GAUGE: 4 sc = 1″; 4 rows = 1″.

Note: Use double strand of knitting worsted for back of hand and one strand for palm.

LEFT MITTEN: BACK OF HAND: FLOWER MOTIF: Starting at center with red, ch 5; join with sl st to form ring.

1st rnd: Ch 3, work 11 dc in ring; join with sl st to top of ch-3 (12 dc, counting ch-3 as 1 dc). Break off.

2nd rnd: Attach navy to any dc, ch 1, 2 sc in same dc, work 2 sc in each dc around; join to first ch-1 (24 sc.) Do not break off.

STEM: 3rd row: Ch 5, sc in 3rd ch from hook (bottom lp made), sc in each of next 2 ch sts, sc in next sc on flower. Break off.

4th row: Hold circle with right side facing you and stem on top. Attach red to back lp of 4th sc on circle to the right of stem, ch 1, working in back lps only, work sc in same place, sc in each of next 3 sc, sc in each of next 3 sts on stem, work 3 sc in lp at tip of stem, working along opposite side of stem work sc in each of next 3 sc, sc in each of next 4 sc on circle. Break off. Mark center sc of the 15 navy sc unworked.

LEAVES:

5th row: With right side facing you, attach lime to back lp of 5th red sc on 4th row, ch 1, working in back lps only, work sc in same place, sc in each of next 2 sc, in next sc work sc, ch 1 and sc, work 3 sc in next sc, in next sc work sc, ch 1 and sc, sc in each of next 3 sc. Break off.

Background: 6th rnd: With right side facing you, attach rust to back lp of 8th navy sc of flower (top center), ch 1, working in back lps only, work sc in same sc, work 2 sc in each of next 7 sc, sc in each of next 4 red sc, sc in each of next 4 lime sc, in ch-1 sp work sc, ch 2 and sc, sc in each of next 5 sc, in next ch-1 sp work sc, ch 2 and sc, sc in each of next 4 lime sc, sc in each of next 4 red sc, work 2 sc in each of next 7 navy sc; join.

7th rnd: Working in back lps only, work sc in each of next 18 sc, hdc in each of next 6 sc, in ch-2 corner lp work 2 dc, ch 2 and 2 dc, sk next sc, sc in each of next 5 sc, sk next sc, in next ch-2 lp work 2 dc, ch 2 and 2 dc, hdc in each of next 6 sc, sc in next 18 sc; join. Break off.

8th row (wrist edge): With right side facing you, holding wrist edge up, attach navy to first ch-2 sp, ch 1, sc in same place; working in back lps only, work sc in each of next 2 dc, sc in each of next 5 sc, sc in each of next 2 dc, sc in ch-2 lp; ch 1, turn.

9th through 13th rows: Sc in each sc across; ch 1, turn, omitting last ch-1; ch 3, turn.

14th row: Work dc each st across. Break off.

PALM: With navy, work as for Palm of girl's mitten.

FINISHING: Sew thumb opening. Place Back of Hand and Palm pieces together right sides out and, with double strand of navy, join with sc over both layers evenly along outer edges, except wrist edges. Break off.

WRIST EDGING;

1st rnd: With right side facing you, attach double strand of navy to wrist edge of Palm, ch 3, dc in each st around; join to top of ch-3. Break off.

RIGHT MITTEN: Work as for Left Mitten. The stitches for Palm are reversible. Turn thumb inside out before sewing thumb opening and joining Palm to Back of Hand.

VICTORIAN CAP SET

SIZES: Children's 4–6.

MATERIALS: Knitting worsted, 8 oz. bronze, 4 oz. cardinal, small amounts gold and purple; for cap only, 3 oz. bronze, small amounts of gold, purple, and cardinal; for scarf only, 5 oz. bronze, 2 oz. cardinal, small amounts of gold and purple; for mittens only, 2 oz. cardinal, small amounts bronze, gold, and purple; aluminum crochet hook size G (or English/Canadian hook No. 9) *or the size that will give you the correct gauge.*

CAP

GAUGE: 3 sc = 1″; 3 rows of sc = 1″.

Note: Use two strands of knitting worsted throughout.

Starting at top of crown with purple, ch 5, join with sl st to form ring.

1st rnd (right side): Ch 3, work 9 dc in ring; join with sl st to top of first ch-3 (10 dc, counting ch-3 as 1 dc).

2nd rnd (right side): Ch 3, work dc in same place as sl st, work 2 dc in each dc around; join to top of first ch-3 (20 dc, counting ch-3 as 1 dc). Break off. Circle should measure 2½″ in diameter.

3rd rnd: With right side facing you, attach bronze to last sl st, ch 3, dc in same place as sl st, work 2 dc in each dc around; join to top of first ch-3 (40 dc, counting ch-3 as 1 dc). Break off.

4th rnd: With wrong side facing you, attach gold to last sl st; ch 1, working in top lps only, work sc in each dc around; join to first ch-1 (40 sc). Break off.

5th rnd: With right side facing you, attach bronze to last sl st; ch 1, working in both lps work * sc in each of next 4 sc, 2 sc in next sc. Rep from * around; join to first ch-1 (48 sc). Break off. Piece should measure 5″ in diameter.

6th rnd: With right side facing you, working in back lps only, attach cardinal to last sl st, * ch 3, keeping last lp of each dc on hook work 2 dc in same place, yo, draw through all 3 lps on hook (3-dc cl made, counting ch-3 as 1 dc), ch 3, sc in 3rd ch from hook (p made), sc in same sp as cl (p-cl made), ch 5, sk 5 sc, sl st in next sc. Rep from * around, ending with sl st in base of first ch-3 (8 p-cl made). Break off. Piece should begin to cup.

7th rnd: With right side facing you, attach bronze to first free sc after any p-cl, ch 3, working in back lps only, work dc in each of next 3 sc, 2 dc in next sc, * sk next p-cl, dc in each of next 4 sc, work 2 dc in next sc. Rep from * around; join to top of first ch-3 (48 dc, counting ch-3 as 1 dc). Do not break off.

8th rnd: Ch 3, working in both lps work dc in each of next 4 dc, 2 dc in next dc, * dc in each of next 5 dc, 2 dc in next dc. Rep from * around; join with sl st to top of first ch-3 (56 dc, counting ch-3 as 1 dc). Break off.

9th rnd: With right side facing you, attach gold to last sl st, ch 1, working in both lps work sc in each of next 6 dc, ch 3, sc in 3rd ch from hook for p, * sc in each of next 7 dc, work p. Rep from * around; join to first ch-1 (8 p made). Break off.

10th rnd: With right side facing you, attach bronze to 2nd sc after any p, ch 1, sc in same place, sc in each of next 4 sc, * ch 1, sk next sc, p and following sc, work sc in each of next 5 sc. Rep from * around, ch 1, sk next sc, last p and following sc; join with sl st to first ch-1. Break off.

11th rnd: With right side facing you, attach purple to any ch-1 sp, ch 3, dc in same sp, working in back lps only, work dc in each of next 5 sc, * work 2 dc in next ch-1 sp, dc in each of next 5 sc. Rep from * around; join to top of first ch-3 (56 dc, counting ch-3 as 1 dc.)

12th rnd: Ch 1, sc in each dc around; join to first ch-1 (56 sc). Break off.

13th rnd: Attach bronze to any sc, ch 1, working in both lps work sc in each sc around; join to first ch-1.

14th row: Ch 3, (sk next sc, keeping last lp of each dc on hook, work 3 dc in next sc, yo and draw through all 4 lps on hook—cl made, ch 1) 3 times, omitting last ch-1; sk next sc, dc in following sc (3 cl made); ch 3, turn.

15th row: (Work cl in sp between next 2 cl, ch 1) twice, omitting last ch-1; dc in top of turning ch; ch 3, turn.

16th row: Work cl in sp between next 2 cl, dc in top of turning ch. Break off. First earflap completed. Sk 18 sc (front of hat) to left of earflap just completed and attach bronze to next sc. Rep 14th through 16th rows for 2nd earflap. Do not break off or turn.

17th rnd: Working along side of 2nd earflap, work 2 sc over end of each of next 3 rows, sc in each of next 20 sc (back of hat) across to first earflap, work 2 sc over end of each of next 3 rows, ch 2, sk top cl, work 2 sc over end of each of next 3 rows, sc in each of next 18 sc across to 2nd earflap, work 2 sc over end of each of next 3 rows; ch 2; join to first sc. Break off.

18th row: With wrong side facing you, attach gold to 2nd sc after ch-2 lp on 2nd earflap, ch 1, working in top lps only, work sc in each of next 3 sc, sk next sc, work 3-dc cl in next sc, sk next sc, sc in each of next 14 sc across front, sk next sc, work 3-dc cl in next sc, sk next sc, sc in each of next 4 sc. Break off.

19th row: With right side facing you, attach bronze to ch-2 lp of first earflap, ch 1, work 2 sc, ch 2 and 2 sc in same lp; working in top lps only, work sc in each of next 4 sc, sk cl, work 3 dc in sp after cl, work dc in each of next 14 sc, work 3 dc in sp before cl, sk cl, sc in each of next 4 sc, in next ch-2 lp work 2 sc, ch 2 and 2 sc. Break off.

20th rnd: With right side facing you, sk 6 sc on left side of 2nd earflap, attach cardinal to back lp of next sc, ch 1, working in back lps only, work sc in each of next 20 sc of back edge, * ch 3, sc in 3rd ch from hook for p, sc in next st. Rep from * around; join to first ch-1. Break off.

SCARF

GAUGE: 3 cl = 2″; 2 rows = 1″.

Note: Use single strand of knitting worsted for scarf and double strand for borders.

1st loop row (right side): Starting with bronze at 1 end after border, ch 3, dc in 3rd ch from hook (first lp made), (ch 3, turn, dc in 3rd ch st of previous ch-3) 10 times (11 lps made); ch 3. Do not turn, but continue to work along one side of lps.

2nd row (right side): Keeping last lp of each dc on hook, work 3 dc in first lp (the last lp made), yo, draw yarn through all 4 lps on hook (first cl made), (ch 1, work 3-dc cl in next lp) 10 times; ch 1, dc in first ch st of first lp made (11 cl made); ch 3, turn.

3rd row (wrong side): Sk first cl, work 2 sc in next ch-1 sp, (ch 2, sk next cl, work 2 sc in next ch-1 sp) 9 times, ch 2, sc in turning ch (11 ch-2 lps made); ch 3, turn.

4th row (right side): Work 3-dc cl in first lp, (ch 1, work 3-dc cl in next lp) 10 times (11 cl made); ch 1, dc in first ch st of turning ch-3; ch 3, turn.

Rep 3rd and 4th rows 28 times more or to length

desired.

Last loop row (wrong side): Sk first cl, sc in next ch-1 sp, (ch 2, sk next cl, sc in next ch-1 sp) 9 times; ch 2, sc in turning ch (11 lps made). Break off.

BORDER: 1st row: With wrong side facing you, attach purple to first ch-2 lp of last lp row, ch 3, dc in same lp, work 2 dc in each of next 10 lps (22 dc, counting ch-3 as 1 dc); ch 3, turn.

2nd row (right side): Sk first dc, dc in each dc across and in turning ch. Break off.

3rd row: With right side facing you, attach bronze to top of turning ch, ch 3, dc in next dc and each dc across (22 dc, counting ch-3 as 1 dc). Break off.

4th row: With wrong side facing you, attach gold to first dc (last dc made on last row), ch 1, sc in same dc, sc in next dc, * ch 3, keeping last lp of each dc on hook, work 2 dc in 3rd ch from hook, yo, draw yarn through all 3 lps on hook (3-dc cl made, counting ch-3 as 1 dc), sk 2 dc, sc in next 2 dc. Rep from * across, ending with sc in top of ch-3 (5 cl made). Break off.

5th row: With right side facing you, attach bronze to last sc made on last row, ch 3, work 2 dc in next sc, * ch 1, sk cl, work 2 dc in each of next 2 sc. Rep from * 3 times more; ch 1, sk cl, work 2 dc in next sc, dc in last sc. Break off.

Work edging in same manner along opposite end.

FRINGE: Using cardinal, cut sixteen 12″ lengths for each tassel. Knot 5 tassels across each end of scarf as follows: Hold lengths together and fold in half. Draw folded end through a ch-1 sp; draw ends through loop and tighten.

MITTENS

GAUGE: 7 hdc = 2″.

Note: Use double strand of knitting worsted for back of hand and one strand for palm.

LEFT MITTEN: BACK OF HAND: 1st rnd (right side): Starting at center with purple, ch 16, hdc in 3rd ch from hook and in each of next 12 ch sts, work 5 hdc in last ch st; continuing along opposite side of foundation ch, work 1 hdc in each of next 12 ch sts, 3 hdc in last ch st; join with sl st to top of turning ch-2 (34 hdc, counting turning ch-2 as 1 hdc). Break off. Completed center panel should measure 1″ x 5″.

2nd rnd: With right side facing you, attach bronze to back lp of hdc to left of last sl st, ch 1, working in back lps only, work sc in same st, sc in each of next 13 hdc, work 2 sc in each of next 3 hdc (top), sc in each of next 15 hdc, ch 1 and mark this ch, 2 sc in each of next 2 hdc, ch 1; join to first ch-1 (41 sts). Break off.

3rd rnd: With wrong side facing you, working in top lp only of each st, attach gold to marked ch-1, ch 1, sc in same sp, sc in each of next 14 sc, work 2 sc in each of next 6 sc, sc in each of next 15 sc, in next ch-1 sp work sc, ch 1 and sc (mark last ch-1 made), sc in each of next 4 sc, sc in next ch-1 sp, ch 1; join to first ch-1 (51 sts). Break off.

4th rnd: With right side facing you, attach bronze to marked ch-1 sp, ch 1, sc in same place, sc in each of next 17 sc, work 2 sc in each of next 9 sc, sc in each of next 17 sc, in next ch-1 sp work sc, ch 1 and sc, sc in each of next 6 sc, sc in next ch-1 sp, ch 1; join to first ch-1 (64 sts). Break off.

PALM: Starting at tip of little finger, with burgundy ch 22.

1st (inc) row: Sc in 2nd ch from hook and in each ch across, working 2 sc in last ch st (22 sc); ch 1, turn. Piece should measure 5¾″.

2nd row: Sc in each sc across; ch 1, turn (22 sc).

3rd (inc) row: Sc in first sc and in each sc across, working 2 sc in last sc (23 sc); ch 1, turn.

Rep 2nd and 3rd rows twice more (25 sc), then rep 2nd row once more.

TO SHAPE THUMB: 9th row: Sc in each of next 11 sc, ch 9 for thumb, sc in 2nd ch from hook and in each ch across, continue to sc in each sc across remainder of row; ch 1, turn.

10th (dec) row: Dec 1 sc at beg of row (to dec, pull up lp in next 2 sts, yo, draw yarn through all 3 lps on hook), sc in each of next 19 sc, work 3 sc in turning ch at tip of thumb; then working along opposite side of thumb ch, sc in each ch across, sc in each remaining sc across; ch 1, turn.

11th (dec) row: Sc in each sc across, dec 1 sc at end of row; ch 1, turn.

12th (dec) row: Dec 1 sc at beg of row, sc in each sc across; ch 1, turn.

13th (dec) row: Rep 11th row, omitting last ch-1. Break off.

FINISHING: Sew thumb opening. Place Back of Hand and Palm pieces together right sides out. With double strand of cardinal, join with sc through both layers evenly along outer edges. Break off.

WRIST EDGING: With right side facing you, attach cardinal to wrist edge. * Ch 3, sc in 3rd ch from hook (p made), sc in next sc. Rep from * around; join. Break off.

RIGHT MITTEN: Work as for Left Mitten. The Palms are reversible. Turn thumb inside out before sewing thumb opening and joining Palm to Back of Hand.

Dog Coat

Man's best friend will enjoy this coat, complete with collar and buttoned front, made in strips which are crocheted together. Worked in double strand for added warmth, the coat is composed of single crochet and chain stitches.

SIZE: Large. Coat measures 18″ from back neck edge to bottom and 26″ around body at under front legs.

MATERIALS: Knitting worsted, used double throughout, 3 (4-oz.) skeins navy, 1 skein each yellow, green, red, and lavender; aluminum crochet hook size H (or English/Canadian hook No. 8) *or the size that will give you the correct gauge.*

GAUGE: 4 sc = 1¼″; 3 rows of sc = 1″.

BACK: Strip 1: 1st row: With green, ch 9, in 4th ch st from hook work sc, (ch 1, sk 1 ch st, sc in next ch st) twice, ch 3, turn.

2nd row: Sk first sc st, (sc in next ch sp, ch 1, sk next sc) twice, sc over turning ch-3, ch 3, turn. Rep 2nd row until there are 63 rows. Fasten off.

Right Edging: Hold strip horizontally with foundation ch edge on your right.

1st row: With yellow, working along long edge of Strip, sc over each end-of-row st (total 63 sts); ch 2, turn (ch 2 counts as sc).

2nd row: Working back lps only, sc in each st across. Fasten off. Turn.

3rd row: Use red. Starting in last sc made, working back lps only, sc in each st across. Fasten off. Mark this side as right side.

Left Edging: Hold Strip horizontally with right side facing and last row edge of Strip on your right. Working opposite long edge of Strip, rep 1st through 3rd rows of Right Edging.

Strip 2: 1st row: With navy, ch 11, work sc in 4th ch st from hook, (ch 1, sk 1 ch st, sc next ch st) 3 times, ch 3, turn.

2nd row: Sk first sc st, (sc next ch sp, ch 1, sk next sc) 3 times, sc over turning ch-3, ch 3, turn. Rep 2nd row until there are 63 rows. Fasten off.

Right Edging: Hold Strip horizontally with foundation ch edge on your right. With navy, working on long edge of Strip, sc in each end-of-row st (total 63 sts). Fasten off. Mark this as right side.

Left Edging: Hold Strip horizontally with right side facing and last row edge of Strip on your right.

1st row: Working opposite long edge of Strip, with lavender, sc in each end-of-row st, ch 2, turn.

2nd row: Work back lps only, sc each st across. Fasten off.

Joining Strip 1 to Strip 2: Mark foundation ch edges of strips as bottom edge and last row edges of strips as neck edge. Place Strip 2 on top of Strip 1, with right sides tog, and foundation ch edges on your right. Working on wrong side with red, sc Strips tog, working top lps only.

Strip 3: Rep Strip 1.

Strip 4: Rep Strip 2. Join Strip 3 to Strip 4 same as for joining Strips 1 and 2.

Joining Strip 3 to Strip 2: Place Strip 3 on top of Strip 2, with right sides tog, and foundation ch edges on your right. With red, sc strips tog working tops lps only.

Seam Edges: With navy, working back lps only, work 3 rows of sc even on left edging of Strip 1 (right seam) and 2 rows of sc even on right edging of Strip 4 (left seam). On each seam edge, count down 6 stitches from the neck edge and mark the 6th st.

LEFT FRONT: Strip: With lavender, ch 7, sc in 4th ch st from hook, ch 1, sk 1 ch st, sc next ch st, ch 3, turn.

2nd row: Sk first sc st, sc next ch sp, ch 1, sk next sc, sc over turning ch-3, ch 3, turn. Rep 2nd row until there are 32 rows. Fasten off.

Right Edge: Hold strip horizontally with foundation ch edge on your right. With navy, working on long edge of strip, sc in each end-of-row st (total 32 sts). Fasten off. Mark this as right side. Mark foundation ch edge as bottom and last row edge as neck edge.

Left Edge: Hold Strip horizontally with right side facing and last row edge of Strip on your right.

1st row: Working opposite long edge of Strip with red, sc in each end-of-row st. Fasten off. Do not turn.

2nd row: With front side facing, begin in first st of last row. With yellow, working back lps only, sc each st across. Fasten off. Do not turn.

3rd row: With green, work as for 2nd row.

4th row: With navy, work as for 2nd row. Do not fasten off; ch 2, turn.

Lapel: Work 6 more rows of sc, working back lps only, increasing 1 sc at neck edge on each row. Fasten off.

RIGHT FRONT: Rep Left Front through 4th row of left edge. Fasten off.

Lapel: Hold piece with right side facing and foundation ch edge on your right. With navy, working back lps only, across right edge work 3 rows of sc, increasing 1 sc at neck edge on each row.

Next row: Work sc in same sp as turning ch, sc next 10 sts, (ch 2, sk 2 sc, sc next 6 sc) 3 times (buttonholes formed); ch 2, turn. Work 2 more rows of sc, working back lps only, increasing 1 sc on each row at neck edge.

JOINING FRONTS TO BACK: Hold Back and Left Front tog, with right sides facing and left seam edges meeting. Place Left Front neck edge at marker on Strip 4. Starting at marker, with navy, sc sections tog for 10 sts. Fasten off. Sk next 12 corresponding sts (Sleeve opening);

continue joining with sc. Hold Back and Right Front tog with right sides facing and right seam edges meeting. Place Right Front neck edge at marker on Strip 1. Join same as for opposite side.

SLEEVES: Hold piece with right side facing.

1st rnd: With navy, beg in either seam at Sleeve opening, work sc, sc in next 12 sts, sc in next seam, sc in remaining 12 sts, sl st in beg sc; ch 2, turn. Working back lps only, work 5 more rnds of sc even. Fasten off. Work 4 more rnds of sc, working back lps only, as follows: Work one each in green, yellow, red, and lavender, turn for each rnd. Work opposite Sleeve in same manner.

COLLAR: Hold piece, with right side facing.

1st row: Begin on Right Front, omit 6 rows of lapel, with navy, sc in next end-of-row st, sc in each of 2 ch sps on Strip, sc in each of next 4 end-of-row sts of strip edging, in seam work 2 dc, sk next 3 sts on Back seam edge, sc next 3 sts, work sc along Back neck edge, working only in ch sps on strips and in each end-of-row st of strip edgings, sc next 3 sts on Back seam edge, sk 3 sts, 2 dc in seam, working on Left Front, sc in next 4 end-of-row sts, sc in each of 2 ch sps, sc in next end-of-row st; ch 2, turn.

2nd row: Work both lps. Work next 2 sts as 1 (dec), sc to within dc, 2 dc in each dc, sk next 3 sc on seam edge, working along neck edge of Back sc across working 1 dec every 6th st, sk 3 sc on seam edge, 2 dc in each dc, sc across working last 2 sts as 1; ch 2, turn.

3rd and 4th rows: Work back lps only for remainder of collar. Work 2 rows of sc even.

5th and 6th rows: Sc across working an inc of 1 sc every 6th st.

7th and 8th rows: Work 2 rows of sc even.

FINISHING: Final Edging: With navy, work sc edging around entire jacket, working 3 sc to turn each corner.

BUTTONS: Make 3. With navy, ch 4, join to form ring with sl st in first ch st.

1st rnd: Work 8 sc in ring, sl st in beg sc.

2nd rnd: Ch 2, working through center of ring over 1st rnd, work 6 long sc; sl st in beg ch-2. Fasten off. Attach buttons to correspond with buttonholes.

Afghans

SHIRVAN AFGHAN

This afghan, based on mosaic patterns of the Caucasian rug style, is easy to make. It is created by repeating just one motif with color variations.

SIZE: Approximately 50″ x 58″.

MATERIALS: Knitting worsted, 2 (4-oz.) skeins each red (color A), Wedgewood blue (B), burgundy (C), 3 skeins each navy (D) and scarlet (E), 4 skeins each royal blue (F) and camel beige (G); aluminum crochet hook size H (or English/Canadian hook No. 8) *or the size that will give you the correct gauge;* small tags for marking rectangles.

GAUGE: Rectangles measure 6″ x 10″. 8 dc = 3″.

Note: Afghan is composed of 35 rectangles. These are numbered on the Diagram according to color combinations given in the directions. Rectangles are joined and border is added to complete afghan.

Work with yarn double throughout.

RECTANGLE NO. 1: First Circle: Starting at center with A, ch 6, join with sl st to form ring.

1st rnd: Ch 3, work 13 dc in ring, join with sl st to top of ch-3. Break off. Mark ring "First Circle" and put it aside. Make another circle in same manner, break off and mark it "2nd Circle."

2nd rnd: 2nd Circle: With right side facing you, using D, work 2 dc in sl st, * work 2 dc in next dc. Rep from * around (28 dc); sl st in top of first dc. Do not break off. Pick up First Circle and, with right side facing you, work 2nd rnd around it in same manner as for 2nd Circle; mark with pin the last dc made (28 dc). Break off. Both circles are now joined and each should measure 3½″ in diameter.

3rd rnd: With wrong side facing you, sk marked dc on first circle, using F, * work 2 sc in next dc, sc in next dc. Rep from * around Circle to within last dc before sl st (38 sc). Do not break off, sk first free dc on 2nd Circle, 2 sc in next dc, sc in next dc; continue around as for First Circle (38 sc); sl st in first sc on First Circle. Break off.

4th rnd: With right side facing you, working in back lp only of each st, sk first 3 sc on 2nd Circle, using A, * sc in each sc around Circle to within last 3 sc (32 sc); work dc over 3rd rnd connection link between 2 Circles, work long dc (draw up 1½″ lp for long dc) in st connecting Circles on 2nd rnd, work another dc over link *, sk next 3 sc on First Circle. Rep from * to * around Circle; sl st in first sc. Break off.

5th rnd: With right side facing you, sk sl st and next 2 sc on 2nd Circle, using B, * sc in next 7 sc, in next sc work sc, ch 2 and sc (corner made; mark this corner with pin), sc in next 10 sc, work corner in next sc, sc in next 7 sc, sk next 3 sc, work 2 dc in next dc, 3 dc in next dc, 2 dc in next dc *, sk next 3 sc on First Circle. Rep from * to * around; sl st in first sc. Break off.

6th rnd: With right side facing you, using D, in a marked corner sp work 3 dc, ch 2 and 3 dc, * sk 3 sc, sc in next 6 sc, sk next 3 sc, in next corner sp work 3 dc, ch 2 and 3 dc, sk next 3 sc, sc in next 17 sts *, sk next 3 sc, work corner in corner sp. Rep from * to * around; sl st in first dc. Break off. Rectangle completed. Mark with tag #1.

Using same colors as Rectangle No. 1, make 9 more rectangles. Then make 25 more rectangles in the following color combinations and mark them:

Home Decoration

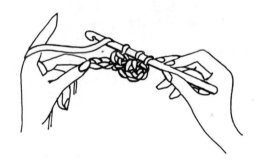

RECTANGLES NO. 2 (make 15): 1st rnd: color G.
    2nd rnd: F.
    3rd rnd: E.
    4th rnd: D.
    5th rnd: F.
    6th rnd: E.

RECTANGLES NO. 3 (make 6): 1st rnd: color D.
    2nd rnd: G.
    3rd rnd: A.
    4th rnd: D.

    5th rnd: G.
    6th rnd: A.

RECTANGLES NO. 4 (make 4): 1st rnd: color E.
    2nd rnd: C.
    3rd rnd: B.
    4th rnd: E.
    5th rnd: C.
    6th rnd: B.

TO JOIN RECTANGLES: Hold a No. 1 and a No. 2

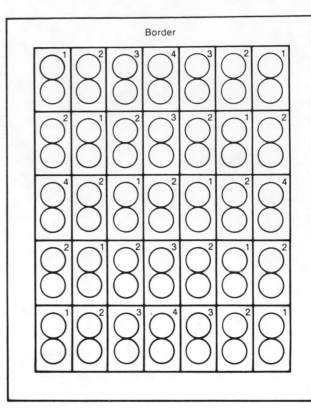

Border

Rectangle together, wrong sides facing, and join across 1 long edge as follows: With C, work 1 sc in 2nd ch st of both pieces at corner; working through back lp of each sc, work sc in each pair of matching sc across to within ch-2 of next corner, sc in next ch st. Break off. When pieces are opened out, a ridge will form on right side.

Join a No. 3 Rectangle to opposite long edge of No. 2. Then complete strip, joining No. 4, No. 3, No. 2, and No. 1 as shown across top of Diagram. Join 4 more strips as shown; then join the strips to complete afghan, except for border.

BORDER: 1st rnd: With right side facing you, using C, work sc, ch 1 and sc in a corner sp; * working through back lp only of each st, sc in each st across to within next corner sp, work sc, ch 1 and sc in sp. Rep from * around afghan to within first sc in first corner; join with sl st in sc. Break off.

2nd rnd: With right side facing you, using F, work 2 dc, ch 2 and 2 dc in a corner sp of last rnd; * working in back lp of each st, dc in each sc across to within next corner sp, work 2 dc, ch 2 and 2 dc in sp. Rep from * around to within first dc; join to dc. Break off.

3rd rnd: With wrong side facing you, using G, work 2 dc, ch 2 and 2 dc in a corner sp; * working in front lp only of each st, dc in each st across to within next corner sp, work 2 dc, ch 2 and 2 dc in sp. Rep from * around to first dc; join, ch 3, turn.

4th rnd: Sk first dc, dc in each dc to corner sp, * work dc, ch 2 and dc in sp, dc in each dc to next corner sp. Rep from * around, work corner; join to top of ch-3. Break off.

5th rnd: With wrong side facing you, using C, work hdc, ch 2 and hdc in a corner sp; * working in front lp only of each st, hdc in each dc across to within next corner sp, work hdc, ch 2 and hdc in sp. Rep from * around to first hdc; join to hdc. Break off.

6th rnd: With right side facing you, using E, work sc, ch 2 and sc in a corner sp, * working in back lp only of each st, sc in each hdc across to within next corner sp, work sc, ch 2 and sc in sp. Rep from * to first sc; join. Break off.

7th and 8th rnds: Rep 3rd and 4th rnds.

MIHRAB AFGHAN

Made in panels, this afghan is inspired by the Turkish prayer rug on which each family member had his own place. Three pattern stitches are used in the panels to create a design with texture as well as color.

SIZE: Approximately 44" x 73".

MATERIALS: Knitting worsted, 6 (4-oz.) skeins dark blue-green (color A), 4 skeins light gold (B), 2 skeins each light rust (C), dark sea green (D), dark rust (E), emerald green (F), light sea green (G), dusty pink (H), and dark gold (I); aluminum crochet hook size H (or English/Canadian hook No. 8) *or the size that will give you the correct gauge.*

GAUGE: 3 dc = 1"; 1 dc row = 1".

Note: The afghan is composed of 6 Panels, each consisting of 3 Sections. The sections of each panel are made separately and joined. Then the panels are joined to form the completed afghan.

Work with yarn double throughout.

PANEL 1: SECTION 1: See Diagram 1.

Flower Strip: 1st row: With color I, ch 7 to measure 2¼", * sc in 4th ch from hook for p, sk next 2 ch, work 3 dc in next ch; ch 3, turn. Sc in first dc (2nd p made), holding back on hook the last lp of each dc, work dc in

each of next 2 dc and in next sc, y o, draw yarn through all 4 lps on hook (flower made); ch 10 to measure 3″. Rep from * 8 times more (2 completed flowers should measure 4¼″); work ch 1 instead of ch 10 at end of last rep (9 flowers made). Piece should measure 23¾″. Break off.

2nd rnd (right side): Attach B to last ch-1; ch 5, * holding back on hook the last lp of each dc, work 2 dc in 4th ch from hook, y o, draw yarn through all 3 lps on hook (3-dc cl made, counting ch-3 as 1 dc), ch 1, sc in next p, ch 4, holding back on hook the last lp of each dc, work 3 dc in 4th ch from hook, y o, draw yarn through all 4 lps on hook (4-dc cl made, counting ch-3 as 1 dc), ch 1, sc in same p, ch 4, make 3-dc cl in 4th ch from hook, ch 1, sc in center ch of ch-3 between flowers, ch 4. Rep from

* 8 times more, ending last rep with sl st in beg of first flower, ch 4; do not break off, but continue to work along opposite side in same manner, ending with sl st in beg of rnd; omit last ch-4. Break off.

3rd rnd: With right side facing you, attach A to last sl st, ch 4, * sk next cl, working in back lp only of each st, work 4 dc in next sc (4-dc group made), ch 1, sc in 4th ch of ch-4 of next cl, ch 1, work 4-dc group in next sc, sk next cl, tr in next sc. Rep from * 7 times more; sk next cl, work 4-dc group in next sc, ch 1, sc in 4th ch of ch-4 of next cl, ch 1, work 4-dc group in next sc, ch 4, sc in next sc at end of piece, ch 4; do not break off, but continue to work along opposite side to match first side, ch 4, sl st at beg (piece should measure 4½″ x 25¼″). Break off.

Flower Strip completed.

Field (a): 1st row: With right side facing you, counting to left of last sl st, sk ch-4, attach E to first dc of first 4-dc group; ch 4, sk next 2 dc, 2 sc in next dc, sk next ch-1, 2 sc in next sc, sk next ch-1, 2 sc in next dc, * sk 3 dc, work 3 tr in next tr, sk next 3 dc, 2 sc in next dc, sk next ch-1, 2 sc in next sc, sk next ch-1, 2 sc in next dc. Rep from * 7 times more; sk 2 dc, tr in next dc; ch 3, turn.

2nd row (wrong side): Sk first tr, working in top lp only of each st, dc in next st and in each st across, ending with dc in top of last ch-4 (80 dc, counting turning ch as 1 dc); ch 3, turn.

3rd row: Sk first 2 dc, working in top lp of each st, dc in each of next 2 dc, dc loosely in 2nd skipped dc (cross group made, with 1 dc crossed around 2 dc), * sk next dc, dc in each of next 2 dc, dc in skipped dc (another cross group made). Rep from * across; dc in top of turning ch (26 cross groups made); ch 3, turn.

4th row: Sk first dc, working in top lp of each st, dc in next dc and in each dc across, ending with dc in top of turning ch (80 dc, counting turning ch as 1 dc); ch 3, turn.

5th row: Rep 3rd row.

6th row: Rep 4th row, omitting last ch-3. Break off.

7th row (Leaf Row): With wrong side facing you, attach B to top of turning ch at beg of last row, ch 1, * work sc and 2 dc in next dc, sk next 2 dc. Rep from * across, ending with sc in last dc (26 leaves made). Break off.

8th row (Field b): With right side facing you, attach E to last sc made on last row; ch 4, * sk next 2 dc, work 3 dc in next sc. Rep from * across, ending with dc in first ch-1 made on last row (80 dc, counting turning ch as 1 dc). Piece should measure 9¾" x 25¼". Break off.

Field (c): Work along opposite side of Flower Strip as follows:

1st row: With right side facing you, attach E to first dc of 4-dc group at right end; rep first row of Field (a) across. Then rep 2nd, 3rd, and 4th rows. Omit ch-3 at end of 4th row. Break off.

Edging: With right side facing you, attach A to last dc made on 8th row (Field b); ch 1, working along short side of rectangle, work 3 sc over post of same dc, sc in first ch-1 of Leaf Row, 3 sc over post of each of next 5 sts, 4 sc over post of next st, 3 sc over post of each of next 2 ch-4 lps, 4 sc over post of next st, 3 sc over post of each of next 3 sts, ch 2; continue across long side of rectangle, working in top lp of each st, sc in each dc across and in turning ch, ch 2; work along remaining 2 sides to match first 2; join with sl st to first ch-1. Rectangle should measure 12¼" x 25½". Break off. Section 1 completed.

SECTION 2: Rising Sun: Starting at center of Sun (X on Diagram 1), with H, ch 6. Join with sl st to form ring.

1st row: Ch 3, work 9 dc in ring (10 dc, counting ch-3 as 1 dc); ch 3, turn.

Work in top lp only of each st.

2nd row (right side): Dc in first dc, 2 dc in each of next 8 dc, 2 dc in top of turning ch (20 dc, counting ch-3 as 1 dc. Fan shape formed.) Ch 3, turn.

3rd row: Sk first dc, * work 2 dc in next st, dc in skipped st (cross group), sk next st *. Rep from * to * 8 times more; dc in top of turning ch (9 cross groups made). Piece should measure 5" across base; ch 3, turn.

4th row: Sk first dc, dc in next dc and each dc across, dc in top of turning ch (29 dc, counting ch-3 as 1 dc); ch 3, turn.

5th row: Sk first 2 dc, rep from * to * on 3rd row, dc in turning ch (13 cross groups made). Piece should measure 8¼" across base. Break off. Sun completed.

Rainbows: Work in top lp only of each st.

1st row: With right side facing you, using A, work sc in last dc made on last row; sc in each dc across, ending with sc in turning ch (41 sc). Break off.

2nd row: With wrong side facing you, attach I to last sc made on last row, ch 2, hdc in each of next 2 sc, sk next sc. Rep from * to * on 3rd row of Rising Sun across to within last 4 sc, sk next sc, work hdc in each of next 3 sc (17 cross groups made). Break off.

3rd row: With right side facing you, attach B to last hdc made on last row; ch 3, dc in next and each st across, ending with dc in top of ch-2 (57 dc, counting ch-3 as 1 dc). Piece should measure across the base the same as narrow end of Section 1, without edging. Break off.

4th row: With wrong side facing you, using A, and counting from right to left, work sc in 7th dc and in each dc across to within last 6 dc (45 sc), leaving 6 sts unworked. Break off.

5th row: With right side facing you, using B, and counting from right to left, work sc in 3rd sc and in each of next 2 sc, dc in next 35 sc, sc in each of next 3 sc, leaving 2 sts unworked. Break off.

6th row: With wrong side facing you, sk last sc made on last row, using I, work sc in each of next 2 sc, sk next dc. Rep 3rd row of Rising Sun from * to * across to within last 4 sts, sk next dc, sc in each of next 2 sc (17 cross groups made). Break off.

7th row: With right side facing you, using A, and counting from right to left, sk 2 sc and 3 dc of cross group, work sc in next dc and in each dc across to within last 5 sts (45 sc). Break off.

8th row: With wrong side facing you, sk last 2 sc made on last row, using I, work sc in next 2 sc, dc in each of next 37 sc, sc in each of next 2 sc. Break off.

9th row: With right side facing you, using A, work sc in each st across (41 sc). Break off. Rainbows completed.

Air: Work in top lp only of each st.

1st row: With wrong side facing you, using H, sk last

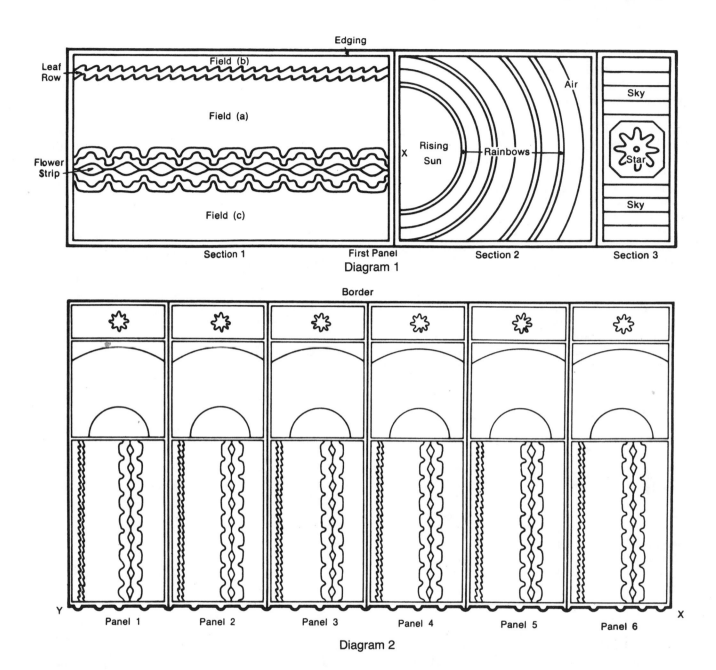

Edging

Field (b)

Leaf Row

Field (a)

Air

Rising Sun

Rainbows

Sky

Flower Strip

X

Star

Field (c)

Sky

Section 1   First Panel   Section 2   Section 3

Diagram 1

Border

Y   X

Panel 1   Panel 2   Panel 3   Panel 4   Panel 5   Panel 6

Diagram 2

sc made on last row and sc in next 3 sc, dc in next sc, ch 2, dc in next 31 sc, ch 2, dc in next sc, sc in next 3 sc; ch 1, turn.

2nd row: Sk first sc, sc in each of next 2 sc, sc next dc, in ch-2 lp work 2 dc, ch 2 and 3 tr, sk next 3 dc, dc in each of next 3 dc, hdc in each of next 3 dc, sc in each of next 13 dc, hdc in each of next 3 dc, dc in each of next 3 dc, sk next 3 dc, in ch-2 lp work 3 tr, ch 2 and 2 dc, sc next dc, sc in next 2 sc, sl st in next sc. Break off. Air completed.

Edging: With right side facing you, attach A to first H

tr in top right corner, ch 4, sk 2 tr, sl st in next dc, (ch 3, sk next 2 sts, sl st in next st) 9 times; in next ch-2 corner lp work 2 sc, ch 2 and 2 sc, work 25 sc evenly spaced along side of piece to next corner, ch 2, continue along bottom edge and work 3 sc over post of next dc, work 2 sc over post of next hdc, sc in next A sc, work 3 sc over post of each of next 10 dc or turning chs, sc in next A sc, 2 sc over post of next hdc, 3 sc over next ch-3 lp (42 sc along base of Sun), ch 2, work 25 sc along side to match opposite side, in ch-2 lp work 2 sc, ch 2 and 2 sc; join with sl st to first ch of ch-4. Piece should measure 10½" x 12¼". Break off. Section 2 completed.

SECTION 3: Star: Starting at center with E, ch 6. Join with sl st to form ring.

1st rnd (right side): Ch 3, work 15 dc in ring; join with sl st to top of ch-3 (16 dc, counting ch-3 as 1 dc).

2nd rnd: Ch 1, sc in same space, work 2 sc in next dc and each dc around; join to first sc (32 sc).

3rd rnd: * Ch 5, sc in 3rd ch from hook, hdc in next ch, dc in next ch, sk next 3 sc, sl st in back lp of next sc. Rep from * 7 times more (8 points made). Star should measure 4¾″ in diameter. Break off. Star completed.

Octagonal Rnd: With right side facing you, attach A to last sl st; ch 3, working in back lp of each st, work dc, ch 2 and 2 dc in same sl st, sc in top ch of next point, * in next sl st between 2 points work 2 dc, ch 2 and 2 dc, sc in top of next point. Rep from * around; join to top of first ch-3. Break off.

Sky: 1st rnd: With right side facing you, and working in back lp of each st, using B and counting from right to left, work sc in 2nd ch st of any ch-2 sp, sc in each of next 6 sts, * sk next ch and 2 dc, in next sc work 3 dc, ch 2 and 3 dc (corner made), sk next 2 dc and first ch of ch-2, sc in each of next 7 sts. Rep from * twice more; sk next ch and 2 dc, work corner in next sc; join to first sc (4 corners made). Break off.

2nd row: With right side facing you and working in back lp of each st, attach B to first ch of a ch-2 corner lp; ch 3, * sk next st, work dc in each of next 2 sts, dc loosely in skipped st (cross group). Rep from * 4 times more (5 cross groups made), dc in 2nd ch st of next corner; ch 3, turn.

3rd row: Sk first dc, working in top lp of each st, dc in each dc across, ending with dc in top of ch-3 (17 dc, counting turning ch as 1 dc); ch 3, turn.

4th row: Sk first 2 dc, working in top lp of each st, dc in each of next 2 dc, dc in 2nd skipped dc (cross group), * sk next dc, dc in each of next 2 dc, make cross group. Rep from * 3 times more (5 cross groups made), dc in top of turning ch; ch 3, turn.

5th row: Rep 3rd row, omitting last ch-3. Break off.

Work sky along opposite side in same manner, repeating 2nd through 5th rows. Sky completed. Piece should measure width of Section 2, without edging.

Edging: With right side facing you, using A, work sc in top lp of last dc made on last row; * working in top lp of each st, sc in each dc across end of piece, ending with sc in top of turning ch (17 sc), ch 3, working along side of piece, work 3 sc over post of same turning ch and each of next 3 sts, working in back lp of each st work 2 sc in each of next 2 dc, sc in each of next 9 sts, 2 sc in each of next 3 dc, 3 sc over post of each of next 3 sts (41 sc along side), ch 3. Rep from * around; join to first sc. Piece should

measure 5¾″ x 12¼″. Break off. Section 3 completed.

Block sections carefully so that they fit together as shown in Diagram 1.

Joining: Hold Sections 1 and 2 with right sides facing. Sl st them together with A along 12¼″ edge, joining matching sts through top lps only. When pieces are opened out, the front lps will form a slight ridge along each edge on right side and the sl sts will form a heavy ridge on wrong side. If desired, the sections can be whipped together with needle and yarn through top lps on wrong side. Join Section 3 to Section 2 as shown. First Panel completed. Panel should measure 12¼″ x 43½″.

Make 5 more Panels in same manner as before, using the following colors: All Flower Strips, Leaf Rows, Rainbows, Skies, Octagonal Rnds and Edgings are worked with the same colors as for First Panel. Remaining areas are worked in the following colors:

PANEL 2: Field and Star, color F; Rising Sun and Air, color C.

PANEL 3: Field and Star, color D; Rising Sun and Air, color E.

PANEL 4: Field and Star, color G; Rising Sun and Air, color F.

PANEL 5: Field and Star, color H; Rising Sun and Air, color D.

PANEL 6: Field and Star, color C; Rising Sun and Air, color G.

Following Diagram 2, crochet or whip panels together in same manner as sections were joined.

BORDER: 1st rnd: With right side facing you, using A, work 3 sl sts in corner ch-2 lp (X on Diagram 2), working along short side of afghan, sl st in each st to next corner lp, work 3 sl sts in corner, work sl st in each st across top edge, work sl st on corner, sl st in each st along opposite short side to Y, work corner. Now work along lower edge (Y to X) as follows: * (Ch 2, sk next 2 sc, working in both lps of each st, sl st in next sc) 14 times; ch 2, sk seam, sl st in first sc on next panel. Rep from * across, ending with sl st in first sl st; ch 3, turn.

2nd row: Work 2 dc in each of next 2 ch-2 lps, * work 2 dc in next lp, ch 3, sc in top of last dc made (p), work 2 dc in each of next 2 ch-2 lps. Rep from * across, ending with dc in ch-2 corner lp. Break off.

SHIRAZ AFGHAN

Reflecting the Persian rug's botanical forms in its undulating vinelike pattern and stylized central flower, this afghan is for the experienced crocheter, since it combines an intricate construction with a variety of stitches.

SIZE: Approximately 47" x 68".

MATERIALS: Knitting worsted, 6 (4-oz.) skeins each hunter green (color A), dark purple (B), and green-gold (C), 3 skeins dark lavender (D), 2 skeins each chartreuse (E), dark cream (F), and copper (G); aluminum crochet hook size H (or English/Canadian hook No. 8) *or the size that will give you the correct gauge;* small tags to mark sections.

GAUGE: 3 dc = 1"; 3 dc rows = 2".

Note: The afghan is composed of 3 center sections, a background, 4 border strips and 4 corners.
Work with yarn double throughout.

SECTION 1: CENTER MEDALLION: See Diagram 1. Starting at center of Section 1, with color A, ch 6. Join with sl st to form ring.

1st rnd: Ch 3, work 15 dc in ring (16 dc, counting ch-3 as 1 dc); join with sl st to top of ch-3. Continue, following Diagram 2 for color placement.

2nd rnd: Ch 3, dc in same place as sl st, work 2 dc in

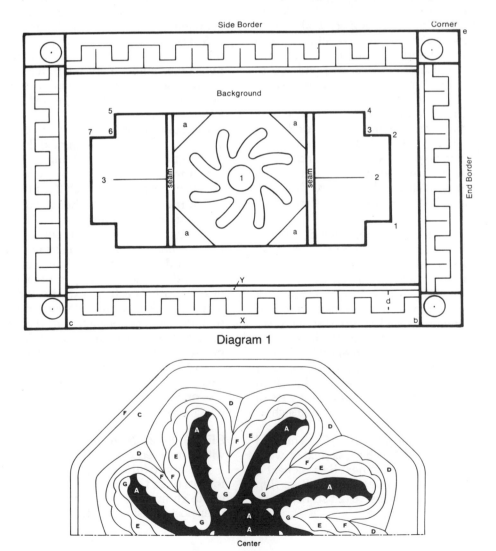

Diagram 1

Diagram 2

169

each dc around (32 dc, counting ch-3 as 1 dc); sl st in top of ch-3. Piece should measure 3½" in diameter.

3rd rnd (first spoke): Ch 1, sc in next dc, * (ch 4, dc in 3rd ch from hook) 7 times (7 lps made), ch 3, being careful not to twist lps, work into lps as follows: Work 2 dc over post of last dc made, work 3 dc over post of each dc on remaining 6 lps (21 dc, counting ch-3 as 1 dc) (6½" spoke made). Sk next 2 dc on circle, sc in each of next 2 dc. Rep from * 7 times more, omitting last 2 sc on last rep, sk 2 dc, sl st in beg ch-1 (8 spokes made). Break off.

4th rnd: With right side facing you, using G, work 2 sc in a ch-3 lp at top of any spoke, * ch 2, working in back lp of each st, sc in next 20 dc along side of spoke, sk 2 sc on circle, work 2 dc over each ch-3 lp on next spoke (14 dc); ch 2, work 2 sc in ch-3 lp at top of spoke. Rep from * around each spoke, omitting last 2 sc on last rep; sl st in first sc. Break off.

5th rnd: With right side facing you, using E, work 2 sc in last ch-2 lp made, * sc in each of next 2 sc (top of spoke), 2 sc in next ch-2 lp, (ch 1, sk 2 sc, work 5 dc in next sc—shell made—sk 2 sc, sc in next sc) 3 times (3 shells made); sk next 2 sc and 4 dc on next spoke, sc in back lp of next 9 dc, in next dc work sc, ch 1 and sc, 2 sc in next ch-2 lp. Rep from * around, omitting last 2 sc on last rep; sl st in first sc. Break off.

6th rnd: With right side facing you, using F, sc in ch-1 sp before first shell made on last rnd, * ch 2, (sk 2 dc of shell, sc in next dc, sk 2 dc, work 5-dc shell in next sc) twice; sk next 2 dc, sc in next dc, sk next 2 dc and 5 sc on next spoke, sc in next 6 sc, in next ch-1 sp work sc, ch 1 and sc, sc in next 7 sc, sc in ch-1 sp before next shell. Rep from * around, omitting last sc on last rep; sl st in first sc. Break off.

7th rnd: With right side facing you, using D, work sc in center st of first dc shell made on last rnd, * sk 2 dc, work 5-dc shell in next sc, sk 2 dc, sc in next dc, sk next 2 dc and 5 sc, sc in each of next 3 sc, in ch-1 sp work sc, ch 1 and sc, sc in next 8 sc, ch 1, sc in next sc, ch 4, sk ch-2, sc in next sc, ch 3, sc in center dc of next shell. Rep from * around, omitting last sc on last rep; sl st in first sc.

8th rnd: Ch 1, * sc in each of next 2 dc, sk next 3 dc and 5 sc, sc in ch-1 sp of next spoke (mark this sc), sc in next 9 sc, in next ch-1 sp work sc, ch 1 and sc, 4 sc over next ch-4 lp, sc in next sc, 3 sc over next ch-3 lp, sc in next sc. Rep from * around without marking any sts of repeats. End omitting last sc on last rep; sl st in first ch-1. Break off.

9th rnd: With right side facing you, using C, sk marked sc and next 2 sc, * sc in each of next 8 sc, sk next sc, work sc, ch 1 and sc in next ch-1 sp, sc in next 8 sc, sk next 3 sc, work 3 dc in next sc (shell made), sk next 3 sc. Rep from * around, ending with sl st in first sc (21 sts between ch-1 sps on each side of octagon).

10th rnd: Ch 3, dc in each of next 8 sc, * work dc, ch 1 and dc in ch-1 sp, dc in next 9 sc, work 2 tr in each of next 3 dc of shell, dc in next 9 sc. Rep from * around, omitting last 9 dc on last rep; sl st in ch-3 (26 sts between ch-1 sps on each side). Break off.

11th rnd: With wrong side facing you, using F and working in top lp of each st, sc in last sl st made, sc in next 9 sts, * ch 1 (mark this st), sc in next 26 sts. Rep from * around, ending sc in last 17 sts; sl st in first sc (26 sc on each side). Break off. Medallion completed.

TRIANGLES (a):

1st row: With right side facing you, using B and working in back lp of each st, work hdc in sc after a marked sp, sk next st, hdc in next st, sk next st, hdc in next 18 sts, sk next st, hdc in next st, sk next st, hdc in next st (22 hdc); ch 2, turn.

2nd row: Sk first st, hdc in next st, sk next st, hdc in next 14 sts, (sk next st, hdc in next st) twice (18 hdc, counting ch-2 as 1 hdc); ch 2, turn.

3rd row: Sk first st, working in back lp of each st, work hdc in next st, sk next st, hdc in next 10 sts, (sk next st, hdc in next st) twice (14 hdc); ch 2, turn.

4th row: Sk first st, hdc in next st, sk next st, hdc in next 6 sts, (sk next st, hdc in next st) twice (10 hdc); ch 2, turn.

5th row: Sk first st, working in back lp of each st, hdc in next st, sk next st, hdc in next 2 sts, (sk next st, hdc in next st) twice (6 hdc); ch 2, turn.

6th row: Sk first st, hdc in each of next 2 sts, sk next st, hdc in next st (4 hdc); ch 2, turn.

7th row: Sk first 2 sts, hdc in back lp of next st. Break off. First triangle completed. Make 3 more triangles in same manner on every other side of octagon so that piece forms square. Work around square as follows:

1st rnd: With right side facing you, using B, work 3 dc, ch 2 and 3 dc in corner sp at point of a triangle, work 2 dc over post of each of next 6 sts, (hdc or ch-2) along side of triangle, sk ch-1 on Medallion, sc in back lps of next 26 sc, 2 dc over post of each of next 6 sts along side of next triangle. Continue around remaining 3 sides in same manner, sl st in first dc (56 sts on each side); ch 1, turn.

2nd rnd: Sc in next 2 dc * work 4 sc in ch-1 sp, sc in each st to next corner sp. Rep from * around, omitting last 2 sc on last rep; sl st in first sc (60 sts on each side). Break off. Section 1 completed.

SECTION 2: Note: Be sure to mark where indicated with numbered markers.

1st row (right side): Make 24 foundation ch lps as follows (area C-X on Diagram 3): With C, (ch 4, work dc in 4th ch from hook) 24 times (24 lps); ch 3, work 2 dc over post of last dc made (first dc group), 3 dc over post

of next dc (2nd dc group), 3 dc over post of each of next 4 dc (6 groups made in all), place marker #1 in last dc of 3rd group, place marker #2 in last dc of 4th group; ch 3, 3 dc over post of each of next 12 dc; ch 3, 3 dc over post over each of next 2 dc, 3 dc over post of next dc and place marker #3 in first dc of this group, 3 dc over post of next dc and place marker #4 in first dc of this group, 3 dc over post of next dc and place marker #5 in first dc of this group, 3 dc over post of last dc (24 groups). Break off.

2nd row: With right side facing you, working in back lp of each st, using A, work dc in marked dc #5, dc in each of next 5 dc (last 5 dc made on last row), ch 2, work 6 dc over post of last st worked into, ch 2; working along opposite side of foundation ch lps work 3 dc in each of next 5 ch-3 lps, 2 dc in next lp, sk next lp, work 3 sc in each of next 10 lps, sk next lp, 2 dc in next lp, 3 dc in each of next 5 lps, ch 2, 6 dc over post of ch-3, ch 2, dc in top of ch-3, dc in back lp of each of next 5 dc, place marker #6 in last dc made. Break off.

3rd row: With right side facing you, using G, work dc in first dc made on last row, dc in each of next 5 dc, work 2 dc, ch 2 and 2 dc in ch-2 lp, dc in each of next 6 dc, work 2 dc, ch 2 and 2 dc in next ch-2 lp, dc in next 17 dc, sk next 4 sc, sc in next 22 sc, sk next 4 sc, dc in next 17 dc, (work 2 dc, ch 2 and 2 dc in next ch-2 lp, dc in next 6 dc) twice; ch 1, place marker #7 in ch-1. Turn.

4th row: Sk first dc, sc in next 7 dc, work sc, ch 1 and

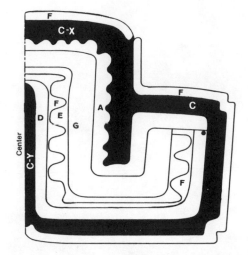

sc in ch-2 lp (first corner), sc in next 10 dc, work corner in ch-2 lp, sc in next 17 dc, sk next 2 dc and 1 sc, sc in next 20 sc, sk next sc and 2 dc, sc in next 17 dc, work corner in next lp, sc in next 10 dc, work corner in next lp, sc in next 8 dc. Break off.

5th row: With wrong side facing you, using E, work sl st in marked ch-1 #7, ch 5, sc in 3rd ch from hook, hdc in next ch, dc in next ch (triangle made), sk 3 sc, sl st in next sc, work triangle, sk 3 sc, sl st in next sc, in ch-1 sp work sc, ch 1 and sc (first corner), sc in next 12 sc, work corner in next ch-1 sp, sl st in next sc, (work triangle, sk 3 sc, sl st in next sc) 4 times; sk 2 sc, sc in next 18 sc, sk 2 sc, sl st in next sc, (work triangle, sk 3 sc, sl st in next sc) 4 times; work corner in next ch-1 sp, sc in next 12 sc, work corner in next ch-1 sp, sl st in next sc, (work triangle, sk 3 sc, sl st in next sc) twice. Break off. Turn.

6th row: With right side facing you, using F, work 2 dc in last sl st made on last row, sl st in top of triangle, 3 dc in sl st between triangles, sl st in top of next triangle, 3 dc in next sl st, dc in next sc, dc in next ch-1 sp, ch 3, sc in next 14 sc, ch 3, dc in next ch-1 sp, dc in next sc, 3 dc in next sl st, (sl st in top of next triangle, 3 dc in sl st between triangles) 3 times; sl st in top of next triangle, sk next sl st and 4 sc, sc in next 10 sc, sk next 4 sc and 1 sl st, (sl st in top of next triangle, 3 dc in next sl st) 3 times; sl st in top of next triangle, 3 dc in next sl st, dc in next sc, dc in ch-1 sp, ch 3, sc in next 14 sc, ch 3, dc in ch-1 sp, dc in next sc, 3 dc in next sl st, sl st in top of triangle, 3 dc in next sl st between triangles, sl st in top of next triangle, 2 dc in last sl st. Break off.

7th row: With right side facing you, using D, work dc in first dc made on last row, dc in next 11 sc, work 2 dc, ch 2 and 2 dc in next ch-3 lp (corner shell), dc in next 14 sts, work corner shell in next ch-3 lp, dc in next 18 sts, sk next 3 sc, sc in next 4 sc, sk next 3 sc, dc in next 18 sts, work corner shell in next ch-3 lp, dc in next 14 sc, work corner shell in next lp, dc in next 12 sts (108 sts, not

counting corner loops). Break off.

8th row: With right side facing you, place piece before you so that it resembles an archway. With A, work 3 dc over post of last dc made at right (dot on Diagram 3), 3 dc over post of next dc, dc in marked ch st #7, 3 dc over post of each of next 2 dc, sk 2 dc, sl st in marked dc #1. Break off. Working on opposite side of "archway," sl st in dc marked #4, sk 2 dc, 3 dc over post of each of next 2 dc, dc in next sc, work 3 dc over each of next 2 posts (13 dc on each side). Break off.

9th row: With right side facing you, using C, sl st in marked dc #3, sk next 3 sts, dc in next 13 sts of 8th row, ch 2, 3 dc over post of last dc worked into, dc in next 13 dc, work dc, ch 1 and 3 dc in next ch-2 lp, dc in next 18 dc, work 3 dc, ch 1 and dc in next ch-2 lp, ch 1, tr in next 20 dc, sk next 3 sc, sl st in next sc; to close seam (C-Y on Diagram 3), fold piece right side out with tr's on last row matching color D dc's, join with 20 sc working in back lp of each st (seam joined) ending in last dc before ch-2; work dc, ch 1 and 3 dc in next ch-2 lp, dc in next 18 dc, work 3 dc, ch 1 and dc in ch-2 lp and place marker #8 in lp, dc in next 13 dc, work 3 dc over post of next dc, ch 1, dc in top of same dc and in next 12 dc, sk next 3 sts, sl st in marked dc #2. Break off.

10th row: With wrong side facing you, using F, work 2 dc, ch 2 and 2 dc in marked lp #8, working in front lp of each st, work sc in next 24 dc, 2 hdc in next ch-1 sp, sk seam, 2 hdc in next ch-1 sp on other side of seam, sc in next 24 dc, work 2 dc, ch 2 and 2 dc in ch-1 sp and place marker #9 in ch-2 lp, sc in next 17 dc, work sc, ch 1 and sc in next ch-1 sp, sc in next 12 dc, sk next dc, sl st and dc, sc in next 5 dc, work 4 sc in next ch-3 lp, ch 2, sc in next 36 dc, ch 2, 4 sc in next ch-3 lp, sc in next 5 dc, sk next dc, sl st and dc, sc in next 12 dc, work sc, ch 1 and sc in ch-1 sp, sc in next 17 dc, sl st in first dc. Break off. Turn.

11th row: With right side facing you, working in back lp of each st, using B, work 4 dc in marked lp #9, dc in next 56 sts, 4 dc in next ch-2 lp, dc in next 20 sts, work dc, ch 2 and dc in next ch-1 sp, dc in next 12 sc, sk 4 sts, sc in next 6 sts, work 2 sc, ch 2 and 3 dc in next ch-2 lp, sk next 3 sc, sc in next 30 sc, sk next 3 sc, work 3 dc, ch 2 and 2 sc in next ch-2 lp, sc in next 6 sts, sk next 4 sts, dc in next 12 sc, work dc, ch 2 and dc in next ch-1 sp, dc in next 20 sts; sl st in first dc. Break off. Section 2 completed.

SECTION 3: Work in same manner as for Section 2.

TO JOIN SECTIONS: With right sides together, match 60 sts of Section 1 to 60 sts of Section 2 (seam on Diagram 1); working in back lp of each st on both pieces, using B, sc in pairs of sts across. Break off. Join Section 3 to opposite edge of Section 1 in same manner.

BACKGROUND: 1st rnd: With wrong side facing you, using B, work hdc, ch 2 and hdc (corner) in corner sp 1 on Diagram 1, * hdc in next 36 sts to corner 2, work corner in corner sp, hdc in next 7 sts to inner point 3, sk next 2 sts, hdc in next 12 sts to corner 4, work corner in corner sp, hdc in next 23 sts, sk seam, hdc in next 60 sts to next seam, sk seam, hdc in next 23 sts to corner 5, work corner in corner sp, hdc in next 12 sts to inner point 6, sk 2 sts, hdc in next 7 sts to corner 7, work corner in corner sp; complete rnd to match side just finished; sl st in first hdc. Ch 2, turn.

2nd rnd: Working in back lp of each st, hdc in each st around working 2 dc, ch 2 and 2 dc in each corner sp and skipping 2 sts at each inner point (42 sts from 1 to 2, 9 sts from 2 to 3, 14 sts from 3 to 4, 112 sts from 4 to 5, 14 sts from 5 to 6, 9 sts from 6 to 7, etc.); join. Ch 2, turn.

3rd rnd: Work hdc in each st around working 2 dc, ch 2 and 2 dc in each corner sp and skipping 2 sts at each inner point (46 sts from 1 to 2, 10 sts from 2 to 3, 15 sts from 3 to 4, 116 sts from 4 to 5, 15 sts from 5 to 6, 10 sts from 6 to 7); join. Break off. Turn.

4th row: Work in back lp of each st except for sl sts work both lps. With right side facing you, hold piece so that Section 2 is at top. Counting down from corner 2 toward inner point 3, work sl st in 8th hdc, sk next 3 sts, dc in next 14 sts, work dc, ch 1 and dc in corner 4, dc in next 116 hdc, work dc, ch 1 and dc in corner 5, dc in next 14 hdc, sk next 3 sts at inner point 6, sl st in next hdc; sl st in 3 more hdc, turn.

5th row: Sk first dc, dc in next 14 dc, work dc, ch 1 and dc in corner 5, dc in next 118 dc, work dc, ch 1 and dc in corner 4, dc in next 14 dc, sk next dc and 2 hdc, sl st in each of next 3 hdc; turn.

6th row: Sk first dc, dc in next 14 dc, work dc, ch 1 and dc in corner 4, dc in next 120 dc, work corner 4, dc in next 14 dc, sk next dc and the 2 dc at corner 7; sl st in next 2 dc and corner sp; turn.

7th row: Sk first dc, dc in next 14 dc, work dc, ch 1 and dc in corner 5, dc in next 122 dc, work dc, ch 1 and dc in corner 4, dc in next 14 dc; sl st in corner sp. Break off.

Rep 4th row through 7th row on opposite edge of afghan.

8th rnd: With right side facing you, using B, work 2 dc, ch 1 and 2 dc in any corner sp; work dc in each st around working 2 dc, ch 1 and 2 dc in each of the remaining 3 corners (126 dc on long sides, 80 dc on short sides); sl st in first dc.

9th rnd: Ch 3, sk first dc, work dc in each dc around working 2 dc, ch 2 and 2 dc in each corner (130 dc on each long side, 84 sts on each short side); sl st in first ch-3, turn.

10th rnd: (wrong side): Sc in each dc around working

2 sc, ch 2 and 2 sc in each corner (134 sc on long sides, 88 sc on short sides); join. Break off.

With C, work 2 more rnds sc in same manner, working sc, ch 1 and sc in each corner (138 sc on long sides, 92 sc on short sides on last rnd). Break off. Background completed.

BORDER: Side Border: Work 13 lps as follows:

1st row: With A, (ch 4, dc in 4th ch from hook) 13 times; * ch 18, sl st in 6th ch from hook, (ch 2, sk 2 ch sts, sl st in next st) 4 times (5 lps made), (ch 4, dc in 4th ch from hook) 8 times (8 lps made). Rep from * 5 times more; make 5 more lps. Piece resembles a comb (Area X on Diagram 1) having a base of 66 lps with six 5-lp "teeth" widely spaced. The 13-lp extension at each end of base will turn up at a right angle to form an additional "tooth" at each end.

2nd rnd: Ch 3, work 2 dc over post of last dc made, 3 dc over post of each of next 4 dc, ch 3 (Corner b on Diagram 1), 3 dc over posts of next 56 dc along base of "comb," ch 3, (Corner c on Diagram), 3 dc over post of each of remaining 5 dc, * ch 3, sc in same lp, ch 3, 3 dc over ch-3 side of same lp, working along opposite edge of lps, work 3 dc in each of next 3 ch-3 lps, 2 dc in next lp, sk next lp, 3 sc in each of next 6 lps, sk next lp, 2 dc in next lp ("tooth" of "comb"), 3 dc in each of next 4 lps (top of "tooth"). Rep from * 6 times more; ch 3, sc in same lp, ch 3 and place marker #1 in ch-sp, sl st in top of first ch-3. Break off.

3rd row: With wrong side facing you, using G, work 3 sc over marked ch-sp #1, 3 sc over next ch-3 lp, * ch 2, sl st in next dc, (ch 5, sc in 3rd ch from hook, hdc in next ch st, dc in next ch st—triangle made—sk 3 dc, sl st in next dc) 3 times (3 triangles); sk 1 dc and 1 sc, sc in next 16 sc, sk 1 sc and 1 dc, sl st in next dc, (ch 5, make triangle, sk 3 dc, sl st in next dc) 3 times; ch 2, work 3 sc over each of next ch-3 lps. Rep from * 6 times more. Break off.

4th row: With right side facing you, using E, work sc in last sc made, sc in each of next 5 sc, * work sc, ch 3 and dc in ch-2 lp, 2 dc in sl st at base of triangle, sl st in top of triangle, (3 dc in sl st between triangles, sl st in top of triangle) twice; sk next sl st and 2 sc, sc in next 12 sc, sk 2 sc and 1 sl st, (sl st in top of triangle, 3 dc in sl st between triangles) twice; sl st in top of next triangle, 2 dc in next sl st, work dc, ch 3 and sc in ch-2 lp, sc in next 6 sc. Rep from * 6 times more. Break off.

5th row: With wrong side facing you, using F, work sc in last sc made, sc in next 6 sc, * work 2 sc, ch 1 and sc in ch-3 lp, sc in next 11 sts, sk 1 sl st and 1 sc, sc in next 10 sc, sk 1 sc and 1 sl st, sc in next 11 sts, work sc, ch 1 and 2 sc in ch-3 lp, sc in next 8 sc. Rep from * 6 times more, ending last rep with 7 sc instead of 8. Break off.

6th row: With right side facing you, using D, work sc in last sc made, sc in next 8 sc, * work ch 3 and dc in ch-1 sp, dc in next 11 sc, sk 3 sc, sc in next 6 sc, sk 3 sc, dc in next 11 sc, work dc in ch-1 sp, ch 3, sc in next 12 sc. Rep from * 6 times more, ending with 9 sc instead of 12. Break off.

7th rnd: With right side facing you, working in back lp of each st, using C, work sc in first sc made on last row, sc in next 8 sc, * work 2 sc in ch-3 lp, ch 3, tr in next 12 dc, sk 5 sc, sl st in next sc; to close seam (Line d on Diagram 1), fold piece right side out with tr's matching dc's of last row, working in back lp of matching tr's and dc's work 11 sc (seam closed), ch 3, work 2 sc in ch-3 lp, sc in next 12 sc. Rep from * 6 times more, ending last rep with 9 sc instead of 12. All seams are now closed and piece forms rectangular shape. Continue across end of piece, outer edge and other end as follows: Ch 1, work sc in side of each of next 4 row ends (colors D, F, E, G), working in back lp of each st, work sc in next 15 dc, work 3 dc, ch 2 and 3 dc in ch-3 lp, dc in next 168 dc across outer edge, work 3 dc, ch 2 and 3 dc in ch-3 lp, sc in next 15 dc, work sc in side of each of next 4 row ends (colors G, E, F, D), ch 1, sl st in first sc. Break off.

8th row: Work across inner edge of piece (Y on Diagram 1) as follows: With right side facing you, working in back lp of each st, using D, work sc in last ch-1 sp made, sc in next 11 sc, * sk ch-3, work 3 dc in top of tr, working behind next ch-3 work dc in color D ch-3 lp of 6th row, working into color C sts again work sc in next 16 sc. Rep from * 6 times more, ending last rep with 11 sc instead of 16. Break off. One Side Border piece completed. Make another piece in same manner.

End Border: 1st row: Following directions for first row of Side Border, make 13 lps; then * ch 18 and make 5 lps for "tooth" on "comb," make 8 more lps for base of "comb." Rep from * 3 times more, then make 5 more lps ("comb" has a base of 50 lps with four 5-loop "teeth"). Work as for Side Border, working rep on each row 4 times instead of 6. Make another End Border.

CORNERS: Starting at center with B, ch 6. Join with sl st to form ring.

1st rnd: Ch 3, work 11 dc in ring, sl st in top of ch-3.

2nd rnd: Ch 3, working in top of each st, dc in same place as sl st, 2 dc in each of next 11 dc, sl st in top of ch-3 (24 dc, counting ch-3 as 1 dc).

3rd rnd: Ch 3, dc in sl st, working in top lp of each st, work 2 dc in each of next 5 dc, ch 2, (2 dc in next 6 dc, ch 2) 3 times (48 sts); sl st in top of ch-3. Break off.

4th rnd: With right side facing you, using C, work 3 dc, ch 2 and 3 dc in a ch-2 lp, sk 3 dc, working in top lp of each st, work sc in next 6 dc, sk 3 dc, (work 3 dc, ch 2 and 3 dc in next ch-2 lp, sk 3 dc, sc in next 6 dc, sk 3 dc) 3 times; sl st in first 3 dc.

5th row: Ch 3, dc in ch-2 sp, working in top lp of each st, (dc in each st to next corner lp, in lp work 3 dc, ch 2 and 3 dc) twice; dc in each st to next corner lp, dc in lp, ch 3, sl st in same lp. Break off.

6th row: With right side facing you, using C and working in top lp of each st, work sl st in top of first ch-3 made on last row, ch 3, dc in next 16 dc, work dc, ch 2 and dc in lp (Corner e on Diagram 1), dc in next 18 dc, ch 3, sl st in corner lp. Break off. Corner completed. Make 3 more corners.

Crochet borders in place with sl st, working on wrong side. Sc corners in place on right side so that joining forms ridge.

BOKHARA AFGHAN

This afghan dramatizes the geometric motifs of Turkoman rugs by exploding their size and by adding hot color. Its construction plays variations on the theme of the easy single crochet stitch and features the granny square.

SIZE: Approximately 46″ x 71″.

MATERIALS: Knitting worsted, 2 (4-oz.) skeins each lime green (color A), light chocolate (B), and dark chocolate (C), 4 skeins each dark blue-green (D), hunter green (E), camel beige (F), and burnt orange (G); aluminum crochet hook size H (or English/Canadian hook No. 8) *or the size that will give you the correct gauge;* small tags to mark sections.

GAUGE: Granny squares measure 4½″ x 4½″. 3 sc = 1″; 3 sc rows = 1″.

Note: Afghan is composed of 2 major sections (X and Y on the Diagram). Each major section is made up of smaller units and sections. These are numbered on the Diagram. The major sections are joined in the middle and a border is added to complete the afghan.

Work with yarn double throughout.

MAJOR SECTION X: UNIT 1: First Granny Square

(a): Starting at center with color C, ch 6. Join with sl st to form ring.

1st rnd: Ch 3, work 2 dc in ring, (ch 2, 3 dc in ring) 3 times; ch 2, join with sl st to top of ch-3. Break off.

Note: Always work granny squares with right side facing you.

2nd rnd: With G, work 3 sc, ch 2 and 3 sc in any ch-2 sp (first corner made), * ch 1, in next ch-2 sp work 3 sc, ch 2 and 3 sc (another corner). Rep from * twice more; ch 1, join with sl st to first sc. Break off.

3rd rnd: With A, work 3 dc, ch 2 and 3 dc in any corner sp (first corner), * 3 dc in next ch-1 sp (shell made), in next corner sp work 3 dc, ch 2 and 3 dc (another corner). Rep from * twice more; shell in next sp; join with sl st to top of first dc. Break off.

4th rnd: With F, work sc, ch 2 and sc in any corner sp, * sc in each of next 9 dc, in next corner sp work sc, ch 2 and sc. Rep from * twice more; sc in each of next 9 dc; join to first sc. Break off.

Work 3 more Granny Squares (b, c, and d) in same manner. Pin the 4 squares tog to form a 9″ square. With F, crochet edges tog with sl st on wrong side joining matching sts through top lps only. Front lps will form a slight ridge around each square on right side and sl sts will form heavy ridge on wrong side.

5th rnd (border rnd): With D, work sc, ch 2 and sc in any corner sp, * working in back lp only of each st, sc in each of next 11 sc, work sc in each of next 2 ch-2 sps where 2 squares are joined, sc in each of next 11 sc, in next corner sp, work sc, ch 2 and sc. Rep from * around; join to first sc (26 sc on each side). Break off. Unit 1 com-

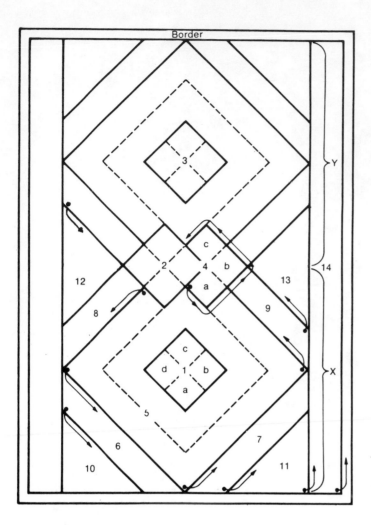

pleted. Mark unit with a numbered tag.

UNITS 2 AND 3: Work in same manner as Unit 1.

UNIT 4: Work 3 Granny Squares (a, b, and c) as for Unit 1 through 4th rnd.

Pin the 3 squares tog to form L-shape. With F, sl st edges tog as before.

5th rnd (border rnd): With D, work sc in corner sp (dot on Diagram), working in back lp of each st in direction of arrows, sc in each of next 11 sc, * in next corner sp work sc, ch 2 and sc, sc in each of next 11 sc, sc in each of next 2 ch-2 sps where squares join, sc in each of next 11 sc. Rep from * once more; in next corner sp work sc, ch 2 and sc, sc in each of next 11 sc; sl st in next sp (border on 4 sides of shape). Break off.

Fit and pin a corner of Unit 2 into inside corner of Unit 4, as shown. With D, sl st pinned edges tog on wrong side as before (Unit 2–4 completed). Put Units 2–4 and 3 aside. Work Section 5 around Unit 1 as follows:

SECTION 5: 1st rnd: With right side facing you, using B, work sc in back lp of center sc on any side of Unit 1,

* working in back lp of each st, sc in each sc to corner sp, in corner sp work sc, ch 2 and sc *. Rep from * to * 3 times more; sc in each sc to first sc; join to first sc (28 sc on each side); ch 1 (ch 1 counts as first sc). Do not turn or break off, but continue in rnds.

2nd through 4th rnds: Rep 1st rnd from * to * 4 times; complete rnd as before (34 sc on each side at end of 4th rnd. Square measures 12½".) Break off.

5th rnd: With wrong side facing you, using A, work sc in back lp of center sc on any side of square. Rep from * to * on 1st rnd, complete rnd as before (36 sc on each side); ch 1, do not turn, but continue in rnds.

6th through 10th rnds: Rep 1st rnd from * to * 4 times; complete rnd as before (46 sc on each side at end of 10th rnd. Square measures 16½".) Break off.

11th rnd: With right side facing you, using C, work dc in any corner sp on square; * working in both lps of each sc, work dc in each of next 5 sc, ch 2, sl st in each of next 8 sc, (ch 2, dc in each of next 6 sc, ch 2, sl st in each of next 8 sc) twice; ch 2, dc in each of next 5 sc; in next corner sp work dc, ch 2 and dc. Rep from * around, ending with dc in first corner sp; ch 2, join to top of first st (48 sts on each side). Break off.

12th rnd: With right side facing you, using B, work sc in any corner sp on square, * working in back lp of each st, sc in each of next 6 dc and in top of ch-2, (sk next sl st, dc in each of next 6 sl sts, sk next sl st, sc in top of ch-2 and in each of next 6 dc and in top of next ch-2) twice; sk next sl st, dc in each of next 6 sl sts, sk next sl st, sc in top of ch-2 and in each of next 6 dc, in next corner sp work sc, ch 2 and sc. Rep from * around, ending with sc in first corner sp; ch 2, join to first sc (50 sts on each side of square). Break off.

13th row: With right side facing you, counting from right to left, sk 8 sc and 4 dc after any corner sp, using G, work sc in back lp of next dc, * working in back lp of each st, sc in each st across to next corner sp, in corner sp work sc, ch 2 and sc. Rep from * twice more; sc in each st across to within last 12 sts (52 sts on each long side, 39 sts on each short side); ch 1, turn (turning ch-1 counts as first sc of next row).

14th row: Working in both lps of each sc, * sc in each sc across to corner, in corner sp work sc, ch 2 and sc. Rep from * twice more; sc in each sc to end; ch 1, turn.

15th row: Working in back lp of each st, rep 14th row from * to end.

16th through 22nd rows: Rep 14th and 15th rows 3 times more, then rep 14th row once again, omitting last ch-1 (70 sc on each long side, 48 sc on each short side). Break off.

23rd row: With right side facing you, using F, work sl st in both lps of last sc made on last row on short side; working in both lps of each st, sl st in each of next 8 sc, (ch 2, dc in each of next 8 sc, ch 2, sl st in each of next 8 sc) twice; ch 2, dc in each of next 7 sc, in corner sp work dc, ch 2 and dc, * dc in each of next 7 sc, ch 2, sl st in each of next 8 sc, (ch 2, dc in each of next 8 sc, ch 2, sl st in each of next 8 sc) 3 times; ch 2, dc in each of next 7 sc, in corner sp work dc, ch 2 and dc. Rep from * once more; dc in each of next 7 sc, (ch 2, sl st in each of next 8 sc, ch 2, dc in each of next 8 sc) twice; ch 2, sl st in each of next 9 sc (72 sts on each long side, 49 sts on each short side). Break off.

24th row: With right side facing you, using E, work dc in back lp of first sl st on last row; working in back lp of each st, dc in each of next 7 sl sts, (sk next sl st, sc in top of ch-2, sc in each of next 8 dc, sc in top of ch-2, sk next sl st, dc in each of next 6 sl sts) twice; sk next sl st, sc in top of ch-2, * sc in each of next 8 dc, in corner sp work sc, ch 2 and sc, sc in each of next 8 dc and in top of ch-2, (sk next sl st, dc in each of next 6 sl sts, sk next sl st, sc in top of ch-2, sc in each of next 8 dc and in top of next ch-2) 3 times; sk next sl st, dc in each of next 6 sl sts, sk next sl st, sc in top of ch-2. Rep from * once more; sc in each of next 8 dc, in corner sp work sc, ch 2 and sc, sc in each of next 8 dc and in top of ch-2, (sk next sl st, dc in each of next 6 sl sts, sk next sl st, sc in top of ch-2, sc in each of next 8 dc and in top of next ch-2) twice; sk next sl st, dc in each of next 8 sl sts (74 sts on each long side, 50 sts on each short side. Long sides should measure 26″, short sides 17″.) Break off. Section 5 completed. Two inside corners are formed into which Unit 2–4 will be fitted later.

SECTION 6: 1st row: With right side facing you, using D, work sc in back lp of first sc on a long side of Section 5 (dot on Diagram): Working in back lp of each st, sc in each st across in direction of arrow to next corner, ending with sc in last sc (74 sc); ch 1, turn.

Note: To dec 1 st: draw up a lp in each of 2 sts, y o, draw through all 3 lps on hook.

2nd row: (dec row): Working in both lps of each st and decreasing 1 sc at beg and end of row, sc in each sc across (72 sc); ch 1, turn.

3rd through 13th rows: Rep last row 11 times more (50 sc). Break off. Section 6 completed. Last row should measure 17″ across.

SECTION 7: Work in same manner as Section 6, on next long side of Section 5.

SECTION 8: 1st row: With right side facing you, using D, work sc in back lp of first sc on short side of Section 5 (dot on Diagram); working in back lp of each st, sc in each st across in direction of arrow to next corner, ending with sc in last sc (50 sc); ch 1, turn.

2nd row: Working in both lps of each st and decreasing 1 st at beg of row, sc in each sc across (49 sc); ch 1, turn.

3rd row: Working in both lps of each st and decreasing at end of row, sc in each sc across (48 sc); ch 1, turn.

4th through 13th rows: Rep 2nd and 3rd rows 5 times more (38 sc). Break off. Section 8 completed.

SECTION 9: Work as for Section 8 on opposite short side of Section 5, reversing shapings by decreasing at end of 2nd row and beg of 3rd row.

CORNER SECTION 10: 1st row: With right side facing you, using E, working in back lp of each st in direction of arrow and decreasing 1 sc at beg and end of row, sc in each st on last row of Section 6 (48 sc); ch 1, turn.

2nd row: Working in top lp of each st and decreasing at beg and end of row, sc in each sc across (46 sc); ch 1, turn. Rep last row 4 times more, omitting ch-1 in last row (38 sc). Break off.

7th row: With right side facing you, using B, rep 2nd row. Rep 2nd row 3 times more, omitting ch-1 at end of last row (30 sc). Break off.

11th row: With right side facing you, using A, rep 2nd row (28 sc). Rep 2nd row twice more, omitting ch-1 at end of last row (24 sc). Break off.

14th row: With wrong side facing you, using G, rep 2nd row (22 sc). Rep 2nd row once more, omitting last ch-1 (20 sc). Break off.

16th row: With wrong side facing you, using E, rep 2nd row (18 sc). Rep 2nd row 8 times more, omitting ch-1 at end of last row (2 sc). Break off. Section 10 completed.

CORNER SECTION 11: Work in same manner as Section 10. Major Section X completed.

MAJOR SECTION Y: Work Major Section Y in same manner as for Major Section X. Fit joined Granny Square Unit 2–4 into center openings and sl st in place on wrong side.

SECTION 12: 1st row: Begin at dot on Diagram. With right side facing you, using F, and working in back lps, sc in first sc of Section 8 on Y, dec 1 st, sc in each sc across to within last 2 sc on this Section, dec 1 st (36 sc), dc in ch-2 sp of Granny Square, dec 1 st on next Section 8 on X, sc in each st to within last 2 sc, dec 1 st; ch 1, turn.

2nd row: Working in top lp of each st and decreasing 1 st at beg and end of Section 8, sc in each sc across (34 sc), work dc in both lps of next dc, decreasing 1 st at beg and end, sc in each sc across next Section 8; ch 1, turn. Rep last row twice more, omitting ch-1 at end of last row (30 sc on each Section 8 edge). Break off.

5th row: With right side facing you, using E, rep 2nd row (28 sc on each edge). Rep 2nd row twice more, omitting ch-1 at end of last row (24 sc on each edge). Break off.

8th row: With wrong side facing you, using B, rep 2nd row (22 sc on each edge). Rep 2nd row 5 times more, omitting ch-1 at end of last row (12 sc on each edge). Break off.

14th row: With wrong side facing you, using C, rep 2nd row (10 sc on each edge). Rep 2nd row 4 times more, omitting ch-1 at end of last row (2 sc). Break off. Section 12 completed.

SECTION 13: Work in same manner as Section 12.

SIDE EDGING 14: 1st row: With right side facing you, using F, work sc in st at corner of Section 11 (dot on Diagram); working in direction of arrow, sc evenly across entire length of joined X–Y sections; ch 1, turn. Work in both lps of each st throughout edging.

2nd row: Sc in each sc; ch 3, turn.

3rd row: Sk first sc, dc in each sc across (ch-3 at beg of row counts as 1 dc). Break off.

4th row: With wrong side facing you, using E, work sc in each dc. Break off.

5th row: With right side facing you, using F, work sc in each sc; ch 1, turn.

6th row: Sc in each sc. Break off.

7th row: With right side facing you, using E, dc in each sc. Break off.

8th row: With wrong side facing you, using B, work sc in each dc. Break off.

9th row: With right side facing you, using C, work dc in each sc across. Break off. Side Edging 14 completed along 1 edge. Work in same manner along opposite edge of X–Y sections.

BORDER: 1st rnd: With right side facing you, using F, work dc in first dc on last C row of Edging 14 (dot on Diagram); working in direction of arrow, work dc evenly around afghan, working dc, ch 2 and dc in each corner, ending last corner with ch 2, sl st in first dc. Break off.

2nd rnd: With right side facing you, using E, work sc in a corner sp, ch 2, sc in same sp, sc in each st around, working sc, ch 2 and sc in each corner space; sl st in first st. Break off.

3rd rnd: With F, rep 2nd rnd.

BABY AFGHAN

Here is a picot-edged afghan for a baby. This delightful clown comes to life when you take all the parts, which are mainly hexagons, and put them together.

SIZE: 26″ x 36″.

MATERIALS: Sport-weight yarn such as Bear Brand Winsom (orlon acrylic yarn), 1 (2-oz.) skein each dark turquoise (color A), peach (B), light olive (C), light blue (D), pale gray (E), and hunter green (F), 3 skeins each jade green (G) and pale yellow (H); knitting worsted weight acrylic yarn such as Bucilla Triple-Tweed, 3 (1¾-oz.) balls red-black-and-gray tweed (I), 2 balls each red-white-and-blue tweed (J) and tangerine (K); aluminum crochet hooks sizes F and G (or English/Canadian hooks No. 10 and 8) *or the sizes that will give you the correct gauge*; tapestry needle.

GAUGE: 7 sc = 2″ with size G hook; 4 sts = 1″ with F hook.

Note: When working with sport-weight yarn, work with 2 strands. Use only 1 strand when working with knitting worsted weight. Label sections as you work.

CLOWN FACE: Starting at center with size G hook and color E, ch 6. Join with sl st to form ring.

1st rnd: Ch 3, work 11 dc in ring (12 dc, counting ch 3 as 1 dc); sl st in top of ch-3.

2nd rnd: Ch 3, turn; dc in same place as sl st, work 2 dc in each sc around (24 dc); sl st in ch-3.

3rd rnd: Ch 3, turn; * 2 dc in next dc, dc in next dc. Rep from * up to last st, 2 dc in last st (36 dc); sl st in ch-3.

4th rnd (right side): Ch 2, turn; sc in each of next 3 dc, * 3 hdc in next dc, place marker, 3 hdc in next dc, sc in each of next 4 dc. Rep from * 4 times more; (3 hdc in next dc) twice; sl st in ch-2. Break off. Piece should measure 5″ from point to point. (Piece has 6 sides of 10 sts each between markers—3 hdc, 4 sc, and 3 hdc.)

BIB: Triangles for Bib are all worked with F hook, using color J yarn. Always work first row of Triangles with right side of work facing you. Start with lp on hook and sc in back lp only of sts throughout. Trim is added between some Triangles as specified and is worked with G hook, using color F (see heavy line on Diagram).

Triangle 1: 1st row: Starting at any marker, sc in each of next 3 hdc, sc in each of next 4 sc, sc in each of next 3 hdc; ch 2, turn.

2nd row: Draw up lp in each of next 2 sts, y o hook, and draw through all 3 lps on hook (1 sc dec), sc in each sc up to last 2 sc, dec 1 sc; ch 2, turn.

3rd and 4th rows: Rep 2nd row twice more (4 sc).

5th row: Sk first st, draw up lp in each of next 3 sts, y o hook, and draw through all 4 lps on hook; ch 1 tightly. Break off. Triangle should measure 2″ from base to tip.

Triangles 2, 3, and 4: Make another Triangle in same manner across each of the next 3 sides of face.

Triangle 5: Work across edges of Triangle 2. Hold piece so that Triangle 1 is at right (see Diagram for placement).

1st row: Working across edge of Triangle 2, work 2 sc over post of st at end of each row to tip of Triangle (10 sc); ch 2, turn.

2nd through 5th rows: Rep 2nd through 5th rows of Triangle 1.

Triangle 6: Starting at tip of Triangle 3, work in same manner as Triangle 5.

First Trim: (See heavy line on Diagram.) With size G hook and color F, starting at base of Triangle 1 with right side facing you, work 10 sc evenly across edge of Triangle 1 to tip, ch 2, work 10 sc across other edge of same Triangle to base. Rep same trim along both edges of Triangle 5, ch 2, work 10 sc across free edge of Triangle 2, work 10 sc across free edge of Triangle 3, ch 2, then continue trim as before across Triangles 6 and 4. Break off.

Triangle 7: With size F hook and color J, starting at tip of Triangle 1, work 1 sc in back lp of each of next 10 sc of trim; ch 2, turn. Complete Triangle as before. With trim color work overcast st, on wrong side, joining left edge of this Triangle to trim on edge of Triangle 5.

Triangle 8: Working across free edge of last Triangle made, work 10 sc; ch 2, turn. Complete Triangle as before.

Triangle 9: Starting at base of Triangle 4 and working across right edge between base and tip, work 1 sc in each of next 10 sc of trim; ch 2, turn. Complete Triangle as before, then sew right edge of this Triangle to trim on adjacent Triangle 6.

Triangle 10: Work as for Triangle 8.

Triangles 11, 12 13, and 14: Working into sc of trim, work Triangles across free edges of Triangles 5, 2, 3, and 6. Join last 2 Triangles as follows: With right side of work facing you, holding Triangles 12 and 13 with wrong sides together and using size G hook and color F, join adjacent edges by working a row of 10 sc through both thicknesses. Break off.

Triangles 15 and 16: Working as before, work Triangles across free edges of Triangles 12 and 13.

2nd Row of Trim: With right side of work facing you and using G hook, attach F with sl st in ch-2 sp of trim at tip of Triangle 1. Work as follows across each of next 6 Triangles, forming outer edge of Bib: Work 10 sc along right side edge, ch 2, work 10 sc along left side edge, sc in next ch-2 sp between Triangles (or sc in st between 2 center Triangles), ending with sl st in ch-2 sp at tip of Triangle 4. With right side facing you and using size F hook and color F, work 1 row sl st around upper edge of Bib adjacent to face. Break off.

EYES: Following Diagram for placement, with size F hook and color F work sl-st Triangles to form eyes.

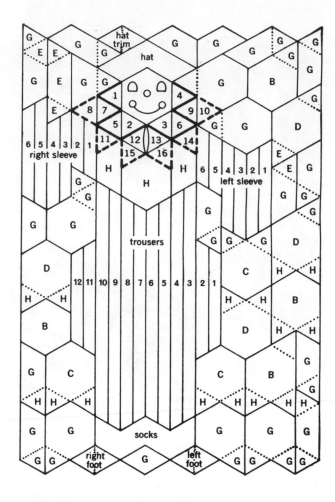

NOSE: With size F hook and I, ch 4. Join with sl st to form ring.

1st rnd: Ch 1, work 5 sc in ring; sl st in ch 1.

2nd rnd: Ch 1, sc in top lp only of each sc around; join. Break off, leaving 12″ end. Thread end in tapestry needle, sew opening on nose and sew in place.

CHEEKS (make 2): With size F hook and color I, ch 4. Join with sl st to form ring.

1st rnd: Ch 2, work 7 hdc in ring; sl st in top of ch-2. Break off. Sew cheeks in place.

MOUTH: With size F hook and color I, sl st a semicircle between cheeks.

HAT: Hold face with right side facing you and Bib down.

1st row: Working in back lps from right to left across 2 remaining free sides of face, with size G hook and color F work sc in each of first 3 hdc, sc in each of next 4 sc, sc in each of next 3 hdc, ch 2 for center, sc in each of next 3 hdc, sc in each of next 4 sc, sc in each of next 3 hdc; ch 2, turn (ch 2 counts as sc).

2nd row: Working in back lps only, work sc in same sp

as turning ch (inc), sc in each sc to center sp, work sc, ch 2 and sc in center sp, sc in each sc to last sc; work 2 sc in last sc; ch 2, turn (24 sc counting turning ch-2).

3rd row: Working in back lps only, sc in each sc to center sp, work sc, ch 2 and sc in center sp, sc in each remaining sc across; ch 2, turn.

4th through 6th rows: Rep 3rd row 3 times more, omitting last ch-2. Break off. Turn work.

HAT TRIM: Hold Face, Bib, and Hat so that right side is facing you with Hat at top. Work in back lps only throughout.

1st Triangle: 1st row: Starting at first sc to left of center ch-sp of Hat (see Diagram for position), continue using size G hook and color F as for Hat. Sc in this sc and in each of next 7 sc; ch 2, turn.

2nd row: Dec 1 sc, sc in each sc up to last 2 sc, dec 1 sc; ch 2, turn.

3rd Row: Rep 2nd row once more.

4th row: Sk first st, draw up lp in each of next 3 sts, y o hook and draw through all 4 lps on hook, ch 1 tightly. Break off.

2nd Triangle: 1st row: With right side facing you, starting at tip of first Hat Trim Triangle with size G hook and color F, work 8 sc evenly across left edge.

2nd through 4th rows: Work as for first Triangle.

TROUSERS: See directions for individual shell strips, below.

Pattern for Shell Strip: Each strip is worked from top to bottom, with same side (right side of work) always facing you. With size F hook, ch 7. Join with sl st to first ch to form ring. Sc in ring, ch 3, work 5 dc in ring (first shell made). * Ch 2, remove lp from hook, insert hook in top of ch-3, then insert hook in free lp of ch-2 and pull lp through, sc in ch-2 sp, ch 3, work 5 dc in ch-2 sp (next shell made). Rep from * until desired number of shells (see individual strip directions) have been made; ch 2, remove lp from hook, insert hook in top of ch-3, insert hook in free lp of ch-2 and pull lp through. Break off.

To Join Strips: Method 1: To join new Strip that extends below previous Strip, work as follows: Work required number of shells on new Strip before Strips are to be joined, ending with 5 dc of last shell. Holding Strips to be joined with right side facing you and first shell of each Strip at lower edge, sc in starting ring of first shell of previous Strip, * ch 2, remove lp from hook, insert hook in top of ch-3 before 5 dc of last shell worked, insert hook in free lp of ch-2 and pull lp through, sc in ch-2 sp, ch 3, work 5 dc in ch-2 sp (shell made), sc through ch-sp above corresponding shell on previous Strip. Rep from * to end of previous Strip, then rep from * in Pattern for Shell Strip, if necessary, until desired number of shells have been completed.

Method 2: To join new Strip that starts above previous Strip or starts with same first shell work as follows: Ch 3; with right side of previous Strip facing you as before, sc in corresponding ch-2 sp in which shell was worked on previous Strip, ch 2, sl st in first ch of ch-3 to form ring, ch 3, work 5 dc in ring, sc in ch-sp above corresponding shell on previous Strip. Rep from * of Method 1 until desired number of shells have been joined, then rep from * in Pattern for Shell Strip, if necessary, to finish desired number of shells.

Note: Trousers and Sleeves are made upside down. Beginnings of Strips are the top edge, and ends are the bottom edge. Turn Diagram upside down to follow the order of working Strips.

SHELL STRIPS: Following Diagram for order of strips, work from left to right as follows:

1st Strip: With I work 9 shells, marking first shell for top edge of Trousers. Break off.

2nd Strip: With K work 1 shell; then, following Method 1, join next 9 shells to first Strip; work 2 more shells (12 shells). Break off.

3rd Strip: With J work 6 shells; then, following Method 1, join next 12 shells to 2nd Strip; work 6 more shells (24 shells). Break off.

4th Strip: Sk first shell on 3rd Strip; with K, following Method 2, join next 23 shells to 3rd Strip; work 1 more shell (24 shells). Break off.

5th Strip: Sk first shell on 4th Strip. With I, following Method 2, join next 23 shells to 4th Strip (23 shells). Break off.

6th Strip: Sk first shell on 5th Strip. With K, following Method 2, join next 21 shells to 5th Strip (21 shells). Break off.

7th Strip: With K, following Method 2, join each shell of 7th Strip to each shell of 6th Strip, ending sc in ch-sp above corresponding shell in previous Strip, ch 2, remove lp from hook, insert hook in top of ch-3 before 5 dc of last shell worked, insert hook in free lp on ch-2 and pull lp through (21 shells). Break off.

8th Strip: With I work 1 shell; following Method 1, join next 22 shells to 7th Strip; work 1 more shell (23 shells). Break off.

9th Strip: With K work 1 shell; following Method 1, join next 23 shells to 8th Strip, ending as for 7th Strip (24 shells). Break off.

10th Strip: With J work 1 shell. (Mark end of this Strip with pin for start of Socks to be worked later.) Following Method 1, join next 23 shells to 9th Strip, ending as for 7th Strip (24 shells). Break off.

11th Strip: Sk first 6 shells on 10th Strip. With K, following Method 2, join next 12 shells to 10th Strip, ending as for 7th Strip (12 shells). Break off.

12th Strip: Sk first shell on 11th Strip. With I, following Method 2, join next 9 shells to 11th Strip, ending as for 7th Strip (9 shells). Break off. Do not remove marker on first Strip that marks top edge of this entire piece. For placement later, turn this piece upside down with marker at top.

LEFT SLEEVE: Following Diagram and pattern for Shell Strip and joining Strips as for Trousers, work from left to right, using color I throughout, as follows:

1st Strip: Marking first shell for top edge, work 9 shells. Break off.

2nd Strip: Sk first shell on first Strip. Work and join next 8 shells; work 1 more shell (9 shells). Break off.

3rd Strip: Work and join 9 shells, joining shells to 2nd Strip. Break off.

4th Strip: Work 1 shell; then work and join next 8 shells to 3rd Strip (9 shells). Break off.

5th Strip: Work and join 6 shells, joining each shell to each of first 6 shells of 4th Strip (6 shells). Break off.

6th Strip: Work 1 shell; then work and join next 5 shells to 5th Strip (6 shells). Break off.

RIGHT SLEEVE: Working as for Left Sleeve, work as follows:

1st Strip: Marking first shell for top edge, work 6 shells. Break off.

2nd Strip: Work 1 shell; then work and join next 5 shells to first Strip (6 shells). Break off.

3rd Strip: Work and join 6 shells, joining shells to 2nd Strip; work 3 more shells (9 shells). Break off.

4th Strip: Sk first shell of 3rd Strip. Work and join next 8 shells to 3rd Strip; work 1 more shell (9 shells). Break off.

5th Strip: Work 3 shells; then work and join next 8 shells to 4th Strip (11 shells). Break off.

6th Strip: Sk first shell of 5th Strip. Work and join next 9 shells to 5th Strip. Break off.

Do not remove markers placed on first Strip of each Sleeve. They will be needed for placement.

SOCKS: With right side facing you, hold Trousers so that marked lower edge is at top.

1st row: With size G hook and color H and starting at pin marker, work 4 sc over ch-2 sp at end of 10th Strip, work 4 sc over ch-2 sp at end of 9th Strip, ch 2, (work 4 sc over ch-2 sp at end of next Strip) 4 times; ch 2, (work 4 sc over ch-2 sp at end of next Strip) twice (last 4 sc are worked across 3rd Strip); ch 2, turn (ch 2 counts as sc).

2nd row: Working in back lps only, dec 1 sc over next

2 sc, sc in each of next 5 sc; work sc, ch 2 and sc in next ch-2 sp; sc in each of next 7 sc, sk next 2 sc, sc in each of next 7 sc; work sc, ch 2 and sc in next ch-2 sp; sc in each of next 6 sc, dec 1 sc over last 2 sc; ch 2, turn.

3rd through 6th rows: Rep 2nd row 4 times more. Break off; attach F. With F, ch 2; turn and work as follows for first Triangle of right foot.

RIGHT FOOT: 1st Triangle: 1st row: With G hook and color F, working in back lps only, sc in each of next 7 sc of last row of Socks; ch 2, turn. Complete as for first Triangle of Hat Trim.

2nd Triangle: 1st row: With size G hook and color F, starting at base of first Triangle, work 8 sc evenly spaced along right side edge; ch 2, turn. Complete as for first Triangle.

LEFT FOOT: 1st Triangle: 1st row: With right side of work facing you and using G hook and color F, sc in each of last 8 sc on last row of Socks. Complete as for first Triangle of Hat Trim.

2nd Triangle: Starting at tip of first Triangle, work another Triangle as before along left side edge of first Triangle.

Fill-In Between Feet: With right side facing you, hold Socks so that the free sts (between the feet) of last row of Socks are at top edge.

1st row: With F hook and color G, working in back lps only, sc in each of 16 free sc between feet; ch 2, turn.

2nd row: Working in back lps only, dec 1 sc, sc in each sc up to 2 center sc, sk 2 center sc, sc in each sc up to last 2 sc; dec 1 sc; ch 2, turn.

3rd and 4th rows: Rep 2nd row twice more.

5th row: Sk first sc, draw up lp in each of next 3 sc, y o hook and draw through all 4 lps on hook; ch 1 tightly. Break off.

HEXAGON MOTIF: Starting at center with size F hook, ch 4. Join with sl st to form ring.

1st rnd: Ch 3, work 11 dc in ring (12 dc, counting ch-3 as 1 dc); sl st in top of ch-3.

2nd rnd: Ch 2, turn; hdc in same place as sl st, work 2 hdc in each dc around (24 hdc, counting ch-2 as 1 hdc; sl st in top of ch 2).

3rd rnd: Ch 2, turn; hdc in same place as sl st, hdc in next hdc, * 2 hdc in next hdc, hdc in next hdc. Rep from * around (36 hdc); sl st in top of ch-2.

4th rnd: Ch 2, turn; sc in each of next 3 hdc, 2 hdc in next hdc, place marker, 2 hdc in next hdc, * sc in each of next 4 hdc, 2 hdc in next hdc, place marker, 2 hdc in next hdc. Rep from * 4 times; sl st in top of ch-2. Piece should measure 4½" from point to point. **Note:** Piece has 6 sides of 8 sts each between markers—2 hdc, 4 sc, and 2 hdc. Work 18 Hexagons in the following colors: 4 B, 3 C, 4 D, 6 G and 1 H.

HALF-HEXAGON: With size F hook ch 4. Join with sl st to form ring.

1st row: Ch 3, work 5 dc in ring (6 dc, counting ch-3 as 1 dc); ch 2, turn.

2nd row: Hdc in base of ch-2, (2 hdc in next dc) 4 times; 2 hdc in top of turning ch (12 hdc, counting ch-2 as 1 hdc); ch 2, turn.

3rd row: Hdc in base of ch-2, hdc in next hdc, (2 hdc in next hdc, hdc in next hdc) 5 times (18 hdc); ch 2, turn.

4th row: Hdc in base of ch-2, sc in each of next 4 hdc, 2 hdc in next hdc, (place marker, 2 hdc in next hdc, sc in each of next 4 hdc, 2 hdc in next hdc) twice. Break off.

Work 18 Half-Hexagons in the following colors: 1 E, 15 G and 2 H.

TO JOIN BODY: Following Diagram for position, with right sides of pieces facing you, whipstitch adjacent pieces of body together as follows: Working through back lps of Hexagon, sew Hexagon H and 2 Half-Hexagon H's tog and to Bib, then add Trousers and Sleeves.

BACKGROUND: Triangles Crocheted to Hexagons and Half-Hexagons: Following Diagram for placement and colors, work fill-in triangles to complete background as follows: On background, dotted lines represent sides of Hexagons and Half-Hexagons to which Triangles are crocheted. Solid lines represent sides where adjacent pieces are whipstitched together, sewing through back lps only when joining Hexagons and Half-Hexagons.

Starting at top of blanket, work fill-in triangles and sew adjacent pieces together as you go along.

Fill-In Triangle: 1st row: With right side of Hexagon facing you, using size F hook and working through back lps only, sc in each of 8 sts along one side of motif; ch 2, turn.

2nd row: Working in back lps only, dec 1 sc over next 2 sc, sc in each sc up to last 2 sc, dec 1 sc over last 2 sc; ch 2, turn.

3rd row: Rep 2nd row once more.

4th row: Sk first sc, draw up lp in each of next 3 sc, y o hook and draw through all 4 lps on hook. Break off.

EDGING: 1st rnd: With right side of blanket facing you and using size F hook and color A, work sc evenly spaced around outer edge as follows: Work sc in each sc along sides of Hexagons, work 2 sc over post of st at end of each row on Triangles and Half-Hexagons, work 2 sc over each shell on Left Sleeve. Join with sl st.

2nd rnd: * Sc in next 2 sc, ch 4, sc in 3rd ch from hook (p made), sk 2 sc. Rep from * around; sl st in next st. Break off.

Pillows

ARROWHEAD PILLOW

If you can make a granny square, you can make this pillow, a dramatic assemblage of sixteen small spear-shaped units. The units are mostly single crochet. When finished, the pillow cover will fit around a standard bed pillow.

SIZE: 18″ x 24″.

MATERIALS: Knitting worsted, 2 (4-oz.) skeins each dark peach (color A), off-white (B), light green (C), bright red (D), navy (E); aluminum crochet hook size H (or English/Canadian hook No. 8) *or the size that will give you the correct gauge;* bed pillow, about 18″ x 24″, or 1½ yds. 45″-wide muslin and 3 lbs. Dacron polyester to make pillow form.

GAUGE: 3 sc = 1″; 3 rows = 1″.

Note: Use yarn double throughout. Work in both lps of each st except where otherwise stated.

UNIT ONE (make 8): Starting at base of triangle (see Diagram) with color A, ch 12.

1st row: Sc in 2nd ch from hook and in each ch across (11 sc); turn.

2nd row: Draw up lp in each of first 2 sc, y o, draw through all 3 lps on hook (1 sc dec), sc in each sc to last 2 sc, dec 1 sc (9 sc); ch 1, turn.

3rd row: Sc in each sc; turn.

4th through 9th rows: Rep 2nd and 3rd rows 3 times more (3 sc).

10th row: Draw up lp in each sc, y o and draw through all 4 lps on hook (1 sc).

11th rnd (right side): Ch 2; working down left side of triangle over ends of sts, work 13 sc evenly to base; ch

2 at corner; work 12 sc across base of triangle; ch 2 at corner (mark this st); working up right side of triangle over ends of sts, work 13 sc evenly to tip; sl st in ch-2. Break off.

12th row: Make lp on hook with B and work 2 sc in marked st; sc in next sc, (ch 2, dc in each of next 3 sc, ch 2, sc in each of next 3 sc) twice; ch 2; work 3 dc in top ch-2 of triangle, (ch 2, sc in each of next 3 sc, ch 2, dc in each of next 3 sc) twice; ch 2, sc in next sc; work 2 sc in ch-2 sp. Break off.

13th row: Make lp on hook with C and dc in each of first 3 sc of previous row; * sk ch-2 and, working in back lps only, work sc in each of next 3 dc, sk ch-2; working in both lps, dc in each of the next 3 sc. Rep from * once more; sk ch-2, sc in back lp of next dc; in next dc (center dc at tip) work sc, ch 2 and sc; sc in next dc, (sk ch-2 and, working in both lps, dc in each of next 3 sc, sk ch-2; working in back lps only, sc in each of next 3 dc) twice; sk ch-2; working in both lps, dc in each of last 3 sc; ch 3, turn.

14th row: Sc in last dc; sc in each of next 16 sts; in ch-2 sp at tip work sc, ch 2 and sc; sc in each of next 16 sts; work 2 dc in last sc. Break off.

15th row: Make lp on hook with D, y o hook, work 2 dc in ch-3, dc in each of next 5 sts, sc in each of next 8 sc, dc in each of next 5 sc, in ch-2 sp (tip) work 3 dc, ch 2 and 3 dc; dc in each of next 5 sc (mark last dc), sc in each of next 8 sc; dc in each of next 5 sts; work 2 dc in last sc. Break off.

16th row: Turn work to right side. Make lp on hook with E, work 2 sc in marked st, sc in each of next 7 sts, ch 2, work sc in ch-2 sp at tip, ch 2, sc in each of next 7 dc, work 2 sc in next dc; ch 1, turn.

17th row: 2 sc in first sc, sc in each of the next 8 sc, in ch-2 sp work sc, ch 2 and sc; sc in next sc, in ch-2 sp work sc, ch 2 and sc; sc in each of next 8 sc, work 2 sc in last sc; ch 1, turn.

18th row: 2 sc in first sc, sc in each of next 10 sc, in ch-2 sp work sc, ch 2 and sc; sc in each of next 3 sc, in ch-2 sp work sc, ch 2 and sc; sc in each of next 10 sc, work 2 sc in last st; ch 1, turn.

19th row (wrong side): 2 sc in first sc, sc in each of next 12 sc, in ch-2 sp work sc, ch 2 and sc; sc in next 5 sc, in ch-2 sp work sc, ch 2 and sc (mark the ch-2 sp); sc in each of next 12 sc, work 2 sc in last sc. Break off.

UNIT TWO (make 8): Work same as Unit One using the following colors:

1st through 11th rows: color D.
12th row: color B.
13th and 14th rows: color C.
15th row: color A.
16th through 19th rows: color C.

ASSEMBLING: Line up 8 units as in Diagram. Working through back lp of each st, sc sides of units together on right side to form strip (seams will form ridges). Fit ends

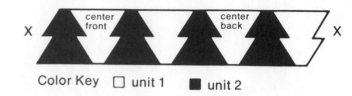

Color Key ☐ unit 1 ■ unit 2

(X) together and join with sc to form tube. Make another tube with remaining 8 sections.

Borders for tubular sections: Make lp on hook with B and work sc in marked ch-2 sp on right side of any unit tip. * Work cl as follows: (y o hook, pull up lp in next sc, y o hook and pull through 2 lps on hook) 7 times; y o hook and pull through all 8 lps on hook, ch 1 (cl completed); sc in next ch-2 sp; work 2 sc over each of next 3 end sts, sc over next end st, sc in next 12 sc (base of original triangle), sc over next end st, 2 sc over each of next 3 end sts, sc in next marked ch-2 sp. Rep from * 3 more times, omitting last sc in marked sp; join with sl st. Break off. Work border around both edges of both tubes.

Center seam: After all 4 borders are finished, turn both sections inside out. Line up (right sides together) so that center front and back units match. With B, sc tog, working through front lps only (2 ridges formed on right side); join. Break off (wide tube formed).

Bottom seam: Turn right side out. With B, sc edges of tube tog to form cover open at one end. Break off. Slide in bed pillow or make pillow form as for Aubusson pillow.

Top seam: Same as bottom seam.

INTARSIA PILLOW

This subtle rendering of geometric motifs resembles Renaissance wood-inlay work. The pattern uses a fine mélange of inventive crochet stitches.

SIZE: About 18" square.

MATERIALS: Knitting worsted, 2 (4-oz.) skeins dark apricot (color A), 1 skein each dark rust (B), light peach (C), forest green (D), and light rust (E); aluminum crochet hook size H (or English/Canadian hook No. 8) *or the size that will give you the correct gauge;* 1¼ yds. 45"-wide muslin; 3 lbs. Dacron polyester for stuffing.

GAUGE: 3 sc = 1".

Note: Use yarn double throughout.

SIDE ONE: Starting at first zigzag row at top of pillow with A, ch 71.

1st row (wrong side): Work sc in 2nd ch from hook, sc in each of next 2 ch; in next ch work sc, ch 2 and sc; sc in each of next 3 ch, * sk 2 ch, sc in each of next 3 ch; in next ch work sc, ch 2 and sc; sc in each of next 3 ch. Rep from * across; ch 1, turn.

2nd row (right side): Draw up lp in each of first 2 sc, y o and draw through all 3 lps on hook (a 2-joined sc made), sc in each of next 2 sc; in ch-2 sp work sc, ch 2 and sc; * sc in each of next 3 sc, sk 2 sc, sc in each of next 3 sc; in ch-2 sp work sc, ch 2 and sc. Rep from * across to last 4 sc, sc in each of next 2 sc, draw up lp in each of last 2 sc, y o and draw through all 3 lps on hook (another 2-joined sc made); ch 1, turn.

Rep 2nd row twice more, omitting ch 1 at end of last row. Break off. Do not turn.

5th row (right side): Make lp on hook with B and, starting at beg of last row, work a 2-joined sc in first 2 sts,

Arrowhead (top) and Intarsia Pillows

sc in each of next 2 sts; in ch-2 sp work sc, ch 2 and sc; * sc in each of next 2 sts; long sc in next st (to work long sc insert hook in next st 1 row below, y o and draw up lp so that st lies flat, y o and complete sc), sk 2 sts, work long sc in next st 1 row below, sc in each of next 2 sts; in ch-2 sp work sc, ch 2 and sc *. Rep from * to * across to last 4 sts, sc in each of next 2 sts, work a 2-joined sc in last 2 sts. Break off; do not turn.

6th row: With C, rep 5th row.

7th row: With D, rep 5th row.

8th row: Make lp on hook with A. Starting at beg of last row, in first 4 sts work half-cl as follows: Y o and draw up lp in first st, y o and pull through 2 lps on hook, (y o and draw up lp in next st, y o and pull through 2 lps on hook) 3 times; y o and pull through all 5 lps on hook, ch 2; work 3 sc in ch-2 sp (3-sc group made); * form cl as follows: (Y o and draw up lp in next st, y o and pull through 2 lps on hook) 3 times; sk 2 sts, (y o and draw up lp in next st, y o and pull through 2 lps on hook) 3 times; y o and pull through all 7 lps on hook, ch 2, work 3-sc group in ch-2 sp *. Rep from * to * 6 times more. In last 4 sts work half-cl as follows: (Y o and draw up lp in next st, y o and pull through 2 lps on hook) 4 times; y o and pull through all 5 lps on hook; ch 4, turn.

9th row: Work 3 dc in 4th ch from hook, sl st in center st of next 3-sc group, * 5 dc in top of next cl, sl st in center st of next 3-sc group *. Rep from * to * 6 times more; 4 dc in top of last half-cl. Break off, turn.

10th row: Make lp on hook with D and work sc in each of first 3 sts, sk next st, * insert hook in ch-2 sp of 7th row (last color D row) and, working over sl st of 9th row and sc's of 8th row, work 2 long sc, sk next st, sc in next st; in next st work 2 sc, ch 2 and 2 sc; sc in next st, sk next st *. Rep from * to * 6 times more; work 2 long sc in st on 7th row as before, sk next st, sc in each of next 2 sts, sc in top of turning ch-4. Break off; do not turn.

11th row: Make lp on hook with C and, starting at beg of last row, work 2 sc in first sc, sc in each of next 2 sc, * sk 2 sts, sc in each of next 3 sc; in ch-2 sp work sc, ch 2 and sc; sc in each of next 3 sc *. Rep from * to * 6 times more; sk 2 sts, sc in each of next 2 sc, 2 sc in last sc; ch 1, turn.

12th row: Work 2 sc in first sc, sc in each of next 2 sc. Rep from * on 11th row, omitting ch 1 at end of row. Break off. Turn.

13th row: Make lp on hook with D and work 2 sc in first st, y o and draw up lp in same st as last 2 sc worked, y o and pull through 2 lps on hook, (y o and draw up lp in next st, y o and pull through 2 lps on hook) twice; sk 2 sts, (y o and draw up lp in next st, y o and pull through 2 lps on hook) 3 times; y o and pull through all 7 lps on hook, ch 2, work 3 sc in ch-2 sp. Rep from * to * of 8th row, ending last rep with 2 sc in same place as last st worked; ch 1, turn.

14th row: Sc in first sc, rep from * to * of 9th row 8 times, ending last rep with sc in last st. Break off. Turn.

15th row: Make lp on hook with C, sc in first st, sk 1 st, sc in next st; in next st work 2 sc, ch 2 and 2 sc; sc in next st, sk next st. Rep from * to * of 10th row 7 times (working long sc into ch-2 sp of 12th color C row), sc in last sc. Break off; do not turn.

16th row: Starting at beg of last row with B, work sc, rep 2nd row.

17th row: With B rep 2nd row, omitting ch 1 at end of row. Break off, turn.

18th row: With C work a 2-joined sc in first 2 sts, sc in each of next 2 sc; in ch-2 sp work sc, ch 2 and sc. Rep from * to * of 5th row to within last 4 sc, sc in each of next 2 sc, work a 2-joined sc in last 2 sts. Break off. Do not turn.

19th row: With D, rep 5th row.

20th row: With B, rep 5th row.

21st row: With E, rep 8th row.

22nd row: With E, rep 9th row; turn.

23rd row: With A, rep 10th row, working long sc in ch-2 sp of 20th (B) row.

24th row: Starting at beg of last row with E, rep 13th row.

25th row: With E, rep 14th row; turn.

26th row: With A, rep 15th row.

27th row: With B, rep 5th row.

28th row: With C, rep 5th row.

29th row: With D, rep 5th row.

30th row: With B, rep 5th row.

31st row: With C, rep 5th row.

32nd row: With D, rep 5th row. Break off.

33rd row: With D, rep 8th row. At end of row, ch 1, turn.

34th row: With D, sc in each st across. Break off.

Next row: Working along foundation ch at beg of work (top of pillow) with A, rep 13th row, skipping only 1 st between cl's; ch 1, turn.

Following row: Sc in each st across; ch 1, turn. Rep last row 3 times more, omitting ch 1; turn at end of last row. Break off.

SIDE TWO: Rep Side One.

FINISHING: Block both sides together to ensure equal dimensions. Make an inner pillow form by cutting 2 pieces of muslin ½" larger all around than blocked piece; sew ½" seams on 3 sides; turn and stuff; blindstitch last side. With right sides of crochet facing, sl st 3 sides tog; turn and slide in pillow form. Sl st last side closed. Break off.

GREEK KEY PILLOW

Consisting of four sections—two for the front and two for the back—this is the easiest of the four pillows. It goes quickly and uses single, double, and treble crochet stitches.

SIZE: About 21" square.

MATERIALS: Knitting worsted, 3 (4-oz.) skeins off-white (color A), 1 skein each bright sky blue (B), dark lavender (C), copper (D); aluminum crochet hooks sizes H and I (or English/Canadian hooks No. 8 and 11) *or the sizes that will give you the correct gauge;* 1¼ yds. 45"-wide muslin; 3 lbs. Dacron polyester for stuffing.

GAUGE: 3 sc = 1"; 2 rows = 1".

Greek Key (top) and Aubusson Pillows

Note: Use yarn double throughout. Work in both lps of each st unless otherwise stated.

SECTION ONE: Starting at outer edge of pillow, using size H hook with color A, ch 62.

1st row: Work sc in 2nd ch from hook, sc in each ch to end (61 sc); ch 3, turn.

2nd row: Sk first sc, work dc in each sc across; drop lp from hook but do not cut.

3rd row: Do not turn work. Make lp on hook with B.

4th row: Pick up dropped A lp, ch 3, turn. Sk first dc, dc in next 2 dc, * sc in next B sc; working over ch-3, work dc in next 3 A dc. Rep from * 13 times more; sc in next sc, dc in last dc (61 sts), ch 1, turn.

5th row: Sc in each st across; drop lp but do not cut.

6th row: Do not turn work. Make lp on hook with B. Sc in 3rd st from beg, * ch 3, sk 3 sc, sc in next sc. Rep from * 13 times more. Break off.
Sc in 4th st from beg, * ch 3, sk 3 dc, sc in next dc. Rep from * 13 times more. Break off.

7th row: Pick up dropped A lp, ch 3, turn. Sk first sc, dc in next sc, * sc in next B sc; working over ch-3, work dc in next 3 A sc. Rep from * 13 times more; sc in next sc, dc in each of last 2 sc; ch 1, turn.

8th row: Sc in each st across, drop lp but do not cut.

9th through 14th rows: Rep 3rd through 8th rows once more. Break off.

15th row: Beg key motif as follows: Make lp on hook with C. Sc in first 10 sc, * sl st in next sc (mark this sc), ch 10, sl st in 5th ch from hook, ch 2, sk 2 ch, sl st in next ch, ch 2, sl st in marked st (this forms a spoke of 3 circles), sc in next 19 sc. Rep from * twice more, ending with 10 sc on last rep (3 spokes are formed); ch 1, turn.

16th row: Sc in first 7 sc, * sl st in next sc, sk next 2 sc, work 3 dc in each of the first 2 circles of spoke; in top circle of spoke work 3 dc, ch 2, 3 dc, ch 2 and 3 dc; working down other side of spoke work 3 dc in each of the next 2 circles, sk next 2 sc, sl st in next sc, sc in next 13 sc. Rep from * twice more, ending with 7 sc on last rep; ch 1, turn.

17th row: Sc in next 7 sc, * sk next sl st and next dc on spoke, sc in next 8 dc on spoke; in ch-2 sp work sc, ch 2 and sc; work sc in each of next 3 dc across top of spoke; in ch-2 sp work sc, ch 2 and sc; sc in next 8 dc; sk next dc and next sl st, sc in next 13 sc. Rep from * twice more, ending with 7 sc on last rep. Break off.

18th row: Make lp on hook with A. Start at beg of last row. Sc in first 6 sc, * sk next sc and next dc on spoke, sc in next 8 dc on spoke; in ch-2 sp work sc, ch 2 and sc; sc in each of next 5 sc across top of spoke; in ch-2 sp work sc, ch 2 and sc, sc in next 8 dc, sk next dc and next sc, sc in next 11 sc. Rep from * twice more, ending with 6 sc on last rep; ch 1, turn.

19th row: Sc in next 5 sc. Rep from * on last row 3 times with 7 sc across top of each spoke, 9 sc between spokes, and ending with 5 sc on last rep. Break off. Turn.

20th row: Make lp on hook with B. Sc in last 4 sc worked. Rep from * on 18th row 3 times with 9 sc across top of each spoke, 7 sc between spokes and ending with 4 sc on last rep. Break off.

21st row: Change to size I hook. Make lp on hook with D. Sc in first sc on last row, sl st in next sc, sk next 3 sc, dc in next 8 sc; in ch-2 sp work dc, ch 2 and sc; sc in next 11 sc across top of spoke; * in ch-2 sp work sc, ch 3 and tr; tr in next 9 sc, sk next 3 sc, sc in next sc (center sc between spokes), sk 3 sc, (tr in next 3 sc, sl st in corresponding tr on other spoke) 3 times; in ch-2 sp work tr, ch 3 and sc; sc in next 11 sc. Rep from * once more; in ch-2 sp work sc, ch 2 and dc; dc in next 8 sc, sk next 3 sc, sl st in next sc, sc in next sc; turn.

22nd row: Sk first 3 sts, sc in next 8 dc; in ch-2 sp work sc, ch 2 and sc; * sc in next 13 sc, 4 sc in each of next 2 ch-3 sps. Rep from * once more; sc in next 13 sc; in ch-2 sp work sc, ch 2 and sc; sc in next 8 dc, sk next 3 sts, sl st in last st. Break off.

SECTIONS 2, 3, and 4: Rep Section 1.

FINISHING AND ASSEMBLING: Hold Sections 1 and 2 with right sides facing. With D, sc together along last row of each by working through front lp of each st. Join Sections 3 and 4 in same manner. Block pieces together to ensure same size. Make an inner pillow form as for Aubusson Pillow. Whipstitch crocheted pieces together around 3 sides, using matching yarns. Insert pillow form; whipstitch closed.

AUBUSSON PILLOW

A great circular puff of a pillow is crowned with an ornate star pattern. You start in the center, then make rounds that eventually branch out into spokes. There are shells and other decorative stitches along the way.

SIZE: 20″ diameter.

MATERIALS: Knitting worsted, 1 (4-oz.) skein each peach (color A), pale rose (B), light blue (C), light olive (D), chocolate (E), cream white (F); aluminum crochet hook size H (or English/Canadian hook No. 8) *or the size that will give you the correct gauge;* 1 yd. 45″-wide muslin, 2 lbs. Dacron polyester for stuffing.

GAUGE: Measurements are indicated at several stages.

Note: Use yarn double throughout. Work in both lps of each st except where otherwise indicated.

SIDE ONE: Starting at center with color A, ch 6; join with sl st to form ring.

1st rnd (right side): Ch 3, work 11 dc in ring (12 dc, counting ch-3 as 1 dc); join with sl st in 3rd ch of ch-3. Ch

3, turn.

2nd rnd (wrong side): Work dc in same st as ch-3; work 2 dc in each dc around; sl st to join (24 dc). Ch 3, turn.

3rd rnd: Working in back lps only, * work 2 dc in next dc, dc in next dc. Rep from * around, ending with 2 dc (36 dc); join. Break off. Piece should measure 4½" in diameter.

4th rnd: Make lp on hook with B. Work spoke as follows: Work sc in any dc, * ch 9, work sc in each of 3rd and 4th ch from hook, work dc in each of next 5 ch, make sc in same st as sc at base of spoke (spoke completed); work sc in each of next 6 dc on circle. Rep from * until 6 spokes are formed; sc in each remaining 5 dc; join. Break off.

5th rnd: Make lp on hook with C. * Working along right edge of a spoke, work sc in first ch of spoke, work 2 dc in each of next 4 ch, sc in each of next 2 ch; in next sp (tip of spoke) work sc, ch 1 and sc; sc in each of next 2 sc, work 2 dc in each of next 4 dc (**Note:** dc's should line up with dc's on other side of spoke), sc in next dc, sk next sc, work sc in each of next 5 sc on circle, sk next sc. Rep from * around; join. Break off. Piece should measure 11½" across from tip to tip.

6th rnd: Make lp on hook with D. Start at tip of any spoke. * In tip sp work sc, ch 2 and sc; work sc in each of next 6 sts, work 3 dc in each of next 2 dc, sk next 3 dc, work sc in next sc (base of spoke), work cl as follows: (Y o hook, draw up lp in next sc, y o hook, draw through 2 lps on hook) 5 times; y o hook and draw through remaining 6 lps on hook, ch 1 (cl completed); work sc in next sc, turn work, sl st in sc before cl, turn work, sk next 3 dc on next spoke, work 3 dc in each of next 2 dc, sc in each of next 6 sts. Rep from * to end of rnd; join. Break off.

7th rnd: Make lp on hook with E. Start at tip of any spoke. * In tip sp work sc, ch 2 and sc; sc in next 10 sts, sk next 2 dc, y o twice, insert hook in next dc, draw up lp, sk st over cl, insert hook in next st, pull up lp (5 lps on hook), y o hook, pull through 3 lps on hook, (y o hook, pull through 2 lps on hook) twice (long st made); sk next 2 dc, sc in next 10 sts. Rep from * around; join. Break off.

8th rnd: Make lp on hook with F. Start at tip of any spoke and work in back lp only of each st around. * In tip sp work sc, ch 2 and sc; work sc in next 8 sc, form cl as follows: (Y o hook and draw up lp in next sc, y o hook and draw through 2 lps on hook) 3 times; sk long st; rep directions in parentheses 3 times; y o hook and draw through all 7 lps on hook, ch 1, sc in next 8 sc. Rep from * around; join. Break off. Piece should measure 14½" across from tip to tip.

9th rnd: Make lp on hook with D. Start at any tip. * In tip sp work sc, ch 2 and sc; sc in next 8 sc, sk next sc, 3 dc into side of cl, 3 dc in ch-1 over cl, sk next sc, sc in next 8 sc. Rep from * around.

10th rnd: Using Color D, * in tip sp work sc, ch 2 and sc; sc in next 9 sc, sk next 2 dc, work 3 dc in each of next 2 dc (center sts of cl), sk next 2 dc, sc in next 9 sc. Rep from * around; join. Break off.

11th rnd: Make lp on hook with E. Start at any tip. * In tip sp work sc, ch 2 and sc; sc in next 7 sc, sk next 3 sc, work 2 dc in each of the next 3 dc (first 3 sts of cl), ch 4, sl st in 4th ch from hook to form ring; work 2 dc in each of next 3 dc (last 3 sts of cl; fan shape formed with ring above); sk next 3 sc, sc in each of next 7 sc. Rep from * around; join. Break off. Piece should measure 17½" across from tip to tip.

12th rnd: Make lp on hook with C, y o hook. Start in ring above any fan. * Work 7 dc in ring to form shell, sk next 2 dc, sc in each of next 2 dc, form cl in next 6 sts as follows: (Y o hook, draw up lp in next st, y o hook and draw through 2 lps on hook) 6 times; y o hook and draw through all 7 lps on hook, ch 2, sc in each of next 2 sc, sk next 2 sc, work 7 dc in tip to form shell, sk next 2 dc, sc in each of next 2 sc, form cl in next 6 sts, sc in next 2 dc, sk next 2 dc. Rep from * around; join. Break off.

13th rnd: Make lp on hook with A. Start in last dc of any shell (above tip). * Work sc in dc, sc next sc, sk next sc; in ch above cl work shell of 6 dc, sk next sc, sc in each of next 2 sts, ch 5, pass the ch-5 behind shell on previous rnd and sk next 5 dc of shell. Rep from * around; join. Break off.

14th rnd: Make lp on hook with B. Start in center dc of any C shell on 12th rnd (3rd dc of 5 dc skipped on previous rnd). * Work sc in center dc, sk next 2 C dc, work 3 dc in each of next 2 A sc, sk next 2 dc, sc in each of next 2 dc (center 2 sts on shell), sk next 2 dc, work 3 dc in each of next 2 sc, sk next 2 C dc. Rep from * around; join. Break off.

15th rnd: Make lp on hook with E. Start in any dc and work sc in each dc around (sk all sc); join.

16th rnd: Using E, sc in every sc around; join. Break off. Piece should measure 20" across.

SIDE TWO: Repeat Side One.

FINISHING: Block both sides together to ensure equal dimensions. To make inner pillow form, cut a pattern the size of the blocked piece, adding ½" all around for seam allowance. Cut 2 muslin pieces from the pattern. Stitch ½" seam, leaving 6" opening for stuffing. Clip seam allowance every inch or so for easy turning. Turn inside out and stuff with polyester. Blindstitch opening. With wrong sides of crochet facing, using E, join edges halfway around with sc in back lps. Slide in pillow form. Continue sc to end. Sl st to join. Break off.

Rugs

OCTAGON RUG

Dramatic octagons and triangles interlock to create a marvelous contemporary mosaic of line and color. The rug is done mostly in easy single crochet.

SIZE: About 44" x 72".

MATERIALS: Heavy rug yarn such as Aunt Lydia's rug yarn (rayon/cotton), 6 (70-yd.) skeins each wheat yellow (color F) and navy (N), 5 skeins medium orchid (O), 4 skeins forest green (G), 3 skeins each light blue (B), medium blue (M), and pale orchid (L), 2 skeins each dark red (R), and light aqua (T); aluminum crochet hook size H (or English/Canadian hook No. 8) *or the size that will give you the correct gauge.*

GAUGE: 3 sc = 1".

Note: Sections 1, 2, and 3 on Diagram are octagons to which small triangles are added (see dotted lines), forming squares or parts of squares.

SECTION 1 (make 2): Octagon: Starting at center with color F, ch 5. Join with sl st to form ring.
1st rnd (wrong side): Ch 3, work 11 dc in ring (12 dc, counting ch-3 as 1 dc); join with sl st to top of ch-3. Work in back lps only from now on and mark beg of each rnd.
2nd rnd: Work 2 sc in sl st, 2 sc in each st around; join with sl st to first sc.
3rd rnd: Work 2 sc in sl st, * sc in each of next 2 sc, 2 sc in next sc. Rep from * around, ending with sc in each of last 2 sc (32 sc); join.
4th rnd: Work 2 sc in sl st, * sc in each of next 3 sc, 2

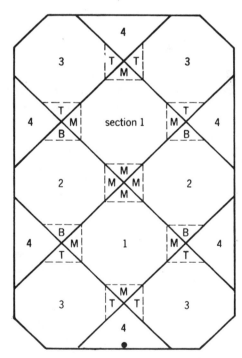

sc in next sc. Rep from * around, ending with sc in each of last 3 sc (40 sc); join.
5th rnd: Work 2 sc in sl st, * sc in each of next 4 sc, 2 sc in next sc. Rep from * around, ending with sc in each of last 4 sc (48 sc); join. Break off; turn. There are 8 corners

forming around edge of piece.

6th rnd (right side): Working in front lps only, with B, make lp on hook and sc in last sl st and in each of next 5 sts, ch 1, (sc in each of next 6 sc, ch 1) 7 times (ch 1 made at each corner); join.

Note: Work in back lp only of each st from now on.

7th rnd: Sc in sl st, (sc in each sc to within next ch 1, work 2 sc in ch-1 sp) 8 times (64 sc); join. Break off.

8th rnd: With M make a lp on hook, sc in last sl st, sc in each sc around, working ch 1 between the 2 sc at each corner; join.

9th rnd: Sc in sl st, sc in each sc around, working 2 sc in each ch-1 sp at each corner (8 sc inc). Break off M; with R make a lp on hook, sc in last sl st. Rep 8th and 9th rnds 6 times more, working rnds in the following colors:

10th rnd: R
11th rnd: M
12th through 14th rnds: N
15th rnd: L
16th through 18th rnds: F
19th rnd: T
20th and 21st rnds: G

22nd rnd: Rep 8th rnd with O once (22 sc on each side of Octagon, 176 sc in all at end of last rnd). Break off.

Small Triangles: See dotted lines on Diagram.

1st row: Make lp on hook with M; with right side of an Octagon facing you, working in back lps only, sk first sc on side of Octagon (mark skipped sc with pin) and work next 2 sc as 1, as follows: Pull up lp in each of next 2 sc, y o and draw through all 3 lps on hook (1 sc dec); sc in each of next 16 sc, dec 1 sc (18 sc); ch 2, turn. Turning ch-2 counts as first sc of next row.

Note: Work in front lps only from now on.

2nd row: Dec 1 sc, sc in each st to within last 2 sc, dec 1 sc (16 sc); ch 2, turn. Rep 2nd row 6 times more (4 sts remain at end of last row).

Next row: Pull up lp in each of next 3 sts, y o and draw through all 4 lps on hook. Break off.

Border: Make a lp on hook with N, sc in marked sc on side of Octagon. Working along side of Triangle, * work 2 sc over side of first sc, (sc over side of next sc, 2 sc over side of next sc) 4 times *, sc in top of Triangle; working along opposite side, rep from * to * once; sc in next sc on side of Octagon. Break off. (Following Diagram, sk next side of Octagon, work M Triangle with N Border on next

side) 3 times so that completed Section 1 forms a square.

SECTION 2 (make 2): Follow directions for Octagon in Section 1. With B follow directions for small Triangle, using O for Border. Sk next side of Octagon and using M work Triangle with O Border. Sk next side and work another B Triangle with O Border.

SECTION 3 (make 4): Follow directions for Octagon in Section 1. With T follow directions for small Triangle, using O for Border. Sk next side of Octagon and work another T Triangle with O Border.

SECTION 4: Make 6 large Triangles as follows: Starting at center of base of Triangle (dot on Diagram) with N, ch 4.

1st row (right side): In 4th ch from hook work 2 hdc, 1 dc and 3 hdc (7 sts, counting turning ch as 1 st); ch 3, turn. Work in front lps only from now on.

2nd row: Sc in first st (1 st inc), sc in each of next 2 sts; work sc, ch 1 and sc in next dc (corner made); sc in each of next 2 sts, 2 sc in top of turning ch (1 st inc); ch 3, turn.

3rd row: Sc in first st, sc in each st to within ch 1; in ch 1 work corner; sc in each st to within last st, 2 sc in last st; ch 3, turn.

4th row (double inc row): Sc in first st, 2 sc in next st, sc in each st to within ch 1, work corner in ch 1, sc in each st to within last 2 sts, 2 sc in each of last 2 sts; ch 3, turn. Continuing in established pattern and working double inc row every 4th row, work rows in the following colors:

5th through 8th rows: N
9th and 10th rows: L
11th through 16th rows: O. Do not break off O and do not ch 3 or turn.

Border: With same side facing you, work 2 sc over post of last sc made, * work 2 sc in post of next row, sc over post of next row, rep from * across base of Triangle ending 2 sc over last post; sl st in top of same st (49 sts). Break off.

FINISHING: Following Diagram for placement, join Sections as follows: Hold 2 Sections with right sides together and edges matching. With O crochet 1 row of sl st through top lps only of corresponding sts. Join remaining Sections in same manner. Break off.

HEXAGON RUG

Surprisingly easy and quick to finish, only nine of the hexagon modules in this rug involve changing colors; the rest are solid. The result is a versatile, colorful design that lends itself to contemporary or period decor. The hexagons are worked mainly in double crochet.

SIZE: About 51″ x 92″.

MATERIALS: Heavy rug yarn such as Kentucky rug yarn (rayon/cotton), 15 (70-yd.) skeins dark old rose (color A), 14 skeins light chocolate (B), 11 skeins each light old rose (C) and taupe (D), 8 skeins burgundy (E), 2 skeins bright red (F), 1 skein light avocado (G); aluminum crochet hook size H (or English/Canadian hook No. 8) *or the size that will give you the correct gauge.*

GAUGE: 3 sc = 1″. Each hexagon measures 5¾″ across from point to opposite point.

HEXAGON: Starting at center with color A, ch 5, join with sl st to form ring.
   1st rnd (right side): Ch 3, work 11 dc in ring (12 dc, counting ch-3 as 1 dc); join with sl st to top of ch-3.
   2nd rnd: Ch 3, work dc in sl st, 2 dc in each dc around (24 dc); join. Ch 3, turn.
   3rd rnd (wrong side): Work dc in sl st, work 2 dc in each dc around (48 dc); join. Ch 1, turn.
   4th rnd (right side): Working in back lps only, sc in sl st, sc in each of next 5 dc, 2 hdc in each of next 2 dc, (sc in each of next 6 dc, 2 hdc in each of next 2 dc) 5 times (60 sts); join with sl st to beg ch-1. Break off.
   Make 37 more A Hexagons in the following colors: 34 B, 32 D, 24 E, 18 C, and 6 F.
   Make 9 C-G Hexagons as follows: Starting with C, follow directions for solid-color Hexagon through 2nd rnd, omitting ch 3 at end. Break off; turn.
   3rd rnd (wrong side): Make lp on hook with G, y o and work dc in any dc, work 1 more dc in same st, work 2 dc in each dc around (48 dc); join. Break off; turn.
   4th rnd (right side): Make lp on hook with C and, working in back lps only, sc in any st, sc in each of next 5 sts, (work 2 hdc in each of next 2 sts, sc in each of next 6 sts) 5 times; 2 hdc in each of last 2 sts; join. Break off.

TO ASSEMBLE: Note: The Diagram shows half the rug and center strip only. Rug is symmetrical. Assemble Hexagons as shown, then assemble on other side of center strip to correspond to first side. Join Hexagons into vertical strips as follows: Hold 2 Hexagons together with right sides facing and edges matching. Working along 1 side, crochet 1 row of sl sts through matching 2 hdc, 6 sc, and 2 hdc, working through top lp only of each st (heavy ridge formed by sl sts on wrong side; there are 2 light ridges on right side, one on each side of sl sts formed by unworked lps). Continue in this manner until 9 Hexagons are joined into strip (heavy lines on Diagram separate strips). Make strip with 8 Hexagons. Alternating 9- and 8-Hexagon strips, join strips in same manner as individual Hexagons were joined.

FINISHING: End Border: Work with right side facing you and in back lp only of each st. Starting at dot on Diagram, make lp on hook with B and work sc in first hdc of 4-hdc corner group on E Hexagon, sc in each of next 2 hdc, * dc in next 6 sts, (y o hook twice, pull up lp in next st, y o, draw through 2 lps on hook, y o, draw through 2 more lps on hook) 3 times, leaving 4 lps on hook; sk the seam between 2 Hexagons, then rep directions in parentheses 3 times on adjacent Hexagon, y o and draw

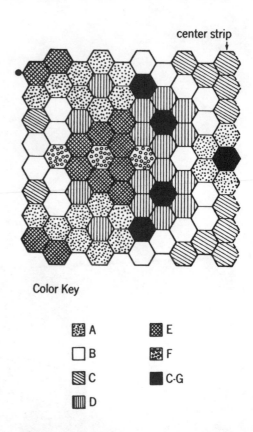

center strip

Color Key

A		E	
B		F	
C		C-G	
D			

through all 7 lps on hook (joined 6-tr cl made); dc in next 6 sts, sc in each of next 2 sts, ending at corner of Hexagon. Rep from * 6 times more. Do not break off.
   Side Border: Continuing around, sc in next 10 sts, ending at corner; dc in each of next 6 sts, work joined 6-tr cl, dc in each of next 6 sts, ending at corner; * sc in each of next 12 sts, ending at corner; dc in each of next 6 sts, work joined 6-tr cl, tr in next 4 sts, work joined 6-tr cl, dc in each of next 6 sts, ending at corner. Rep from * 7 times more, dc in each of next 6 sts, work joined to 6-tr cl, dc in each of next 6 sts, sc in next 10 sts.
   Starting at * on end border, work across next end and opposite long edge of rug to correspond to other 2 sides; join with sl st to first sc. Break off.

Wall Hangings

WHEEL OF FORTUNE

Small touches of color spin through the openwork of this seven-panel piece. The strips are worked in single and double crochet and are quite simple to make.

SIZE: About 66″ long.

MATERIALS: Heavy rug yarn such as Aunt Lydia's rug yarn, 12 (70-yd.) skeins beige (color A), 2 skeins each forest green (B), light brown (C), and brick red (D); aluminum crochet hook size I (or English/Canadian hook No. 7) *or the size that will give you the correct gauge;* two 45″-long dowels ¾″ in diameter. (You can stain them brown.)

GAUGE: See dimensions for circular motifs.

Note: Each panel is composed of similar circular motifs and strips. They vary only in the length of the strips and the colors of the motifs. Follow Diagram for placement.

PANEL NO. 1: Circular Motif X: Starting at center with color D, ch 6. Join with sl st fo form ring.
Note: Right side is always facing you as you work motifs.
1st rnd: Ch 3, work 14 dc in ring (15 dc, counting ch-3 as 1 dc); join with sl st to top of ch-3. Break off.
2nd rnd: With A, make a lp on hook, y o, work dc in any st, dc in same place, work 2 dc in each dc around (30 dc); join with sl st to beg dc. Break off.
3rd rnd: With D, work 2 sc in any dc; * ch 5, sc in 2nd ch from hook, hdc in next ch, dc in next ch, tr in next ch (triangle made), sk 4 dc, work 2 sc in next dc. Rep from * 4 times more; make triangle; join to first sc (6 triangles completed). Break off.

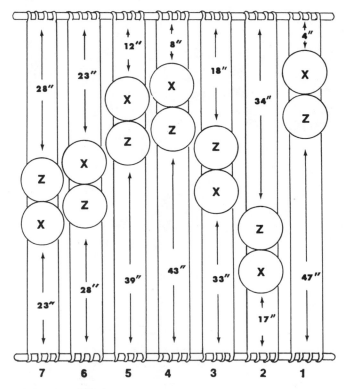

4th rnd: With A, make a lp on hook, y o twice, work tr in first sc of any 2-sc group, tr in same st, ch 3, sc in 3rd ch from hook (p made), 2 tr in next sc, ch 2, work sc, ch

1 and sc in point of triangle, ch 2, (work 2 tr in next sc between triangles, p, 2 tr in next sc, ch 2, work sc, ch 1 and sc in point of next triangle, ch 2) 5 times; join to first tr (24 tr's). Break off A. Piece should measure approximately 7½" in diameter.

Circular Motif Z: Starting with color B, work same as for Motif X through 3rd rnd, using B for all 3 rnds. Break off B.

4th rnd (joining rnd): With C, work 2 tr in first sc of any 2-sc group, ch 1, holding Motifs X and Z with wrong sides together and p's matching, with Motif Z facing you, remove hook from ch-1, insert hook through top of matching p on Motif X and draw lp of ch-1 through, y o hook, draw through both lps on hook, ch 1, sc in first ch for p (p joining made), work 2 tr in next sc, ch 2, sc in point of next triangle, remove hook from sc, insert through matching ch-1 sp on Motif X and draw lp of sc through, y o hook, draw through both lps on hook (ch-1 joining made), sc in same st at point of triangle, ch 2, work 2 tr in next sc, work a p joining (2 p and 1 ch-1 joining made in all), work 2 tr in next sc, complete rnd in pattern. Break off.

4" Strip: Hold joined Motifs X and Z with Motif X at top. Make a lp on hook with A, sk 2 free D triangles at right, sc in p between next 2 A tr's.

1st row: Ch 6, sc in ch-1 sp at top of next triangle, ch 6, sc in next p; ch 4, turn.

2nd row: Dc in 3rd ch of ch-6, ch 1, dc in next ch, ch 3, sc in 3rd ch from hook for p, work tr, ch 1 and tr in next sc, p, dc in 4th ch of ch-6, ch 1, dc in next ch, tr in end sc; ch 4, turn.

3rd row: (Work dc, ch 1 and dc in next ch-1 sp, p) twice; work dc, ch 1 and dc in next ch-1 sp, tr in top of ch-4; ch 4, turn. Rep 3rd row once more. Break off.

47" Strip: Holding piece with Motif Z at top, sk 2 free B triangles at right, attach A to p between next 2 C tr's.

Work upper strip in same manner as 4" lower strip, repeating 3rd row for pattern until piece measures 47" from beg (entire panel should measure about 66", stretched). Break off.

Work remaining panels in same manner, with the following variations in color and placement of circular Motifs X and Z. Follow diagram for lengths of strips.

PANEL NO. 2: For Motif X, work first rnd with B, 2nd rnd A, 3rd rnd B, 4th rnd A. For Motif Z, work first, 2nd, and 3rd rnds with D, 4th rnd with C.

PANEL NO. 3: Work Motifs X and Z same as for X and Z on Panel No. 1.

PANEL NO. 4: Work Motifs X and Z same as for Panel No. 2, working X as for Z and Z as for X.

PANEL NO. 5: Work Motifs X and Z same as for Panel No. 4.

PANEL NO. 6: Work Motifs X and Z same as for Panel No. 1.

PANEL NO. 7: Work Motifs X and Z same as for Panel No. 1, working X as for Z and Z as for X.

After all Panels are completed, weave dowel through lps formed by last row on each strip at each end of Panels, making sure that the right sides of all Panels are facing the same way.

Note: For a long-lasting crisp appearance, the panels can be starched before hanging. For starching instructions see p. 206

DEVA'S WEB

A lacy butcher's twine creation evokes nature's magical forms. It is an intricate design worked in sections with a variety of pattern stitches.

SIZE: Approximately 71".

MATERIALS: 24-ply cotton wrapping cord (a soft, loosely twisted butcher's twine sold in hardware and stationery stores), two 2-lb. cones; aluminum crochet hook size H (or English/Canadian hook No. 8) *or the size that will give you the correct gauge;* 2 dowels, one piece 35" long ⅜" in diameter, and one piece 26½" long ⅜" in diameter.

GAUGE: Half-circles measure about 14" across straight edge.

Note: The wrapping cord comes in white only. If you prefer a colored hanging, you can dye it with any commercial dye, or you can substitute Lily Sugar-'n-Cream cotton yarn (worked double), which comes in an assortment of colors. You will need 16 (125-yd.) skeins.

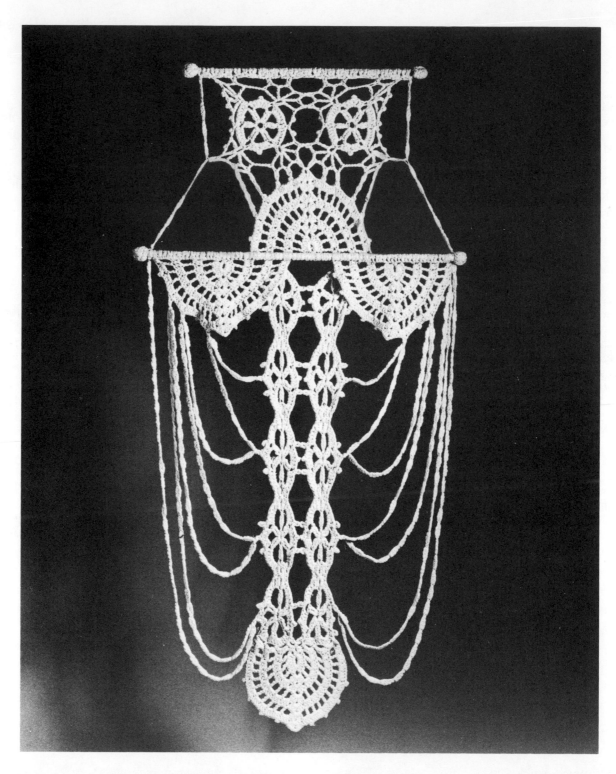

HALF-CIRCLE A (see Diagram 1): Starting at center of straight edge, ch 8. Join with sl st to form ring.

1st rnd: Ch 3, work 6 dc in ring, ch 2, 7 dc in ring (14 dc, counting ch-3 as 1 dc), do not join; ch 6, turn.

2nd row: (Sk next dc, tr in next dc, ch 2) 3 times; sk next dc, work 3 dc, ch 2 and 3 dc in ch-2 sp (double shell made), (ch 2, sk next dc, tr in next dc) 4 times; ch 3, turn.

3rd row: Work 2 dc over next ch-2 sp, work 3 dc over next ch-2 sp (3-dc shell made), shell in each of next 2 ch-2 sps, double shell in next ch-2 sp, shell in each of next 4 sps (30 dc, counting starting ch-3 as 1 dc); ch 6, turn.

4th row: (Sk next dc, tr in next dc, ch 2) 6 times; sk next 2 dc, work double shell in next ch-2 sp, ch 2, sk next 2 dc, tr in next dc, ch 2, (sk next dc, tr in next dc, ch 2)

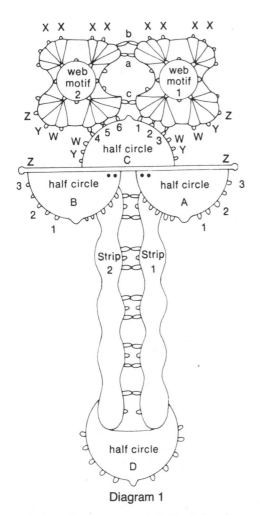

Diagram 1

as shown in Diagram 1, and place markers Nos. 1 and 2 in corresponding sts on Half-Circle B. The 4 dots show approximate locations of the markers on the 2 Half-Circles.

HALF-CIRCLE C: Work as for Half-Circle A, omitting markers. Put Half-Circles aside.

CENTER STRIP 1: Loop row: Working along center of strip, ch 4, tr in 4th ch from hook (first lp made), (ch 4, tr in 4th ch from hook) 22 times (23 lps, counting first lp made).

1st rnd: Ch 6, working over tr posts of lps, sk first lp, * work 2 tr, ch 6 and 2 tr over next lp, (ch 6, sk next lp, work 4 sc over each of next 2 lps, ch 6, sk next lp, work 2 tr, ch 6 and 2 tr over next lp) 4 times; * ch 6, 2 sc in end of next (first) lp. Working down opposite side of ch lps (ch 4 side of lps), ch 6, rep from * to * once more; ch 6, sl st to end of 23rd lp to join; ch 3.

2nd rnd: * (6 dc over next ch-6 lp, ch 6, sl st in 6th ch from hook—long p made, work 3 dc, short p and 3 dc over next ch-6 lp, long p, 6 dc over next ch-6 lp, sk 3 sc, sc in each of next 2 sc) 4 times; * 6 dc over next ch-6 lp, long p, work 3 dc, short p and 3 dc over next ch-6 lp, long p, 6 dc over next ch 6 lp, dc in each of next 2 sc. Rep from * to * once more. 6 dc over next ch-6 lp, long p, work 3 dc, short p and 3 dc over next ch-6 lp; join next long p to marked dc No. 1 on Half-Circle A as follows: Ch 3, remove hook from st, insert through 2 lps on post of marked dc and pull dropped lp through, ch 3, sl st in first ch to complete p (joined long p made), 6 dc over next ch-6 lp, sl st last dc to post of marked dc No. 2; sl st to top of first ch-3 to join. Break off.

STRIP 2: Work as for Strip No. 1 through the first rnd.

2nd rnd: Sl st to marked dc No. 2 on Half-Circle B, 6 dc over next ch-6 lp, work a joined long p to marked dc No. 1; (work 3 dc, short p and 3 dc over next ch-6 lp, long p, 6 dc over next ch-6 lp, sk 3 sc, sc in each of next 2 sc, 6 dc over next ch-6 lp, long p) 4 times; work 3 dc, short p, and 3 dc over next ch-6 lp, long p, 6 dc over next ch-6 lp; dc in each of 2 sc, 6 dc over next ch-6 lp (see Diagram 2 which shows joined long p's), work joined long p in corresponding long p (inside edge) on Strip No. 1, (work 3 dc, short p and 3 dc over next ch-6 lp, make joined long p, 6 dc over next ch-6 lp, sk 3 sc, sc in each of next 2 sc, 6 dc over next ch-6 lp, make joined long p) 4 times; work 3 dc, short p and 3 dc over next ch-6 lp, make joined long p, 6 dc over next ch-6 lp; join to top of beg ch-3. Break off.

HALF-CIRCLE D: Work as for Half-Circle A, omitting markers. Do not break off at end of 7th row.

5 times; sk next dc, tr in top of ch-3; ch 3, turn.

5th row: Work 2 dc over next ch-2 sp, shell in each of next 6 sps, double shell in next sp, shell in each of next 7 sps, shell in ch-6 sp, place marker No. 1 in last dc (48 dc, counting ch-3 as 1 dc); ch 6, turn.

6th row: (Sk next dc, tr in next dc, ch 2) 10 times; sk 3 dc, double shell in ch-2 sp, ch 2, sk 3 dc, tr in next dc, ch 2, (sk next dc, tr in next dc, ch 2) 9 times; tr in top of ch-3; ch 3, turn.

7th row: Work 2 dc over ch-2 sp, shell over next ch-2 sp, ch 3, sc in 3rd ch from hook (short p made), (shell in each of next 2 ch-sps, p) 4 times; shell in next ch-sp, double shell in next ch-sp, shell in next ch-sp, (p, shell in each of next 2 ch-sps) 5 times; place marker No. 2 in last dc. Break off. Piece should measure approximately 14″ across straight edge.

HALF-CIRCLE B: Work as for Half-Circle A, omitting markers 1 and 2. Place Half-Circles A and B in position,

8th row (joining row): Working across top straight edge, sc over post of last st made (see Diagram 2 where lines at lower edge of Strips 1 and 2 represent dc's; the dc's to be joined are marked by dots); sl st in first dc dot on Strip No. 1 (arrow), 1 sc over same post on Half-Circle, * (2 sc over next post, skipping 3 dc on Strip, sl st in next dc dot, 2 sc over next post) 3 times; * sl st between joined p's (center dot); rep from * to * once more; 2 sc over next post, sl st in last dc dot; sl st in post to join. Break off.

UPPER SECTION: WEB MOTIF NO. 1: Starting at center of circle, ch 6. Join with sl st to form ring.

1st rnd: Ch 4, tr in ring, (ch 6, 2 tr in ring) 5 times; ch 6, sl st in top of first ch-4 (6 spokes).

2nd rnd: Ch 3, * work 6 dc over next ch-6 lp, make long p, * work 3 dc, short p, and 3 dc over next ch-6 lp, long p, 6 dc over next ch-6 lp, * dc in next tr; rep from * to * once more; join with sl st in top of ch-3 (38 dc, counting ch-3 as 1 dc). Piece should measure about 6″ in diameter.

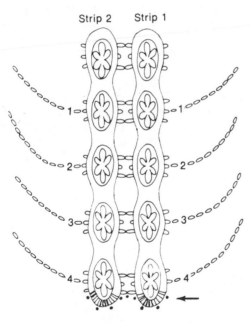

Strip 2   Strip 1

Diagram 2

3rd rnd (joining rnd): Ch 4, sc in 3rd ch st from hook (ch 1 and short p made), ch 1, * tr in next long p, (ch 1, short p, ch 1, tr in same long p) 4 times *; ch 5. Rep from * to * once more; ch 1, short p, ch 1, sk 6 dc, sc in next dc, ch 1, short p, ch 1, tr in next long p, ch 1, short p, ch

1, tr in same long p, ch 1, work a joined long p in ch-2 sp of double shell on Half-Circle C (see No. 1 on Diagram 1), ch 1, tr in same long p, (ch 1, work a joined long p in next p on Half-Circle C, ch 1, tr in same long p on web) twice (joinings 1, 2 and 3 made); ch 5, tr in next long p, (ch 1, short p, ch 1, tr in same long p on web) 4 times; ch 1, short p, ch 1; sl st in first ch-1. Break off.

WEB MOTIF NO. 2: Work as for Web Motif No. 1 through the 2nd rnd.

3rd rnd (joining rnd): Ch 4, sc in 3rd ch st from hook (ch 1 and short p made), ch 1, tr in next long p, ch 3, sl st in p marked A on Web Motif No. 1 (see Diagram 1), ch 1, sl st in 2nd ch of ch-3 (joined short p made), ch 1, tr in same long p, work a joined short p in p marked B on Web Motif No. 1, ch 1, (tr in same long p, ch 1, short p, ch 1) twice; tr in same long p, ch 5, tr in next long p, * (ch 1, short p, ch 1, tr in same long p) 4 times *; ch 1, short p, ch 1, sk 6 dc, sc in next dc, ch 1, short p, ch 1, tr in next long p. Rep from * to * once more; ch 5, tr in next long p, ch 1, work a joined long p over p 4 (see Diagram 1) on Half-Circle C, ch 1, tr in same long p, ch 1, work joined long p over p (5), ch 1, tr over same long p, ch 1, work joined long p (6) in ch-2 sp of double shell, ch 1, tr in same long p, ch 1, work joined short p over p marked C on Diagram 1 on Web Motif No. 1, ch 1, tr in same long p, ch 1, short p, ch 1; sl st in first ch-1. Break off.

DOWEL LOOPS (Mid-Section): Work on right sides of Half-Circles. Work across top straight edge of Half-Circle A as follows: (Sc over post of dc on first shell, ch 4) 4 times—4 lps made over post—(sc over post of next st on tr row, ch 4) 6 times (6 lps made). Continue in this manner working 4 lps over posts on shell rows and 6 lps over posts on tr rows (lp pattern) over the next 7 posts; then holding Half-Circles C and A with straight edges together, as in position on Diagram 1, work 4 lps over first shell post on Half-Circle C, (sk corresponding post on Half-Circle A, work 6 lps over next post on A, work 4 lps on next shell post on Half-Circle C) twice; sc in tip of last post on Half-Circle A (Half-Circle A and C joined by lps). Work lps in pattern over each of the next 4 posts of Half-Circle C, then holding Half-Circles B and C together, work sc in top of first post on Half-Circle B, work 4 lps over corresponding shell post on Half-Circle C (work 6 lps over next tr post on B, work 4 lps on next shell post on C) twice; sk corresponding shell post on B, (Half-Circle B and C joined by lps), work lps in pattern over each of the next 9 posts of Half-Circle B. Break off.

TO COMPLETE UPPER SECTION: 1st row: Ch 4, tr in 4th ch from hook (1 lp made), sc to first right-hand p marked X on Web Motif No. 1 (see Diagram 1), * make

2 lps, sc to next p X, make 3 lps, sc to next p X, make 2 lps, sc to next p X *, make 3 lps, sc to next X (on Web Motif No. 2); rep from * to * once more; make 1 lp (19 lps made and 8 joinings completed); ch 6, turn.

2nd row: Work over ch side of lps (sc over lp, ch 4) 5 times (4 dowel lps made); continue across lp row working (sc and ch 6) 4 times over each lp to end of row. Break off.

ROPE JOININGS (Upper Section): 1st joining: Attach yarn with sc to p marked W on Half-Circle C, (ch 4, tr in 4th ch from hook) twice (2 lps made); sc to p W on Web Motif No. 1, ch 4, sl st to p Y on Web Motif No. 1, make 4 lps, sc to p Y on Half-Circle C. Break off. Work rope joining to correspond on Web Motif 2.

2nd joining: On Half-Circle A, attach yarn with sc to top of post on right end at Z, make 5 lps, 2 sc in picot Z on Web Motif No. 1, make 4 lps, sc to end dowel lp of top section. Break off. Rep joining on opposite side.

ROPE JOININGS (Lower Section): Note: Before beginning ropes see Diagram 2 and mark p's numbered 1, 2, 3, and 4 shown on Strips 1 and 2. Then, looking at Diagram 1 mark p's 1, 2, 3, and 4 on Half-Circles A and B. Attach yarn with sc to p 1 on Strip 1, make 5 lps, sc to p 1 on Half-Circle A, make 8 lps, sc to p 2 on Strip 1, make 14 lps, sc to p 2 on Half-Circle A, make 17 lps, sc to p 3 on Strip 1, make 23 lps, sc to p 3 on Half-Circle A, make 29 lps, sc to p 4 on Strip 1, make 35 lps, sc to corner of Half-Circle A (Z). Break off.

Rep ropes on opposite side, connecting strip No. 2 and Half-Circle B.

FINISHING: Insert 35″ dowel through dowel lps on Mid-Section, and 26½″ dowel through lps on Upper Section.

Dowel Knobs: Ch 6. Join with sl st to form ring. Ch 3, work 11 dc in ring (ch-3 counts as dc), sl st top of ch-3. Ch 3, holding last lp of each dc back on hook, work dc in next 5 sts, y o, pull through all lps on hook (6-dc cl made, counting ch-3 as 1 dc); work 1 more 6-dc cl over remaining 6 sts, ch 1, sl st knob to sc at end dowel lp. Break off. Put knob over dowel end. Make 3 more knobs in same manner, placing each one on a remaining exposed dowel end.

TRELLIS

The narrow rug-yarn panel is inspired by a vine-covered lattice. Composed of little circles and half-circles, it is crocheted together with single and treble crochet and chain stitches.

SIZE: Approximately 9½″ x 44½″.

MATERIALS: Heavy rug yarn such as Aunt Lydia's rug yarn, 2 (70-yd.) skeins each mint green (color A); forest green (B), cinnamon (C); aluminum crochet hook size I (or English/Canadian hook No. 7) *or the size that will give you the correct gauge;* two 12″-long dowels ⅝″ in diameter (you can stain the ends green).

Note: Work with yarn double throughout, unless otherwise specified.

GAUGE: Circles measure 4″ in diameter.

CIRCLES (make 6): Starting at center with A, ch 8. Join with sl st to form ring.

1st rnd: Ch 3, work 11 dc in ring, pulling up lp of each dc about 1″ (12 dc, counting starting ch-3 as 1 dc); join with sl st to top of ch-3.

2nd rnd: Work sc, ch 1 and sc in same place as sl st, (ch 3, sk 2 dc, work sc, ch 1 and sc in next dc) 3 times; ch 3; sl st to first sc. Break off.

DIAMONDS (make 11): Starting at center with B, ch 10. Join with sl st to form ring.

1st rnd: Work (3 sc in ring, ch 3) 4 times; join with sl st to first sc. Break off.

HALF-CIRCLE (make 5): Starting at center with A, ch 8. Join with sl st to form ring.

1st row (right side): Work 6 dc in ring, pulling lp of each dc up about 1″ (7 dc, counting starting ch-3 as 1 dc); ch 1, turn.

2nd row: Work sc, ch 1 and sc in next dc, (ch 3, sk 2 dc, work sc, ch 1 and sc in next dc) twice. Break off.

FIRST STRIP JOINING CIRCLES AND DIAMONDS: Holding a circle with right side facing you, with B make a lp on hook. Join with sc to any ch-1 sp.

Outside edge: Ch 8, * sc in next ch-1 sp, ch 4, y o hook twice, insert hook in next ch-1 sp, y o, pull up a lp, y o, pull through 2 lps on hook (3 lps remain on hook), holding Diamond with right side facing you, insert hook in any ch-3 sp on Diamond, y o, pull up a lp, y o, pull through 2 lps on hook (first joining made—3 lps remain

Inside Edge: 1st row: Attach C with sc to last ch-1 sp worked. Holding piece with right side facing you, ch 8, * sc in next ch-1 sp, ch 4, work a first joining, y o, work remaining lps off hook as for dc, ch 4, sc in next ch-3 sp, ch 4, work a 2nd joining, y o, work off remaining lps as for dc, ch 4. Rep from * until inside edge of Circles and Diamonds are joined; sc in next ch-1 sp, ch 4, tr in next ch-1 sp; ch 4, turn.

2nd row (wrong side): * Work tr, ch 8 and tr in next sc, tr in next tr, ch 4, work tr, ch 1 and tr in next sc, ch 4, tr in next tr. Rep from * along side, ending last rep with tr, ch 8 and tr in next sc (place marker No. 1 in last tr), ch 4, sl st in 4th ch of starting ch-8 of first C row. Break off C.

SECOND STRIP JOINING DIAMONDS AND HALF-CIRCLES:

Hold a Diamond with right side facing you, with B, make a lp on hook and join to any ch-3 sp (place marker No. 2 in this sp).

Outside edge: Ch 8, * sc in next ch-3 sp, ch 4, y o hook twice, insert hook in next ch-3 sp, y o, pull up a lp, y o, pull through 2 lps on hook (3 lps remain on hook), holding a Half-Circle with right side facing you, insert hook in first ch-1 sp, y o, pull up lp, y o, pull through 2 lps on hook (first joining made—3 lps remain on hook), y o, work off remaining lps as for dc, ch 4, sc in next ch-1 sp, ch 4, y o hook twice, insert hook in next ch-1 sp, y o, pull up lp, y o, pull through 2 lps on hook (3 lps remain on hook), insert hook in any ch-3 sp on another Diamond, y o, pull up lp, y o, pull through 2 lps on hook (2nd joining made—3 lps remain on hook), y o, work off remaining lps as for dc, ch 4. Rep from * until 6 Diamonds and 5 Half-Circles are joined, then work sc in next ch-3 sp, ch 8, sc in last ch-3 sp (place marker No. 3 in this sp). Break off B.

TO JOIN FIRST AND SECOND STRIPS:

Holding both strips with right side facing you, attach B with sl st to marked tr No. 1; ch 4, tr in marked No. 3 ch-3 sp, ch 4.

1st row: * Sl st in next ch-3 sp on triangle, sc over color C ch-8 lp of first strip, ch 4, tr in next tr, ch 4, sl st into center of Half-Circle, tr in next ch-1 sp (between tr's in first strip), ch 4, tr in next tr, ch 4. Rep from * until both Strips are joined, ending last rep with sl st in ch-3 sp on Diamond, sc over ch-8 lp, ch 4, tr in next tr, ch 4, sc in marked No. 2 ch-3 sp. Break off B.

FINISHING:

With a single strand of B, make lps along top and bottom edge of piece in the following manner: With right side facing you, beginning at corner ch-8 sp, * sc in sp, ch 10, sc in same sp (first lp made). Rep from * 5 times more. There are 6 lps in each sp along edge (36 lps made). Break off. Work other end in same manner. Insert dowels through lps.

on hook); y o, work remaining lps off hook as for dc, ch 4, sc in next ch-3 sp, ch 4, y o hook twice, insert hook in next ch-3 sp, y o, pull up a lp, y o, pull through 2 lps on hook (3 lps remain on hook), insert hook in any ch-1 sp on another circle, y o, pull up lp, y o, pull through 2 lps on hook (2nd joining made—3 lps remain on hook); y o, work off remaining lps as for dc, ch 4. Rep from * until 6 Circles are joined to 5 Diamonds; sc in next ch-1 sp of last Circle, ch 8, sc in next ch-1 sp. Break off B.

Christmas Decorations

WREATH

To make your holiday bright create a permanent addition to your Christmas collection. This wreath, a unique crochet sculpture, is made with picots in double and treble crochet shells, worked on a tube base of double crochet and chain loops. It comes complete with crocheted ornaments, cones, and berries. It is an ideal gift for your home and friends.

SIZE: Diameter measures 15".

MATERIALS: Knitting worsted weight, 12 oz. forest green, 4 oz. bright green, small amounts of gold, red, lavender, teal, pale turquoise, sea green, pale blue, and bright rose; rug or bulky yarn weight, 8 oz. emerald green and 4 oz. hunter green; aluminum crochet hooks F, G, and H (or English/Canadian hooks No. 10, 9, and 8) *or the size that will give you the correct gauge;* a piece of green fabric 50" long by 9" wide; 2 lbs. polyester stuffing; large-eyed tapestry needle.

GAUGE: With H hook 5 dc = 1⅛".

BASE: With forest green, using H hook, ch 30, join with sl st in first ch st to form ring.
  1st rnd: Ch 3 (equals dc), work dc in each ch st around, sl st top of beg ch-3 (total 30 sts).
  2nd rnd: Working back lps only throughout, * ch 6, sl st in each of next 5 dc, rep from * 5 times (6 lps formed).
  3rd rnd: Ch 3, * sk ch-6 lp, working behind ch-6 lp, dc in next 5 sl sts, rep from * 4 times, sk last ch-6 lp, dc in remaining 4 sl sts, sl st top of beg ch-3.
  4th rnd: Sl st in each of next 3 dc, * ch 6, sl st next 5 dc, rep from * 4 times, ch 6, sl st next 2 dc, sl st in beg sl st.

5th rnd: Ch 3, dc in each of next 2 sl st, * sk ch-6 lp, dc in each of next 5 sl st, rep from * 4 times, sk last ch-6, dc in each of next 2 sl sts, sl st in top of beg ch-3. Rep 2nd through 5th rnds consecutively 23 times (total 97 rows). Fasten off.

BRANCHES: 1st row: With hunter green, using H hook, work in first lp rnd (2nd rnd). In any lp work sc, * ch 3 and sc in 3rd ch st from hook (p made), dc in same lp, rep from * 3 times, ** in next lp, work sc and (p, dc) 4 times; rep from ** around (6 dc shells made).
  2nd rnd: In next lp on next lp-rnd, * work sc and (p, tr) 4 times, rep from * in each lp around. Rep 1st and 2nd rnds, sc in next lp on next lp-rnd. Fasten off. Rep 1st and 2nd rnds alternately to end of tube with color changes as follows: (3 rnds of forest green, 4 rnds of bright green, 3 rnds of emerald green, and 4 rnds of hunter green) 3 times; end with 3 rnds of bright green. When ending off color always sc in next lp on next rnd of lps, then fasten off. Begin new color in same lp with last sc.

FIRST ORNAMENT: Note: Work double strand.
  Bottom: With lavender, using G hook, ch 5, sl st in first ch st to form ring.
  1st rnd: Ch 3, 9 dc in ring, sl st top of beg ch-3.
  2nd rnd: Ch 2, * 2 hdc next st, hdc next st, rep from

* around ending 2 hdc last st, sl st in top of beg ch-2 (total 15 sts).

3rd rnd: Ch 2, * 2 hdc next st, hdc next st, rep from * around, sl st in top beg ch-2 (total 22 sts). Fasten off.

4th rnd: With bright rose, sc in each st around, sl st in beg sc.

5th rnd: * Work p, sk 1 st, sl st next st, rep from * around. Fasten off.

6th rnd: With lavender, begin in any sl st sp between p's; * working over sl st, sc in sc of previous rnd, working behind next p, sc in skipped sc under p, rep from * around; sl st in beg sc. Fasten off.

Top: Rep Bottom through 3rd rnd. With lavender and tapestry needle sew 2 halves tog leaving 1″ opening; stuff with polyester and sew closed.

SECOND ORNAMENT: Work as for first ornament. Rep Bottom through 3rd rnds with pale blue; rep 4th and 5th rnds using teal and rep 6th rnd and Top using pale blue.

THIRD ORNAMENT: Use H hook. Rep Bottom through 3rd rnds with pale turquoise; rep 4th and 5th rnds using sea green and rep 6th rnd and Top using pale turquoise.

CONES (Make 6): Leave 2″ ends at beg and end. With gold, using hook size F, ch 13, beg in 2nd ch st from hook, work 4 sc in each of next 3 ch sts, 4 hdc in each of next 3 ch sts, 4 dc in each of next 3 ch sts, 4 trc in each of next 3 ch sts, ch 3, sl st in same ch sp. Fasten off.

BERRIES (Make 6): Leave 2″ ends at beg and end. With red, using G hook, * work (p) 3 times, sl st in base of 1st p, rep from * twice. Fasten off.

FINISHING: Sew length of cloth with ½″ seam to form tube. Stuff with polyester filling. Slide Wreath over stuffed tube and sew ends of the tube tog. Then crochet ends of the Wreath tog. Tie on Cones and Berries with 2″ ends. Sew on ornaments.

TREE

This festive replica, a true evergreen, is replete with picot berries and curlicue single crochet cones. You begin with a cover made of double crochet and chain-3 loops, which will be placed over a plastic-foam cone. Then come the branches—crocheted into the chain loops—which run the gamut of stitches from single crochet to double treble crochet.

SIZE: 12″ in height x 5″ in width.

MATERIALS: Knitting-worsted-weight yarn, 5 oz. emerald green (color E), 2 oz. forest green (F), 1 oz. each dark gold (G) and red (R); aluminum crochet hook size H (or English/Canadian hook No. 8) *or the size that will give you the correct gauge;* plastic-foam cone 12″ high x 5″ diameter at base.

GAUGE: 3 dc = 1″.

FOUNDATION: Starting at tip with E, ch 5. Join with sl st to form ring.

1st rnd: Ch 3, work 5 dc in ring; sl st in top of ch-3.

2nd rnd: Ch 3, work 2 dc in next dc (dc in next dc, 2 dc in next dc) twice; sl st in ch-3.

3rd rnd (lp rnd): * Ch 6, sc in next 3 dc. Rep from * around, ending sc in last 2 dc; sl st in sl st at base of first lp (3 lps).

4th rnd: Ch 3, dc in same place as sl st; * holding lp forward, sk next ch-6 lp, dc in next 2 sc, 2 dc in next sc. Rep from *, ending dc in last 2 sc; sl st in ch-3.

5th rnd: Rep 3rd rnd (4 lps).

6th rnd: Ch 3, * sk next ch-6 lp, dc in next 3 sc. Rep from *, ending dc in last 2 sc; sl st in ch-3.

7th rnd: Rep 3rd rnd (4 lps).

8th rnd: Rep 4th rnd.

9th rnd (lp rnd): * Ch 6, sc in next 4 dc. Rep from *, ending sc in last 3 dc; sl st in sl st (4 lps).

10th rnd: Ch 3, dc in same place as sl st, * sk next ch-6 lp, dc in next 3 sc, 2 dc in next sc. Rep from *, ending dc in last 3 sc; sl st in ch-3.

11th rnd: Rep 9th rnd (5 lps).

12th rnd: Ch 3, * sk next ch-6 lp, dc in next 4 sc. Rep from *, ending dc in last 3 sc; sl st in ch-3.

13th rnd: Rep 9th rnd (5 lps).

14th rnd: Rep 10th rnd.

15th rnd (lp rnd): * Ch 6, sc in next 5 dc. Rep from *, ending sc in last 4 dc; sl st in sl st (5 lps).

16th rnd: Ch 3, dc in same place as sl st, * sk next ch-6 lp, dc in next 4 sc, 2 dc in next sc. Rep from *, ending dc in last 4 dc; sl st in ch-3.

17th rnd: Rep 15th rnd (6 lps).

18th rnd: Ch 3, * sk next ch-6 lp, dc in next 5 sc. Rep from *, ending dc in last 4 sc; sl st in ch-3.

19th rnd: Rep 15th rnd (6 lps).

20th rnd: Ch 3, dc in same place as sl st, * sk next ch-6 lp, dc in next 4 sc, 2 dc in next sc. Rep from *, ending dc in last 4 sc; sl st in ch-3.

21st rnd (lp rnd): * Ch 6, sc in next 6 dc. Rep from * around, ending sc in last 5 sc; sl st in sl st (6 lps).

22nd rnd: Ch 3, dc in same place as sl st, * sk next ch-6 lp, dc in next 5 sc, 2 dc in next sc. Rep from *, ending

dc in last 5 sc; sl st in ch-3.

23rd rnd: Rep 21st rnd (7 lps).

24th rnd: Ch 3, * sk next ch-6 lp, dc in next 6 sc. Rep from *, ending dc in last 5 sc; sl st in ch-3.

25th rnd: Rep 21st rnd (7 lps).

26th rnd: Rep 22nd rnd.

27th rnd: * Ch 6, sc in next 7 dc. Rep from *, ending sc in last 6 dc; sl st in sl st (7 lps).

28th rnd: Ch 3, dc in same place as sl st, * sk next ch-6 lp, dc in next 6 sc, 2 dc in next sc. Rep from *, ending dc in last 5 sc; sl st in ch-3.

29th rnd: Rep 27th rnd (8 lps).

30th rnd: Ch 3, * sk next ch-6 lp, dc in next 7 sc. Rep from *, ending dc in last 6 sc; sl st in ch-3.

31st rnd: Rep 27th rnd (8 lps).

32nd rnd: Rep 28th rnd. Break off.

BRANCHES: Hold piece with 1st rnd of Foundation on bottom.

1st rnd: Starting in any lp of first lp rnd, with E, sc in lp; * (ch 3, sc in 3rd ch from hook—p made—sc in same lp) twice; in next lp work sc. Rep from * in each lp around, ending sc in next lp on next rnd.

2nd rnd: Rep 1st rnd from * in each lp of next lp rnd. Break off.

3rd rnd: Attach F in last st made, * hdc in next lp on next lp rnd, (make p, hdc in same lp) 4 times. Rep from * around. Break off.

4th rnd: Attach E in last st made, work as for 3rd rnd.

5th rnd: * Dc in next lp, on next lp rnd, (make p, dc in same lp) 5 times. Rep from * around. Break off.

6th rnd: Attach F in last st made, rep 5th rnd.

7th rnd: Attach E in last st made; work as for 5th rnd.

8th rnd: * Tr in next lp (make p, tr in same lp) 6 times. Rep from * around. Break off.

9th and 10th rnds: Attach F in last st made. Working as for 8th rnd, work 2 rnds. Break off.

11th rnd: Attach E in last st made, rep 8th rnd.

12th rnd: Attach F in last st made, work as for 8th rnd.

13th rnd: * Dtr in next lp, (make p, dtr in same lp) 7 times. Rep from * around. Break off.

14th rnd: Attach E in last st made, rep 13th rnd.

15th rnd: Attach F in last st made, rep 13th rnd, sl st in top of first dtr. Break off.

CONES (make 5): Leaving 3" ends at beg and end, with G, ch 6, 5 sc in 2nd ch from hook and in each ch across. Break off.

BERRIES (make 5): Leaving 3" ends at beg and end, with R, make lp on hook, (make p) 3 times, sl st in sc of first p. Break off.

Tie on cones and berries with 3" ends. Make as many as desired and tie on where desired. Slip tree over cone. For tighter fit, add tissue paper.

FOUR SNOWFLAKES

You will be assured of a white holiday season with these starched, lacy, cotton snowflakes. Just as in nature, each six-pointed star has a unique design, here created from a variety of intricate stitches.

MATERIALS: Mercerized knit and crochet "bedspread" cotton, 1 (175-yd.) spool ecru; steel crochet hook size 6 (or English/Canadian hook No. 9) *or the size that will give you the correct gauge.*

GAUGE: 5 dc = ½"; 3 dc = 1".

SIZE: Snowflakes measure approximately 4" at widest point.

Directions for Starching

Dissolve ½ cup of laundry starch in ¾ cup of cold water. Boil slowly over a low flame. As it thickens, stir in gradually about 1¼ cups of hot water. Stir constantly until starch clears. The mixture should be thick and pasty. As soon as starch is cool enough to handle, dip snowflake and squeeze starch through it thoroughly. Pin snowflake in position and leave it to dry thoroughly.

CLUSTER SNOWFLAKE (No. 1): 1st rnd: Ch 10, join to form ring, ch 3, work 23 dc in ring, sl st in top of beg ch-3.

2nd rnd: ** Sc next st, ch 6, working both lps of ch st, dtr in 6th ch st from hook, * ch 5, in 5th ch st from hook, working both lps of ch st, work 3 tr holding back last lps on hook, y o, pull through all 4 lps on hook (3-tr cl made), ch 4, sl st in same ch st as base of cl, rep from * twice, sl st in top of dtr, ch 5, sl st in same ch st as base of dtr, (ch 4, working both lps of ch st, work 3-dc cl in 4th ch st from hook) 3 times, sk 3 sts, rep from ** 5 times, sl st in beg sc. Fasten off.

TREFOIL TIP SNOWFLAKE (No. 2): 1st rnd: Ch 8, join with sl st to form ring; ch 3, work 23 dc in ring, sl st top ch-3.

2nd rnd: Ch 5, work 3-dtr cl in same sp as follows: Work 3 dtr in same sp, holding back last lp on hook, y o,

Snowflakes (starting from left): Numbers 1, 2, 3, and 4

pull through all 4 lps on hook. * Ch 8, sk 1 st, sc in next st, ch 8, sk 1 st, ** 4-dtr cl in next st, rep from * 4 times, rep from * to **, sl st in top of beg cl.

3rd rnd: Ch 3, 3 dc in same sp, ch 3, 4 dc in same sp, * over ch-8 work 3 sc, over next ch-8 work 3 sc, ** in top of next cl, work 4 dc, ch 3 and 4 dc, rep from * 4 times, rep from * to **, sl st in top of beg ch-3.

4th rnd: Working back lps only, sl st in next 3 dc, ** in ch-3 sp work sc, * ch 5, sc in 3rd ch st from hook, dc in each of next 2 ch sts, sc in same ch-3 sp *, ch 7, sc in 3rd ch st from hook, hdc next ch st, dc in each of next 3 ch sts, sc in same ch-3 sp, rep from * to *, working back lps only, sl st in each st to within next ch-3 sp, rep from ** 5 times except on last rep sl st in beg sl st. Fasten off.

STAR POINT SNOWFLAKE (No. 3): 1st rnd: Ch 12, join with sl st to form ring, ch 1, work 23 sc in ring, sl st in beg ch-1.

2nd rnd: * Sc next st, ch 6, sk 3 sts, rep from * 5 times, end sl st in beg sc.

3rd rnd: Work 4 sc, ch 3 and 4 sc over each ch-6 lp, end sl st in first 2 sc sts.

4th rnd: * Sc next st, ch 6, sk sc, ch 3 and sc, sc next st, ch 16, sk last 2 sc on this lp and first 2 sc on next lp, rep from * 5 times, end sl st in beg sc.

5th rnd: * Over ch-6 lp work 4 sc, ch 5 and 4 sc, over ch-16 work 7 sc, ch 5, 6 sc, ch 5, sc, ch 7, sc, ch 5, 6 sc, ch 5, 7 sc, rep from * 5 times, sl st beg sc. Fasten off.

RING OF RINGS SNOWFLAKE (No. 4): 1st Ring: * Ch 7, join with sl st in 7th ch st from hook to form ring, ch 1, 3 sc in ring, ch 3, 4 sc in ring, rep from * 4 times, (5 triangles formed), mark ch-3 sp on last triangle made, sl st in beg ch-1 of first triangle (joining st) to form triangle ring. **Note:** This is right side. Fasten off.

2nd Ring: ** Ch 7, join with sl st to form ring, ch 1, 3 sc in ring, ch 1, pick up triangle ring just completed, hold with right side facing and joining st on bottom, sl st in marked ch-3 sp, ch 1, in ch ring work 4 sc, * ch 7, join with sl st to form ring, ch 1, 3 sc in ring, ch 3, 4 sc in ring, rep from * 3 times, mark ch-3 sp on last triangle made, sl st in beg ch-1 of first triangle on this ring. Fasten off.

3rd, 4th, and 5th Rings: Rep 2nd Ring.

6th Ring: Rep 2nd Ring from ** to *; (ch 7, join with sl st to form ring, ch 1, 3 sc in ring, ch 3, 4 sc in ring) 3 times; ch 7, join with sl st in first ch st to form ring, ch 1, 3 sc in ring, ch 1, sl st in ch-3 sp of first triangle on first ring, ch 1, 4 sc in ch ring, sl st in beg ch-1 of first triangle in this ring. Fasten off.

Center: 1st rnd: Ch 8, join with sl st to form ring, ch 3, work 23 dc in ring; sl st in top beg ch-3.

2nd rnd: Sc next 3 sts; in next st work dc, ch 2, pick up 6 joined triangle rings, work sl st in joining st of any ring, ch 2, dc in same dc on center circle, * sc next 3 sts, dc next st, ch 2, sl st in joining st of next triangle ring, ch 2, dc in same sp, rep from * 4 times, sl st in beg sc. Fasten off.

Appendix

MANUFACTURERS AND DISTRIBUTORS OF YARN

American Thread Company
Hi Ridge Park
Stamford, Connecticut 06905

Armen Corp.
P. O. Box 8348
Asheville, North Carolina 28804

Belding Lily Co.
Lily Mills
Shelby, North Carolina 28150

Emile Bernat & Sons, Inc.
230 Fifth Avenue
New York, New York 10001

Stanley Berroco, Inc.
140 Mendon Street
Uxbridge, Massachusetts 10569

Brunswick Worsted Mills
230 Fifth Avenue
New York, New York 10001

Bucilla Yarn Co.
30-20 Thompson Avenue
Long Island City, New York 11101

Coats & Clark, Inc.
75 Rockefeller Plaza
New York, New York 10019

Columbia Minerva Corp.
295 Fifth Avenue
New York, New York 10016

Coyote
Box 2159
GPO New York, New York 10001

Craft Yarns of Rhode Island, Inc.
P. O. Box 385
Pawtucket, Rhode Island 02862

Fredrick J. Fawcett, Inc.
129 South Street
Boston, Massachusetts 02111

Fibre Yarn Co., Inc.
840 Sixth Avenue
New York, N.Y. 10001

Joseph Galler, Inc.
149 Fifth Avenue
New York, New York 10001

Kentucky Yarns
January and Wood Co.
Maysville, Kentucky 41056

Paternayan Yarn Co.
312 East 95th Street
New York, New York 10028

Plymouth Yarn Co.
Box 28
Bristol, Pennsylvania 19007

Reynold Yarns Inc.
15 Ozer Avenue
Hauppauge, New York 11787

Lawrence Schiff Silk Mills, Inc.
79 Madison Avenue
New York, New York 10038

Scott's Woolen Mill
Hecla Street and Elmdale Road
Uxbridge, Massachusetts 01569

Tahki Imports
62 Madison Street
Hackensack, New Jersey 07601

William Unger & Co., Inc.
230 Fifth Avenue
New York, New York 10001